An Introduction to Literature, Criticism and Theory

Second Edition

For Anna
and
For Kati

An Introduction to Literature, Criticism and Theory

Second Edition

Andrew Bennett and Nicholas Royle

An imprint of **Pearson Education**

Harlow, England · London · New York · Reading, Massachusetts · San Francisco
Toronto · Don Mills, Ontario · Sydney · Tokyo · Singapore · Hong Kong · Seoul
Taipei · Cape Town · Madrid · Mexico City · Amsterdam · Munich · Paris · Milan

Pearson Education Limited
Edinburgh Gate
Harlow
Essex CM20 2JE
England
and Associated Companies throughout the world
Visit us on the world wide web at: http://www.pearsoneduc.com

First published 1995
This second edition published 1999

© Prentice Hall Europe 1995, 1999

Typeset by Wyvern 21 Ltd, Bristol
Printed and bound in Great Britain by MPG Books, Bodmin, Cornwall

---

Library of Congress Cataloging-in-Publication Data

Available from the Publisher
Andrew Bennett, 1960. Nicolas Royal 1957.

British Library Cataloguing in Publication Data

A catalogue record for this book is available from the British Library

ISBN 0-13-010914-2

---

10 9 8 7 6 5 4 3
04 03 02 01 00

Contents

Preface to the first edition

This is a new kind of book. It offers new ways of thinking about literature and about what is involved in reading critically. It is designed to be clear and accessible to those who are beginning to study literature, as well as to more advanced students. Although written with university students in mind, we dare to hope that it might also be of interest to other readers.

Literary theory is an unavoidable part of studying literature and criticism. But theory—especially when it takes the form of 'isms'—can often be intimidating or else, frankly, boring. We have tried to avoid simply giving potted summaries of *isms*. Instead we present brief essays on a range of key critical concepts all of which have more or less familiar names. We put these concepts into practice through readings of particular literary texts. Our primary focus, in other words, is on what is powerful, complex and strange about literary works themselves. Our aim is to explain, entertain, stimulate and challenge.

The book is divided into twenty-four chapters and looks as if it has a certain order or progression. It begins with 'The beginning' and ends with 'The end'. But it has been put together in such a way that it can also be read starting from any one chapter. 'The end', for example, is not a bad place to begin. Each chapter concludes with some suggestions for further reading. There is a glossary of critical and theoretical terms at the back of the book, plus a full bibliography of the texts discussed.

Preface to the second edition

This new edition of *An Introduction to Literature, Criticism and Theory* has been thoroughly revised and, we hope, improved. We have revised all existing chapters, updated and expanded the further reading sections, the glossary and the bibliography, and also added four new chapters: 'Monuments', 'Ghosts', 'Queer' and 'The colony'. These additional chapters reflect the importance of certain new or emerging areas of literary studies, such as queer theory, postcolonial theory, debates about 'the canon' and spectrality. We also hope, however, that the new chapters may complement and reinforce what we believe was already distinctive about the first edition of this book, namely its preoccupation with literature and the literary as such. Our foremost desire has been to explore and analyze the strange, protean forms and effects of the literary and of literature as an institution. This second edition, then, attempts to make explicit in new ways our continuing fascination with literary works themselves—with, for example, their monumental, ghostly, queer and colonizing power.

We are grateful to Michael Ayers for permission to reproduce copyright material, 'Bittersweet', on page 217.

The beginning

When will we have begun?

Where—or when—does a literary text begin? This question raises a series of fundamental problems in literary criticism and theory. Does a text begin as the author puts his or her first mark on a piece of paper or keys in the first word on a word processor? Does it begin with the first idea about a story or poem, or in the childhood of the writer, for instance? Or does the text only begin as the reader picks up the book? Does the text begin with its title, or with the first word of the so-called 'body' of the text?

The only way to begin is with some literary texts. John Milton's great epic poem *Paradise Lost* (1667) begins by returning to the beginning:

> Of man's first disobedience, and the fruit
> Of that forbidden tree, whose mortal taste
> Brought death into the world, and all our woe,
> With loss of Eden, till one greater Man
> Restore us, and regain the blissful seat,
> Sing Heav'nly Muse, that on the secret top
> Of Oreb, or of Sinai, didst inspire
> That shepherd, who first taught the chosen seed,
> In the beginning how the heav'ns and earth
> Rose out of chaos: or if Sion hill
> Delight thee more, and Siloa's brook that flowed
> Fast by the oracle of God; I thence
> Invoke thy aid to my advent'rous song,
> That with no middle flight intends to soar
> Above th'Aonian mount, while it pursues
> Things unattempted yet in prose or rhyme.

This extraordinary opening sentence is all about beginnings. Thematically, it establishes the poem to be about the *first* disobedience of Adam and Eve which 'Brought death into the world, and all our woe'. But it is also about itself *as* a beginning: it assures us that this is the first time that such a project has been attempted ('Things unattempted yet in prose or rhyme'). It is as if the opening to a poem could be the equivalent of a moon-landing—one small step for John Milton . . . Rather differently, the opening sentence is about itself as a beginning in the sense that it is asking the 'Heav'nly Muse' for inspiration. It is about the way that poems are conventionally thought to begin—in inspiration. This produces a strange paradox of beginnings: the origin of the poem, inspiration, comes *after* the beginning of the poem. In other ways, too, Milton's opening distorts and ungrounds any simple notion of opening or beginning. Not only does the poem talk about a beginning, the eating of the apple of knowledge, but it also refers to a return to a time before that beginning ('regain the blissful seat'), a restoration which will be both the beginning of a new age and a repetition of a previous state.

There is another way in which this beginning is not a beginning: it repeatedly refers us back to other texts. Milton refers to Moses ('That shepherd') in the belief that he 'taught' the children of Israel the creation story—in other words, that he wrote the opening books of the Old Testament. In this respect, the muse that Milton's poem addresses and invokes is a second-hand muse. Contrary to its claims to originality, this opening echoes and alludes to various other openings. 'Of man's first disobedience . . . Sing Heav'nly Muse' repeats the conventional apostrophe of such classical openings as Homer's *Iliad* and Virgil's *Aeneid*. 'In the beginning' repeats the opening to the Gospel according to St John ('In the beginning was the Word') and so on. Finally, the very syntax of Milton's sentence displaces the beginning of the poem, in particular by holding back the main verb of the sentence—'Sing'—until line six.

Despite the complications of Milton's opening, however, at least it tries (or pretends to try) to begin at the beginning, rather than in the middle. Beginning in the middle—*in medias res*—is the other way to begin. One of the most famous beginnings-in-the-middle is Dante's opening to *The Divine Comedy* (*c*.1307–20):

> Nel mezzo del cammin di nostra vita
> mi ritrovai per una selva oscura,
> che la diritta via era smarrita.
> (Midway in the journey of our life I found myself in a dark
> wood, for the straight way was lost.)

There are at least three different middles here: the middle of 'our life', the middle of a dark wood, the middle of a narrative. Dante conflates life, journey and narrative, and suggests the uncanny terror of *beginning* at such a moment of middling. In particular, the uncanniness of 'mi ritrovai' suggests the hallucinatory terror of (re-)finding, of retrieving oneself. But Dante's opening might also suggest that there are *no* absolute beginnings—only uncanny originary middles. No journey, no life, no narrative ever really begins: all are 'always already' begun. But this is not to say that we can do without the concept of the beginning. Where would a text be without a beginning?

The paradox of the beginning as always already begun is wittily presented by Laurence Sterne in the opening of his novel *The Life and Opinions of Tristram Shandy, Gentleman* (1759) in terms of both the beginning of a narrative and the beginning of a life:

> I wish either my father or my mother, or indeed both of them, as they were in duty both equally bound to it, had minded what they were about when they begot me; had they duly consider'd how much depended upon what they were then doing;—that not only the production of a rational Being was concern'd in it, but that possibly the happy formation and temperature of his body, perhaps his genius and the very cast of his mind;—and, for aught they knew to the contrary, even the fortunes of his whole house might take their turn from the humours and dispositions which were then uppermost:— Had they duly weighed and considered all this, and proceeded accordingly,—I am verily persuaded I should have made a quite different figure in the world, from that, in which the reader is likely to see me. (5)

This opening is a comic version of Philip Larkin's equivocal opening line to his poem 'This Be The Verse' (1974): 'They fuck you up, your mum and dad'. Tristram Shandy complains because his parents were thinking of something else at the moment of his conception and he is afraid that in consequence his whole life has been fucked up. As his uncle Toby remarks a few pages later, 'My Tristram's misfortunes began nine months before ever he came into the world' (7). *Tristram Shandy* famously confronts the intractable problem of how to end an autobiography: such a text can never catch up with itself because it takes longer to write about life than it takes to live it. In this sense, autobiography can never end. But *Tristram Shandy* is also about how to begin—how to begin at the beginning—and how we begin. Both narrative and life are always already begun, their beginnings displaced to another time.

If beginnings always have a context and are therefore determined by what comes before, the opening to *Tristram Shandy* also makes it clear that, in turn, beginnings determine what comes after. This is true of literary as of other beginnings: beginnings augur, acting like promises for what is to come. Such is the force of many well-known literary beginnings. The opening to Jane Austen's *Pride and Prejudice* (1813) is apparently unequivocal: 'It is a truth universally acknowledged, that a single man in possession of a good fortune, must be in want of a wife' (1). This sets the stage for the whole novel. The topic is marriage, the tone is ironic. Austen proclaims the values of universalism ('a truth universally acknowledged'), while satirizing them: what is acknowledged as a truth for heterosexual men in early nineteenth-century England is not necessarily acknowledged universally. Before going on to provide an 'Explanatory' note on its dialect, Mark Twain's *The Adventures of Huckleberry Finn (Tom Sawyer's Comrade)* (1885) begins with a 'notice':

NOTICE

Persons attempting to find a motive in this narrative will be prosecuted; persons attempting to find a moral in it will be banished; persons attempting to find a plot in it will be shot.

BY ORDER OF THE AUTHOR
PER G.G., CHIEF OF ORDNANCE

At once witty and baffling, the sentence is both an entrance and a barrier to the novel. It reads something like the sentence 'Do not read this sentence', in that it both acknowledges that readers *do* try to find motives and morals in narratives and comically prohibits such a reading. Herman Melville's *Moby Dick; or, The Whale* (1851) is also framed by a number of what Gérard Genette calls 'peritexts' (Genette 1987)—by a contents page, a dedication, an 'Etymology' (of the word 'Whale') and 'Extracts' (several pages of quotations about whales)—before it begins with the famous words 'Call me Ishmael'. Satirical prevarication and pedantry, combined with blustering assertiveness, characterize the whole novel. Virginia Woolf's *Orlando* (1928) opens (after a dedication, preface, contents page and list of illustrations) with a sentence that equivocates by appearing not to do so: 'He—for there could be no doubt of his sex, though the fashion of the time did something to disguise it—was in the act of slicing at the head of a Moor which swung from the rafters' (13).

The sentence begins a book about a person of uncertain gender in a tone of strange uncertainty, with a suggestive mixture of decapitation and castration. By appearing not to, this opening sentence, like the novel as a whole, subtly undermines conventional ideas about gender identity. The first sentence of Ford Madox Ford's *The Good Soldier* (1915) is sheer heart-tugging seduction: 'This is the saddest story I have ever heard' (7). It is the sort of sentence from which a novel might never recover. And Proust's famous understated opening to *Remembrance of Things Past* (1913–27) implies that there is no single beginning: 'Longtemps, je me suis couché de bonne heure' ('For a long time I used to go to bed early', 13). A studied reflection on the past, a sense of intimacy, the power of habit and repetition are what characterize Proust's 3,000-page novel. As these examples suggest, one of the peculiarities of literary openings is that they are never single. The openings to *Huckleberry Finn*, *Moby Dick* and *Orlando* produce multiple beginnings through their 'peritexts', but the other examples are also multiple: *The Good Soldier* suggests both a story and its retelling, while Proust's opening gives a sense that narrative begins in repetition, that no single event can be said to be a beginning.

As we have begun to see, one of the ways in which a literary text multiplies its beginning is through the deployment of peritexts—titles, subtitles, dedications, epigraphs, introductions, 'notices' and so on. A classic example would be the opening of T.S. Eliot's *The Waste Land* (1922). Before we arrive at the first words of Eliot's poem we encounter a series of multilingual hurdles. To start with, there is the title. The title, like all titles, is uncertainly poised between inside and outside. It both names the poem, as if from outside, and forms part of that poem. 'The Waste Land' both refers to a place or predicament—post-1918 Europe, for example—and names the strange 'land' that Eliot's poem creates (like a waste land, the poem is full of debris from the past, fragmentary memories and quotations). Next we encounter the Latin and Greek of Petronius: 'Nam Sibyllam quidem Cumis ego ipse oculis meis vidi in ampulla pendere, et cum illi pueri dicerent: Σίβυλλα τί Θελεις; respondebat illa: ἀποθανευιν Θέλω' ('For once I myself saw with my own eyes the Sibyl at Cumae hanging in a cage, and when the boys said to her "Sibyl, what do you want?" she replied, "I want to die"'). As an epigraph, this quotation too may be said to be both inside and outside the poem, both a commentary on and a part of the text. The next hurdle is a tribute in Italian to Ezra Pound: 'il miglior fabbro' ('the better craftsman'). Pound, as editor, was responsible for much of the final shape of Eliot's poem and therefore is in part the craftsman of what follows. Even this tribute is a quotation: it comes from Dante's *Purgatorio* and is thus both part of Eliot's poem and not part of it. Finally, there is a subtitle: '1. The Burial of the Dead'. This is a quotation from the Anglican burial service. But even when we arrive at what we might think of as the first words of the poem—'April is the cruellest month . . .'—we find that they are a pastiche or reworking of the opening to another poem, Chaucer's *The Canterbury Tales* (*c*.1387–1400) ('Whan that April with his shoures sote / The droghte of Marche hath perced to the rote, / And bathed every veyne in swich licour, / Of which vertu engendred is the flour'). In these and other ways, Eliot's poem displaces its own beginnings. The beginning of the poem is no longer the first stroke of the pen or keyboard. Through emphatic effects of *intertextuality* in particular, Eliot's poem suggests that originality, the notion of beginning as singular, definable, stable is severely problematic. To ask where or when Eliot's poem begins is to meet with a series of questions concerning the identity of the author, the text and reader, and finally of the Western literary tradition generally.

The Waste Land may seem to be unusually concerned with questions of origins and their displacement. But the kinds of effects of intertextuality that this opening explores are in fact fundamental to literary texts more generally. Literary texts, that is to say, are always constructed by and within a context or tradition. (We explore this idea in greater detail in 'Monuments': see Chapter 6.) In his well-known essay 'Tradition and the Individual Talent' (1919), Eliot himself argues that 'No poet, no artist of any art, has his [*sic*] complete meaning alone': rather, what is important is the poet's 'relation to the dead poets and artists' (Eliot 1975, 38). A poem, novel or play that does not in some sense relate to previous texts is, in fact, literally unimaginable. The author of such a text would have to invent everything. It would be like inventing a new language from scratch, without any knowledge of already existing languages. In this sense, intertextuality (the displacement of origins to other texts, which are in turn displacements of other texts and so on) is fundamental to the institution of literature. No text makes sense without other texts. Every text is what Roland Barthes calls 'a new tissue of past citations' (Barthes 1981, 39).

Two of the most compelling and most persistent myths of literary texts concern their origins. The first is the idea that the most important aspect of any reading is an imagined meeting of the reader's mind with that of the author—an idea that exemplifies what has been known for the past fifty years as the 'intentional fallacy' (the mistaken belief that what the author intended is the 'real', 'final' meaning of the work and that we can or should know what this is). In this respect, readers attempt to find the origin of the text, its beginning, in the author's consciousness. But if we cannot know the beginnings of a text in terms of what is available to us on the page, how much more difficult it would be to discover the origins of the thought which impels the text. Does an author know where these thoughts come from? Are they thoughts (conscious, coherent, consistent)? Whose 'thoughts' do we read when we read the beginning of *The Waste Land*? Eliot's, Chaucer's, Pound's, Petronius', Dante's? Are they still the poet's thoughts if the poet is said to be 'inspired'? (See Chapter 3 for more on these issues.) The second common myth involves the priority often given to an individual reader's first reading of a text. According to this myth, all literary criticism involves a corruption of the original 'experience' of reading. Although we often talk about literary texts as though they have been subjected only to one reading, we all know that this is many respects simply a convenient fiction. Roland Barthes, in his book *S/Z* (1970), makes a point about the act of rereading as 'an operation contrary to the commercial and ideological habits of our society' and suggests that it is 'tolerated only in certain marginal categories of readers (children, old people and professors)' (Barthes 1990b, 15–16). Professors—who are usually old people, very seldom children, though not infrequently an undecidable mixture of the two—include Roland Barthes, of course, and it is part of his aim to question the very idea of a single or first reading. Rereading, he argues,

> contests the claim which would have us believe that the first reading is a primary, naïve, phenomenal reading which we will only, afterwards, have to 'explicate', to intellectualize (as if there were a beginning of reading, as if everything were not already read: there is no *first* reading . . .). (Barthes 1990b, 16)

Once again, Eliot's poem suggests some of the complexities involved in a first reading. If the opening to Eliot's poem refers to Chaucer's, then when can we properly be said to read 'April is the cruelest month'? Surely we must reread it, once we have read it, with Chaucer's words in mind. In which case the first reading is inadequate. Less dramatically, perhaps, the same may be said of any other literary text: every reading (even a so-called 'first reading') is at least in part a learned or programmed response, conditioned by other and others' readings. In this respect, reading critically is, in T.S. Eliot's words, 'as inevitable as breathing' (Eliot 1975, 37).

The present book is, fundamentally, about questions of origins, about beginning. It is concerned with how we might begin to read, to think about and write about literary texts. In particular, the book is about those uncertain origins—the author, the reader and the text—none of which can ever be taken for granted. Neither author nor reader nor text constitutes a beginning. As with the idea of 'beginning literary studies' (which we have always already begun and continue to begin), the idea that everything begins with the author or with the reader or with one particular text is both deeply compelling and deeply false.

Further reading

The classic exploration of literary beginnings is Edward Said's *Beginnings* (1975), an exuberant and theoretically astute exploration of openings, originality and origins in literature and theory. A more recent and perhaps more accessible book on beginnings is A.D. Nuttall's *Openings* (1992), which eschews theoretical discussion in favour of a concentrated focus on a small number of classic literary openings. On intertextuality, see the collection of essays edited by Judith Still and Michael Worton, *Intertextuality* (1990), which includes a useful introduction. For a different perspective on these questions, see Françoise Meltzer's recent study of the idea of literary originality, *Hot Property* (1994). On inspiration and, and as, the origin of creative thinking, see Timothy Clark's inspirational book, *The Theory of Inspiration* (1997).

Readers and reading

What do you do when you come across a poem like this?

> I met a traveller from an antique land,
> Who said—'Two vast and trunkless legs of stone
> Stand in the desert . . . Near them, on the sand,
> Half sunk a shattered visage lies, whose frown,
> And wrinkled lip, and sneer of cold command,
> Tell that its sculptor well those passions read
> Which yet survive, stamped on these lifeless things,
> The hand that mocked them, and the heart that fed;
> And on the pedestal, these words appear:
> My name is Ozymandias, King of Kings,
> Look on my Works, ye Mighty, and despair!
> Nothing beside remains. Round the decay
> Of that colossal Wreck, boundless and bare
> The lone and level sands stretch far away'.

In Percy Bysshe Shelley's famous sonnet 'Ozymandias' (1818) the narrator speaks of meeting a traveller who reports having seen a vast shattered statue strewn across the desert. The statue is of Ozymandias, the thirteenth-century BC King Rameses II of Egypt (Ozymandias is the Greek name for this king). All that remains of the King of Kings and of his 'works' are a few broken fragments, a couple of legs and an inscription which commands the reader to despair. The poem, then, is about monuments, survival and about the transience of even the greatest of us. But we might also notice that the poem is about readers and reading—the traveller reads a piece of writing, an inscription on the pedestal of a fragmented statue. The inscription *commands* the reader. And, rather differently, the word 'read' appears in line six, referring to the way that the sculptor understood the 'passions' of Ozymandias and was able to immortalize them in stone. Both the traveller and the sculptor are explicitly figured as readers, and we might also think about the 'I' of the first line as another kind of reader—a listener to the traveller's tale.

The poem, then, concerns a series of framed acts of reading. The sculptor reads the face of the king, the traveller reads the inscription, the narrative 'I' listens to the tale and, finally, we read the poem. One of the things that we might do with this poem is to think about these acts of reading. The poem can be thought about as what Paul de Man calls an 'allegory of reading': it is not only a poem which can be read, it is also a poem which tells an allegory or subtextual story about reading. One of the crucial questions of reading, for example, is how we can justify any particular reading: how can we tell if a particular reading or interpretation is valid? This is a question that goes to the heart of almost every debate in criticism and theory. In this respect the poem presents a paradox in that the traveller says that only a few fragments of the statue remain, that this is all that is left of Ozymandias and his great works. But if this is the case, then the traveller cannot know that the sculptor read the king's passions 'well'. In this way Shelley's poem can be understood as telling a story or allegory about one of the central paradoxes of reading. To read 'well' is generally taken as meaning to read accurately or faithfully. But the question of which reading of a text is the most accurate is itself a question of reading.

'Ozymandias', then, opens up a series of questions concerning readers and reading. In addition to the crucial question of how we can validate any reading (how we can know whether it is true or faithful), the poem also engages with other questions. Who is this traveller who reads the inscription, for example? And who is the 'I' who listens to, or 'reads', his story? Is the sculptor's 'mocking' of the king's face a kind of reading? What do such questions lead us to think about the power relations of any reading? Is it in the king's power to command his readers to despair? Is the traveller's reading of the inscription different from how that inscription might have been read while the king was alive? And does reading therefore change over time—is reading historically specific? What do these acts of reading, embedded within the poem, suggest about reading more generally and about our reading of this poem in particular? In this chapter we shall begin to explore some of these questions, referring to Shelley's poem as a way of summarizing some of the developments in literary criticism and theory over the past few decades.

Some of the most widely publicized developments in literary theory of the second half of the century have gone under the umbrella term 'reader-response criticism'. Such developments are usually understood as a reaction against Anglo-American 'new criticism' of the post-war period. Before we discuss reader-response criticism itself, then, it might be useful briefly to outline the position of new criticism with regard to readers and reading. Associated with such US critics as Cleanth Brooks, W.K. Wimsatt and Monroe Beardsley, and indebted also to the principles of 'practical criticism' associated with the British critics I.A. Richards and F.R. Leavis, new criticism involved a way of reading that emphasized form—the importance of considering 'the words on the page'—rather than factors such as the life of the author and his or her intentions, or the historical and ideological context in which the text was produced. New critics considered that such questions, while no doubt interesting, were irrelevant to a consideration of the text itself: they thought of literary texts as 'autonomous', as self-sufficient and self-contained unities, as aesthetic objects made of words. Correspondingly, new critics argued that to try to take account of the reactions or responses of readers in the context of, for example, a poem, was to introduce an alien and fundamentally extraneous factor. They even invented a term for what they saw as the 'error' involved in talking about a reader's response in discussions of literary texts: they called it the 'affective fallacy'. For new critics, then, what was important was to pay scrupulous attention to the words of texts themselves, and to go beyond the subjective impressionism of the reader's response.

Like all critical movements, new criticism created its own special canon of literary works and authors. Shelley, notoriously, was not in the new critical canon: in his influential book *Revaluation* (1936), F.R. Leavis had set the trend by caustically opining that Shelley is 'almost unreadable', and that the effect of his eloquence is 'to hand poetry over to a sensibility that has no more dealings with intelligence than it can help' (Leavis 1972, 171, 175). One of the peculiar characteristics of broadly 'new critical' approaches to 'Ozymandias' is that they tend to see the poem as entirely straightforward and unambiguous. As Graham Hough says, in his only comment on the poem in his book *The Romantic Poets: 'Ozymandias* is an extremely clear and direct poem, advancing to a predetermined end by means of one firmly held image' (Hough 1967, 142). Such a reaction to the poem is curious, not least because of the fact that irony, ambiguity and paradox are key elements in the new critical weaponry of reading, and that all three are dramatically at stake in lines ten and eleven of the poem, the inscription on the pedestal. 'Look on my Works, ye Mighty, and despair!' is ironic, for example, from at least two perspectives. First, the line can be read as an example of 'hubris' or excessive pride on the part of Ozymandias, who is thus shown to be absurd. Second, it can be read as ironic from Ozymandias's point of view: knowing that even he will die, Ozymandias inscribes these words for future generations, reminding us that even the greatest will be forgotten in time. These conflicting ironies produce both ambiguity and paradox—ambiguity concerning which reading is more valid, and paradox in the fact that the inscription appears to say two conflicting things.

Beginning in the late 1960s and becoming increasingly influential in the 1970s and early 1980s, reader-response criticism directly questions the principles of new criticism. For critics and theorists such as Wolf-gang Iser, Stanley Fish and Michael Riffaterre, questions of the literary text and its meaning(s) cannot be disengaged from the role that the reader takes. Although these and other reader-response critics have widely different approaches to literary texts, they all agree that the meaning of the text is created through the process of reading. What they object to in the new critical approach is the notion that a certain quality or 'meaning' of a literary text simply lies there in the text waiting for the reader or critic to come along and pull it out. Graham Hough's apparently objective assertion that 'Ozymandias' is 'extremely clear and direct', for example, elides the question of 'to whom?' Hough appears to generalize what is, in fact, his particular view of the poem. As we have tried to suggest, the poem may also be read very differently, as syntactically complex and semantically dense. The new critics' sense that the meaning of a poem is simply *there* involves thinking of meaning (in Terry Eagleton's memorable metaphor) as like a wisdom tooth, 'waiting patiently to be extracted' (Eagleton 1996, 77). Reacting against what we might call the dentistry school of criticism, reader-response critics recognize that the meanings of a text rely, in a dynamic way, on the work of the reader. Given that reading is a necessary dimension of any text, these critics attempt to plot the process of reading and the role of the reader.

Rather than closing down the questions of 'who reads?' and 'what is reading?', however, reader-response criticism has opened a postmodern Pandora's box. Critics such as Norman Holland and David Bleich, for example, are interested in investigating ways in which particular indi-viduals respond to texts, and with exploring ways in which such responses can be related to those individuals' 'identity themes', to their personal psychic dispositions—the individual character of their desires, needs, experiences, resistances and so on. This is often referred to as 'subjective criticism' or 'personal criticism'. Such critics would not be interested in deciding which reading of line eleven of 'Ozymandias' is 'correct' because such correctness or accuracy is beside the point. Norman Holland, for example, argues that 'interpretation is a function of identity' and that 'all of us, as we read, use the literary work to symbolize and finally to replicate ourselves' (Holland 1980, 123, 124). To parody the logic of subjective criticism, we might suppose that a reader whose irregular potty-training has resulted in a pathological hatred of authority-figures will delight in the ironic treatment of the King of Kings in Shelley's poem, while another reader who has early come to associate father-figures with absence and unreliability will see the poem as a poignant confirmation of the inevitable disappearance of all fathers. Although Holland assures his reader that he is not 'positing an isolated solipsistic self' (Holland 1980, 131), this is precisely the danger that other critics have seen in this kind of criticism: such a reliance on the autonomy of the reader's thoughts and feelings seems to lead to a state of delusion epitomized by Ozymandias's hollow words.

Theorists such as Stanley Fish on the other hand argue that any individual reader is necessarily part of a 'community' of readers. Every reader, he suggests, reads according to the conventions of his or her 'interpretive community'. In other words, an individual reader's response, according to this model, is determined by the conventions of reading that he or she has been educated into within a certain socio-historical context. Our recognition of the equivocality of 'Ozymandias', for example, is determined by the fact that we have been taught to recognize multiple meanings of texts whenever possible; polysemia is, in a sense, the very 'logo' of contemporary university English Studies.

A third influential strand of reader-response criticism is exemplified by the work of Wolfgang Iser. Iser elaborates ways in which the work of reading involves an interaction between elements of the text and the act of reading itself. He explores ways in which the text is 'concretized'—given shape or meaning in the act of reading. For Iser, neither the text nor the reader should be studied in isolation. Rather, the text produces certain 'blanks' or 'gaps' that the reader must attempt to complete: the reader 'is drawn into the events and made to supply what is meant from what is not said' (Iser 1995, 24). For Iser, the fact that we know nothing about the traveller in Shelley's poem, for example, 'spurs the reader into action' (24). 'Who is this traveller?', we might ask. 'What does he or she think about what is described in the poem?' The text prompts us imaginatively to fill in or fill out such hermeneutic or interpretative 'gaps'.

During the 1980s and 1990s, the political dimensions of reading became increasingly central to critical debate. Literary texts have been read in terms of power relations, in accordance with Michel Foucault's suggestion that 'power is everywhere' (Foucault 1981, 93)—even in reading. 'Ozymandias', in fact, produces multiple representations of the relationship between power and reading. Most explicitly there is the sculptor's 'reading' of the power of the king. The crucial lines here are lines four to eight:

> Half sunk a shattered visage lies, whose frown,
> And wrinkled lip, and sneer of cold command,
> Tell that its sculptor well those passions read
> Which yet survive, stamped on these lifeless things,
> The hand that mocked them, and the heart that fed . . .

The word 'mocked' means both 'imitated' or 'copied' and 'ridiculed' (a *mis*representation that represents more accurately or more cruelly). The commanding power of the king—his power, not least, to make the sculptor 'read' his face and to copy it onto stone—is resisted in that very reading, in that mockery. The sculptor's 'reading' is both a copy, a faithful representation, and a reading which makes ridiculous. Reading here is figured as *both* faithful, an action of subservience, *and* a subversive act of resistance to power, a transfer and transformation of power. Alternatively, we might consider ways in which the poem suggests that acts of reading are bound up in the historical specificity of power relations. The reading of the statue and the inscription, in this sense, changes over time. Someone contemporary with the King of Kings might read the commanding inscription—'Look on my Works, ye Mighty, and despair!'—as a statement of omnipotence. By contrast, a reader who, like the traveller, reads the inscription surrounded by the 'lone and level sands', by the *absence* of those works, their *non*-survival, can only read them ironically. What has remained, what has survived, is the work of the sculptor, the *represented* 'passions' of the king (itself a kind of reading) not his works. The power relations of text and reader have shifted decisively over time. Reading, in this sense, is not always and everywhere the same. As Robert Young comments, Shelley's poem 'demonstrates that meaning, like power, is not stable or fixed, and that even power cannot guarantee a tyranny of meaning: although authors may have intentions when they write, once they have written they cannot control and fix the meaning of any reading' (Young 1991a, 238). Finally, we might extrapolate from this to think about the way in which any reading produces a certain relation of power. Shelley's poem might itself be read as a kind of 'cold command'—a command to read. But any reading of the poem must constitute a form of resistance to such a command, a 'mockery' of that command, by the imposition or 'stamping' of its own interpretation on the poem. Reading *survives* the command of the text.

As part of this emphasis on power-relations, recent criticism has also given increased attention to questions of gender and race. Judith Fetterley, for example, has argued that female readers of classic US fiction (and, by implication, of other literary texts) have been 'immasculated', by which she means that they have traditionally been taught to read 'as men' (Fetterley 1978). Writing in the late 1970s, Fetterley argues that women should begin to liberate themselves from the notion of a 'universal' reader (who is implicitly male) and from an identification with male viewpoints in reading, and to develop specifically female models of reading. At stake here is, in Jonathan Culler's terms, the question of what it would mean to read 'as a woman' (Culler 1983, 43–64): how might 'reading as a woman' be different from 'reading as a man'? And do we know what it means to read 'as a man'? It might be possible to think about Shelley's poem in terms of gendered reading. If we can assume that the traveller is male (after all, few solitary European travellers were female in the early nineteenth century), then one can see that the poem is not only about male pride, but also about male reading. The poem, indeed, is overwhelmingly masculine, a text from which women have been excluded. Yet few critics have been troubled by questions of sexual difference in relation to 'Ozymandias': in this respect, we might suggest, the critical response has been 'immasculated'. From Fetterley's perspective, we might ask how a non-immasculated reading would respond to the masculine power-play of Shelley's poem.

Critics concerned with questions of race and ethnicity have also developed specific strategies of reading and talking about reading. Theorists such as Gayatri Chakravorty Spivak, Henry Louis Gates, Jr and Edward Said, for example, have transformed the nature of contemporary literary studies through their emphasis on questions of colonization, ethnic difference, racial oppression and discrimination, the position of the subaltern, the West and its construction of the 'other', imperialism and Orientalism. Edward Said, for instance, argues for what he calls 'contrapuntal reading' whereby, in reading a text, one 'open[s] it out both to what went into it and to what its author excluded' (Said 1993, 79). Our reading of *Jane Eyre* in terms of race and slavery in Chapter 22 suggests one such 'contrapuntal' reading. Similarly, Henry Louis Gates makes questions of reading central to black literary criticism and theory when he argues that black people in the United States have had to develop particular strategies of reading and interpretation for survival:

> Black people have always been masters of the figurative: saying one thing to mean something quite other has been basic to black survival in oppressive Western cultures. Misreading signs could be, and indeed often was, fatal. 'Reading', in this sense, was not play; it was an essential aspect of the 'literacy' training of a child. (Gates 1984, 6).

A reading concerned with questions of race might start from the fact that this English poem deals with a racial other—Egypt—and explore the way in which such otherness is inscribed in the poem. The fact that Egypt is referred to as an 'antique' land, for example, entirely effaces any possibility of a contemporary civilization and culture in that land. There is nothing beside the barrenness of the 'lone and level sands'. For this poem, Africa only signifies in terms of a mythical past.

Finally, a poststructuralist or deconstructive reading of 'Ozymandias' might, in addition to these concerns, trace the dispersal or dissolution of the reader's identity in the act of reading and affirm the sense of a radical otherness which undermines all claims to interpretive mastery. For poststructuralists, there is a dynamic significance in the question of which comes first—the text or the reader? Is reading simply something that happens to a text as if by chance, something which leaves a text fundamentally unaltered? If so, then the role of the reader would appear to be determined by the text itself: each literary text would be like a set of instructions, a kind of recipe, for how it should be read. By contrast, the text may be understood as fundamentally incomplete, to be constructed in the act of reading. In this case the text is remade in every reading. Rather than choosing between these two hypotheses, deconstructive theories of reading argue that *both* models are operative, in a peculiar double bind of reading: the reader makes the text and the text makes the reader. Deconstruction explores the space between these two possibilities and it seeks to highlight ways in which every reading and every text is unpredictable. Thus deconstruction is interested in the fact that while any text demands a 'faithful' reading, it also demands an *individual* response. Put differently, reading is at once singular (yours and nobody else's) and general (conforming to patterns of meaning dictated by the text—a text that does not require *you* in order to function). Through analysis of these and other paradoxes, critics such as Paul de Man and J. Hillis Miller suggest ways in which reading is strange, unsettling and even 'impossible'.

How should we read the word 'appear' in line nine of Shelley's poem ('And on the pedestal, these words appear'), for example? What makes these words appear? The word 'appear' might be shown to challenge all conventional preconceptions concerning reading. In particular, it challenges us to rethink the relationship between a text on the one hand simply *appearing*, simply being there like a monument, to be read, appearing from nowhere, and on the other hand a text appearing in the sense of 'seeming', an apparition, made in reading. Is the text *there*, or do we make it appear, do we imagine it? Jacques Derrida has referred to the *delireium* of reading, a pun or 'portmanteau' word which combines the French 'lire' ('to read') with 'delirium', to suggest ways in which reading can be delirious or hallucinatory (Derrida 1979, 94, quoting Blanchot). Just as we can never know how 'well', how accurately or faithfully the sculptor has read the king's passions, neither can we escape the dynamics of reading and delirium. In short, we can never stop reading because we can never finally know if what 'appears' in this poem is us reading or us being read. This is not to suggest we should therefore give up, either in despair or in indifference. Our very lives and identities are at stake. If, as we have argued, 'Ozymandias' is as much about readers and reading as about anything else, then we might see that the relation between reading and being read is shaken up in this poem: not only do we read the poem but the poem reads us. Like Ozymandias himself, we are fragmented, mute, immutable and transient: our 'passions' are read, and perhaps mocked, by the sculptor, in the form of the poem itself. After all, in reading this poem, we cannot avoid a ventriloquistic articulation, silent or not, of the king's words—

> My name is Ozymandias, King of Kings,
> Look on my Works, ye Mighty, and despair!

How do you read *that*? What happens to you, to your name?

Further reading

Andrew Bennett, ed., *Readers and Reading* (1995), collects some of the most significant essays in reading theory of recent years and includes a wide-ranging introduction to the field; for an important collection of earlier essays, see Suleiman and Crosman, eds, *The Reader in the Text* (1980). Sara Mills, ed., *Gendering the Reader* (1994) approaches reading theory from the perspective of gender and feminism. Two recent collections of essays which consider reading from a historical perspective are Raven, Small and Tadmor, eds, *The Practice and Representation of Reading in England* (1995) and James L. Machor, ed., *Readers in History* (1993). A concise and accessible summary of reader-response criticism and theory is Elizabeth Freund's book *The Return of the Reader* (1987). For a brilliant if difficult discussion of how reading is figured in literary texts, see Paul de Man's *Allegories of Reading* (1979), and see J. Hillis Miller's *The Ethics of Reading* (1987), for a consideration of the act of reading as a response to an ethical call. Two important books from a psychoanalytically oriented feminist perspective are Mary Jacobus's *Reading Woman* (1986) and Shoshana Felman's *What Does a Woman Want? Reading and Sexual Difference* (1993). For an accessible and entertaining history of reading practices and theories from the earliest records to the present, see Alberto Manguel, *A History of Reading* (1997).

3

The author

> If you really want to hear about it, the first thing you'll probably
> want to know is where I was born, and what my lousy childhood
> was like, and how my parents were occupied and all before they had
> me, and all that David Copperfield kind of crap, but I don't feel like
> going into it. (5)

The opening sentence of J.D. Salinger's *The Catcher in the Rye* (1951)
suggests a number of ways of thinking about the figure of the author. It
is at once compellingly straightforward and strangely cryptic. The sentence gives the impression of a spontaneous, candid speaking voice, directly addressing us and showing a specific concern for our wishes and
desires ('If you really want . . . you'll probably want'): we are being
addressed very much *on the level*—nothing pretentious here, none of
'that David Copperfield kind of crap'. Despite appearances, however,
this opening sentence tells us nothing, gives nothing away, rather it is
furtive and evasive: 'I don't feel like going into it'. The most important
word in this famous opening sentence may indeed be the word 'it': 'it'
is the emphatic but equivocal subject ('If you really want to hear about
it . . . I don't feel like going into it'). Is the 'it' at the beginning of the
sentence the same as the 'it' at the end?

The ambiguity of 'it' corresponds to another kind of uncertainty. For
what is also unclear from this opening sentence is *who is speaking* or,
more accurately, *who is writing*. After all, despite the seductiveness of
the confiding, colloquial voice here, it would be somewhat naive or at
least reductive to pretend that this is *not* writing. The sentence is playing
a type of literary game with conventions of novel-openings. Of course
we quickly learn that the 'I' here is a 16-year-old American boy called

19

Holden Caulfield, but this is not something that is made clear in the first sentence. All we can presume at this point is that we are reading that particular kind of text called a novel and that it has been written by J.D. Salinger. The literary game that is set in motion by this opening sentence has to do with the relationship between fiction (a novel) and truth (biography or autobiography) on the one hand, and with the strange relationship between an author, a narrator and a reader, on the other. This is suggested by the apparently deprecating reference to David Copperfield ('all that David Copperfield kind of crap'). There is, then, a *metafictional* dimension in this seemingly simple opening sentence: the narrator invokes the protagonist of one of the 'classic' English nineteenth-century novels and implies, even by denying it, a correlation with *another* literary text.

Both *David Copperfield* and *The Catcher in the Rye* offer a mixing of novel and (auto)biography. In doing so, they provoke a series of fundamental questions about the relationship between literary texts, narrators, characters and authors. Above all, they provoke the question: who is speaking? In presenting us with the voice of a fictional speaker, these texts draw attention to the figure of the author as a sort of concealed or cryptic, haunting but unspecified presence. Who is behind this 'I'? The opening of *The Catcher in the Rye* thus introduces a general question for literary criticism and theory, the question of the presence of another 'I'—the haunting absent-presence of the 'I' who writes, of the author. The author is a kind of ghost. Salinger's novel provides more than one illustration of this. A few pages further on, for example, Holden Caulfield tells us:

> What really knocks me out is a book that, when you're all done reading it, you wish the author that wrote it was a terrific friend of yours and you could call him up on the phone whenever you felt like it. That doesn't happen much, though. I wouldn't mind calling this Isak Dinesen up. And Ring Lardner, except that D.B. [Holden's brother] told me he's dead. You take that book *Of Human Bondage*, by Somerset Maugham, though. I read it last summer. It's a pretty good book and all, but I wouldn't want to call Somerset Maugham up. I don't know. He just isn't the kind of a guy I'd want to call up, that's all. I'd rather call old Thomas Hardy up. I like that Eustacia Vye. (22)

Again this passage is delightfully straightforward and yet extraordinarily suggestive. It presents us with what is in many respects an undeniable truth, as well as what constitutes one of the curious effects of literature: literary texts can and do generate feelings of identification, not only between reader and character but also, perhaps more enigmatically, between reader and author. You really can be drawn into the feeling that the author is 'a terrific friend of yours' or at least that your appreciation and understanding of an author is so intense it touches on the telepathic. In a sense, Holden's reference to getting on the phone to the author is uncannily apposite: the rapport that exists between you and your favourite author is indeed like a sort of surreal tele-link. The author is an absent presence, both there and not there. You may feel that you understand like nobody else what it is that the author is saying; and you may be willing to acknowledge that this author can express your opinions, thoughts and feelings as well as or even better than you yourself could. This is, in fact, precisely how the greatness of Shakespeare is often described. It is what William Hazlitt says, for example, in his 1818 lecture on dramatic poetry: 'the striking peculiarity of Shakespeare's mind' is 'its power of communication with all other minds' (Hazlitt 1910, 47).

At the same time, however, this passage from *The Catcher in the Rye* prompts us to reflect on at least two other points. First, it is not (usually anyway) a two-way friendship that a reader enjoys with an author. Indeed, this one-waywardness is part of the fantasy of reading: the 'author' is generally *not* someone whose telephone number you can readily acquire and with whom you really can become terrific friends in the way that Caulfield is suggesting. The author, in other words, is not so much an 'actual' author at all: rather, it is your personal projection, *your idea* of the author. Second, it is also the case that the author not only *may be* dead, but in some respects always already *is* dead. Part of the irony and humour of this passage from Salinger's novel consists in the blurring of the distinction between living authors and dead ones. For despite his concern with the problem of giving Ring Lardner a ring, given that Ring Lardner cannot be rung (since he is dead), Holden Caulfield concludes his 'call-an-author' fantasy by saying he would like to 'call old Thomas Hardy up'—as if Hardy, though 'old', still lived. As we might all be reasonably expected to know, Thomas Hardy is (and was, well before 1951) unequivocally dead.

A lot has been said and written over the past few decades about 'the death of the author'. This paradoxical idea refers not to the empirical or literal death of a given author, but to the fact that, in a radical sense, the author is absent from the text. 'The death of the author' became a catch-phrase primarily on account of an essay of that title, written by the French poststructuralist Roland Barthes and first published in 1968. Barthes's essay is flamboyant and provocative. In part, he is arguing against the very common ascription of authority to the figure of the author. People often ask, for example: 'Is that what Shakespeare (or Brontë or Dickens) really meant? Is that what the author intended? Such questions reflect what W.K. Wimsatt and Monroe Beardsley described, in an essay first published in 1946, as 'the intentional fallacy' (Wimsatt and Beardsley 1972). In what became a conceptual cornerstone of Anglo-American New Criticism, they argued that 'the design or intention of the author is neither available nor desirable as a standard for judging the success of a literary work' (Wimsatt and Beardsley 1972, 334). All we have, they argued, are the 'words on the page'—which may indicate intention but can never finally prove it. Even if we were to go to a living author and ask what he or she meant by a particular text, all we would get would be another *text* (his or her answer), which would then, in turn, be open to interpretation. Just because it comes 'from the horse's mouth' does not mean that the horse is telling the truth, or that the horse *knows* the truth, or indeed that what the horse has to say about the 'words on the page' is any more interesting or illuminating than what anyone else might have to say. We could also ponder the question of 'authorial intention' in the light of psychoanalysis. 'Conscious intention', in this respect, can always be considered as subject to the unconscious workings of the mind. With psychoanalysis, it is no longer possible simply to privilege consciousness as the sombre judge of what is intended. The jurisdiction of 'authorial intention' falters here: what is not meant can still (in another sense) be meant. 'I didn't mean to hurt you' can always mean 'I did'. Correspondingly, it is important to acknowledge some of the implications of twentieth-century linguistics (Saussure, Chomsky, Pinker) as regards this question of the author and his or her authority. Rather than say that the author is in control of the language that he or she uses, we might consider the idea that the language is as much in control of the author. In this respect, language can be thought of as a kind of system within which any writer must take a designated place: the system and rules of language inevitably dictate the possibilities of what someone can say. An author is not God, after all.

Barthes's essay provides a strong sense of the ways in which we need, if not to ridicule, at least to be sceptical about the idea of the author as the origin and end of the meaning of a text. But rather than solving the problem of interpretive authority, 'The Death of the Author' in certain respects simply transfers it. In particular, Barthes argues that 'the death of the author' is synonymous with 'the birth of the reader' (Barthes 1977a, 118). But as we suggest in the preceding chapter, such a claim is manifestly problematic: after all, the critique of the notion of the Author (to which Barthes wittily gives a capital 'A', thus highlighting the putatively god-like attributes of this figure) is just as valid as a critique of the notion of the reader (who, in effect, simply acquires in Barthes's account a capital 'R' instead). Nevertheless his essay does offer some crucial and succinct remarks on the idea of the author and it remains a valuable account. Barthes writes:

> We know now that a text is not a line of words releasing a single 'theological' meaning (the 'message' of the Author–God) but a multi-dimensional space in which a variety of writings, none of them original, blend and clash. The text is a tissue of quotations drawn from the innumerable centres of culture ... Once the Author is removed, the claim to decipher a text becomes quite futile. To give a text an Author is to impose a limit on that text, to furnish it with a final signified, to close the writing. (Barthes 1977a, 146)

In a sense the problem here is evident simply from the two words which frame the above quotation: 'Barthes writes'. We are still talking in terms of the author and there could be little more persuasive indication of the idea that the author is *not* dead (though Roland Barthes, sadly, is) than the use of the present tense: Barthes *writes*. But at the same time we need to be careful here. The 'death of the author', in Barthesian terms, is explicitly figurative or metaphorical, and we could say, by way of a sort of corrective to possible misreading in this context, that the author cannot die precisely because, as we've been suggesting, the author is— always has been and always will be—a ghost. Never fully present or fully absent, a figure of fantasy and elusiveness, the author only ever haunts. It is also important to stress that Barthes is not in fact talking about 'the author' but 'the Author'. Insofar as the metaphorical death makes sense, then, it is the death of a particular *concept* of the Author that is at stake. In this respect Barthes's essay has to be seen in its cultural and historical context, as providing a simplified but valuable articulation of a variety of intellectual positions that have emerged over the past few decades, in France and elsewhere.

Barthes's essay should be read alongside Michel Foucault's 'What Is an Author?' (1969), an essay that is undoubtedly more systematic and rigorous than Barthes's in many respects. More drily but more carefully than Barthes, Foucault provides (but note the present tense: Foucault, too, is dead) an extraordinary sense of the figure of the author as a *historical construction*. The idea of the author is not a timeless given: the figure and significance of the author varies across time, and from one culture to another, from one discourse to another and so on. As regards works of literature, Foucault is concerned to criticize the notion of the author as 'the principle of a certain unity of writing' (Foucault 1979, 151). In other words, like Barthes, he puts into question the idea that the author is a god-like or (in more Foucauldian terms) saint-like figure, that the author is the presiding authority or principle of coherence for the understanding of a text. He does this primarily by focusing on the historical and ideological determinations of the notion of the author. He notes, for example, that

> There was a time when the texts that we today call 'literary' (narratives, stories, epics, tragedies, comedies) were accepted, put into circulation, and valorized without any question about the identity of their author; their anonymity caused no difficulties since their ancientness, whether real or imagined, was regarded as a sufficient guarantee of their status. (Foucault 1979, 149)

And he emphasizes that, more recently, literary authorship has been integrally bound up with changes in law and questions of copyright and ownership of texts. Finally, like Barthes, Foucault is interested in the potentially revolutionary effects of writing. 'What Is an Author?' affirms the jubilatory—because anti-authoritarian (here the correlations between 'author' and 'authority' become explicit)—energies of a writing or discourse freed of the conventional impositions of authorship. Foucault emphasizes the paradox that, while we think of the author as 'a perpetual surging of invention', in fact 'we make him [or her] function in exactly the opposite fashion'. While we think of the author as endlessly creative, in other words, our practice of reading and criticism makes him or her into a locus of authority which confines meaning and significance to a single univocal strand. Foucault thus concludes: 'The author is therefore the ideological figure by which one marks the manner in which we fear the proliferation of meaning' (159). We want there to be an identifiable author for a text because this comforts us with the notion that there is a particular sense to that text.

Barthes and Foucault, among many others, are quire rightly concerned with ways of thinking about literature that do not depend on regarding the author as the origin of the meaning of a text or as the authoritative 'presence' in that text. Contemporary literary theory draws together threads from psychoanalysis (the 'I' is in many ways *by defini-tion* not in control of itself, since it is determined by what it cannot control, in other words, the unconscious), linguistics (language *speaks us* as much as we speak language), ethnology (creativity, authorship, etc. are differently constructed and conceived in different cultures) and feminism (the Author with a capital A is in many respects clearly male: God, the Father, the patriarchal Presence). Nevertheless, the figure of the author remains a decisive force in contemporary culture—for all kinds of reasons, some of them entirely admirable. Thus in women's writing, for example, or in the study of supposedly non-mainstream (i.e. non-white, non-European, non-male, non-middle class, non-heterosexual) writing, there has been and continues to be an emphasis on the person of the author, an emphasis that is in some ways remarkably conventional and 'conformist'. This emphasis is particularly character-istic of what has come to be known as identity politics. Such 'conform-ism' is understandable especially if, as theorists of such writing some-times claim, it is presented as the initial step in a longer-term strategy of disturbing, dislocating and transforming anthropocentric, patriarchal, white, bourgeois, 'straight' values. It is also true that what we think about a particular text, how we read and understand it, can probably never be simply dissociated from what we know (or think we know) of its author. The fact that we know (assuming that we do) that John Keats died of tuberculosis at the tragically early age of 25 cannot but affect the way we read those prophetically poignant lines from 'Ode to a Nightingale' (1819), written only two years before his death:

> Now more than ever seems it rich to die,
>   To cease upon the midnight with no pain,
>   While thou art pouring forth thy soul abroad
>   In such an ecstasy!
> Still wouldst thou sing, and I have ears in vain—
>   To thy high requiem become a sod.

Similarly, the fact that Ezra Pound made fascist propaganda broadcasts on Italian radio cannot but affect the way that we read Pound's *Cantos*. But it is still important to bear in mind that all such more or less conven-tional valorizations of the author are deeply problematic. In particular, the attempt to settle questions of interpretation through appeals to the intended meaning of the author should always be viewed with at least deep suspicion. It is not a question (as Barthes polemically argued) of 'removing' the author or of the death of the author: the author was always already dead. Specifically, as Jacques Derrida argues, an author is 'dead insofar as his [or her] text has a structure of survival even if he [or she] is living' (Derrida 1985a, 183). This acknowledgement that the death of the author is written into every word she or he publishes is evident in copyright law, which is explicitly concerned with the text as legal property, regardless of whether the author is alive or not.

As we have attempted to show, then, the idea of an author-centred reading is in various ways problematic. No doubt it will never be possible to give up the sense of phantasmatic identification with an author ('I love Emily Brontë', 'John Webster is my hero'). Nor, indeed, are we likely to stop reading literary biographies and being interested in the apparently tangential issues of authors' love affairs, their compositional practices or even, if all else fails, their laundry lists. But it is well to be aware that the relationship between life and work is at least highly complex and highly mediated, and that a key to the authorial life is by no means necessarily a key to the literary text. Our identifications with and ideas about authors are, in the final analysis, themselves forms of fiction. To adapt Holden Caulfield's analogy here, a ghost does not have a telephone number. In keeping with the notion that the author is necessarily a ghost, we could suggest that the greatest literary texts are indeed those in which the author seems most ghostly. (We develop this idea in greater detail in Chapter 15.) The most powerful works of literature are those which suggest that they are singular, that no one else could have written them, *and yet* that their authorship is, in more than one sense, a phantom issue. One need think only, for example, of Chaucer's *Canterbury Tales*, the plays of Shakespeare, Emily Brontë's *Wuthering Heights*, Toni Morrison's *The Bluest Eye* or of course J.D. Salinger's *The Catcher in the Rye*, to realize that in a sense they tell us nothing about their authors, even if they are texts in which we feel their elusive and strange presence in an especially powerful way. What is true of authors generally is true of Keats's remark about the poet. The poet as poet has no identity: he or she lives, and lives on, in the strange space of writing.

Further reading

The brief essay entitled 'The Intentional Fallacy' (Wimsatt and Beardsley 1972) remains a valuable critical reference-point for thinking about authorial intention. For a concise and thought-provoking more recent essay on 'Intention', see Annabel Patterson (1990). On the figure of the author more generally, Roland Barthes's 'The Death of the Author' (1977a) is vigorous and entertaining but ultimately perhaps not as helpful as his somewhat later essays, 'From Work to Text' (Barthes 1977b) and 'Theory of the Text' (in Young 1981). For two good wide-ranging collections of critical and other material on the author, see Sean Burke, ed., *Authorship: From Plato to the Postmodern* (1995) and Maurice Biriotti and Nicola Miller, eds, *What is an Author?* (1993). Kevin Pask's *The Emergence of the English Author* (1996) presents a useful detailed account of the history of the author in the early-modern period. For a contrast to Michel Foucault's now classic essay 'What Is an Author?' (1979), see Karl Miller's very much more traditional study, *Authors* (1989). Similarly, for a recent book that seeks to refute Barthesian thinking on authorship, see Sean Burke's *The Death and Return of the Author* (1992).

The text and the world

All of the chapters in this book are, in different ways, about the relationship between texts and the world. How do texts represent the world? Where does a text begin and end? Is an author an inhabitant of the world or the creation of a literary text? To what extent is history a kind of text? And what implications does this have for thinking about literature? Can literary texts do things to the world as well as simply describe it? These are some of the questions with which we engage in this book.

The relation between literary texts and the world has been a central problem in criticism and theory at least since Plato. The very phrase 'the text and the world', however, immediately presents a questionable distinction: its very formulation presupposes a difference between a text on the one hand and the world on the other. This distinction is, of course, a very common way of thinking about literature: it is implicit in notions of mimesis or imitation, of realism and naturalism, and of representation, as well as in metaphors which figure literary texts as offering a window onto the world or (in Hamlet's words) as holding a mirror up to nature. All of these ways of thinking about literary texts start from an assumed separation of the literary work, the text, from the world. They imply that a literary text is not, in essence, part of the world. Actually, various writers have been trying to drive a stake into the heart of this assumption for centuries: the text–world dichotomy is like a vampire that will not lie down. The latest and most persistent of these vampire-killers are called poststructuralists. Poststructuralism (including new historicism, feminism, deconstruction) consistently undermines the very terms of this text–world dichotomy. Michel Foucault puts the point in a Nietzschean way: 'if language expresses, it does so not in so far as it is an imitation and duplication of things, but in so far as it manifests ... the fundamental will of those who speak it'

(Foucault 1970, 290). Poststructuralists ask what it means to say that a literary text is different from, separate from the world. Shouldn't we say, rather, that such texts actually make up our world? How can an act of inscription or an act of reading *not* be part of the world? Is there a world without such acts? In a later chapter, we consider the way in which texts may be considered as performative speech-acts, acts of language which themselves *do* things, as well as just talk about things. In this chapter in particular, we shall try to explore the idea that literary texts are acts that destabilize the very notion of the world and disturb all assumptions about a separation between world and text.

In order to consider this proposition, we shall discuss Andrew Marvell's poem 'To His Coy Mistress' (1681). The poem presents itself as a work of seduction. The speaker addresses his 'coy mistress' and attempts to persuade her to go to bed with him:

> Had we but world enough, and time,
> This coyness, lady, were no crime.
> We would sit down, and think which way
> To walk, and pass our long love's day.
> Thou by the Indian Ganges' side
> Shouldst rubies find: I by the tide
> Of Humber would complain. I would
> Love you ten years before the flood:
> And you should, if you please, refuse
> Till the conversion of the Jews.
> My vegetable love should grow
> Vaster than empires, and more slow.
> An hundred years should go to praise
> Thine eyes, and on thy forehead gaze.
> Two hundred to adore each breast:
> But thirty thousand to the rest.
> An age at least to every part,
> And the last age should show your heart:
> For, lady, you deserve this state,
> Nor would I love at lower rate.
>
> But at my back I always hear
> Time's winged chariot hurrying near:
> And yonder all before us lie
> Deserts of vast eternity.
> Thy beauty shall no more be found;
> Nor, in thy marble vault, shall sound

> My echoing song: then worms shall try
> That long-preserved virginity:
> And your quaint honour turn to dust;
> And into ashes all my lust.
> The grave's a fine and private place,
> But none, I think, do there embrace.
>
> Now, therefore, while the youthful hue
> Sits on thy skin like morning dew,
> And while thy willing soul transpires
> At every pore with instant fires,
> Now let us sport us while we may,
> And now, like amorous birds of prey,
> Rather at once our time devour,
> Than languish in his slow-chapped power.
> Let us roll all our strength, and all
> Our sweetness, up into one ball:
> And tear our pleasures with rough strife,
> Thorough the iron gates of life.
> Thus, though we cannot make our sun
> Stand still, yet we will make him run.

As soon as we ask even the simplest questions about this poem we come up against the problem of representation, the problem of the relationship between the text and the world. Perhaps the most obvious question that we would want to ask is whether the poem should be read as *really* a poem of seduction: is the speaker the same as the poet and, if so, is this text really addressed to a woman Andrew Marvell knew? Or should we understand the speaker to be a fictional construction and the 'real' addressee to be another reader—us, for example—a reader or readers not explicitly addressed but nevertheless implied by the text? Most readings of the poem assume that the latter is the case, that rather than attempting to seduce a woman, this poem presents a fictional dramatization of such an attempt. In this sense, it may seem that the poem is categorically separate from the 'real' world and from 'real' people. But this poetic attempt at seduction does not just take place between a fictive woman and speaker. In various ways, 'To His Coy Mistress' dislodges any stable opposition of fiction and the real. For example, regardless of whether the mistress is conceived as real or fictive, the poem has effects on us. In particular, as we argue more fully in Chapter 24, such a poem can be considered as performative—in the sense that it performs an act not so much of sexual as of textual seduction. It tries to entice us to read and to read on and to draw us into another world—a world of reading that is both fictional and real.

But Marvell's poem does not stop here. It can be shown to engage with the world through the use of a number of specific discourses. The seduction is mediated not only by reference to other kinds of literary texts (poems of seduction, love poems, the *blazon*, the *carpe diem* or *memento mori* motif and so on), but also in terms of other kinds of discourse (biblical, classical, colonial, philosophical, scientific, military). In this respect, the poem could be seen as an example of what the Russian critic M.M. Bakhtin calls 'heteroglossia', in that it embraces a series of overlapping codes and discourses. This complex jumble of references to different discourses positions the text in relation to 'the world'—even if we try to read the poem as simply fictional.

Indeed, rather than thinking of texts on one side and 'the world' on the other, we might reflect on the idea that everything human that happens in the world is mediated by language. Language, as Jean-Jacques Lecercle puts it, 'always reminds us that it, and no one else, is speaking, that whenever we believe we rule over our words, we are in the grip of an unavoidable but nevertheless delusive illusion' (Lecercle 1990, 265). In this way we could attempt to clarify the notoriously controversial statement by Jacques Derrida, in his book *Of Grammatology* (1976, 163), that 'There is nothing outside the text'. This much quoted and much misunderstood slogan is, in fact, a misleading translation of the French sentence 'Il n'y a pas de hors-texte', which might be better translated as 'There is no outside-text'. The latter version is preferable because it is easier to see that it is saying something credible: Derrida's point is not that there is no such thing as a 'real world' but that there is nothing outside context, there is no perception or experience which is not bound up with effects of text or language. This might suggest at least two different things: first, with respect to 'To His Coy Mistress', that there is no reading of this poem that is not dependent on previous reading conventions. Reading, in this sense, is not *outside* the text being read. But nor is it outside *texts* more generally. Our experience of reading Marvell's poem is itself a kind of text. Second, Derrida's axiom can help us to think about the fact that there is no way to conceive, imagine or even perceive 'the world' without that world being contaminated by language. Put very crudely, there is no access to 'the world' except, in the broadest sense, through language. 'Language' here need not be simply verbal, but may include everything that works as a system of signs. Even without words, for example, seduction is an affair of language—there is the language of eyes, gestures, touch, a complex olfactory system of signs and so on. Derrida and other theorists of deconstruction, then, regard the text–world opposition as unavoidable but untenable. In this respect, those critics of Derrida who argue that his is a 'pure' textualism which cannot account for power or politics are simply failing to recognize the extent to which political, social, economic and historical forces are bound up in language, in discourse, in representation.

Some of these points may become clear if we take a closer look at a few details of Marvell's poem. The poem explicitly plays upon an opposition between text and world. It begins by claiming that if there were 'world enough, and time', the speaker would spend many hundreds of years praising the woman's beauty. Thus the opening verse-paragraph immediately establishes an opposition between words and deeds, between talking and making love, between language and the body—between the text and the world. And, in a self-consuming rhetorical gesture, the poem argues against any more discourse, any more talk. It argues for the disposal or rejection of speech in favour of action—the action of the joining of two bodies. In this sense, the whole poem may be read in terms of a conflict played out between the text and the world, an attempt to go beyond its own discourse to the body of the woman. At the same time, however, and paradoxically, the poem appears to suggest that this separation of text and world is itself impossible. The poem culminates in a rejection of speech or discourse and in a militaristic metaphor for the violent exchange between two bodies ('Let us roll all our strength, and all / Our sweetness, up into one ball: / And tear our pleasures with rough strife / Thorough the iron gates of life'). But this final rejection of speech in favour of action simply results in silence, the end of the poem: it does not, cannot, go beyond talk to the body of the woman. For the speaker, there is no escape from talk, language, discourse, no pure body without, outside of, this poem.

Nevertheless, at various points in the poem, the speaker does attempt to point beyond language, to refer to the woman's body—here and now. At the beginning of the third verse-paragraph, for example, he describes a blush which suffuses the woman's body:

> Now, therefore, while the youthful hue
> Sits on thy skin like morning dew,
> And while thy willing soul transpires
> At every pore with instant fires,
> Now let us sport us while we may . . .

What we might call the poem's 'fiction of immediacy' (the sense that the speaker is addressing a woman who is present and that the action of this poem takes place in 'real time') becomes fully apparent at this point, when the speaker refers directly to the altering state of the woman's body. In addition to the insistent deixis of 'Now . . . Now', this sense of immediacy is generated through complex *rhetorical* strategies. For example, the blush or sweat which 'transpires / At every pore' is read as a sign of the inner 'fires' produced by the 'willing soul' of the woman. In its most direct reference to the woman's body, at this 'instant', here and now, the poem is highly figurative. The complicated metaphoricity of these lines dissolves any possible illusion of corporeal presence. Moreover, as we have suggested, the speaker *interprets* the woman's blush just as we interpret his lines. This interpretation translates the woman's body into a text to be read. Indeed, part of the irony of this section of the poem lies in the fact that the speaker's reading is highly questionable. A different interpretation would be that the woman is angry, repulsed or shocked, rather than amorous. After all, the speaker has just referred, in a lewd and outrageous way, to the woman's 'quaint honor' being invaded by worms—she will not be able to keep her purity or virginity in the grave, but will be penetrated by worms. Another 'reading' of the text of the woman's body, of her blush and of the poem, then, would highlight the speaker's blind misogyny, his capacity for a violent mis-reading of his 'coy mistress'. The poem's fiction of immediacy, its attempt to get to a world supposedly beyond language, a world embodied in and as the body of the woman, is compromised at precisely that moment that it is most explicitly asserted.

'The text and the world' names a false opposition. Texts cannot but be part of the world. To talk about texts as 'representing' reality simply overlooks ways in which texts are already part of that reality, and ways in which literary texts *produce* our reality, make our worlds. In this respect we may be prompted to ask what is at stake not only in the narrator's but in Marvell's and in Western culture's representations of the female body. In particular, we might ask what is involved in the violence embedded within Marvell's figuration of the woman as a body and as dead—as a corpse. What is the relationship between aesthetic and erotic contemplation in this representation on the one hand and its imagining of the woman's death on the other? In her book *Over Her Dead Body: Death, Femininity and the Aesthetic* (1992), Elisabeth Bronfen has explored the multiple ways in which patriarchy figures the conjunction of femininity with death and the aesthetic, and the fact that the female body as an object of aesthetic contemplation is also bound up with a certain violence towards femininity, towards women. According to this thinking, the very status of Marvell's poem as a classic, as a showcase poetic urn in the imaginary museum of English literary history, its reproduction in classrooms, lecture theatres, anthologies and in books such as our own, produces and reinforces the cultural construction of 'woman' as allied with death and with the aesthetic. Indeed, Bronfen would argue that such a poem and its reception have a crucial social and cultural function since, like other representations of the death of a beautiful woman, the poem exemplifies patriarchy's repression of the fact of the (male) subject's own death by the displaced representation of that death in the 'other' (the woman). The linguist Roman Jakobson famously defines the 'poetic function' of language as 'a focus on the message for its own sake' (Jakobson 1960, 365), and the critical tradition has tended to respond to Marvell's poem in just this way, reading it as a self-reflexive, autonomous work of art which transcends the interests of the world. But if instead we read it as a powerful and influential expression of the cultural construction of femininity, we see that the distinction that is embedded in our chapter title—between the text and the world—has dissolved.

Further reading

Edward Said's *The World, the Text, and the Critic* (1983), especially the title essay, persuasively argues for a recognition of the fact that 'a text in being a text is a being in the world'. An earlier and now classic argument for a similar position is contained in the influential work of Raymond Williams, whose 1961 book *The Long Revolution* (1992) has been deeply influential for British cultural materialism in particular. Roland Barthes's classic book *Mythologies* (1972) demonstrates the cultural construction of 'reality' or 'nature' in fascinating analyses of anything from soap powder to wrestling. Roger Fowler's *Linguistic Criticism* (1986) takes a linguistic perspective on questions raised in this chapter. Whiteside and Issacharoff, eds, *On Referring in Literature* (1987) collects a number of essays on the problem of reference in relation to literary texts. Alongside and rather more accessible than Bronfen's *Over Her Dead Body* (1992) is Peter Brooks's lucid and thought-provoking *Body Work* (1993), which also considers the representation of bodies—especially female bodies—in nineteenth- and twentieth-century art and literature. For two powerful and very different accounts of writing and/ through the body of a woman, see Luce Irigaray, 'This Sex Which is Not One' (1985) and Hélène Cixous's 'The Laugh of the Medusa' (1990).

The uncanny

Literature is uncanny. What does this mean? To try to define the uncanny is immediately to encounter one of its decisive paradoxes, namely that 'the uncanny' has to do with a *troubling* of definitions, with a fundamental disturbance of what we think and feel. The uncanny has to do with a sense of strangeness, mystery or eeriness. More particularly it concerns a sense of unfamiliarity which appears at the very heart of the familiar, or else a sense of familiarity which appears at the very heart of the unfamiliar. The uncanny is not just a matter of the weird or spooky, but has to do more specifically with a disturbance of the familiar. Such a disturbance might be hinted at by way of the word 'familiar' itself. 'Familiar' goes back to the Latin *familia*, a family; as an adjective it means 'well acquainted or intimate', 'having a thorough knowledge', etc.; but as a noun 'familiar' carries the more unsettling, supernatural sense of 'a spirit or demon supposed to come to a person *esp* a witch, etc, at his or her call' (*Chambers Dictionary*). We might think here, for example, of the demonic 'familiar' that is said to haunt Bertha Mason in Charlotte Brontë's *Jane Eyre* (1847) or, more comically, of the 12-year-old Maud's 'supernatural companion' in Elizabeth Bown's superb novel *A World of Love* (1955).

Here are a couple of examples of the uncanny. First: you walk into a room in a house you have never visited before and suddenly you have the sense that you *have* been there before and that you even seem to know what will happen next. This kind of experience has even developed its own name, *déjà vu*. Or, second example: you are in some public place (a shop perhaps or a train) and you catch sight of someone whom you think looks rather disturbing, and then you realize that you have caught sight of this person reflected in a window or a mirror and that this person is yourself.

These examples could be described as so-called 'real life' occurrences.

But are they in fact 'real life'? If, as we shall see, the uncanny is especially relevant to the study of literature, it also has to do with how the 'literary' and the 'real' can seem to merge into one another. On the one hand, uncanniness could be defined as occurring when 'real', everyday life suddenly takes on a disturbingly 'literary' or 'fictional' quality. On the other hand, literature itself could be defined as the discourse of the uncanny: literature is the kind of writing which most persistently and most provocatively engages with the uncanny aspects of experience, thought and feeling. In some ways this is in keeping with the sort of conception of literature theorized by the Russian formalists of the early twentieth century, especially Viktor Shklovsky. Literature, for the Russian formalists, has to do with *defamiliarization* (*ostranenie*): it makes the familiar strange, it challenges our beliefs and assumptions about the world and about the nature of 'reality'. Bertolt Brecht's argument that theatre should produce 'alienation effects' is an obvious analogy here. For Brecht, no actor is supposed to identify completely with the character he or she plays. Likewise the spectator is encouraged to feel dissociated, uneasy, alienated. In accordance with this, Brecht's concern is to demonstrate that the 'real' is not something that is simply a *given*: it is not something definite and immutable, but is constructed through human perception, language, beliefs and assumptions, and consequently it is something that can be changed. In Brechtian terms, the alienating or defamiliarizing power of drama—and art and literature more generally—lies in its capacity to transform us and the world around us. In this chapter we shall argue that these ideas about the power of art to disturb, defamiliarize or shake our beliefs and assumptions are intimately bound up with the uncanny. The uncanny—in particular as first elaborated by Freud, in his essay of that title (Freud 1985b)—is central to any description of the literary.

The uncanny has to do with making things *uncertain*: it has to do with the sense that things are not as they have come to appear through habit and familiarity, that they may challenge all rationality and logic. Nevertheless, it is possible to suggest a few forms that the uncanny takes:

1. The uncanny involves, above all, strange kinds of repetition: repetition of a feeling, situation, event or character. Two obvious examples of the uncanny, in this respect, would be the experience of *déjà vu* (the sense that something has happened before), and the idea of the double (or *doppelgänger*).
2. Odd coincidences and, more generally, the sense that things are *fated* to happen.

3. Animism. This is the rhetorical term referring to a situation in which what is inanimate or lifeless is given attributes of life or spirit. In the last sentence of Emily Brontë's *Wuthering Heights* (1847), for example, we read of 'the soft wind breathing through the grass'—a potentially uncanny instance of animism.

4. Anthropomorphism—that is to say, a more specific (because specifically human) form of animism. It is the rhetorical figure that refers to a situation in which what is not human is given attributes of human form or shape: the legs of a table or the face of a cliff would be examples of anthropomorphism, though they might not immediately or necessarily provoke a feeling of uncanniness. More immediately uncanny, perhaps, would be the descriptions of the wallpaper in Charlotte Perkins Gilman's story *The Yellow Wallpaper* (1892). There is, for example, the moment when the narrator tells us about the 'kind of sub-pattern' in the wallpaper: 'in the places where [the wallpaper] isn't faded and where the sun is just so—I can see a strange, provoking, formless sort of figure, that seems to skulk about behind' (18).

5. Automatism. This is a term that can be used when what is human is perceived as merely mechanical: examples of this would be sleepwalking, epileptic fits, trance-states and madness. The narrator of *The Yellow Wallpaper* would clearly fit into this category (especially when she is 'creeping' round and round her room at the end), but a sufficiently careful reading of, say, Keats's trance-like 'Ode to a Nightingale' (1819) might also prove interesting in this context. The question at the end of Keats's poem is about trance and, perhaps, madness. In a sense it is a question that haunts literature in general: 'Do I wake or sleep?' To suggest briefly one other example, the writing of D.H. Lawrence is full of people in states of trance and seizure. Towards the end of 'The Rocking-Horse Winner' (1912), for instance, there is a description of Paul and his mother: 'The Derby was drawing near, and the boy grew more and more tense. He hardly heard what was spoken to him, he was very frail, and his eyes were really uncanny. His mother had sudden seizures of uneasiness about him' (745). Robots and other automata (such as Terminator), on the other hand, are also uncanny, for the opposite reason: what is perceived as human is in fact mechanical.

6. A sense of radical uncertainty about sexual identity—about whether a person is male or female, or apparently one but actually the other. This is made dramatically clear, for instance, in the uncanny revela-

tion in the course of Neil Jordan's film *The Crying Game* (1992), when an apparently female character turns out to have the genitalia of a man; but we could also think of the uncanniness of gender in, for example, Virginia Woolf's *Orlando* (1927) or, more recently, Jeanette Winterson's *Sexing the Cherry* (1989) or *Written on the Body* (1992).

7. A fear of being buried alive. This is in itself perhaps a somewhat 'refined' example of the uncanny, but it is relevant insofar as it is related more broadly to images or experiences of claustrophobia, of being unexpectedly and unpleasantly stuck (for instance in an elevator, or in a swamp, or simply in a room with the last person in the world you would like to be left alone with). An extreme but fascinating instance of the uncanny in this context would be Edgar Allan Poe's story 'The Premature Burial' (1844)—about a man who has an obsessive fear of being buried alive and goes to great trouble and expense to have his family crypt designed in such a way as to allow him to escape, in the (one might have thought laughably unlikely) event of being buried alive by mistake. In a broader sense, however, we could reflect on the uncanny feelings encountered in all the incidents of being locked in, of enclosure and confinement, in Brontë's intensely claustrophobic *Wuthering Heights*.

8. Silence. Intriguingly, this is an example proposed by Freud, though he himself is effectively silent on the subject of what makes it uncanny. The potentially uncanny qualities of silence are particularly evident in a work such as Henry James's *The Turn of the Screw* (1898). There is, for example, the strangely silent encounter on the stairs, between the governess and the dead Peter Quint:

> It was the dead silence of our long gaze at such close quarters that gave the whole horror, huge as it was, its only note of the unnatural. If I had met a murderer in such a place and at such an hour we still at least would have spoken. Something would have passed, in life, between us; if nothing had passed one of us would have moved. The moment was so prolonged that it would have taken but little more to make me doubt if even *I* were in life. I can't express what followed it save by saying that the silence itself . . . became the element into which I saw the figure disappear. (135)

9. Telepathy. This is an uncanny idea not least because it involves the thought that your thoughts are perhaps not your own, however

private or concealed you might have assumed them to be. Literature is pervaded by examples of the telepathic. Alongside some of the texts already mentioned, such as *Jane Eyre*, *Wuthering Heights*, 'The Rocking-Horse Winner' and *The Turn of the Screw*, we might think, for instance, of George Eliot's *The Lifted Veil* (1878)—the very title of which gestures towards uncanny relevation. Eliot's narrator, Latimer, describes how he suddenly becomes capable of reading others' thoughts. In this way he presents an uncanny example of one of the most fundamental characteristics of narrative fiction: he becomes an omniscient (or nearly omniscient) narrator.

10. Death. In particular, death as something at once familiar—'all that lives must die', as Gertrude puts it (*Hamlet*, I, ii, 72)—and absolutely unfamiliar, unthinkable, unimaginable.

In sum, then, the uncanny can be described as the thoughts and feelings which may arise on those occasions when the homely becomes unhomely, when the familiar becomes unfamiliar or the unfamiliar becomes strangely familiar. Alternatively, the uncanny is—in the words of the German philosopher F.W.J. Schelling—that which 'ought to have remained ... secret and hidden but has come to light'. Schelling's definition of the uncanny is quoted by Sigmund Freud in his essay, published in 1919, entitled 'The "Uncanny"' ('Das Unheimliche'). In fact, most of the account of the uncanny which we have given so far is indebted to this extraordinary text. When Freud chose to write an essay on the uncanny he was opening up a very strange can of worms.

Freud's essay is largely focused on literature and in particular on a reading of E.T.A. Hoffmann's story 'The Sand-Man' (1816). In this respect it is slightly unusual, since Freud wrote comparatively little that could be described as literary criticism or literary theory. But few of Freud's essays have had a more pervasive and exciting impact on literary studies. What is especially fascinating about Freud's essay is the way in which it prompts us to ask various questions about *boundaries* and *limits*: How much of Freud's essay is psychoanalysis and how much is literature? Where does reason become imagination and imagination reason? Where does science become fiction and fiction science? Where does literature end and literary criticism or literary theory begin?

It has become something of a truism now to note that Freud's writings can be thought about in at least two basic and quite different ways. First, there is the Freud of the so-called popular imagination: Freud the patriarchal, bourgeois, nineteenth-century Viennese Jew, who believed that everything has to do with sex. This Freud has very firm views and spouts these in the form of rather mechanically predictable theories, the most celebrated and fundamental of which is perhaps the Oedipus complex. Second, however, there is the other Freud, a Freud who did not fully realize what he was saying, who was for various reasons (historical as much as personal) unable to see or develop the implications of what he was saying, not least because these implications regularly run counter to his own proposed themes and assumptions. This second Freud is a Freud who is, we could say, different from himself, and who constitutes what is sometimes referred to as 'the new Freud' or 'French Freud' (in acknowledgement of the work done by the French psychoanalyst Jacques Lacan and others), a result in other words of what has been called 'the rereading of Freud' or 'the return to Freud'.

Freud's 'The "Uncanny"' provides what is perhaps the most dramatic and stimulating manifestation of these two Freuds. On the one hand there is the Freud who believes (and in some sense *needs* to believe) that literature and psychoanalysis can be simply and clearly separated off from each other, and that psychoanalysis can significantly contribute towards a scientific and objective understanding of literary texts. On the other hand there is the Freud who shows (often only inadvertently) that the 'literary' is stranger and more disturbing than psychoanalysis, science or rationalism in general may be able or willing to acknowledge. The essay gives us two Freuds, or a kind of double-Freud, and this double spends the essay investigating the importance among other things of the idea of the double. What makes the double uncanny? According to Freud's essay, the double is paradoxically both a promise of immortality (look, there's my double, I can be reproduced, I can live forever) and a harbinger of death (look, there I am, no longer me here, but there: I am about to die, or else I must be dead already). The notion of the double undermines the very logic of identity.

All of this is suggested, in fact, by the English title of Freud's essay, where the word 'uncanny' is in quotation marks. This putting-into-quotation-marks itself constitutes potential breeding grounds for the uncanny—for the 'uncanny' is always in quotation marks. The uncanny might thus be thought of as a kind of ghost-effect that haunts all words, however self-evident or 'familiar' they may appear to be. We could illustrate this most easily perhaps by trying to imagine what it would be like if proper names (such as 'London', 'Bill Clinton', 'God') were suddenly used only in quotation marks—thus giving a new sense to the phrase 'scare quotes'. Language itself, then, becomes uncanny. Indeed, very often the more *familiar* a word, the more uncanny it can become. Every 'word', for example, is capable of being put into quotation marks and the act of putting it into quotation marks makes that word a little strange, as if different from itself, referring to something or somewhere else. This is a general point, also, about repetition: repetition of a word ('Words, words, words', as Hamlet says) can give rise to a sense of hollowness, strangeness, even spookiness.

Repetition is a key aspect of the uncanny, as Freud's essay makes clear. The uncanny is not simply a matter of the mysterious, bizarre or frightening: as we have tried to suggest, it involves a kind of *duplicity* (both doubling and deception) within the familiar. This logic of the uncanny, whereby the familiar turns into, or becomes contaminated by, the unfamiliar, is evident in the word 'uncanny' (or, in German, '*unheimlich*') itself. 'Uncanny' is the opposite of 'canny', meaning 'skil-ful', 'shrewd', 'knowing' (from Old English *kunnan*, 'to know', especially in the sense 'to know how to be able to do something'). But the word 'canny' shades into its opposite: in Scottish English in particular, 'canny' can suggest *unnatural* or *excessive* skilfulness, shrewdness or knowing. This capacity for a word to contain or to turn into its opposite is what Freud elsewhere talks about as the 'antithetical' meanings of 'primal words' (see Freud 1957a). We consider another example of this in Chap-ter 27, where 'pleasure' can be seen—at least in certain contexts—to entail its opposite ('pain'). Masochism is the term conventionally used to gloss this contradictory logic according to which pain can be pleasure or pleasure pain.

Analysis of the word 'uncanny' seems ineluctably, even fatalistically, bound up with an experience *of* the uncanny, an experience which dis-turbs any attempts to remain analytically detached and objective. This is strikingly clear from the early pages of Freud's essay, in which he seeks to show how the German word for 'homely' ('*heimlich*'), with its connotations of 'private', 'hidden', 'secret', inevitably conceals its oppos-ite—the 'unhomely' or *unheimlich*. From this it may be concluded that the uncanny cannot readily be avoided or denied: ultimately, as was hinted by putting it last on our list of ten, the uncanny is aligned with death. As a form of strange disruption, questioning and uncertainty, the idea of the uncanny may be frightening, but it also continues to be a crucially important and productive area for literary study.

The uncanny, then, is an experience—even though this may have to do with the unthinkable or unimaginable. It is not a theme which a writer uses or which a text possesses. The uncanny is not something simply present like an object in a painting. It is, rather, an effect. In this respect it has to do with how we read or interpret (interestingly, it makes no difference here whether we are talking about something in a book or something in the so-called outside world). In other words, the uncanny has to do, most of all, with effects of reading, with the experience of *the reader*. The uncanny is not so much *in* the text we are reading: rather, it is like a foreign body within *ourselves*.

Further reading

For two accessible and rather different discussions of the uncanny in literature, see Terry Apter's chapter in *Fantasy Literature* (1982) and J. Hillis Miller's essay on the uncanny and *Wuthering Heights*, in his *Fiction and Repetition* (1982). On the historical background to the concept of the uncanny in English literature, see Terry Castle's *The Female Thermometer* (1995). Hillel Schwartz's *The Culture of the Copy* (1996) offers some fascinating perspectives on doubles and dual-thinking, from 'identical twins' to 'parallel universes'. For a good collection of essays on various aspects of the uncanny, including the first English translation of Ernst Jentsch's 'On the Psychology of the Uncanny' (1906), see *Home and Family* (1995), ed. Sarah Wood. On defamiliarization, the classic essay is Shklovsky's 'Art as Technique' (1965), but for an earlier engagement with similar ideas, see Shelley's crucial and widely reprinted 1821 essay 'A Defence of Poetry'. On theatre and alienation, 'A Short Organum for the Theatre' (Brecht 1978) is terse and stimulating. On telepathy and the uncanny, see Nicholas Royle's *Telepathy and Literature* (1991). Freud's 'The "Uncanny"' remains a rich and surprising text (see Freud 1985b). For some of the more challenging readings of Freud's essay, see Samuel Weber (1973), Hélène Cixous (1976), Neil Hertz (1979) and Jane Marie Todd (1986). On 'the return to Freud', see Samuel Weber's fine study of that title (1992). For general introductions to psychoanalysis and literature, see Wright, *Psychoanalytic Criticism: A Reappraisal* (1998) and Ellmann, ed., *Psychoanalytic Literary Criticism* (1994).

Monuments

Thou art a monument without a tomb,
And art alive still while thy book doth live,
And we have wits to read, and praise to give.

Ben Jonson's poem 'To the Memory of My Beloved, The Author, Mr. William Shakespeare, And What He Hath Left Us' was originally published as a preface to the First Folio edition of Shakespeare's collected plays in 1623, just seven years after the Bard's death. In these lines Jonson addresses the topic of this chapter: the nature of the literary monument and the way in which the writings of living authors are posthumously transformed into monuments to those authors' lives and work. The poet is, in Jonson's seemingly paradoxical formulation, a 'monument without a tomb', and is 'alive still' despite his death. The paradox that Jonson explores involves the idea that the poet is both alive and dead: after his death the poet still 'lives' through the 'life' of his 'book', which itself lives just as long as we read it and praise it. Exploring this paradox of the literary afterlife, the poem is performative. It *performs* an act of monumentalization, since it is designed not only to remind the reader of the value of Shakespeare's work (the word 'monument', we may remind ourselves, originates in the Latin *monere*, to remind) but also, in so doing, to establish that value. In fact, the publishing venture to which Jonson contributes his poem plays a crucial part in the monumentalization of the poet: the publication of a posthumous 'Collected Works' is itself a sign of the importance of the dead poet's work, an index of his genius. In spite of Dryden's sense that the poem was 'an insolent, sparing, and invidious panegyric' (quoted in Donaldson 1988, 718), Jonson's intention seems to have been to 'honour' Shakespeare. This is the first stage in the poet's transcendence of his time and in his establishment as a 'classic'. Shakespeare 'was not of an age', Jonson asserts, 'but for all time!' (l.43).

The Second Folio of Shakespeare's plays, published nine years later in 1632, included an anonymous sixteen-line poem (written in fact by John Milton) entitled 'An Epitaph on the Admirable Dramatic Poet, W. Shakespeare'. Like Jonson's poem, Milton's begins by remarking on the fact that the poet had been buried in Stratford rather than, as might be thought more appropriate, Westminster Abbey (where, as Jonson notes, Chaucer, Spenser and Francis Beaumont are buried). Milton also plays on the opposition of life and death in the idea that Shakespeare has built for himself a 'live-long monument'. But he develops Jonson's notion of the relationship between reading and monumentalization by exploring the idea that we, readers, through our 'wonder and astonishment' at Shakespeare's art, are made 'marble with too much conceiving'. For Milton, we ourselves are monuments to the poet's genius, his living tomb:

> What needs my Shakespeare for his honoured bones
> The labour of an age in piled stones,
> Or that his hallowed relics should be hid
> Under a star-ypointing pyramid?
> Dear son of memory, great heir of fame,
> What need'st thou such weak witness of thy name?
> Thou in our wonder and astonishment
> Hast built thyself a live-long monument.
> For whilst to the shame of slow-endeavouring art,
> Thy easy numbers flow, and that each heart
> Hath from the leaves of thy unvalued book,
> Those Delphic lines with deep impression took,
> Then thou our fancy of itself bereaving,
> Dost make us marble with too much conceiving;
> And so sepulchred in such pomp dost lie,
> That kings for such a tomb would wish to die.

Both Jonson and Milton, then, articulate a series of questions around the idea of the monument, around the idea of the monumentalization of literary texts. How does an author enter the 'canon'? What is the relationship between monumentalization and reading? Do literary texts become static, frozen into their own tombs of eternity, or do they change with time and with each new generation? What is at stake in the literary critical process of canonization and monumentalization? What is gained and what lost? Literary texts, as the epitaphs by Jonson and Milton suggest, are themselves places where such questions are inaugurated, first posed and first pondered.

As we have seen, Jonson and Milton both express a certain ambivalence in their sense of the value of the monument and the process of monumentalization. They assert that Shakespeare needs no physical tomb, a structure that is at once a reminder of life and signifier of death. The third and fourth lines of Milton's poem sneer at the idea that Shakespeare's 'hallowed relics should be hid / Under a star-ypointing pyramid'. The lines suggest that the act of remembering, of monumentalizing the poet, is also an act of hiding, disguising, defacing him, and they remind us that this is precisely what we do when we bury the dead: by burying them we honour them but at the same time we hide them from sight, as if they are as much objects of terror and taboo as they are of veneration and awe. As Jonson and Milton recognize, the acts of monumentalization in which they are engaged when they write on Shakespeare are also acts of burial. And it might be argued that we are engaged in a similar dynamic whenever we read, talk and write about literary texts—not least, of course, when we write books of literary criticism. As Paul de Man has argued in an essay on Shelley, the transformation of literary texts into 'historical and aesthetic objects' involves a certain burial of those texts: what we do with dead poets, he remarks, 'is simply to bury them, to bury them in their own texts made into epitaphs and monumental graves' (de Man 1984, 121). The impulse to honour the dead, that is to say, is at the same time an impulse to bury them, to do away with them, to forget them, to be done with them. This, it might be said, is the fundamental tension of what we have called the 'institution' of literary studies, an irreducible conflict between at once remembering and forgetting the dead.

The paradox is broached rather differently in Frank Kermode's *The Classic* (1975), a book that has itself become a minor classic in discussions of literary value, the canon and the nature of the institutionalization of literature. Kermode comments on the tension between endurance and changeability that constitutes the canon: 'the books we call classic possess intrinsic qualities that endure, but possess also an openness to accommodation which keeps them alive under endlessly varying dispositions' (Kermode 1975, 44). Just as Jonson defines Shakespeare as 'not of an age but for all time', so Kermode is attempting to think about the way that such a text or such an oeuvre 'speaks' to all generations and is as such 'timeless'. But he also suggests that it can only be 'timeless' by signifying differently at different times, so that it is, as such, time-bound. For Kermode, it is the possibility of a certain 'openness' to inter-pretation, what he terms the text's 'accommodation', which allows what we call a 'classic' to survive. Kermode evokes a sense of the classic as the living dead, surviving endlessly on new readers. His account has certain implications for notions of authorial intention and for ideas about the limits of interpretation: if a literary text can be read and reread at different times, in accordance with their varying (conscious *and* unconscious) interests, prejudices, ideas and conventions, then it would seem that the text cannot be limited to a single or univocal interpreta-tion. If this position is correct, Kermode comments, we must somehow 'cope with the paradox that the classic changes, yet retains its identity'. And this has the further consequence that the text must be 'capable of saying more than its author meant', even if it were the case that saying 'more than he meant was what he meant to do'. Strange as it might seem, a 'classic' author may have meant what he or she cannot have known that he or she meant. Ultimately, Kermode suggests, 'the text is under the absolute control of no thinking subject' and is 'not a message from one mind to another' (Kermode 1975, 80, 139).

These ideas about the canon, about literary survival and about the nature of the 'classic', bring us back to issues of concern in other chap-ters in the present book, questions of meaning, interpretation and authorial intention which are engaged with most closely in our chapters on 'Readers and reading', 'The author', 'God' and 'Secrets'. But in addi-tion to these issues, the present chapter is concerned with another ques-tion, one that is equally fundamental to this book and to the practice and discipline of literary criticism more generally: the question of liter-ary value. Readers will no doubt have noticed the way in which Bennett and Royle repeatedly employs terms of valuation: we refer, for example, to Milton's 'great epic poem' in Chapter 1, to Elizabeth Bowen's 'superb' novel in Chaper 5, to the opening paragraph of *Middlemarch* as 'extraordinary' in Chapter 8, to Sheridan's *The School for Scandal* as 'one of the greatest eighteenth-century English comedies' in Chapter 11. We also repeatedly use such terms as 'haunting', 'powerful', 'disturbing', 'singular' to suggest our positive valuation of texts, and seem to ascribe value, more or less explicitly, to texts that we see as funny, complex, undecidable, disturbing, and so on. In other words, Bennett and Royle, like any other work of literary criticism or theory, is benetted and embroiled in value judgements. This situation is unavoidable: even if we were to exclude value-laden terms from our critical vocabulary, we (have to) choose certain texts to read and talk about and such choices can in themselves be taken to imply judgements of value. Indeed, it may be said that the primary aim of critical discourse, the impulse for talking about books, is to persuade someone else to appreciate what the critic finds valuable about a literary text.

The bases on which judgements about literary value are made, however, are not easy to define. One of the most intriguing things about T.S. Eliot's classic essay 'What is a Classic?' (1945) is the way that he repeatedly uses the word 'mature' as a kind of talisman to express what he sees as valuable in literary texts. Indeed for Eliot, in this essay at least, it amounts to the very definition of a classic: 'If there is one word on which we can fix, which will suggest the maximum of what I mean by the term "a classic" it is the word *maturity*' (Eliot 1975, 116). He then goes on to use the words 'mature' (as adjective and verb) and 'maturity' a total of 23 times in the same paragraph: ripeness is certainly all, it would seem, as far as Eliot is concerned. Eliot's essay was written in 1944: it would be strange now to find a critic so confident about the values to be ascribed to the notion of 'maturity'. In general, it might be said, 'mature' is no longer part of the critical vocabulary of value. And what strikes us now about Eliot's use of the word is the fact that he nowhere says what he means by it, what he means when he says that a literary text is 'mature'. We can all tell when a peach is ripe but can we tell a mature poem from an immature one? What do we do with it— squeeze it? Is Shelley's *Adonais* mature? Is it more or less mature than Pope's *Essay on Man*, or Spenser's *Epithalamion*, or Eliot's *The Waste Land*? Is maturity even seen as valuable any more? As a critical term, 'mature' has become risible. And yet, for Eliot, it is crucial to his project of exploring the notion of the 'classic' and to his concept of literary value. This is not to say that Eliot was foolish or irresponsible in his terminology: rather, it exemplifies the fact that critical vocabularies change over time while always being in any case somewhat porous, unstable, contentious. In the eighteenth century, the vocabulary of value included ideas of proportion, probability and propriety; the Romantics developed a vocabulary of the sublime, imagination and originality; while nearer to our time, the New Critics valued complexity, paradox, irony and tension in poems, and postmodern critics valorize disjunction, fragmentation, heteroglossia, aporia, decentring.

Alongside changes in critical vocabulary, there are changes in how literary monuments are perceived and valued. The most obvious example would be the reception of Shakespeare himself. While Jonson and Milton declared, very soon after his death in 1616, that Shakespeare had earned a place in the literary canon, in fact his reputation developed much more slowly than this would suggest. Indeed, during much of the eighteenth century his work was criticized as brilliant but faulty: he was seen as a poet of 'nature' rather than learning, and as at fault in terms of proprieties of versification and diction, his endless punning, his handling of plot and characterization, the improbability of his narratives, for his not obeying the unities of time and place and so on (see Vickers 1981, 1–86). It was only towards the end of the eighteenth century that an unalloyed and arguably uncritical sense of Shakespeare's eternal and towering genius became commonplace. Indeed, throughout the eighteenth and even into the nineteenth century his plays were regularly rewritten to iron-out his faults and make him more amenable to contemporary tastes. Thus, famously, *King Lear* was never performed on the English stage in its original form during the eighteenth century because its ending was held to be too gloomy—a happier, more appropriate ending was written for it by Nahum Tate in 1681 and became the standard acting text. In the present day, the perception and valuation of Shakespeare remains deeply indebted to the Romantic conception of his work as sublime, even sacred. At the same time, this conception of the Shakespearean monument has undergone radical demystification and deconstruction in the work of such critics as Terence Hawkes, Jonathan Dollimore, Joel Fineman, Catherine Belsey, John Drakakis, Margreta de Grazia and others.

In recent years, much attention has been given to the construction of the literary canon. In particular, critics have explored the ways in which the canon is bound up with questions of education, class, economics, race, ethnicity, colonization, sexual and gender difference, and so on. This has led to a large-scale reassessment of both the canon itself and how evaluations take place. The notion of literary value as an inviolable essence has disintegrated. Our sense of the apparently impersonal and autonomous realm of the aesthetic has been irrevocably complicated. More than ever we are made aware of how far our own individual judgements are subject to social, political and institutional constraints. More than ever we are made aware of how far the canon is a fabrication. Thus, for example, critics have devoted much energy in recent years to discovering or rediscovering women writers and writers from different racial and ethnic backgrounds whose work has been neglected. In the case of women writers, it is often argued that such authors have been overlooked precisely because they are women, since, with a few notable exceptions (Austen, the Brontës, Woolf, Plath), the patriarchal ethos of the literary critical establishment has tended to efface or marginalize women's writing in general. The publication of such anthologies as Gilbert and Gubar's *Norton Anthology of Literature by Women* (1985), Roger Lonsdale's *Eighteenth-Century Women Poets* (1989), Andrew Ashfield's *Romantic Women Poets* (1995, 1998), and Angela Leighton and Margaret Reynolds's *Victorian Women Poets: An Anthology* (1995), have altered the shape of the canon in and beyond the academy. More generally, what Elaine Showalter calls 'gynocriticism' and publishing ventures such as Virago and the Woman's Press have altered our literary historical maps by rediscovering numerous forgotten (or never recognized) authors, and critics have devoted a great deal of energy to the work of re-editing their writings, as well as to the critical, biblio- and biographical tasks of new evaluations.

Such reassessments and rediscoveries force us to face a series of difficult and complex questions concerning literary value and critical evaluation. Is literary value eternal and unchanging or is it contingent and dependent on readers and the institutions of criticism? Are we simply constructing new, exclusive canons when we discover 'neglected' writers, or are we rethinking the whole idea of 'the canon' and canonization? Is there such a thing as literary value? If so, how can it be described and defined? What are we doing when we make such judgements? Is there, as Steven Connor argues, an 'imperative' or 'necessity' of value (Connor 1992, 8)?

The recent rethinking of the canon, then, involves both a reassessment of which texts should be in the canon and a rethinking of the idea of the canon itself. Such reassessments have hardly gone unchallenged. One of the most stubbornly provocative challenges to what, in his view, has become the modern critical orthodoxy, is Harold Bloom's *The Western Canon* (1994). Bloom's 'single aim', is to 'preserve poetry as fully and purely as possible' against the politicizing of what he calls the 'school of resentment', by which he means those critics who argue that the literary critical institution has valorized the work of 'dead white males' at the expense of the work of marginalized writers—women, say, or Afro-Caribbeans or Hispanics or gays or the working classes (Bloom 1994, 18). For these 'resentful' critics, the work of criticism cannot be disengaged from the work of social and political critique since the traditional canon operates as an ideological justification of the values (often racist, heterosexist, patriarchal, colonial and elitist) of the male, Western, establishment figures which it enshrines. For Bloom, by contrast, literature is and should be an antisocial body of work. Literary texts, he argues, even work *against* political and social improvement: indeed, for Bloom, great writers 'are subversive of all values'. Reading their work with a view to forming our 'social, political, or personal moral values' would merely make us 'monsters of selfishness and exploitation' (29). The canon, for Bloom, is élitist and discriminatory or it is nothing. Accordingly, his book is itself élitist. Bloom lists the 3,000 books and authors that he claims make up the Western canon. He then narrows this down to 26 books/authors to which his volume is devoted. In the final analysis, though, Bloom's canon comes down to a single author by whose work all else must be judged. We will not be surprised by now to learn that that author is William Shakespeare. Bloom's argument for the Western canon relies, finally, on Shakespeare's unique genius:

> Shakespeare's eminence is, I am certain, the rock upon which the School of Resentment must at last founder. How can they have it both ways? If it is arbitrary that Shakespeare centres the Canon, then they need to show why the dominant social class selected him rather than, say, Ben Jonson, for that arbitrary role. Or if history and not the ruling circles exalted Shakespeare, what was it in Shakespeare that so captivated the mighty Demiurge, economic and social history? Clearly this line of inquiry begins to border on the fantastic; how much simpler to admit that there is a *qualitative* difference, a difference in kind, between Shakespeare and every other writer, even Chaucer, even Tolstoy, or whoever. Originality is the great scandal that resentment cannot accommodate, and Shakespeare remains the most original writer we will ever know. (Bloom 1994, 25)

Bloom is compelling. The apparent continuity of response to Shakespeare from the eighteenth century to the present does indeed seem to validate such a judgement of his work as a unique and uniquely original phenomenon, and this is confirmed by what seems to be our instinctive sense on reading him that we are encountering something original, unique, 'for all time'. It is hard to get round our sense, our intuitive sense, on reading Shakespeare, that his work is simply, unquestionably richer, more complex, more endlessly fertile, than that of other writers, even of other 'canonical' writers.

And yet, and yet . . . Still we might have nagging doubts. How do we know that our 'intuition' is not itself a learned response, that our 'instinctive' sense of Shakespeare's genius is not, itself, a result of our schooling? If we see our appreciation of Shakespeare as an effect of social conditioning, we might feel that his work does not have the eternal qualities we thought it did. Moreover, we might notice that Bloom's 'explanation', his offering of the case of Shakespeare as a final arbiter for his judgement about aesthetic judgement, tells us nothing about the grounds for such claims: indeed, the questions that Bloom poses for the 'school of resentment' might also be asked of his own work, since his account of Shakespeare as *different*, as *original* and so on, is no more an explanation than the 'history' or 'class' which his opponents offer. Bloom's is, finally (and proudly), a monumentalizing gesture: his very language allies Shakespeare with the material of the tomb itself in its metaphor of the 'rock', and eternalizes him and abstracts him from history in its comment that he is 'the most original writer we will ever know'. We are led back, then, to the question with which we began this chapter: is that what we want of our writers? Monuments?

It might seem ironic that what would appear to be the deeply conservative, reactionary, élitist position of Harold Bloom should find confirmation in the writings of that monument of socialism, Karl Marx. And yet Marx himself affirms the sense that, as far as art goes, the crucial question is not how artists reflect on or are influenced by their time but rather just the strange fact of their survival:

> . . . the difficulty lies not in understanding that the Greek arts and epic are bound up with certain forms of social development. The difficulty is that they still afford us artistic pleasure and that in a certain respect they count as a norm and as an unattainable model. (Quoted in Guillory 1993, 322)

This, then, is what remains to be explained: the way that literary works remain with us, haunt us, still, beyond the conditions of their production, whatever may be our legitimate concerns for human and social justice. Just this remaining, this endurance of the haunting singularity of the literary text, is what keeps us coming back to it as our preoccupations, desires, prejudices and commitments change. What baffles and enthrals—what Bloom is responding to in his flawed but deeply productive defence of the canon—is the singularity and uncanny *force* of the literary. It is this characterization of Shakespeare as a 'monument without a tomb'—a monumentalizing *and* anti-monumentalizing phrase—that Bloom shares with Jonson. And it is the undecidable nature of such gestures, the sense that we bury poets as we raise monuments of reading to them and our sense that, still, they hold over us an uncanny, haunting power, which brings us to them, brings us back to them.

Further reading

Much, often highly polemical work, has been published on the so-called 'canon wars' in the last few years, evincing the high institutional and pedagogical stakes involved in how canons are formed and regarded. Barbara Herrnstein Smith's *Contingencies of Value* (1988) offers a persuasive proposal for a pragmatic sense of literary value and the canon. John Guillory's *Cultural Capital* (1993) is a densely argued polemic for the 'inevitability of the social practice of judgement' and of the inextricability of aesthetic and economic 'value'; Guillory is influenced by the work of the French sociologist Pierre Bourdieu, whose *Distinction: A Social Critique of the Judgement of Taste* (1984) offers an important account of the social, cultural, economic and political issues embedded in decisions about the value of literary and other works. Henry Louis Gates's *Loose Canons* (1992) engages with issues raised in this chapter, especially regarding racial and ethnic difference. Within the specifically English critical tradition of the twentieth century, perhaps the most influential and opinionated work is that of F.R. Leavis, who is happy in, for example, *The Great Tradition* (1948), sweepingly to dismiss great swathes of literature (an author such as Laurence Sterne is relegated to a dismissive footnote) and to try to reduce the novel tradition to just four writers: an amusing and enlightening book to read, still, as an insight into the rhetoric of *doxa* and unreflective prejudice in canon formation.

Narrative

Stories are everywhere: in movies, sitcoms, cartoons, commercials, poems, newspaper articles, novels. We all make use of stories every day and our lives are shaped by stories—stories about what happened in our dreams or at the dentist, stories about how we fell in love or the origins of the universe, stories about war and about peace, stories to commemorate the dead and to confirm a sense of who we are. In this chapter, we propose to circle around the following propositions:

1. Stories are everywhere.
2. Not only do we tell stories, but stories tell us: if stories are everywhere, we are also in stories.
3. The telling of a story is always bound up with power, with questions of authority, property and domination.
4. Stories are multiple: there is always more than one story.
5. Stories always have something to tell us about stories themselves: they always involve self-reflexive and metafictional dimensions.

Roland Barthes suggests that falling in love involves telling ourselves stories about falling in love: in this sense, he argues, 'mass culture is a machine for showing desire' (Barthes 1990c, 136). Disagreements, arguments, even wars, are often the result of conflicting stories concerning, for example, the rights to a piece of land: the real reason for the Gulf War may have been oil, but the technical justification for going to war turned on the story of who owned or should own a particular piece of Kuwait. Academic, 'objective' or 'scientific' discourses are constructed as stories. The historian Hayden White has given special emphasis to the fact that history is written in the form of certain kinds of narrative, that the task of the historian is to 'charge . . . events' with 'a comprehensible plot structure' (White 1978, 92). Science is composed of stories: astronomy attempts to narrate the beginnings of the universe, biology the narrative of animal life in its various forms, and physics the consequences of one moving body coming into contact with another. For many centuries, millions of people in the West understood their place in the world largely through the story of Adam and Eve, the life of Christ and other biblical stories. The story of class struggle and emancipation from peasant society to the dictatorship of the proletariat has had a profound influence in the past 150 years. And in the twentieth century, Sigmund Freud has produced a new and scandalous story about the nature of childhood. To say that Christianity, Marxism and psychoanalysis involve stories is not to suggest that they are merely fictive. Rather, it is to register the fact that there are few aspects of life which are not bound up with strategies and effects of narrative.

The simplest way to define narrative is as a series of events in a specific order—with a beginning, a middle and an end. We might think about James Joyce's short story 'The Dead', from *Dubliners* (1914), to illustrate the point. Put very simply, the story begins with the arrival of Gabriel and his wife Gretta at a party, tells of the events of the party and the couple's walk home, and ends as they fall asleep in their hotel. What is important in this description is the temporal ordering of what happens. By contrast, lyric poems, for example, are not typically thought to express or depict a series of temporally ordered series of events. One of the ways in which lyric poetry is defined, in fact, is by the absence of any such representation of events—lyric poems characteristically use the present tense and exploit a sense of the presence of the speaker in the act of meditating or speaking. Percy Bysshe Shelley's 'To a Sky-Lark' (1820) recounts no events, but is an effusion of the poet's sense of the bird's 'unpremeditated art' which he attempts both to define and in some ways to reproduce. Similarly, while Seamus Heaney's 'bog poems' from *North* (1975) might dig up buried narratives of victimization, sacrifice and atonement, their lyric tone gives a sense of an individual poet responding, now, to what he sees. Narrative, however, is characterized by its foregrounding of a series of events or actions which are connected in time. What happens at the end of 'The Dead' is determined by what happened earlier. The events are recounted more or less chronologically in Joyce's story, in that the order of the telling follows the order of the told: first we learn of Gabriel and Gretta's arrival, then of the party and finally of the hotel. But narratives also invariably involve what the narratologist Gérard Genette has called anachronisms—flashbacks, jumps forwards (or prolepses), the slowing down and speeding up of events and other distortions of the linear time-sequence (Genette 1986). Texts such as Virginia Woolf's 'The Mark on the Wall' (1921) dislodge our sense of temporal sequence. The story begins: 'Perhaps it was the middle of January in the present year' (Woolf 1982, 41). This suggests that the events recounted span a number of months, but by the end we have the sense that the story follows the wanderings of the narrator's consciousness over only a number of minutes or, at most, hours. Despite this and many other distortions of chronological order, however, Woolf's text is only readable insofar as it exploits our *expectations* of narrative sequence. Indeed, these distortions themselves can only be conceived against a background of linear chronological sequence.

Time, then, is crucial to narrative. But as the novelist E.M. Forster recognizes in *Aspects of the Novel* (1927), the temporal ordering of events is not the whole story. Forster makes a memorable distinction between 'The king died and then the queen died' on the one hand, and 'The king died, and then the queen died of grief' on the other (Forster 1976, 87). While the first 'narrative' includes two events related in time, the second includes another 'connection', the crucial element of causality. The first simply lists two events, while the second provides the thread of a narrative by showing how they are related. The logical or causal connections between one event and another constitute fundamental aspects of every narrative. An obvious example would be detective stories. Detective stories rely, above all, on our expectation and desire for connection. They produce quite complex routes to a revelation of whodunnit, routes both determined and detected by the logic of cause and effect.

The beginning–middle–end sequence of a narrative also tends to emphasize what is known as a teleological progression—the *end* (in Greek, *telos*) itself as the place to get to. A lyric poem does not seem to rely on its ending to provide coherence: the end is not typically the place where all will be resolved. By contrast, we often think of a good story as one that we just cannot put down, a novel we compulsively read to find out what happens at the end. The narrative theorist Peter Brooks has studied ways in which readers' desires are directed towards the end, ways in which narratives are structured towards, or as a series of digressions from, an ending:

> we are able to read present moments—in literature and, by extension, in life—as endowed with narrative meaning only because we

read them in anticipation of the structuring power of those endings
that will retrospectively give them the order and significance of plot.
(Brooks 1984, 94)

Likewise, Brooks has elaborated the paradoxical ways in which the
dénouement or tying up of a story is worked towards through the paradox of digression. Thus, for example, while we may find a novel, film
or play frustrating if it contains too many digressions from the main
plot, we enjoy the suspense involved in delaying a dénouement. 'Suspense' movies, thrillers and so on, in particular, exploit this strangely
masochistic pleasure that we take in delay. One of the paradoxical attrac-
tions of a good story, in fact, is often understood to be its balancing of
digression, on the one hand, with progression towards an end, on the
other.

But what is this end which we so much desire? (We may find out in
more detail below, in Chapter 28.) Brooks and others have suggested
that narratives move from a state of equilibrium or stasis through a
disturbance of this stability, and back to a state of equilibrium at the
end. The end of a narrative, the state of equilibrium, occurs when the
criminal is discovered, when the lovers get married, or when the tragic
hero dies. In addition, this end is characteristically the place of revelation
and understanding. A part of the equilibrium that endings apparently
offer is the satisfaction of epistemophilia, the reader's desire to know.
And because of the conventional emphasis on hermeneutic discovery at
the end, endings tend to be particularly over-determined places: we look
to the end to provide answers to questions that the text has raised. In
modernist narratives such as Woolf's 'The Mark on the Wall', however,
these answers tend to be withheld or else treated ironically. The ending
of Woolf's story is paradoxical, in fact, in that it resolves the question
with which the story starts out—what is the mark on the wall?—by
telling us that it is a snail. But this 'answer' to the question simply
parodies those conventional realist endings that seem to clear up our
confusions and satisfy our curiosity. So what if it is a snail? To say that
the mark is a snail, is an example of what is called an *aporia*—an
impassable moment or point in narrative, a hole or opening that produces a hermeneutic abyss. If we ask what Woolf's story is 'about', we
realize that it is about itself as a story. The ending tells everything, it
gives us 'the answer', and it tells us nothing: it is not for this 'answer'
that we have read the story. Our epistemophilia proves to be perverted.

One of the most fundamental distinctions in narrative theory is that between 'story' and 'discourse'. As Jonathan Culler has suggested, a fundamental premiss of narratology is that narrative has a double structure: the level of the told (story) and the level of telling (discourse) (Culler 1981). These levels have been given different names by different theorists—the Russian formalists call them *fabula* and *sjuzhet*; the French structuralists call them either *récit* (or *histoire*) and *discours*, and so on. 'Story', in this sense, involves the events or actions which the narrator would like us to believe occurred, the events (explicitly or implicitly) *represented*. 'Discourse', on the other hand, involves the way in which these events are recounted, how they get told, the organization of the *telling*. In fact, of course, these two levels can never be entirely separated, and much narrative theory has been concerned to describe ways in which they interact. Thus Charlotte Brontë's *Jane Eyre* and Joyce's 'The Dead', for example, present the events of the narrative more or less in the order that they are alleged to have occurred. By contrast, texts such as Emily Brontë's *Wuthering Heights* and Woolf's 'The Mark on the Wall' move forward and backward in time and shift from the level of telling to that of the told in complex and unnerving ways. Many modernist and postmodernist texts experiment with the relation between these two levels, to denaturalize or defamiliarize our sense of how narratives function. A text such as Robert Coover's short story 'The Babysitter' from *Pricksongs and Descants* (1969), for instance, presents several slightly different accounts of what appears to be the same evening from a number of different perspectives: the contradictions and dislocations produced within and between these accounts, however, make it impossible, finally, to determine the precise nature or order of the evening's events. Alain Robbe-Grillet's novels, such as *The Voyeur* (1955) and *Jealousy* (1957), also recount the 'same' series of events over and over again, but from the 'same' narratorial perspective: each telling, however, is subtly different, thus dissolving our sense of any one, true, narrative of events. Rather than reading such texts simply as exceptions or aberrations, we might consider ways in which they metafictionally reflect on the multiplicity of any narrative—its susceptibility to different readings, its differing narrative perspectives, its shifting senses of place and time.

Everything that we have said about narrative up to this point has concerned the sense of its linearity: narrative involves a linear series of actions connected in time and through causality. In addition to this linearity, we might consider another important aspect of narrative, namely the relation between teller and listener or reader. Indeed, rather than appealing to the idea of a sequence of events, Barbara Herrnstein Smith has argued that we need to ground our understanding of narrative in terms of 'someone telling someone else that something happened' (Smith 1981, 228). The significance of this proposition is that it redirects our focus from the events or actions themselves to the relationship between the author or teller and the reader or listener. As Jonathan Culler has put it, 'To tell a story is to claim a certain authority, which listeners grant' (Culler 1997, 89). Much of the work in narrative theory has involved attempts to discriminate among different kinds of narrators (first person or third person, objective or subjective, reliable or unreliable, omniscient or not, together with questions concerning his or her 'point of view', his or her 'voice' and so on). Our understanding of a text is pervaded by our sense of the character, trustworthiness and objectivity of the figure who is narrating. Moreover, it is often very important to discriminate between the narratorial point of view and that of the so-called implied author—a particularly important distinction in certain ironic texts, for example. Although Jonathan Swift's essay 'A Modest Proposal' (1729) would not usually be considered as a narrative, it does provide one of the classic examples of narratorial irony. In this essay, the narrator proposes that in order to deal with poverty and hunger in Ireland and to prevent children of the poor from being a burden to their parents, such children should be sold to the rich as food—a solution that would be 'innocent, cheap, easy, and effectual' (509). The narrator appears to make his proposal seriously but we necessarily conceive of an 'implied author' who has very different views and motives, and who is making a political point about the immorality of the English government in its attitude towards poverty in Ireland. Our understanding of the ironic force of the text necessitates a discrimination between the two voices or personae of the narrator and the implied author.

A consideration of the relationship between teller and listener or reader leads in turn to questions of power and property. One of the most famous storytellers is Scheherazade from *A Thousand and One Nights*. In these classical Arabic narratives, Scheherazade has been sentenced to death by the king but is able to stave off her execution by telling him stories. By ending her story each night at a particularly exciting point, she is able to delay her death for another day because the king wants to find out what happens next. What makes *A Thousand and One Nights* so intriguing for narrative theorists has to do with its enactment of forms of power. As Ross Chambers proposes, 'To tell a story is to exercise power' (Chambers 1984, 50). Chambers argues that storytelling is often used, as in the case of Scheherazade, as an 'oppositional' practice, a practice of resistance used by the weak against the strong: 'oppositional narrative', he claims, 'in exploiting the narrative situation, discovers a power, not to change the essential structure of narrative situations, but to *change its other* (the 'narratee' if one will), through the achievement and maintenance of authority, in ways that are potentially radical' (Chambers 1991, 11). In this respect, we might consider the motives and effects of Gretta's story of her dead lover in 'The Dead': perhaps the ending of Joyce's narrative should be understood in terms of the diffusion of Gabriel's egoistic, domineering and even rapacious desire for his wife by Gretta's narration of her love story. Gretta, subject to patriarchal society's insistence on the husband's rights to the wife's body, displaces her husband's unwanted attention by telling him a story. The violence of Gabriel's desire is expressed in references to his longing 'to be master of her strange mood . . . to cry to her from his soul, to crush her body against him, to overmaster her' (248). By the middle of Gretta's narration, Gabriel sees himself, by contrast with the lover of her story, as a 'ludicrous figure . . . idealizing his own clownish lusts' and a 'pitiable fatuous fellow' (251). And by the end, all lusts and all passions and anger, all mastery and desire, have dissolved: 'Gabriel held her hand for a moment longer, irresolutely, and then shy of intruding on her grief, let it fall gently and walked quietly to the window' (253). This conflict of stories—Gabriel's about himself and Gretta's about her dead lover—results in a disturbance of power relations. In this sense, just as much as 'The Mark on the Wall', or the stories of Coover and Robbe-Grillet, 'The Dead' is self-reflexively about the power of stories. More often, of course, it is the dominant ideology which is able to tell stories about, for example, how it got to be the dominant ideology. In the Soviet Union, it was the Bolsheviks and later the Stalinists who got to write the history books. But there is an important difference between these two forms of power: the power exerted by Scheherazade and by Gretta is a specifically *narrative* power. The only way that these storytellers can avoid death on the one hand and violent passion on the other is by making their stories good, by making them 'readable'. By contrast, as far as the Soviet Union was concerned, the Stalinist version of history did not have to be readable (indeed, it did not even have to be plausible), because its reading would be enforced in other ways. *Narrative* power, then, may be the only strategy left for the weak and dispossessed: without narrative power, they may not be heard.

The social and political importance of stories is eloquently expressed by the old man in Chinua Achebe's novel *Anthills of the Savannah* (1987): 'The sounding of the battle-drum is important; the fierce waging of the war itself is important; and the telling of the story afterwards— each is important in its own way' (123–4). But, the man continues, the story is 'chief among his fellows':

> 'The story is our escort; without it we are blind. Does the blind man own his escort? No, neither do we the story; rather it is the story that owns us and directs us. It is the thing that makes us different from cattle; it is the mark on the face that sets one people apart from their neighbours.' (124)

Stories own us, and tell us, Achebe suggests, as much as we own or tell stories.

There are many questions of narrative, then, which may be considered in relation to literature: temporality, linearity and connectivity, narrative perspective, desire and power. But most of all, perhaps, it is the relation between narrative and 'non-' or 'anti-narrative' elements that fascinate and disturb. Aspects such as description, digression, suspension, aporia and self-reflection, temporal and causal disorders are often what are most compelling in narrative. A text such as Woolf's 'The Mark on the Wall', indeed, *has* no narrative outside of description and aporetic reflections on the nature of narrative. Correspondingly, Joyce's 'The Dead' depends to a large extent on moments of what Joyce refers to elsewhere as 'epiphany', moments of revelation or understanding, moments that appear to stand outside time, outside of narrative. As Gabriel watches his wife listening to a piece of music as they prepare to leave the party, there is just such a moment—a moment of revelation which is also a moment of mystery. Gretta, standing listening to a song is, for Gabriel, full of 'grace and mystery . . . as if she were a symbol of something' (240). Like Scheherazade's, Joyce's story-telling holds off, and hangs on, death. And as the snow falls on the world outside the hotel window at the end of the story, as Gabriel falls into unconsciousness and the narrative slips away, there is another moment of epiphany, a dissolution of time, of space, of life, of identity, desire and narrative.

Further reading

Gérard Genette's *Narrative Discourse* (1986) is a systematic and influential account of the structure of narrative. Another modern classic is

Dorrit Cohn's *Transparent Minds* (1978). Wallace Martin's *Recent Theories of Narrative* (1986) provides an excellent and very clear introduction to narrative theory, while J. Hillis Miller's essay 'Narrative' (1990) presents a concise and accessible summary of a number of paradoxes in narrative. Peter Brooks's *Reading for the Plot* (1984) explores ways in which narrative may be thought about in relation to readers' desires. A good short summary of feminist perspectives on narrative theory is Margaret Homans's 'Feminist Fictions and Feminist Theories of Narrative' (1994); see also Lidia Curti, *Female Stories, Female Bodies* (1998). James Phelan has collected some useful and provocative essays on narrative and its relationship to issues of reading in *Reading Narrative* (1989). Seymour Chatman's *Coming to Terms* (1990) is an incisive summary of narrative theory in relation to literary texts and film, and is especially useful in its discussion of ideas of point-of-view and narrative perspective. For a critique of traditional narratology from a poststructuralist perspective, see Andrew Gibson, *Towards a Postmodern Theory of Narrative* (1996).

Character

Characters are the life of literature: they are the objects of our curiosity and fascination, affection and dislike, admiration and condemnation. Indeed, so intense is our relationship with literary characters that they often cease to be simply 'objects'. Through the power of identification, through sympathy and antipathy, they can become part of how we conceive ourselves, a part of who we are. In the *Poetics*, Aristotle argues that character is 'secondary' to what he calls the 'first essential' or 'lifeblood' of tragedy—the plot—and that characters are included 'for the sake of the action' (Aristotle 1965, 40). By contrast, in his essay 'The Art of Fiction' (1884), the novelist Henry James asks, 'What is character but the determination of incident? What is incident but the illustration of character?' (James 1986, 174). While Aristotle makes character 'secondary' to plot, James suggests that the two are equal and mutually defining. Indeed, the novels and plays we respond to most strongly almost invariably have forceful characters as well as an intriguing plot. Our memory of a particular novel or play often depends as much on our sense of a particular character as on the ingenuities of the plot. Characters in books have even become part of our everyday language. Oedipus, for example, has given his name to a condition fundamental to psychoanalytic theory, whereby little boys want to kill their fathers and sleep with their mothers. Mrs Malaprop in Sheridan's play *The Rivals* (1775) has given us the word 'malapropism' when someone uses, for example, the word 'illiterate' to mean 'obliterate' (see I.2.178). A 'romeo' denotes a certain kind of amorous young man resembling the hero of Shakespeare's *Romeo and Juliet* (*c*. 1595). When we refer to someone as a 'scrooge', we mean a miser, but when we do so we are alluding, knowingly or not, to the protagonist of Charles Dickens's *A Christmas Carol* (1843), for whom Christmas is a fatuous waste of time and money. Vladimir Nabokov's novel *Lolita* (1958) has given us a term for what the *OED* defines as 'a sexually precocious schoolgirl', as well as a term ('the Lolita complex') for middle-aged men's sexual desires and fantasies concerning young girls. There is even a day named after a fictional character, 'Bloomsday' (16th June), after Leopold Bloom in James Joyce's *Ulysses* (1922).

But what is a person or a character in a literary work? What does it mean to talk about a character as 'vivid' or 'life-like'? How do writers construct characters and produce the illusion of living beings? What is the relationship between a person in a literary text and a person outside it? As we shall try to demonstrate, these are questions that books themselves—in particular plays, novels and short stories—consistently explore. In this chapter, we shall focus, in particular, on the nineteenth-century realist tradition. It is, we suggest, this tradition which has culminated in the kinds of assumptions that we often hold about people and characters today. And it is against such preconceptions that modernist and postmodernist texts tend to work.

Charles Dickens's *Great Expectations* (1860–1) opens with the orphan-hero, Pip, examining the writing on his parents' gravestones in order to attempt to determine the 'character' of his mother and father:

> As I never saw my father or my mother, and never saw any likeness of either of them (for their days were long before the days of photographs), my first fancies regarding what they were like, were unreasonably derived from their tombstones. The shape of the letters on my father's, gave me an odd idea that he was a square, stout, dark man, with curly black hair. From the character and turn of the inscription, '*Also Georgiana Wife of the Above*', I drew a childish conclusion that my mother was freckled and sickly. (35)

The comedy of this passage is partly produced by the double sense of 'character'—as the shape of an inscribed letter on a tombstone and as the personality of a human being. The text implies that our knowledge of people is determined by writing, by the character of written words. Although he is 'unreasonable', in taking the shape of letters to denote character, Pip is not simply mistaken in recognizing that our sense of our self and of other people is determined by language. For as this passage clearly indicates, we construct ourselves through and in words, in the image-making, story-generating power of language. In this respect, it is significant that the opening to *Great Expectations* explores one of the major themes of literary texts: the question 'who am I?' One fascination of characters in fiction and drama, as well as one of their most 'characteristic' activities, is to suggest answers to this question, not only for themselves, but also for us.

When critics talk about a novel such as *Great Expectations* as 'realist', part of what they mean is that its characters are 'life-like', they are like 'real' people. But what does this mean? The first requirement for such a character is to have a plausible name and to say and do things that seem convincingly like the kinds of things people say and do in so-called 'real life'. The second requirement is a certain complexity. Without this complexity, a character appears merely 'one-dimensional', cardboard or (in E.M. Forster's terms) 'flat' (Forster 1976, 73). To be life-like, a fictional character should have a number of different traits—traits or qualities which may be conflicting or contradictory: he or she should be, to some extent, unpredictable, his or her words and actions should appear to originate in multiple impulses. Thirdly, however, these tensions, contradictions, multiplicities should cohere in a single identity. Thus 'life-likeness' appears to involve both multiplicity and unity at the same time. In the classic nineteenth-century realist text *Middlemarch* (1871–2), for example, there is a character called Lydgate of whom George Eliot observes: 'He had two selves within him', but these selves must 'learn to accommodate each other' in a 'persistent self' (182). It is this tension, between complexity and unity, that makes a character like Lydgate both interesting and credible. The importance of such unity in realist texts is made clear by works like Robert Louis Stevenson's *The Strange Case of Dr Jekyll and Mr Hyde* (1886) or, less melodramatically, Joseph Conrad's 'The Secret Sharer' (1910): these narratives can be called 'limit texts' in that they use the framework of life-like or realistic characters to explore what happens when the self is demonically split or doubled. In doing so, such texts challenge the basis of realism itself.

Realist characterization presupposes a 'mimetic' model of literary texts whereby what is primary or original is a real person, and a character in a book is simply a copy of such a person. Such a model does not allow for a reversal of this relationship: it does not allow for the possibility that, for example, a person in 'real life' might be convincing to the extent that he or she resembles a person in a book. On the face of it, such a reversal may sound rather strange or counterintuitive: we would normally want to give priority to a 'person' and say that characters in books are more or less like 'real' people. In fact, however, as the example of *Great Expectations* suggests, it is easy to demonstrate that things also work the other way round. Indeed, literary history contains various dramatic instances where 'life' copies fiction. After the publication of Goethe's *The Sorrows of Young Werther* in Germany in 1774, for example, there was a fashion among young men in Europe for suicide, an act modelled on the suicide of the eponymous hero of that novel. Similarly, J.D. Salinger's novel *The Catcher in the Rye* (1951) was held responsible for the antisocial behaviour of numerous young men in the United States in the 1950s and early 1960s who identified with the disaffected hero Holden Caulfield. The young, in fact, are often considered (by the old) to be in danger of mimetic dissipation, to endanger themselves, their families and society because they copy the actions and attitudes of disreputable people in books or, more recently, in film and video.

This paradox of character whereby people in books are like 'real' people who are, in turn, like people in books, is suggested by the words 'person' and 'character' themselves. We have been using these words more or less interchangeably, though with an implicit and conventional emphasis on the 'reality' of a person and the 'fictionality' of a character. But the words are worth examining in more detail. According to *Chambers Dictionary*, 'person' signifies both 'a living soul or self-conscious being' and 'a character represented, as on the stage'. Indeed, 'person' goes back to the Latin word *persona*, the mask worn by an actor in a play on the classical stage. The English language uses the word 'persona' to signify a kind of mask or disguise, a pretended or assumed character. The word 'person', then, is bound up with questions of fictionality, disguise, representation and mask. To know a person, or to know who a person is, involves understanding a mask. In this respect, the notion of person is inseparable from the literary. This is not to say that 'real' people are actually fictional. Rather it is to suggest that there is a complex, destabilizing and perhaps finally undecidable interweaving of the 'real' and the 'fictional': our lives, our *real* lives, are governed and directed by the stories we read and write.

There is a similar enigma about the word 'character': just as the word 'person' has a double and paradoxical signification, so 'character' means both a letter or sign, a mark of writing, and the 'essential' qualities of a 'person'. Again, the etymology of the word is suggestive: from the Greek word *kharattein*, to engrave, the word becomes a mark or sign, a person's title and hence a distinguishing mark—that which distinguishes one person from another—and from this a 'fictional' person or a person on stage. Pip's characterological reading of his parents' tombstones, then, is not so far off the mark. And in *Hamlet*, when Polonius tells his son

Laertes that he should remember his 'precepts' or advice, he plays on this double sense, using 'character' as a verb: 'And these few precepts in thy memory / Look thou character' (I.iii.58–9). In this way, Shakespeare's play suggests how intimately 'character' is bound up with inscription, with signs, with writing.

We have argued that the realist novel tends to rely on a particular conception of what a person is—that a person is a complex but unified whole. We might develop this further by suggesting that the realist model of character involves a fundamental dualism of inside (mind, soul or self) and outside (body, face and other external features). The 'inside' that we associate with being human has many different forms. In the nineteenth century this was often described in terms of 'spiritual life' or 'soul', while in the twentieth century it is just as often (and perhaps more helpfully) understood in terms of the unconscious. The following extracts from the first paragraph of George Eliot's novel *Middlemarch* will allow us to explore this in more detail:

> Miss Brooke had that kind of beauty which seems to be thrown into relief by poor dress. Her hand and wrist were so finely formed that she could wear sleeves not less bare of style than those in which the Blessed Virgin appeared to Italian painters; and her profile as well as her stature and bearing seemed to gain the more dignity from her plain garments, which by the side of provincial fashion gave her the impressiveness of a fine quotation from the Bible,—or from one of our elder poets,—in a paragraph from today's newspaper. She was usually spoken of as being remarkably clever, but with the addition that her sister Celia had more common-sense. Nevertheless, Celia wore scarcely more trimmings; and it was only to close observers that her dress differed from her sister's, and had a shade of coquetry in its arrangements; for Miss Brooke's plain dressing was due to mixed conditions, in most of which her sister shared. The pride of being ladies had something to do with it: the Brooke connections, though not exactly aristocratic, were unquestionably 'good' [. . .] Young women of such birth, living in a quiet country-house, and attending a village church hardly larger than a parlour, naturally regarded frippery as the ambition of a huckster's daughter. Then there was well-bred economy, which in those days made show in dress the first item to be deducted from, when any margin was required for expenses more distinctive of rank. Such reasons would have been enough to account for plain dress, quite apart from religious feeling; but in Miss Brooke's case, religion alone would have determined it [. . .] and to her the destinies of mankind, seen by the

> light of Christianity, made the solicitudes of feminine fashion appear
> an occupation for Bedlam. She could not reconcile the anxieties of a
> spiritual life involving eternal consequences, with a keen interest in
> guimp and artificial protrusions of drapery. [. . .] (29–30)

This extraordinary opening paragraph, with its ironic insistence on the
importance of clothes despite Dorothea's spiritual aspirations, clearly
acknowledges that physical appearance (outside) works as a sign of character (inside). What is indicated here is an opposition that is fundamental in realist texts: that there is an inside and an outside to a person,
that these are separate, but that one may be understood to have a crucial
influence on the other. The opening to *Middlemarch* concentrates almost
obsessively on Dorothea's clothes because it is her clothes that allow
us insight into her character. As this suggests, another convention of
characterological realism is that character is hidden or obscure, that in
order to know another person—let alone ourselves—we must decipher
the outer appearance.

From Dorothea's clothes, then, Eliot weaves a fine and intricate web
of character—in terms of the familial, social and political and in terms
of the moral and religious. Indeed, one of the most striking sentences of
the excerpt focuses ironically on this concern with clothes: 'She could
not reconcile the anxieties of a spiritual life involving eternal consequences, with a keen interest in guimp and artificial protrusions of
drapery.' The passage as a whole makes it clear, however, that Dorothea's puritan plainness is simply the reverse side of a 'keen interest in
guimp'. Her preference for 'plain dressing' is itself a complex and considered statement of fashion. It is at this point, in particular, that Eliot's
ironic presentation of Dorothea involves a subtle questioning of the conventional opposition between a 'spiritual life' on the one hand and the
'artificial protrusions of drapery' on the other. The passage suggests that
this opposition is itself artificial, that whatever people 'really' are cannot
be separated from how they appear. It suggests that people are constituted by an interplay of inner and outer, but that it is not a question of
one being the truth and the other mere surface. So while realist conventions of character may rely on the opposition between inner and outer,
mind or spirit and body, and so on, Eliot's description of Dorothea also
shows how this opposition can be questioned from within the realist
tradition itself.

This brings us to one of the central questions raised by many novels:
How can we know a person? As we have seen, realist novels such as

George Eliot's attempt to answer this question by presenting people as knowable by a number of 'outward' signs of 'inner' worth. Appearances, however, can be deceptive. Indeed, many novels and plays are concerned with the problem of deception or disguise, with discriminating between an appearance that is a true sign of inner value and one that is not. The realist tradition often relies on the possibility of such deception, while also presupposing the possibility of finally discovering the worth or value of a person by reading the outward signs. The exposure, despite appearances, of Bulstrode's hypocrisy, for example, and the final validation of Lydgate's good character are central to the plot of *Middlemarch*. But the fact that a 'person' is itself, in some sense, a 'mask', means that even if we think we 'know' the soul or self of a person, his or her true identity, there is always a possibility, even if that person is ourself, that such an identity is itself a form of mask. This irreducible uncertainty may partly account for realism's obsessive concern with the question: 'Who am I?'

The stories of Raymond Carver (1938–88), like many so-called postmodern texts, relentlessly play with such conventions of characterological construction and perception. In 'Cathedral' (1983), for example, the somewhat obtuse, belligerent, intolerant, discriminatory narrator finds it both comic and unnerving to think about how a blind man, a friend of his wife who has been invited to pass the evening in their home, looks—even while (or because) he cannot look. The narrator is struck by the fact that the blind man does not wear dark glasses. This disturbs him, since although at first sight the blind man's eyes 'looked like anyone else's eyes', on closer inspection (and the narrator takes the opportunity for a lengthy session of unreciprocable inspection) they seem 'Creepy': 'As I stared at his face, I saw the left pupil turn in toward his nose while the other made an effort to keep in one place. But it was only an effort, for that eye was on the roam without his knowing it or wanting it to be' (297). The story culminates in a dope-smoking session in which the blind man teaches the narrator the advantages of drawing with closed eyes, of the necessary visual imagination of the blind. On one level, the story performs a conventional reversal of the blind and the seeing, figuring the blind man as the seer. But on another level, Carver explores conventions of characterological construction by querying the equation of the look of someone with their identity (the eyes, conventionally the most telling indicator of character are, for our view of the blind man, just 'creepy' signifiers of mechanical disfunction, disconnected from intention, emotion, will), and by prompting an awareness that in this story it is the one who is *not* seen—either by us as readers or by the blind man—who exposes himself, exposes his 'character', in all its belligerent intolerance, its obtuseness, most fully.

As we have seen, it is difficult in an absolute sense to separate real from fictional characters. To read about a character is to imagine and create a character in reading: it is to create a person. And as we have tried to show, reading characters involves learning to acknowledge that a person can never finally be singular—that there is multiplicity and ambiguity from start to finish. Our final point concerns what it means to 'identify' with characters in fiction. It seems difficult, if not impossible, to enjoy a novel or play without, at some level, identifying with the characters in it. In fact, the most obvious definition of the 'hero' or 'heroine' of a novel or play would be the person with whom we 'identify', with whom we sympathize or empathize, or whose position or role we imaginatively inhabit. But such 'identification' is not as simple as we might think. To identify with a person in a novel or play is to identify *oneself*, to produce an identity for oneself. It is to give oneself a world of fictional people, to start to let one's identity merge with that of a fiction. It is, finally, also to create a character for oneself, to create one's very identity in fiction.

Further reading

Two very good and reasonably accessible accounts of character are Harold Bloom's 'The Analysis of Character' (1990) and Hélène Cixous's 'The Character of "Character"' (1974). A classic if somewhat reductive account of character may be found in Chapters 3 and 4 of Forster's *Aspects of the Novel* (1976), first published in 1927. For a lucid discussion of character in the nineteenth- and early twentieth-century novel, see Martin Price, *Forms of Life* (1983). A very different kind of approach is exemplified in Thomas Docherty's *Reading (Absent) Character* (1983), which focuses in particular on the *nouveau roman* and postmodern writing generally, in order to move beyond a 'mimetic' theory of character to one in which characterization is seen as 'a process of reading and writing'. For an excellent, if difficult, argument for the deconstruction of character which challenges the humanist perspective of a unified self and argues for 'an esthetic and ethic of the fragmented self', see Leo Bersani's important book *A Future for Astyanax* (1978). J. Hillis Miller's chapter on 'Character' in *Ariadne's Thread* (1992) brilliantly weaves literary with critical, theoretical and philosophical reflections on character.

Voice

Nothing is stranger, or more familiar, than the idea of a voice. In George Eliot's *Daniel Deronda* (1876), a character called Mrs Meyrick observes that 'A mother hears something like a lisp in her children's talk to the very last' (423). In Shakespeare's *King Lear* (1605), the blinded Gloucester recognizes Lear from his voice: 'The trick of that voice I do well remember; / Is't not the King?' (IV, vi, 106–7). In both of these examples we have what appear to be confirmations of the persistence of identity, expressed in the singular or peculiar nature (the 'trick') of a person's voice. But in each of these exchanges we are also presented with a kind of strangeness as well: in Eliot's novel, for example, we may reflect on the irony of the fact that what the mother recognizes in her children, what it is in their voice that confirms the persistence of their identity, is something that cannot be heard, a lisp perceived only by the mother. Moreover there is something strange in the idea that an adult's speech should be, in a dream-like or hallucinatory fashion, haunted by the past in this way. In the example from Shakespeare, on the other hand, it is difficult for us not to be aware of the terrible precariousness of recognition and, by implication, of identity: Gloucester may believe that he recognizes, and may indeed recognize, the trick of the king's voice, but we are all too aware of the fact that he can never again *see* the king, never confirm the king's identity by sight. And ironically, Gloucester is only reunited with Lear thanks to help from his son Edgar, whose voice (disguised as Tom o' Bedlam) Gloucester *fails* to recognize.

The examples from Eliot and Shakespeare appear, at least initially, to be about the familiarity and individuality of voice. But like literary texts more generally, they are also concerned with the ways in which a voice may be strange and disturbing. We may enjoy a novel like Chandler's *The Little Sister* (1949) partly on account of the distinctive, gritty, cinematographic voice-over of Marlowe the narrator, but one of the things that makes this novel haunting and powerful, as well as comical, is its sensitivity to the strangeness of voices. Thus for example we have Miss Mavis Weld, apparently concerned about her brother: 'She clutched her bag to her bosom with tight little fingers. "You mean something has happened to him?" Her voice faced off into a sort of sad whisper, like a mortician asking for a down payment' (39). Or we have Marlowe recounting a phone call: 'The phone rang before I had quite started to worry about Mr Lester B. Clausen. I reached for it absently. The voice I heard was an abrupt voice, but thick and clogged, as if it was being strained through a curtain or somebody's long white beard' (41).

The power of a voice is made dramatically clear by the British Government's censorship of the Sinn Fein leader, Gerry Adams: for a number of years (until September 1994) his voice was, in effect, illegal. His words, when broadcast, had to be spoken by an actor. Few voices could be said to have haunted the contemporary British media as forcefully as Gerry Adams's. But a concern with what is powerful, haunting and strange about voices is hardly a recent phenomenon. One need only think of the importance of oracles, and the intimate links between voice and prophecy in the Bible and other classical texts. Consider, for instance, the voice that announces in I Corinthians 13: 'Though I speak with the tongues of men and of angels, and have not charity, I am become as sounding brass, or a tinkling cymbal. / And though I have the gift of prophecy, and understand all mysteries, and all knowledge; and though I have all faith, so that I could remove mountains, and have not charity, I am nothing' (1–2). Or think of the apocalyptic voices at the end of the Bible, in the Book of Revelation—for example of the angel who comes down from heaven, whose 'face was as it were the sun, and his feet as pillars of fire' and who

> cried with a loud voice, as when a lion roareth: and when he had cried, seven thunders uttered their voices.
> And when the seven thunders had uttered their voices, I was about to write: and I heard a voice from heaven saying unto me, Seal up those things which the seven thunders uttered, and write them not.

In both of these biblical quotations voice is described in terms that identify it with the non-human—with musical instruments (sounding brass or tinkling cymbal), with the sound of a lion or with the sound of thunder. It is also presented in terms of multiplicity (speaking in tongues, the voices of the seven thunders) and what we would call the uncanny (the voice that has the gift of prophecy and is omniscient; the voice that is forbidden, that must be sealed up). All of these characteristics are important for thinking about literary texts more generally. Literature, in fact, might be defined as being the space in which, more than anywhere else, the power, beauty and strangeness of the voice is both evoked or bodied forth *and* described, talked about, analyzed. In this respect, reading literary texts involves hearing extraordinary voices.

One of the most obvious extremes of voice in literature is in relation to music—in other words, the idea that voice becomes pure sound, turns into music. Here we may recall Walter Pater's suggestion that all art constantly aspires towards the condition of music: this is as much true of the 'smoky kind of voice' (202) whose singing transfixes and transforms the life of the narrator in Jean Rhys's story 'Let Them Call It Jazz' (1962) as it is of the glozing, serpentine voice that seduces Eve in Milton's *Paradise Lost* (Book IX, 532ff.), or of the song of the skylark or of the nightingale to which Shelley and Keats respectively aspire in their great song-like Odes. At the same time, however, we are all perfectly aware that literary texts are *not* (simply) music or song. Part of what makes texts literary is indeed their peculiar, paradoxical relation to music (not least in lyric poems and ballads, originally performed with or as music). That is to say, poems or short stories or other texts may aspire towards the condition of music, but they are necessarily stuck in their so-called linguistic predicament. Thus Coleridge's 'Kubla Khan' (1798) is concerned with the demonic power of music played by 'A damsel with a dulcimer' and with the paradoxical desire to 'build' the very things that the poem has described (a pleasure-dome and caves of ice) 'with music':

> A damsel with a dulcimer
> In a vision once I saw:
> It was an Abyssinian maid,
> And on her dulcimer she played,
> Singing of Mount Abora.
> Could I revive within me
> Her symphony and song,
> To such a deep delight 'twould win me,
> That with music loud and long,
> I would build that dome in air,
> That sunny dome! those caves of ice!

In Shelley's ode 'To a Sky-Lark' (1820), on the other hand, the speaker ends by implying that he is unteachable:

> Teach me half the gladness
>   That thy brain must know,
> Such harmonious madness
>   From my lips would flow
> The world should listen then—as I am listening now.

Shelley's ode thus aspires to the 'harmonious madness' it can never voice. Similarly, Keats's poem (1819) can acknowledge the 'ecstasy' of the nightingale's 'voice', but the speaker also recognizes that he can never triumph in the desire to 'dissolve' his identity with that voice. No doubt being stuck in this respect is the *condition* of literature and partly explains why literary texts demand to be thought about not only in terms of how they *body forth* voices but also in terms of how they reflect, comment on and analyze what 'voice' *means*. As Eve's temptation by the snaky sibilants of Satan suggests, a voice can be astonishingly seductive. Interestingly, a voice can become *more* seductive by referring to the fact that it is being seductive. (The contemporary commercial success of phone-sex may also testify to this.) Voice seduces: as the etymology of seduction may suggest (*se-*, aside *ducere*, to lead), it leads us aside or draws us away.

What does it mean to talk about voice in relation to literary texts? Take the opening of a short story by Raymond Carver, entitled 'Fat' (1963). It begins:

> I am sitting over coffee and cigarettes at my friend Rita's and I am telling her about it.
> Here is what I tell her.
> It is late of a slow Wednesday when Herb seats the fat man at my station.
> This fat man is the fattest person I have ever seen, though he is neat-appearing and well dressed enough. Everything about him is big. But it is the fingers I remember best. When I stop at the table near his to see to the old couple, I first notice the fingers. They look three times the size of a normal person's fingers—long, thick, creamy fingers. (64)

This is, in some ways at least, a descriptively straightforward opening. But once we reflect on it, we find that it is doing many different and quite sophisticated things. The first point to observe is that this is a first person narration with a strong sense of a speaking voice: we are drawn away by what we might call the 'reality effect' of a speaking voice that is produced in part through the conversational language—the lexical items and syntax, the topic, use of the present tense, repetition—and in part through the explicit reference to the fact that the narrator is speaking and 'telling' us something. The opening sentences, in a quite subtle way, put the reader in the position of the narrator's friend Rita ('I am telling her . . . Here is what I tell . . .'). Despite the seductively 'realistic' or 'everyday' quality of voice here, then, something fairly complex is going on: we are presented with a narrator who, even in the apparently straightforward language of the opening two sentences, makes it clear that this is a self-referential or metafictional story, a story that is at least at some level a story *about* storytelling. The seductiveness of an apparently casual speaking voice tends to distract attention from this quite theoretically sophisticated dimension of the text. Moreover, without really drawing attention to the fact, we have up till now been referring to the 'I' of the story as the narrator. In other words, we have been making an implicit distinction between narrator and author. This is a first-person narration and the narrator, we quickly learn, is a waitress. What we are being presented with, in other words, is the 'voice' of a girl or young woman. At the same time, however, there is a sort of double-voicing here to the extent that we may recognize this text as being characteristic of Raymond Carver's work. In this respect, we could say, there is also the phantasmatic voice of Carver lurking in these lines. We hear the 'voice' of Carver in a figurative, ghostly sense (like a signature tune).

Rather differently, there is Thomas Hardy's poem, 'The Voice':

> Woman much missed, how you call to me, call to me,
> Saying that now you are not as you were
> When you had changed from the one who was all to me,
> But as at first, when our day was fair.
>
> Can it be you that I hear? Let me view you, then,
> Standing as when I drew near to the town
> Where you would wait for me: yes, as I knew you then,
> Even to the original air-blue gown!
>
> Or is it only the breeze, in its listlessness
> Travelling across the wet mead to me here,
> You being ever dissolved to wan wistlessness,
> Heard no more again far or near?

> Thus I; faltering forward,
> Leaves around me falling,
> Wind oozing thin through the thorn from norward,
> And the woman calling.

Written in December 1912, 'The Voice' belongs to the series of so-called '1912–13 poems' that Hardy wrote following his first wife's death earlier that year. It is difficult, in other words, not to read this poem as autobiographical—to understand it as a poem about the poet's experience of mourning following his wife's death. But the poem is more than simply autobiographical: it is about the radical uncertainty of human identity and experience, their faltering. 'The Voice' not only describes the uncanny experience of hearing a dead person's voice but in some sense transfers the call to us in turn. The poem functions as a kind of strange switchboard. Again, we can respond to the poem in quite straightforward terms—it is a poem about someone who is out walking in an autumn or early winter landscape and who thinks he hears the voice of a woman whom he once loved (who was 'all' to him) but who is no longer above ground ('heard no more again far or near'). As its title suggests then, it is about 'the voice' he hears. But it is also a poem about voice more generally, and about the relationship between poetry and hearing voices. (Let us recall, after all, that this is the very form of inspiration in classical Greek and Roman times: hearing women's voices, the voices of the Muses.) This is evident, for example, in the opening line: 'Woman much missed, how you call to me, call to me'. What we are presented with here is an affirmation of the spooky actuality of hearing a dead woman's voice—an affirmation which the poem proceeds to question ('Can it be you that I hear?'), but which it concludes by reaffirming ('Thus I; faltering forward . . . And the woman calling'). This opening line, however, is at the same time grammatically ambiguous: 'how' suggests a questioning as well as an exclamation. 'Call to me, call to me', on the other hand, can be read as an echo (as *two* voices, even if the second is a double of the first) or as changing from an exclamation—'how you call to me'—to a demand: 'call to me'.

The ending of the poem suggests either that the speaker is off his head, hearing voices, or that the dead really do come back and it is indeed possible to hear voices from beyond the grave. But it also suggests something about literary texts in general. Every one of the writers who has been discussed in this chapter is dead. But as we indicate in our discussion of 'the death of the author' (in Chapter 3), every literary text can be thought of as involving a voice from beyond the grave, since every text is at least potentially capable of outliving the person who originally gives voice to it. The woman in Hardy's poem is in this respect a figure of the poet *par excellence.* Do we hear Hardy's voice in 'The Voice' or not? Or—to reflect on the poem in a quite different way altogether, that is to say in the light of what Harold Bloom calls 'the anxiety of influence'—do we perhaps hear Keats's voice in this poem? Bloom's celebrated theory (Bloom 1973) is that what impels poets to write is not so much the desire to reflect on the world as the desire to respond to and to challenge the voices of the dead. For Bloom, any 'strong' poem will always involve an encounter between the 'living' poet—in this case Hardy—and the dead—in this case perhaps most obviously Keats, whose 'Ode to a Nightingale' is also explicitly con- cerned with the 'dissolving' qualities of voice and identity. From a Bloomian perspective, Hardy's reference to 'You being ever dissolved to wan wistlessness' might be read not so much as an address to the poet's dead wife (strange enough as that gesture may itself seem) but rather as an eerie and ambivalent 'replay' of Keats's lines:

> That I might drink, and leave the world unseen,
> And with thee fade away into the forest dim:
> Fade far away, dissolve, and quite forget
> What thou amongst the leaves hast never known . . .

Keats's voice might, in this sense, be said to haunt 'The Voice' as much as it does other Hardy poems, such as 'The Darkling Thrush' (1900)— the very title of which explicitly refers us to Keats's Ode ('Darkling I listen . . .'). In poems such as 'The Voice' and 'The Darkling Thrush', in other words, we can recognize the 'trick' of Hardy's voice in terms of an idiomatic tone (lugubrious, plaintive, ironic etc.) and idiomatic rhymes and neologisms ('listlessness', 'wistlessness'). But this is 'voice' in a figurative, ghostly sense. Moreover, it is 'voice' as plural—haunted by, for example, the voice or voices of other poets such as Keats.

The examples of Carver and Hardy are helpful because they highlight a number of important ideas for thinking about voice in relation to liter- ature. First they suggest that the question of voice is never simple, even (or perhaps especially) when it appears to be. Second, and more spe- cifically, they suggest that literary texts not only *present* voices but also have things to say *about* what voices are and how we might or might not hear them. Third, there is invariably more than one voice in a literary text, even if it is a matter of a voice ostensibly just talking or responding to itself.

This final point can be thought about further in at least two directions. On the one hand—and this has been an important feature of recent literary theoretical concerns—there is the importance of seeing literature as a space in which one encounters multiple voices. Literary texts call upon us to think about them in terms of many voices—for instance, in terms of what M.M. Bakhtin calls *heteroglossia* or of what he, Julia Kristeva, Roland Barthes and others refer to as *polyphony*. Literature is, as Salman Rushdie has observed, 'the one place in any society where, within the secrecy of our own heads, we can hear *voices talking about everything in every possible way*' (Rushdie 1990, 16). Saleem, the narrator of Rushdie's novel *Midnight's Children* (1981), is an excellent example: he is telepathic, like every so-called omniscient narrator in a work of fiction, and he is continually hearing multiple voices. As he remarks: 'I was a radio receiver, and could turn the volume down or up; I could select individual voices; I could even, by an effort of will, switch off my newly-discovered inner ear' (164).

On the other hand—and this has been a related and similarly important feature of recent critical and theoretical concerns—literature encourages us to think about the idea that there may in fact be no such thing as *a* voice, a single, unified voice (whether that of an author, a narrator, a reader or anyone else). Rather, there is difference and multiplicity *within* every voice. There is, then, not only the kind of socio-literary polyphony that Bakhtin describes, and which he illustrates for example by looking at the way Dickens orchestrates, inhabits and detaches himself from the role of various speakers in his novel *Little Dorrit* (Bakhtin 1992, 203–5). But in addition to this, and more fundamentally, any one voice is in fact made up of multiple voices. There is difference and polyphony *within* every voice. We have tried to suggest this by looking at some of the ways in which the voice of an author or poet is always phantasmagoric or ghostly. We might conclude, however, with a thought proffered in one of the 'Adagia' (or 'aphorisms') of the poet Wallace Stevens: 'When the mind is like a hall in which thought is like a voice speaking, the voice is always that of someone else' (168).

Further reading

For two traditional but in some respects still stimulating accounts of voice and literature, see Yvor Winters, 'The Audible Reading of Poetry'

(1957), and Francis Berry, *Poetry and the Physical Voice* (1962). A more recent and theoretically informed account is provided by Furniss and Bath (1996), in their chapter on 'Hearing Voices in Poetic Texts'. Roland Barthes has very engaging, thought-provoking things to say about voice, for example in *S/Z* (Barthes 1990b). On heteroglossia, see M.M. Bakhtin, *The Dialogic Imagination* (1981). For Kristeva and polyphony, see for example the essay 'Word, Dialogue and Novel' (Kristeva 1986). For a challenging but brilliant account of the strangeness of the narrator's 'I' in a literary text, see Maurice Blanchot's 'The Narrative Voice' (Blanchot 1981). On voice in relation to print and reading, see Griffiths, *The Printed Voice of Victorian Poetry* (1989). On poetry, voice and hearing, see Geoffrey Hartman's eclectic and stimulating essay, 'Words and Wounds' (Hartman 1981), and, for a more technical, difficult but fascinating study, see Garrett Stewart's *Reading Voices* (1990). The philosopher David Appelbaum's *Voice* (1990) is a brilliant and idiosyncratic study of such dimensions of 'voice' as the cough, laugh, breath and babble, while Wesling and Slawek's *Literary Voice* (1995) draws on philosophy, linguistics and other disciplines to defend literary voice against 'modern philosophy's critique of the spoken'.

Figures and tropes

It's not for nothing that they call Elvis Presley 'The King' and Eric Clapton 'God'. But the force of these acts of renaming depends on the assumption that no one takes them literally. No one supposes that the United States has become a monarchy and put Elvis Presley on the throne. No one, not even the most loyal of fans, believes that Eric Clapton created the world in six days and rested on the seventh. They may believe that his guitar-playing is transplendent, but even those whose judgement is blurred by an unholy mixture of illegal substances and Clapton's heavenly guitar solos are unlikely to take him for the Almighty Himself. These renamings of Presley and Clapton, then, involve the kind of exaggeration or verbal extravagance known as hyperbole. To refer to Elvis as 'The King' or Clapton as 'God' is to use figurative language.

Literary language is sometimes defined in terms of its deviations from or distortions of ordinary language. Like many generalizations, this idea is both useful and misleading. It suggests that literary texts are characterized by the use of figures of speech or tropes. And it defines figures and tropes in opposition to and as deviations from 'ordinary' or 'literal' language. Thus *Chambers Dictionary* defines a rhetorical figure as 'a deviation from the ordinary mode of expression', and trope as 'a figure of speech, properly one in which a word or expression is used in other than its literal sense'. Such figures include, for example, hyperbole, metaphor, metonymy and anthropomorphism. Metaphor is the general term for the figure of resemblance, whereby one thing is likened to another. Metonymy is a general term for the figure of association or contiguity, whereby one thing is talked about by referring to something associated with it. Anthropomorphism is the general term used to refer to the non-human as if it were human. So-called 'ordinary' language, by contrast, is thought to use far more literal language, language that calls a spade a spade.

As the examples of Presley and Clapton suggest, however, the figurative is by no means restricted to literary texts: rather, it saturates all language. Friedrich Nietzsche famously argued that even truth itself is figurative. In his essay 'On Truth and Lie in an Extra-Moral Sense', Nietzsche asks 'What, then, is truth?' and offers the following answer:

> A mobile army of metaphors, metonyms, and anthropomorphisms— in short, a sum of human relations, which have been enhanced, transposed, and embellished poetically and rhetorically, and which after long use seem firm, canonical, and obligatory to a people: truths are illusions about which one has forgotten that this is what they are; metaphors which are worn out and without sensuous power; coins which have lost their pictures and now matter only as metal, no longer as coins. (Nietzsche 1980, 46–7)

When we think that we speak 'truthfully', without the distortions of figuration, Nietzsche suggests, we only deceive ourselves. The language of truth, language supposedly purified of figures and tropes, is simply language to which we have become so habituated that we no longer recognize it as figurative. This suggests that our world is constituted figuratively, that we relate to ourselves, to other people, to the world, through figures of speech. The manipulation and exploitation of figurative language may therefore be understood to have fundamental implications for the political, social, even economic constitution of our world. The very way that we understand the world may be said to be mediated by the kinds of figures that we use to speak about it. We could think about this in terms of any everyday aspect (aspect is a visual metaphor) of life—for example, the names of newspapers, those 'organs' (a metaphor) that help to *organize* (the same organic metaphor) our world: the *Herald, Guardian, Sun, Mirror, Telegraph, Tribune* and so on. While such discourses as history, philosophy, psychology, economics and so on may, at least in principle, attempt to rid themselves of figurative language, to go beyond figuration in the search for truth, it is precisely figuration, which is anyway unavoidable, which is at the centre of the discipline of literary studies. This unavoidability is suggested in the passage from Nietzsche, with its concluding figuration of metaphors as coins. Nietzsche explicitly relies on figurative language in order to demystify and to formulate a definition of the truth. As Paul de Man remarks, tropes are not 'a derived, marginal, or aberrant form of language but the linguistic paradigm par excellence': figurative language 'characterizes language as such' (de Man 1979, 105).

Central to literary criticism and theory, then, are such questions as: What are the effects of rhetorical figures in literary texts? What purpose do they serve? And how do they function? One of the most common misconceptions about literary texts is that their figurative language is simply decorative, something added to the text to make it more readable, more dramatic, or more 'colourful'. It is certainly true that the presence of figurative language often seems to increase at points of emotional and dramatic intensity, like the soaring violins at scenes of sexual passion or dramatic tension in a Hollywood film. Thus D.H. Lawrence, for example, is known for his so-called 'purple passages'. But simply to suggest that figures are 'added' to literary language like the musical soundtrack to a movie, does not get us very far. Moreover, the soaring violin theory of rhetorical figures is misguided because, as Nietzsche suggests, language is inescapably figurative: the meaning of a text cannot be separated from its expression, its figures.

Figuration is fundamental to our world, to our lives. An alteration in the way we figure the world also involves an alteration in the way that the world works. Take Ralph Ellison's *Invisible Man* (1952), for example. This novel uses invisibility as a metaphor for the marginality, the oppression, effacement and dehumanization of black people in the United States. Here is the opening to the prologue to Ellison's novel:

> I am an invisible man. No, I am not a spook like those who haunted Edgar Allan Poe; nor am I one of your Hollywood-movie ectoplasms. I am a man of substance, of flesh and bone, fiber and liquids—and I might even be said to possess a mind. I am invisible, understand, simply because people refuse to see me. Like the bodiless heads you see sometimes in circus sideshows, it is as though I have been surrounded by mirrors and hard, distorting glass. When they approach me they see only my surroundings, themselves, or figments of their imagination—indeed, everything and anything except me. (3)

Visibility and invisibility work here as metaphors for the social, political and economic effacement and consequent oppression of blacks in the United States. The man is invisible because he cannot escape the preconceptions that others have concerning him. These preconceptions are produced by a 'perception' of his skin colour. This so-called perception is itself an effect of the kind of rhetorical figure we call synecdoche, whereby a part—here, the skin—stands for the whole—a man. But simply to categorize someone as 'black' (or 'white') is in a sense laughably reductive and inaccurate. Likewise, to say that someone is 'coloured' is in a sense to say nothing at all, because the skin, hair, nails, eyes, teeth of each one of us is a multichromatic assemblage of different hues. The categories of black, white and coloured may thus be nothing other than examples of synecdoche. What people 'see' is a form of metaphor, a figment or figure of imagination—a 'phantom in other people's minds . . . a figure in a nightmare which the sleeper tries with all his strength to destroy' (3). It is in this way that Ellison's narrator is invisible, for while people think that they see—they think they see a black man—in fact they see nothing, they are blinded by metaphor. Ellison's novel suggests that such habitual blindness may be challenged and in turn transformed by an act of language. It presents a metaphor or allegory of the invisible man to counter the worn coin of representation. After all, the effacement of the black man is, in a crucial sense, an act of language. Without the vocabulary of prejudice and racism, any such effacement would be inconceivable. Racism is an effect of language. In particular, the passage from Ellison cited above suggests that racism is an effect of synecdochic substitution—skin pigment for personal identity, individual for collective or racial identity. The invisible man can be seen again, his invisibility perceived, through alternative metaphors, through figures.

The opening of Ellison's novel, then, gives us one answer to the question of how figures and tropes function in literary and other texts: they can make us see what is otherwise invisible, concealed by prejudice, effaced by habit. They change the world. To recall the term used by Viktor Shklovsky and other Russian formalist critics writing in the 1920s, figurative language has the capacity to 'defamiliarize' our world—to refigure, reform, revolutionize.

What kinds of effects can be produced through figuration and how far can a reading of such figures go? Let us consider another example, a poem by the nineteenth-century New England poet Emily Dickinson. In Dickinson's work, figures, like language considered more generally, tremble on the edge of meaning. One reason why Dickinson's poetry is particularly appropriate in a discussion of figurative language is that it characteristically 'deconstructs' or defamiliarizes its own rhetorical figures: her poetry constitutes a subtle yet decisive assault on figuration itself. This poem (no. 328) was written around 1862:

A Bird came down the Walk—
He did not know I saw—
He bit an Angleworm in halves
And ate the fellow, raw,

And then he drank a Dew
From a convenient Grass—
And then hopped sidewise to the Wall
To let a Beetle pass—

He glanced with rapid eyes
That hurried all around—
They looked like frightened Beads, I thought—
He stirred his Velvet Head

Like one in danger, Cautious,
I offered him a Crumb
And he unrolled his feathers
And rowed him softer home—

Than Oars divide the Ocean,
Too silver for a seam—
Or Butterflies, off Banks of Noon
Leap, plashless as they swim.

In language at once direct and elusive, the poem describes a bird eating a worm, taking a drink and flying away. The rhetorical figure which stands out in the opening lines is personification or anthropomorphism. Both the bird ('he') and the worm (the 'fellow') of the first stanza are described as if they were human. But the anthropomorphic insistence of the first half of the poem becomes strangely convoluted as it goes on to explore the specificity of simile (a is like b) as a species of metaphor (a is b). In line eleven we learn that the bird's eyes 'looked like frightened Beads'. But this simile is not as simple as it looks. It remains unclear whether 'looked like' means that the eyes actively *looked* (they looked, in the way that beads look, assuming that they do), or whether the bird's eyes, to the narrator, *looked like* beads. The simile is itself ambiguous. Moreover, *what* the eyes looked like—the beads—also undergoes an uncanny metamorphosis. To refer to beads as 'frightened' is to employ the rhetorical figure called animism, whereby an inanimate object is given the attributes of life. Far from clarifying the look of the bird's eyes, the simile makes it *less* concrete, less visible or imaginable, by making a comparison with something that cannot possibly be seen. It is entirely incorrect to say that the bird's eyes 'looked like' frightened beads, since *frightened* beads are not available to the gaze at all, and beads cannot look. The simile, a peculiar example of a 'transferred epithet', disturbs the sense of who or what is frightened and confounds the distinction between the figurative and the literal, image and word, the imagined and the visible.

The last two stanzas of the poem increase these uncertainties. In the penultimate stanza, rowing on an ocean is the 'vehicle' for the metaphor, the 'tenor' or 'meaning' of which is flying. But once again the figure is ambiguous: the ocean metaphor is inadequate, the line suggests, to express the softness, the silvery delicacy of the movement of the bird's flight. Where a boat would leave a wake in the water, a kind of seam, the bird leaves none in the air. But while 'Too silver for a seam' may be 'translated' as meaning something like 'too delicate for a wake or track in water', the line may also be understood to be referring to the delicacy of figurative language and its relation to the world. Critics usually distinguish simile within metaphor more generally by pointing out that phrases such as 'like' or 'as' mark simile as explicitly figurative. Through another kind of figure known as paronomasia—produced by the homophone 'seam'/'seem'—the poem reflects silently on figuration itself. Metaphors seem to be unmarked, too silver, too subtle, for a seam, or for the word 'seem' (or 'as' or 'like'), too delicate for the mark of figuration. Just as there is no seam left behind after the bird's flight—it flies as if by magic—metaphor also leaves no mark, no 'seem' and no seam. Or, to put it more paradoxically but more accurately, like the word 'plashless', a word which negates 'plash' but does so only by referring to it, metaphor both does and does not leave a mark.

The extraordinary ending to the poem involves another metaphor for the bird's flight—the flight of a butterfly—but presents this in terms of swimming. The bird is like a butterfly leaping off a bank into the water so delicately that there is no (s)plash. With the phrase 'Banks of Noon', Dickinson's poem disturbs the basis of metaphorical transformation itself. 'Banks of Noon' is no more comprehensible than the 'frightened Beads' encountered earlier. The metaphorical transitions are short-circuited, for while it is possible to see that a bird's flight is 'like' rowing a boat, it is unclear how a bank of noon can be 'like' anything physical—are we to believe that 'noon' can be a kind of river bank, for example? The phrase highlights the deceptiveness of figuration, its potential for linguistic *trompes l'œil* and hallucinatory effects. It dramatizes the ease, the inevitability with which language slides away from effects of reference. On the other hand, 'Banks of Noon' can be considered in terms of another kind of phenomenon—intertextuality—whereby a text is woven out of borrowed words and phrases. In this respect, the phrase repeats the Shakespearean 'bank and shoal of time' from Macbeth's murderous speech (*Macbeth* I, vii, 6)—giving the sense of the present being a kind of isthmus within the ocean of eternity—and suggests the end or the edge of time, of time strangely suspended or delayed. The ending of Dickinson's poem suggests that figurative language entails a series of displacements and substitutions which both produce and withhold the illusion of reference. In these and other ways, Dickinson's poem suggests that figures make and unmake our world, give us meaning and take it away.

In our discussion of Dickinson's poem, we have drawn attention to the self-reflexive possibilities of figuration, to the way that figures can turn reflexively back on themselves, trope themselves, so that the text remarks on its own language. To end our discussion of figures, we shall turn briefly to another text which may also be shown to register the uncanny potential of figurative language. James Joyce's short story 'The Dead' (1914) begins with this sentence: 'Lily, the caretaker's daughter, was literally run off her feet' (199). In fact, Lily is not *literally* run off her feet at all. Strangely, we say 'literally run off her feet' to mean *not* literally but figuratively run off her feet. The use of the word 'literal' here, like the phrase about feet, is metaphorical. In this respect, we can see that the opening sentence to the story produces a play of figuration which refers indirectly both to the subject of the story, death, and to its telling. 'Literally run off her feet' is a dead metaphor, a metaphor which has become so common that its identity as figurative has largely been lost: dead metaphors are Nietzsche's worn coins of language. We can say 'I was literally run off my feet' without recognizing that we are using a metaphor at all, that far from using the phrase literally, we are exploiting a figure of speech. The metaphorical use of the word 'literal' is a good example of the evocative possibilities of 'catachresis', the rhetorical misuse or abuse of language. 'The Dead', which is above all about death, is also about dead language, dead metaphors.

Joyce's story ends with the return of a 'figure from the dead' (251), the haunting memory of Gretta's dead boyfriend, Michael Furey. In the final pages, Gretta's husband Gabriel looks out of the window of a hotel as his wife sleeps. The last paragraph of the story is couched in intense, swooning, highly figurative prose:

A few light taps upon the pane made him turn to the window. It
had begun to snow again. He watched sleepily the flakes, silver and
dark, falling obliquely against the lamplight. The time had come for
him to set out on his journey westward. Yes, the newspapers were
right: snow was general all over Ireland. It was falling on every part
of the dark central plain, on the treeless hills, falling softly upon the
Bog of Allen and, farther westward, softly falling into the dark
mutinous Shannon waves. It was falling, too, upon every part of the
lonely churchyard on the hill where Michael Furey lay buried. It lay
thickly drifted on the crooked crosses and headstones, on the spears
of the little grate, on the barren thorns. His soul swooned slowly as
he heard the snow falling faintly through the universe and faintly
falling, like the descent of their last end, upon all the living and the
dead. (255–6)

The most remarkable, the most pressing feature of this paragraph is,
perhaps, repetition. In particular, the word 'falling' occurs seven times:
falling obliquely, falling, falling softly, softly falling, falling, falling
faintly, faintly falling. Together with chiasmatic inversion and alliteration, the word's repetition produces a mesmeric sense of descent, sleep,
fading and death. What Joyce appears to be evoking here, through figurative effects of language—repetition, alliteration and assonance, chiasmus—is a fading out, a falling off, of language itself. 'The Dead' is
about the death of (figurative *and* literal) language.

To borrow Joyce's metaphor and reverse it, it is indeed the metaphorical death of language (rather than the death of metaphorical language)
that gives the story life. And it is, more generally, the productive tensions of figurative language that give life to literary texts. In this chapter,
we have tried to suggest that, like literature itself, literary criticism
begins and ends with figuration. In reading we should try to figure out
ways in which figures at once generate and disturb literary texts. Like
Marvell's lover in his desire to stop the sun, if we cannot escape figures,
still we can make them run.

Further reading

See Paul Ricoeur's *The Rule of Metaphor* (1978) for a difficult but comprehensive work on metaphor from the perspective of a philosopher.
For literary critical approaches, see Hawkes's useful book *Metaphor*
(1972) and Brooke-Rose's *A Grammar of Metaphor* (1958). A classic

structuralist account of figuration or 'poetic' language is Roman Jakobson's 'Closing Statement: Linguistics and Poetics' (1960). De Man's *Allegories of Reading* (1979) is a challenging and influential account of the conflicts of rhetoric and grammar produced by close readings of a number of literary and philosophical texts. For an excellent but very demanding series of rhetorical readings in a de Manian vein, see Cynthia Chase, *Decomposing Figures* (1986). Derrida's 'White Mythology' (1982) is a dense and difficult but by now classic argument against the notion that there could be any simple escape from figurative language. Richard Rand's 'Geraldine' (in Young 1981) offers a complex and very stimulating exposition of figures and tropes through a reading of Coleridge. Other useful books are Todorov, *Introduction to Poetics* (1981) and Lakoff and Johnson, *Metaphors We Live By* (1980).

Laughter

'We are very sorry, indeed, to learn what happened,' said a BBC spokesman on hearing about the *death of a Goodies fan while watching the show*. 'He just laughed heartily and too long,' said his wife. 'After 25 minutes of laughing he gave a tremendous belly laugh, slumped on the settee, and died. (He) loved the Goodies, and it was one of the best for a long time' . . . (*The Guardian*, 26 March 1975)

The man's death was, no doubt, a great misfortune. But, as the response of his wife might suggest, there was also something quite funny, and even appropriate about it. The word 'funny' here is oddly ambiguous: how funny it is, after all, that a word ('funny') should mean both 'amusing' and 'strange'. The peculiar appropriateness of the death of this Goodies fan consists not only in the fact that it was a particularly *good* episode of the comedy programme ('one of the best for a long time'), but also in the way in which it is suggestive of a more general and perhaps more intimate link between laughter and death. When we say that someone 'died laughing' or 'laughed themselves to death' we are, in most circumstances, speaking metaphorically. What is funny (in both senses) about the case of the Goodies fan is that it involves a literalization of this metaphor. To take a metaphor literally (which can also be called 'catachresis' or 'misapplication of a word') is an example of a rhetorical device that is often very effective as a means of generating laughter. In this respect it would seem that the man's death conforms to the conventions of comedy. But of course there is also a darker side to this, the side that involves 'funny' in the sense of 'funny peculiar'. In other words, what this newspaper report also prompts us to ask is: *why* do we talk about 'dying with laughter' or 'laughing oneself to death'? Is it *simply* metaphorical? Is there something about laughter that, in a profound if ticklish way, puts it in touch with death? Let us leave these questions in suspense for a little while.

What about laughter and literature? We often think of literature as very (or, dare one say, 'deadly') serious, especially if we are studying it. In part this is because (as we suggest in greater detail in Chapter 17) literature is linked to notions of the sacred, to a sense of hushed respect. But literature is also about pleasure, play and laughter. In this chapter we shall attempt to provide an account of some of the ways in which laughter has been theorized, down the centuries, and attempt to illustrate these theories in relation to particular literary texts. Finally, we shall focus on the idea of literature as a space in which the notion of seriousness itself, and the distinctions between the 'serious' and 'non-serious', are fundamentally unsettled, thrown into question, discombobulated.

There is nothing worse than the prospect of trying to talk about laughter, or trying to define what is humorous. It is something of a lost cause from the start. It automatically seems to put us—if we dare risk a slightly risible analogy at this point—in the position of the frog, in the story about the frog, the chicken and the librarian. A chicken walks into the local town library, goes up to the librarian's desk and says: 'Bok!' So the librarian gives the chicken a book. The chicken goes away, but comes back the next day, goes up to the librarian's desk and says: 'Bok, bok!' So the librarian gives the chicken two books, the chicken goes away, comes back the next day: 'Bok, bok, bok!' So the librarian provides the chicken with three more books. And the next day 'Bok, bok, bok, bok!' and so on until the fifth day, when the chicken comes in and says to the librarian, 'Bok, bok, bok, bok, bok!' The librarian hands over five books but then decides to follow the chicken, at a surreptitious distance, out of the library. The librarian follows as the chicken goes down the street, across the road and down a smaller street, then through an unbolted wooden door, down a passageway, into a garden, across the garden to a small lake, across a narrow bridge to an island in the middle, where the chicken puts the books down in front of a frog who says: 'Reddit, reddit, reddit, reddit, reddit.'

If there is laughter here it would be the result of a number of things. First, there is the ridiculous anthropomorphism: chickens do not go to libraries, librarians do not respond to chickens as if they were simply 'members of the public', frogs do not read books. Second, there is the pleasure of recognition as we realize that the 'bok, bok' of a chicken could after all be heard as a request for a book, or for two books, and that the croaking of a frog might indeed be construed as 'read-it, read-it'. Third, there is the sense of a so-called shaggy dog story, the feeling that the story could go on indefinitely, that the chicken could, at least in principle, order up the entire holdings of the British Library . . . bok, bok, bok. . . . Here laughter would be linked to suspense, and more specifically perhaps to the hysterical effect of a potentially permanent postponement of a resolution. It is this which in part at least constitutes the comic force of a play such as Beckett's *Waiting for Godot* (1953). But by the same token it would also be what haunts or menaces every tragedy: comedy in this sense could be defined as the overturning of the tragic. But there is also, by contrast, something comical about the very corniness (so to speak) of the joke, its 'cheepness' and groan-making quality. In this respect the joke relies on a certain surprise—the surprise of the punchline—*and* a certain recognition: you know that a punchline is going to come and what sort of punchline it will be, but you cannot tell exactly what it will be. There is a child-like pleasure involved in laughing at something at once surprising and familiar. Indeed, Freud argues in his brilliant (but oddly unamusing) book *Jokes and Their Relation to the Unconscious* (1905), 'everything comic is based fundamentally on degradation [or "stepping down"] to being a child' (Freud 1976, 292). Finally, this ridiculous story about the frog, the chicken and the librarian suggests something about the relations between laughter, reading and mystery. For perhaps what is also funny about the story is the implicit hyperbole whereby anyone (let alone a frog) could be expected to have read *everything*. In this respect we can never be in the position of the frog or—to put it more specifically in terms of our argument in this chapter—there is never a truly froglike position from which to provide a serious account of laughter. Any theory of laughter, we would like to suggest, is necessarily infected, undermined, displaced by the experience of laughter itself.

Let us try to be serious for a moment, then, and outline a couple of the basic theories of laughter. The first is the 'masterful frog' or 'complacent librarian' theory, in other words the 'superiority theory' of laughter. It is succinctly and famously formulated by the seventeenth-century English philosopher Thomas Hobbes: 'The passion of laughter is nothing else but *sudden glory* arising from some sudden *conception* of some *eminency* in ourselves, by *comparison* with the *infirmity* of others, or with our own formerly' (Hobbes 1840, 46). We laugh, according to this argument, out of a sense of superiority—the 'sudden glory' or 'conception of eminency' in relation to the stupidity or weakness of others, or of ourselves at some point in the past. Thus, for example, we may laugh at the man who slips over on the banana skin, or we may laugh at Bottom, in *A Midsummer Night's Dream*, because he is such an ass, or we may laugh with Swift at the small-mindedness of other human beings, for example in Book I of *Gulliver's Travels* (1726).

The second theory is what we could call the 'nothing theory' or the 'no theory' theory. This may be illustrated by way of the Monty Python sketch in which a woman called Miss Anne Elk (John Cleese in drag) is interviewed because she is supposed to have a new theory about the brontosaurus. Miss Elk will not disclose her theory but seems instead concerned simply to say over and over again that she *has* a theory and that the theory is hers: 'my theory that I have, that is to say, which is mine, is mine'. Chris, the interviewer (Graham Chapman), becoming exasperated, says: 'Yes, I know it's yours, what is it?' Looking rather nervously around the studio, Anne Elk replies: 'Where?' (Monty Python's Flying Circus 1989, 119) When Miss Elk does finally enunciate her theory it is truly bathetic—in fact, no theory at all:

> *Miss Elk* Ready?
> *Presenter* Yes.
> *Miss Elk* My theory by A. Elk. Brackets Miss, brackets. This theory goes as follows and begins now. All brontosauruses are thin at one end, much much thicker in the middle and then thin again at the far end. That is my theory, it is mine, and belongs to me and I own it, and what it is too.
> *Presenter* That's *it*, is it?
> *Miss Elk* Spot on, Chris. (119)

In more sombre and philosophical terms, the 'nothing theory' or 'no theory' theory is suggested, for instance, by Immanuel Kant's proposition that '*Laughter is an affection arising from a strained expectation being suddenly reduced to nothing*' (Kant 1988, 199). Laughter is nothing more than the bursting of a bubble. When we laugh, according to this argument, we are laughing in a sort of 'absurd' vacuum: 'merely' laughing, with nothing to support us. In a fascinating essay entitled 'The Laughter of Being', Mikkel Borch-Jacobsen suggests a radicalization of this Kantian formulation. Following the work of the French writer Georges Bataille in particular, he argues that 'There is no theory of laughter, only an experience' (Borch-Jacobsen 1987, 742). Moreover, this experience is of a decidedly 'funny' sort—for it is an experience of, precisely, *nothing*.

As Bataille puts it: '[when I laugh,] I am in fact nothing more than the laughter which takes hold of me' (Bataille 1973, 364, cited by Borch-Jacobsen, 744).

Let us turn from 'theory' to consider some literary examples. Laughter can be dependent on the visual—and literature is full of instances of visual comedy. But laughter, at least in literature, is even more fundamentally a matter of language. One of the greatest eighteenth-century English comedies is Richard Brinsley Sheridan's play, *The School for Scandal* (first performed in 1777). It contains numerous classic moments of visual comedy (characters in disguise, characters hiding themselves behind screens, characters being thrust hastily into closets and so on), but the comic power of Sheridan's play consists above all in its language. This starts from the very title of the play—with its satirical implication that scandalmongering is something to be taught—and from the names of its characters—a woman called Lady Sneerwell, her servant, Snake, a gentleman called Sir Benjamin Backbite and so forth. We could consider a brief exchange between Lady Sneerwell and Mr Snake on the subject of her 'superiority' over other slanderers and scandalmongers such as Mrs Clackitt:

> *Lady Sneerwell* Why truly Mrs Clackitt has a very pretty talent—and a great deal of industry.
> *Snake* True, madam, and has been tolerably successful in her day. To my knowledge she has been the cause of six matches being broken off and three sons disinherited, of four forced elopements, and as many close confinements, nine separate maintenances, and two divorces. Nay, I have more than once traced her causing a *tête-à-tête* in the *Town and Country Magazine*, when the parties perhaps had never seen each other's face before in the course of their lives.
> *Lady Sneerwell* She certainly has talents, but her *manner* is gross.
> *Snake* 'Tis very true. She generally designs well, has a free tongue, and a bold invention; but her colouring is too dark and her outlines often extravagant. She wants that delicacy of hint and mellowness of sneer which distinguishes your ladyship's scandal.
> *Lady Sneerwell* You are partial, Snake. (I, i, 10–26)

We can imagine the comic possibilities of the characters' gestures and appearance, but what is most comic is in the language itself—in the satirical observation on what it means to be 'tolerably successful', in the incongruity or absurdity of evaluating who has the more beautiful 'sneer', in the snaking sibilance of Snake's last sentence, in the playful truth of Lady Sneerwell's final remark.

The play called *The School for Scandal* is, then, fundamentally word-play. Indeed, we could say, literature in general has to do with wordplay or—to use a more technical-sounding term—with paronomasia. This is in part what makes it potentially so subversive and disturbing. Could there really be a character called Snake? Or a woman called Lady Sneerwell? What kind of world do they belong to? Literature is a matter of linguistic as well as social scandal. It poses a constant challenge to the realms of so-called 'good sense' and represents an affront to what could be called the ideology of seriousness. Paronomasia is indeed so originary a dimension of literary works that one is tempted to agree with the narrator of Samuel Beckett's *Murphy* (1938) and say: 'In the beginning was the pun' (41). Even Shakespeare becomes open to criticism on this front. Literary critics may not have much of a reputation for being amusing—but critical indignation at Shakespeare's soft spot for the 'quibble' (or 'pun') gives rise to what we think is one of the funniest paragraphs in the history of literary criticism. Here is Samuel Johnson's fascinating and irresistible paragraph from his Preface to Shakespeare (1765):

> A quibble is to Shakespeare what luminous vapours are to the travel-ler; he follows it at all adventures; it is sure to lead him out of his way and sure to engulf him in the mire. It has some malignant power over his mind, and its fascinations are irresistible. Whatever be the dignity or profundity of his disquisition, whether he be enlarging knowledge or exalting affection, whether he be amusing attention with incidents or enchaining it in suspense, let but a quibble spring up before him, and he leaves his work unfinished. A quibble is the golden apple for which he will always turn aside from his career or stoop from his elevation. A quibble, poor and barren as it is, gave him such delight that he was content to purchase it by the sacrifice of reason, propriety, and truth. A quibble was to him the fatal Cleo-patra for which he lost the world and was content to lose it. (Johnson 1969, 68)

We will now consider another, rather different kind of literary work, Geoffrey Chaucer's 'The Miller's Tale'. This is the story set in Oxford, about the superstitious old carpenter John, his beautiful young wife Ali-soun, and their handsome lodger, Nicholas. Along with a rather absurd rival called Absolon, Nicholas is after the young wife. Chaucer's tale recounts, with superb comic concision, how Nicholas persuades John that the end of the world is coming, in order to distract him so that he can get into bed with the old man's wife. John ends up with a broken arm, but Nicholas finally fares worse. That same night, Alisoun has already humiliated Absolon: he craves a kiss from her and she agrees, but in the dark Absolon finds himself kissing her arse, not her mouth. When Nicholas tries to repeat this jape, and indeed embellish it with a thundering fart, he receives a burning hot poker up his bum. In order to try to describe what makes Chaucer's 'The Miller's Tale' one of the greatest comic poems ever written we could point to the visual comedy of John the Carpenter up in the rooftop cutting the cable and crashing down, convinced that the flood is coming and that he'll be safe in the 'kneeding-tubbe' that will be his mini Noah's ark. This fall might be seen as a literalization and structural equivalent of the fall of the tragic hero. In this respect comedy is not the *opposite* of tragedy but the same, viewed from a different perspective. While we identify with the tragic hero or heroine, we stand apart from or above the comic victim. Chaucer's poem, then, offers a clear example of the Hobbesian motif: we laugh because we are not stupid like John the Carpenter. The Carpenter falls. We remain where we are, superior, riding high.

But we must at the same time acknowledge that all of this is in a sense only happening *in language*, as something being narrated. And indeed the comic force of 'The Miller's Tale' is very specifically linguistic. It is not only a matter of the brutally eloquent account of John's cuckolding, or the satirical portrayal of Absolon's fashion-conscious, prancing character, or the bawdy language of pissing and 'letting flee' monumental farts. It is also, and most crucially, that the whole story seems to be structured like a joke condensed from or into the single word, 'water'. The whole text turns on the double signification of the word 'water': for Nicholas it's a screamed request for an anodyne to salve his sizzling arse, for John it signifies that the flood is upon them. The two parts of the story are explosively assembled in the wordplay or paronomasia around this single word:

> The hote culter brende so his toute,
> And for the smert he wende for to dye.
> As he were wood, for wo he gan to crye—
> 'Help! water! water! help, for Goddes herte!'
> This carpenter out of his slomber sterte,
> And herde oon cryen 'water!' as he were wood,

> And thoghte, 'Allas, now comth Nowelis flood!'
> He sit him up withouten wordes mo,
> And with his ax he smoot the corde atwo,
> And doun goth al . . .
>
> (lines 709–18)

The visual comedy of the fall (whether from the roof in Chaucer, or on a banana skin in *Tom and Jerry*), and the accompanying emphasis on high and low, seems to have a 'funny' counterpart in the terms of rhetorical figures and tropes. Thus what creates laughter in a text is often either hyperbole (exaggeration) or litotes (understatement). Some examples of hyperbole would be the sorts of comparative metaphor for which Raymond Chandler's work is celebrated. In *The Little Sister* (1949), for instance, we encounter the gorgeous Miss Gonzales who, Marlowe tells us, 'smelled the way the Taj Mahal looked by moonlight' (70), had a 'mouth as red as a new fire engine' (158) and who proceeds to make 'a couple of drinks in a couple of glasses you could almost have stood umbrellas in' (70). Correspondingly we are told of a man wearing 'sky-blue gaberdine slacks . . . and a two-tone leisure jacket which would have been revolting on a zebra' (84). There is a police lieutenant called Maglachan who 'had a jaw like a park bench' (167), and there is Lee Farrell, 'one of the hottest trouble-shooting lawyers in the country', who 'looked as if it would cost a thousand dollars to shake hands with him' (223). Litotes, on the other hand, is a pervasive trope in Jonathan Swift's *A Modest Proposal* (1729), a text which also illustrates the fundamental, if in many ways disturbing, power of irony as a comic dimension of literary texts. *A Modest Proposal* works by understatement and irony. It modestly (or litotically) proposes that a solution to poverty and population management in Ireland might be the killing of small children, then selling and eating them.

If hyperbole and litotes are both species of irony, to the extent that they involve a sense of saying what is *other than* what is meant, literature in general might suggest not only that irony is capable of generating laughter but that laughter is always ironic. Outside of literature, we might say, it is possible to entertain perfectly serious ideas about laughter, about jokes, comedy and humour. Thus Freud's *Jokes and their Relation to the Unconscious* (Freud 1976) is a fascinating work, not only for the similarities it reveals between the structure of jokes and dreams (and by implication, therefore, the structure of works of literature as well), but also for the basic and in some ways disturbing truth it offers as regards the nature of most jokes. Freud argues that jokes tend to be sexist, 'dirty', violent, racist: they transgress social taboos and 'lift' repression. But literature, conversely, might be defined as the space in which the seriousness of Freud's or anyone else's claims are ironized, satirized, parodied or otherwise put into question. For literature is the discourse that is, perhaps more than any other, concerned with questioning and unsettling assumptions about what is serious and what is not serious. Such a questioning and unsettling is especially characteristic of what is widely referred to as 'the postmodern'. Postmodern works such as the stories of Kafka, the plays of Samuel Beckett or the novels of Ian McEwan present a disquieting, irresolvable mixture of the serious and non-serious, tragic and comic, macabre and laughable. This uncomfortable mixture, however, might also be seen to be at play in Shakespeare's tragedies, for example, or indeed in Chaucer's 'The Miller's Tale', which ends with a scene in which everyone is laughing but where it is no longer clear what kind of laughter it is or who is laughing at what or who. As we have suggested, the study of literature is in various ways policed by a kind of ideology of seriousness. There is a strong tendency to accept the rules, to adhere to boundaries and categories, to say: the study of literature is a serious affair. Or to say: X is a serious text or a serious moment in a text, whereas Y is not serious. No doubt in the context of the novel, 'realism' has been and in many ways continues to be the very embodiment of a certain 'seriousness'. But the postmodern prompts us to ask various questions in this respect: how seriously, for example, should we take 'realism' or 'reality effects' in literature? What does seriousness imply or assume? Who are the police and what is the nature of their authority?

To say that laughter is always ironic is to suggest that laughter (or irony) will always have the last laugh. There is something diabolical about laughter. It can both liberate and mystify. It can be at once offensive (laughing at sexist or racist jokes, for instance) and inoffensive (it was 'only a joke'). It can be cruel, a means of exclusion or of exerting power over people ('then she just laughed in my face'). But it can also be joyous, a means of sharing and of confirming one's sense of 'social community'. As Freud observes of jokes: 'Every joke calls for a public of its own and laughing at the same jokes is evidence of far-reaching psychical conformity' (Freud 1976, 203–4). Laughter can be undecidably 'real' and 'unreal', 'genuine' and 'false'. It can be tiring, it can have you on your hands and knees. It can be uncontrollable, as if with a life of its own. It can be dangerous, as well as exhilarating or ecstatic. In the engulfment of uncontrollable laughter we lose a sense of who or what we are. We are reduced to nothing. Every pretension to mastery or superiority collapses and dissolves. Laughter becomes the obliteration of identity. It is this obliteration—when one is truly engulfed in laughter, when one is nothing *but* this laughter—that perhaps gives laughter its strange intimacy with death.

Further reading

For two classic accounts of laughter and the comic, see Henri Bergson, *Laughter: An Essay on the Meaning of the Comic* (1921) and Sigmund Freud, *Jokes and their Relation to the Unconscious* (1976). Freud also has a short but extremely interesting essay on the nature of humour (in Freud 1985d). Bergson's essay is reprinted in Sypher, ed., *Comedy* (1956) which also reprints George Meredith's eloquent 'An Essay on Comedy' (1877). Arthur Koestler's *The Act of Creation* (1964) contains some engaging and thoughtful material on 'the jester' and the nature of laughter. For a wide-ranging and challenging collection of essays on puns and wordplay, see Jonathan Culler, ed., *On Puns* (1988a). For a varied collection of essays on comedy from a historical perspective, see Cordner, Holland and Kerrigan, eds, *English Comedy* (1994). Borch-Jacobsen's complex but excellent account of theories of laughter, 'The Laughter of Being', appears in a 'Laughter' special issue of *Modern Language Notes* (1987). Of particular interest in the same issue are Samuel Weber's 'Laughing in the Meanwhile' (1987) and Jean-Luc Nancy's 'Wild Laughter in the Throat of Death' (1987); see also Nancy's interrogation of his own question 'Is it possible to be in the presence of laughter?' in 'Laughter, Presence' (1993). From a feminist perspective, see Gray, *Women and Laughter* (1994).

The tragic

Tragedy tears us apart, it shatters our sense of ourselves and the world. The terrifying power of tragedy is suggested by Sir Philip Sidney when he speaks, in *An Apology for Poetry* (1595), of

> high and excellent Tragedy, that openeth the greatest wounds, and showeth forth the ulcers that are covered with tissue; that maketh kings fear to be tyrants, and tyrants manifest their tyrannical humours; that, with stirring the affects of admiration and commiseration, teacheth the uncertainty of this world, and upon how weak foundations gilden roofs are builded . . . (117–18)

Tragedy has to do with strangeness. It involves an overwhelming sense of what Sidney calls 'the uncertainty of this world'. It involves—as Aristotle suggested, more than 2,300 years ago—a paradoxical combination of emotions, at once pity and fear or (as Sidney says) 'admiration and commiseration'. Tragedy involves an encounter not only with the death of a character on stage (or in the pages of a book) but also with the idea of our own deaths. Tragedy resists simple explanations. As A.C. Bradley observed, in 1904: 'tragedy would not be tragedy if it were not a painful mystery' (38). In this chapter we propose to elucidate this sense of 'painful mystery' and to consider some examples of tragic literature, ranging from Shakespeare to the present.

When we think of tragedy in the context of literature in English, no doubt we think first of Shakespeare and especially of the 'great tragedies', *Hamlet* (1600–1), *Othello* (1604), *King Lear* (1605) and *Macbeth* (1606). With such plays in mind we could suggest that tragedy comprises four basic elements. The first is that there is a central character (the protagonist), someone who is 'noble' and with whom we are able to sympathize or identify. The second is that this character should suffer and (preferably) die, and that his or her downfall or death should roughly coincide with the end of the play. The third is that the downfall or death of the central character should be felt by the spectator or reader to be both inevitable and 'right' but at the same time in some sense unjustifiable and unacceptable. The fourth element can be referred to as apocalypticism. As we have already indicated, it is not just the death of the protagonist that we are presented with, in a tragedy: in identifying with the protagonist who dies, we are also drawn into thinking about our own death. And because the protagonist's death is invariably shattering to other characters, tragedy always engages with a broader sense of death and destruction, a shattering of society or the world as a whole.

Without these four elements there cannot be a tragedy. From an Aristotelian perspective we might want to propose additional elements, in particular the notions of *peripeteia* ('reversal'), *anagnorisis* ('revelation' or 'coming to self-knowledge') and *hamartia* ('tragic flaw' or 'error'). *Peripeteia* is a useful term for referring to the reversals or sudden changes in fortune that a character or characters may experience—Lear's being made homeless, for instance, or Othello's being transformed by 'the green-ey'd monster' (III, iii, 166) of jealousy. Aristotle introduced the term in the context of tragedy, though it is also apposite in other contexts, including comedy (where a character experiences a reversal or sudden change for the good). *Anagnorisis* refers to the idea of a moment of revelation or recognition, especially the moment when a protagonist experiences a sudden awakening to the truth or to self-knowledge. A tragic work may contain more than one such moment: Hamlet's life, for instance, might be described as a sort of *anagnorisis* 'block', a ghostly series of apparent but ineffective *anagnorises* starting with his exclamation 'O my prophetic soul!' (I, v, 40) on discovering the murderous truth about his father's death and realizing that this is what he had imagined, deep in his 'prophetic soul'. Classically, though, a tragedy tends to be construed as having one crucial or climactic moment of *anagnorisis*. In Sophocles's *Oedipus the King*, for example, this can be very specifically located in lines 1306–08:

> O god—
> all come true, all burst to light!
> O light—now let me look my last on you!
> I stand revealed at last.

Finally, *hamartia* refers to the idea of tragic characters having a particular flaw or weakness, or making an error of judgment which leads to their downfall or death. Thus, for example, each of the male protagonists of Shakespeare's 'great tragedies' could be considered in terms of a fundamental moral or psychological weakness. Hamlet's irresoluteness, Othello's jealousy, Lear's pride and Macbeth's ambitiousness might then be seen as a key element in each of these works. A primary aim in this chapter, however, is to stress the ways in which the tragic entails a fundamental sense of what remains painful, mysterious or uncertain. That is to say, to focus on character and the idea of 'tragic flaw' or 'error' tends to suggest something straightforwardly *causal*: Hamlet's irresoluteness is the cause of his tragedy and so on. This is not to say that Hamlet's irresoluteness or Othello's jealousy are unimportant: quite the reverse. These 'flaws' or 'weaknesses' are crucial—they are integral to what we think and feel about Hamlet and Othello as characters and therefore to what we think and feel about their tragic fates. But what constitutes the tragic is always stranger and more painful than is suggested by the inevitably moralistic and reductive claim that, for instance, Othello should not have allowed himself to get so jealous and worked up. His jealousy has a crucial but partial and perhaps finally uncertain significance in terms of the tragic power of the play. About to murder his beloved wife, Othello begins what is one of the most anguished and intolerable soliloquies in Shakespeare's work: 'It is the cause, it is the cause, my soul;/Let me not name it to you, you chaste stars,/It is the cause' (V, ii, 1–3). 'Cause' here may mean 'crime', 'legal or other case' or 'reason'. What is conveyed in these lines is a sense of what *cannot be named*, a profound strangeness and uncertainty regarding the very sense of this repeated and equivocal word, 'cause'. Tragedy, we want to suggest, and as *Othello* darkly demonstrates, is not only about the sense of particular causes or explanations but also, and more importantly, about a painful absence or uncertainty of cause.

Tragedy (and here we use the word to embrace both Shakespearean and more recent forms) is not only inimical to the pleasure-button-pushing mentality of Hollywood or Broadway, but also at odds with the very idea of identity and meaning. As Howard Barker puts it, in a series of aphoristic statements entitled 'Asides for a Tragic Theatre' (1986):

> In tragedy, the audience is disunited . . . Tragedy is not about reconciliation . . . Tragedy offends the sensibilities. It drags the unconscious into the public place . . . After the carnival, after the removal of the masks, you are precisely who you were before. After the tragedy, you are not certain who you are. (Barker 1989, 13)

Tragedy is offensive, it generates disunity and exposes disharmony. Like psychoanalytic theory (itself crucially indebted to Sophocles's *Oedipus the King*), tragedy makes the unconscious public. It leaves us uncertain about our very identities, uncertain about how we feel, about what has happened to us.

Finally, there is something apocalyptic about the tragic, not only in the sense that it consistently entails an experience of unmanageable disorder but also in that this experience of disorder is linked to a more general kind of *revelation* (the meaning of the original Greek word 'apocalypsis'). The apocalyptic or revelation at the heart of the tragic has to do with the idea that there is no God or gods looking down on the world to see that justice is done, or that, if there are gods, they are profoundly careless, indifferent, even sadistic. The heavens may be occupied or vacant, but the world is terrible and *makes no sense*. To illustrate this idea in relation to *King Lear*, for example, we could look to a few lines spoken by Albany—addressed to his wife Goneril and concerned with the 'vile' behaviour of herself and her sister Regan towards their father, the King:

> If that the heavens do not their visible spirits
> Send quickly down to tame these vile offenses,
> It will come,
> Humanity must perforce prey on itself
> Like monsters of the deep. (IV, ii, 46–50)

The tragic revelation of *King Lear* concerns the sense that humanity is indeed monstrous and that there are no 'visible spirits' or any other sort of spirits that might properly or profitably be called down from the heavens. One of the shortest, least metrical and yet most powerful lines in Shakespeare—'It will come'—is apocalyptic both in terms of the dark revelation of the idea that there are no gods or divine justice and in terms of the sense of an impending or accumulating cataclysm of general destruction and death. The word 'come' is crucial here—as indeed it is in the final passages of several of Shakespeare's tragedies—in part because it resonates with the apocalypticism of the end of the Bible: 'He which testifieth these things saith, Surely I come quickly. Amen. Even so, come, Lord Jesus' (Revelation 22:20). Tragedy says 'come' in a double sense: it summons us, it engages our feelings of sympathy and identification, it demands that our emotions be involved in what is happening. But at the same time tragedy says: we have to suffer, we are going to die, there is no justice and there is no afterlife. It, death and cataclysm, will come. In this way, tragedy engages with the limits of sense, verges on the senseless. Because what tragedy is about *is* senseless, meaningless—the unjust and yet unavoidable shattering of life. This would be another way of trying to highlight the mysterious and paradoxical nature of the tragic. When Ludovico says, of the bed displaying the corpses of Othello and Desdemona, 'Let it be hid' (*Othello*, V, ii, 365), Shakespeare's play paradoxically conceals or encrypts this intolerable sight that tragedy calls us to witness. Correspondingly, in *King Lear*, the death of Cordelia and Lear's madness of grief are figured in apocalyptic terms—Kent asks, 'Is this the promis'd end?', Edgar retorts, 'Or image of that horror?' (V, iii, 264–5)—but what the tragedy finally and paradoxically reveals is perhaps rather the ethical and spiritual horror of a world in which violence, torture and terror recur unendingly. What is revealed in *King Lear*, in other words, is the sense that there is no image of the end except as this unendingness.

With these rather dark thoughts in mind, let us try to say a little more about the first three elements of a tragedy. First of all, there is the idea of the central character with whom one strongly sympathizes or identifies. 'Sympathy' here entails primarily the idea of 'entering into another's feelings or mind' (*Chambers*). It carries clear connotations of the original Greek terms 'syn', *with*, and 'pathos', *suffering*—that is to say, 'sympathy' as 'suffering with'. It is important to distinguish this from 'feeling sorry for'. In tragedy, sympathy with a character is indistinguishable from a logic of identification, of identifying with that character and experiencing and suffering with her or him. Likewise, it may be useful to distinguish 'sympathy' from 'empathy'. 'Sympathy', 'sympathetic' and 'sympathizing with' are preferable to 'empathy', 'empathetic' or 'empathizing with', if only because the notion of empathy ('I can really empathize with that') tends to suggest that *we know who we are*. The tragic, on the contrary, has to do with a sense of *loss* of identity—the sense that (in Barker's words) 'you are not certain who you are'. We might try to clarify this a little more by remarking on the paradoxical nature of sympathy specifically in relation to drama. Sympathy involves going out of ourselves, and sharing or identifying with the position of another. Putting it slightly differently, it involves a sense of going out of ourselves but, at the same time, *putting ourselves on stage*. In this respect we have an intriguing example of *chiasmus*, which can be formulated as follows: there is no drama without sympathy, but there is no sympathy without drama. This curious proposition may also help us to appreciate why, in historical terms, tragedy has so consistently been associated with the dramatic. More than any other genre, tragedy explores the limits of the experience of sympathy, as it broaches self-obliteration and death. In a manner especially suited to the stage, tragedy is exposure to death—to that extreme of sympathy or identification where, putting oneself on stage, one *becomes* the one who dies.

It is only on the basis of this first element (sympathy) that the second (the suffering and death of a character) can be described as tragic. This seems logical enough, but the third element of a tragedy is distinctly paradoxical: the death that occurs at the end of a tragedy is experienced as being at once unavoidable and unjust. This is sometimes talked about as tragic inevitability. Every tragic work will generate a sense of the inevitable or (to use a term that is perhaps too easily loaded with religious connotations) the *fated*. The tragic invariably concerns a sense of what is *foreseeable* but *unavoidable*. But what is unavoidable (Desdemona in *Othello* must die, Tess in Hardy's novel must die, Ikem and Chris in Achebe's *Anthills of the Savannah* must die) is also unacceptable: the tragic seems to involve a peculiar contradiction whereby death is inevitable and therefore (however painfully) appropriate *but at the same time* unjust, unacceptable and therefore inappropriate. Consider, for example, the moment in the final scene of *Hamlet* when Hamlet confides to Horatio: 'If it be now, 'tis not to come; if it be not to come, it will be now; if it be not now, yet it will come—the readiness is all' (V, ii, 220–2). At this moment we, like Horatio, may not *want* Hamlet to die, but at the same time it is hard to imagine that there could be any other outcome to this dark 'coming' to 'readiness' about which Hamlet is speaking here. The paradoxical nature of this third element of the tragic is analogous to the Aristotelian notion of cartharsis. 'Catharsis' is generally understood to refer to the 'cleansing' effect of watching (or reading) a tragedy and to involve the combination of two kinds of emotion (pity and fear). As we noted earlier, this combination seems contradictory. After all, how can one feel pity and fear at the same time? If there were a simple answer to this question we would no longer be thinking within the terms of the tragic, since the tragic comprises precisely this kind of contradictoriness of feeling. Pity is understood by Aristotle in terms of a movement towards the spectacle of destruction and death on stage (or page), while fear is a movement away from it. In this way, the spectator or reader is torn apart. And it is in this sense that we can say that the tragic is not rationalizable, rather it is an *affront* to our desires for meaning and coherence.

In thinking about a particular drama or other work in terms of the tragic, then, perhaps the most valuable thing to do in the first instance is to consider the question of sympathy and/or identification. One could for example think about such questions as the following: how does a tragic text generate sympathy? Which character or characters elicit our sympathy? What is it that *happens* in the text that produces a feeling of sympathy or identification on our part? It is not only a question of character (what is he or she *like* as an individual?) and plot (what happens to him or her, the poor sod?) but also, and more fundamentally, a matter of how character and plot are created *in language*. In short, it is worth trying to think about which particular passages, which particular speeches, and even which particular phrases or words help to generate sympathy in the spectator or reader. To get a clearer sense of this it may be useful to give an example in which one might reasonably suppose that sympathy is at work, and to offer a paraphrase. Take Lady Macbeth's words of murderous guilt as overheard by the Doctor and Gentlewoman. (It is, by the way, an illustration of the power of this tragedy that Shakespeare is able to make us sympathize or identify with a psychopathic murderer.) Lady Macbeth says: 'Here's the smell of the blood still. All the perfumes of Arabia will not sweeten this little hand. O, O, O!' (V, i, 50–2). Lady Macbeth does *not* say: 'Oh what a bore, this smelly blood. Not even industrial cleansing fluid will get this off my hands. Hell, what am I supposed to do?' There are numerous observations one might make regarding the extraordinary *pathos* of Lady Macbeth's language—in its Shakespearean form, that is. The first word she says, 'Here', is significant precisely because it draws us into absolute proximity with her. 'There' would have a quite different effect. The deictic 'Here' suggests how a play such as *Macbeth* establishes and maintains sympathy or identification through the presentation or indication of psychological interiority, in other words the *inside* perspective of a given character's thoughts and feelings. The 'smell of the blood' and the felt persistency of the word 'still' may be mere somnambulistic hallucination, but the spectator or reader is here being presented with intimate, indeed appalling, knowledge of Lady Macbeth's thoughts and sense-impressions. Through the strangeness of soliloquy (the formal device that most explicitly facilitates our access to the interior world of a character's thoughts and feelings), we feel in turn the pouring out of guilt in 'All the perfumes of Arabia . . .' and the stammering nullity of 'O, O, O!'. We cannot claim to truly understand or identify with Lady Macbeth (that would be sleepwalking madness), but her language, pitifully overheard by other characters and by spectators or readers alike, generates sympathy. Sympathy, in short, is something that calls to be described and analyzed not only at the macro-level of character and plot but also, and more importantly, at the micro-level of individual words, phrases, sentences.

To conclude, we shall consider the question of the tragic in some of its more contemporary forms. One can think of many sorts of literary works that are tragedies of one kind or another—and often showing obvious conformities with the model we have outlined. But it is also evident that tragedy seems to have undergone certain changes in the past century or so. There are various reasons for this. One reason has to do with the notion of 'the death of God'. Tragedy, that is to say, is bound to be different if it is considered, at the outset, from a secular perspective. Shakespearean tragedy might be said to be modern to the extent that it seems to dramatize the terrible revelation of a secular and arbitrary world, a purposeless universe of suffering and death. Thomas Hardy's novels—*The Mayor of Casterbridge* (1886), *The Woodlanders* (1887), *Tess of the d'Urbervilles* (1891) and *Jude the Obscure* (1895), for example—might be regarded as limit-texts in this respect: they are remarkably close to the sort of model of tragedy that we have outlined in this chapter but their tragic force consists less in a dramatic revelation that there is no God or ultimate justice and more in an ironic toying with the very grounds of such a revelation. If, as Paul Fussell has argued, irony is the 'dominating form of modern understanding' (Fussell 1975, 35), this is especially clear in the sort of ironization of tragedy evident in Thomas Hardy's work. The fact that these novels incorporate allusions to what Hardy calls the Immanent Will, the 'intangible Cause' or 'Unfulfilled Intention', as well as to more familiar classical deities, is simply part of this ironization. In terms of drama itself, there have been quite traditional examples of the tragic—one might think of Arthur Miller's great allegorical work, *The Crucible* (1953), for example—but more characteristic of the past century have been the kind of secular tragicomedies of Chekhov or Beckett.

A second reason why tragedy is not what it used to be concerns the transformations that have taken place over the past two hundred years or so regarding the notions of the individual and society. If modern tragedies tend to be about ordinary people rather than kings or queens, they also show how far the lives of such 'ordinary people' are bound up, determined and constrained by broader social, economic and political realities. One of the first modern tragedies in European drama, Henrik

Ibsen's *A Doll's House* (1879), for example, is not simply about the break-up of the 'doll' Nora's marriage: it is about the ways in which the patriarchal institution and conventions of marriage effectively *programme* this tragic break-up. Particularly in the wake of Ibsen's work, in other words, there is a fundamental shift from a classical idea of tragedy as inevitable and beyond human control to the modern idea of a tragedy as something humanly engineered and happening in a world in which something could and should be done, for instance about sexual inequality, racism and so on. In his autobiography, Bertrand Russell remarks that 'One of the things that makes literature so consoling, is that its tragedies are all in the past, and have the completeness and repose that comes of being beyond the reach of our endeavours' (Russell 1967, 169). Russell's observation may be appropriate for thinking about tragedy in its classical modes; but it is quite inadequate and misleading for thinking about modern tragedy. Marxist and poststructuralist critics, in particular, have been concerned to underline what many of the more recent examples of tragic works of literature make clear, namely that what Russell comfortably refers to as 'the past' is precisely what is in question. And if the past is in question, so is the present. Whose past are we talking about? From whose perspective? With whose interests at stake?

We could illustrate this by referring briefly to a couple of contemporary works of tragic literature. The first example is a novel about the United States. Toni Morrison's *The Bluest Eye* (1970) contains the basic elements of tragedy—even if this includes a modification of Shakespearean 'suffering and death' into Morrisonian 'suffering and terrible abuse'. It is set in Ohio, and the narrative begins in 1941. It recounts the story of a young black girl called Pecola and how she comes to be sexually abused by her grimly named father, Cholly Breedlove. Morrison's novel may be set in the past but its power as a tragic text consists partly in the fact that it is making an explicit political statement not only about racism in contemporary US society but also about the perception of history itself. The novel involves a lucid but terrible elaboration of *why* this man called Breedlove should have abused his daughter. By stressing the ways in which Breedlove himself had in the past been racially and physically abused in turn, Morrison's novel provides a complex historical account of racism and violence. *The Bluest Eye* is tragic but the villain is paradoxically part of the tragedy. Morrison's novel broaches a despairing realism quite foreign to Shakespearean tragedy. *King Lear* concludes with Edgar's words:

> The weight of this sad time we must obey,
> Speak what we feel, not what we ought to say:
> The oldest hath borne most; we that are young
> Shall never see so much, nor live so long. (V, ii, 324–7)

His words may sound like a hollow formality or formalism—even as they ironically refer to the importance of saying 'what we feel, not what we ought to say'—but there is at least an implicit affirmation here of some kind of future. Toni Morrison's novel concludes more darkly: 'It's too late. At least on the edge of my town, among the garbage and the sunflowers of my town, it's much, much, much too late' (190).

The second example is Chinua Achebe's *Anthills of the Savannah* (1987). Achebe's novel is at once more and less than a tragedy in a classical or Shakespearean sense. It is set in a semi-fictional present-day African state and recounts the process by which one of the protagonists, a newspaper editor called Ikem Osodi, is 'fatally wounded' (169) by the military authorities, and the other male protagonist, the Commissioner for Information, Chris Oriko, gets shot by a policeman who is apparently about to rape a schoolgirl. The narrator adopts the perspective of Chris's lover, the mourning Beatrice:

> The explanation of the tragedy of Chris and Ikem in terms of petty human calculation or personal accident had begun to give way in her throbbing mind to an altogether more terrifying but more plausible theory of premeditation. The image of Chris as just another stranger who chanced upon death on the Great North Road or Ikem as an early victim of a waxing police state was no longer satisfactory. Were they not in fact trailed travellers whose journeys from start to finish had been carefully programmed in advance by an alienated history? If so, how many more doomed voyagers were already in transit or just setting out, faces fresh with illusions of duty-free travel and happy landings ahead of them? (220)

Though in many respects tragic, *Anthills of the Savannah* suggests a powerful circumscription and questioning of classical notions of tragedy—not least in the light of what Achebe calls 'an alienated history'. Like Morrison's *The Bluest Eye*, it is an explicitly political novel, directly focusing on the contemporary while exploring ways of rethinking the past. Both novels suggest, in their different ways, the extent to which tragedy is—humanly and unacceptably—'carefully programmed'. In its broadest implications, the 'alienated history' to which Achebe's novel refers is perhaps alien to the very forms of Western thought, prompting us to reflect on the idea that 'history' and 'tragedy' are themselves Western concepts.

Further reading

Aristotle's *Poetics* is the single most important account of tragedy in Western history. It is compelling to read, even if this includes acknowledging innumerable difficulties in language and translation. Drakakis and Liebler's *Tragedy* (1998) has a very useful introduction and provides an excellent range of critical material, from Hegel to Derrida. For a psychoanalytic understanding of tragedy, see André Green's now classic *The Tragic Effect* (1979). For an influential account of how the sense of the tragic in the modern world has all but disappeared, see George Steiner's *The Death of Tragedy* (1961). And by way of equally influential riposte, see Raymond William's *Modern Tragedy* (1969), which vigorously demonstrates how tragedy has changed and will continue to do so. Of the most recent studies of the tragic, Jonathan Dollimore's *Radical Tragedy* (2nd edn, 1989) is particularly challenging, exciting and wide-ranging. Specifically on Shakespeare, *Shakespearean Tragedy* (1992), ed. John Drakakis, contains a good deal of valuable critical material.

History

What is the relationship between a literary text and history? Broadly speaking critics have produced four answers to this question:

1. Literary texts belong to no particular time, they are universal and transcend history: the historical context of their production and reception has no bearing on the literary work which is aesthetically autonomous, having its own laws, being a world unto itself.
2. The historical context of a literary work—the circumstances surrounding its production—is integral to a proper understanding of it: the text is produced within a specific historical context but in its literariness it remains separate from that context.
3. Literary works can help us to understand the time in which they are set: realist texts in particular provide imaginative representations of specific historical moments, events or periods.
4. Literary texts are bound up with other discourses and rhetorical structures: they are part of a history that is still in the process of being written.

These four models of literature and history characterize various schools of criticism. The first model is often associated with new criticism or more generally with formalism, especially influential in literary studies in the middle decades of the twentieth century. New critics are concerned with literary texts as artifacts which transcend the contingencies of any particular time or place and which resist what they see as a reduction of the aesthetic whole to a specific historical context. Thus, for example, R.S. Crane argues in an essay first published in 1935 that literary history is essentially part of 'the general history of culture' (Crane 1967, 20), while a 'program of literary studies based on criticism' would focus on 'imaginative works considered with respect to those qualities which can truly be said to be timeless . . . in the sense that they can be adequately discerned and evaluated in the light of general principles quite apart from any knowledge of their origin or historical filiation' (18). The second model is the kind of approach favoured by philological or what we might call 'background' critics. Such critics are concerned to describe and analyze literary texts through a consideration of their historical 'background', whether biographical, linguistic, cultural or political. The titles of Basil Willey's two classic studies from 1934 and 1940 respectively indicate this approach: *The Seventeenth Century Background: Studies in the Thought of the Age in Relation to Poetry and Religion* and *The Eighteenth Century Background: Studies on the Idea of Nature in the Thought of the Period*. For such critics, ignorance of a literary text's historical circumstances is likely to lead to a misreading or misunderstanding of that text. The third model tends to be associated more with traditional historical scholarship than with literary criticism, as it assumes that literary texts are in some respect subordinate to their historical context. It also tends to assume that literary texts provide undistorted 'reflections' of their time. Thus, for example, in his book *Religion and the Decline of Magic* (1971), Keith Thomas appeals to Shakespeare's works on a number of occasions to justify his arguments. Discussing the practice of cursing, Thomas points out that 'In Shakespeare's plays, the curses pronounced by the characters invariably work', and argues that this is 'not just for dramatic effect' but that 'it was a moral necessity that the poor and the injured should be believed to have this power of retaliation when all else failed' (Thomas 1971, 507). We might call this model the 'reflective' approach. The last model is associated with a new kind of concern with the historical dimensions of literary studies particularly since the early 1980s. This model is specifically associated with new historicist critics in the United States and with cultural materialist critics in Britain (for convenience, we shall use the term 'new historicist' in this chapter to cover both varieties). In both cases, this new interest in history has been refracted through the concerns of both Marxism and poststructuralism to produce a complex model of the literary. In this chapter we shall focus on strategies of reading developed by new historicism in order to consider ways in which literary texts may be thought about in historical terms.

New historicists argue that to ask about the relationship between literature and history is the wrong question. The form of the question presupposes that there is literature on the one side and history on the other.

Despite their differences, 'new critics', 'background critics' and 'reflectionists' tend to rely on precisely such a polarity: they assume that the categories of 'literature' and 'history' are intrinsically separate. They distinguish, more or less explicitly, between the need for the interpretation of literary texts on the one hand, and the transparency of history on the other. In an essay entitled 'Literary Theory, Criticism, and History', for example, René Wellek argues that 'Literary study differs from historical study in having to deal not with documents but with monuments' and that the literary critic 'has direct access to his [*sic*] object', while the historian 'has to reconstruct a long-past event on the basis of eye-witness accounts' (Wellek 1963, 14–15). For old-historicist critics, history is not so much textual as more simply a series of empirically verifiable events. And they also assume that it is possible for our knowledge of both historical events and literary texts to be detached and objective, outside the forces of history.

New historicism may be understood as a reaction against such presuppositions: put briefly, it may be defined as a recognition of the extent to which history is textual and as a rejection of the autonomy of the literary text and of the objectivity of interpretation in general. As the quasi-founder of new historicism, Stephen Greenblatt, remarks in an essay entitled 'Toward a Poetics of Culture', 'methodological self-consciousness is one of the distinguishing marks of the new historicism in cultural studies as opposed to a historicism based upon faith in the transparency of signs and interpretive procedures' (Greenblatt 1990a, 158). Thus, new historicists argue that the production of literary texts is a cultural practice different only in its specific mode or formulation from other practices—from furniture-making to teaching to warfare to legal process to printing to basket-weaving to selling double-glazing. No absolute distinction can be made between literary texts and other cultural practices. As Stephen Greenblatt puts it, art is 'made up along with other products, practices, discourses of a given culture' (Greenblatt 1988, 13). Literary texts are embedded within the social and economic circumstances in which they are produced and consumed. But what is important for new historicists is that these circumstances are not stable in themselves and are susceptible to being rewritten and transformed. From this perspective, literary texts are part of a larger circulation of social energies, both products of and influences on a particular culture or ideology. What is new about new historicism in particular is its recognition that history is the 'history of the present', that history is in the making, that, rather than being monumental and closed, history is radically open to transformation and rewriting.

New historicists argue that any 'knowledge' of the past is necessarily mediated by *texts* or, to put it differently, that history is in many respects textual. A number of major consequences follow from this assertion. In the first place, there can be no knowledge of the past without interpretation. (This is one of the ways in which new historicism is specifically Nietzschean: as Nietzsche said, 'facts is precisely what there is not, only interpretations' (Nietzsche 1968, section 481).) Just as literary texts need to be read, so do the 'facts' of history. Thus, theorists such as Hayden White suggest that our knowledge of the past is determined by particular narrative configurations—that in talking about the past we tell stories. 'Properly understood', White remarks,

> histories ought never to be read as unambiguous signs of the events they report, but rather as symbolic structures, extended metaphors, that 'liken' the events reported in them to some form with which we have already become familiar in our literary culture . . . By the very constitution of a set of events in such a way as to make a comprehensible story out of them, the historian charges those events with the symbolic significance of a comprehensible plot structure. (White 1978, 91–2)

In this respect, the strategies and tools of critical analysis—the consideration of figures and tropes, a critical awareness of the rhetorical elements of language and so on—are as appropriate to a critical study of history as they are to literary studies.

From a new historicist perspective, any reading of a literary text is a question of negotiation, a negotiation between text and reader within the context of a history or histories that cannot be closed or finalized. Indeed, Stephen Greenblatt argues that literary works themselves should be understood in terms of negotiation, rather than in the conventional (romantic) sense of a 'pure act of untrammeled creation'—negotiations which are 'a subtle, elusive set of exchanges, a network of trades and trade-offs, a jostling of competing representations' (Greenblatt 1988, 7). 'The work of art', declares Greenblatt, 'is the product of a negotiation between a creator or class of creators, equipped with a complex, communally shared repertoire of conventions, and the institutions and practices of society' (Greenblatt 1990a, 158). Greenblatt and other new historicist critics reject any attempt to produce a 'whole' or final reading and argue for readings which are apparently disjunctive or fragmented. Similarly, questioning the boundaries of text and world, of art and society, such critics work 'at the margins of the text' in order to gain 'insight into the half-hidden cultural transactions through which great works of art are empowered' (Greenblatt 1988, 4). A critic might study legal documents, for example, or arguments concerning the politics of kingship, or handbooks on the education of children, or accounts of exotic travels and exploration and so on, in order to get a purchase on a particular work of literature. But such texts are not to be understood as the background to or context of the literary text. Rather, like plays, poems and novels, they are to be understood as texts through which questions of politics and power must be negotiated.

Such negotiation concerns, not least, our reading. If 'history' necessarily entails reading or interpretation, then such acts of reading will themselves be embedded within a particular social and cultural situation. There is no escape from history even if this history is regarded as multiple and in a process of unceasing transformation. New historicism argues that we are inescapably implicated—even in the fantasy of academic objectivity and detachment—in structures and strategies of power. Power is produced and reproduced in research, teaching and learning as it is in any other practice or discourse. As Michel Foucault remarks, power is 'omnipresent', it is 'the moving substrate of force relations which, by virtue of their inequality, constantly engender states of power, but the latter are always local and unstable'. 'Power', Foucault goes on, 'is everywhere' (Foucault 1981, 93).

In order to consider how such an approach might work in practice, we propose to discuss a poem by the English romantic poet William Wordsworth entitled 'Alice Fell, or Poverty'. The poem was written on the 12th and 13th March 1802, and first published in 1807. It is a seemingly uncomplicated account of an incident that was recounted to Wordsworth by his friend Robert Grahame. As the subtitle indicates, the poem presents itself as an allegory concerning poverty:

> The Post-boy drove with fierce career,
> For threat'ning clouds the moon had drowned;
> When suddenly I seemed to hear
> A moan, a lamentable sound.
>
> As if the wind blew many ways
> I heard the sound, and more and more:
> It seemed to follow with the Chaise,
> And still I heard it as before.

At length I to the Boy called out,
He stopped his horses at the word;
But neither cry, nor voice, nor shout,
Nor aught else like it could be heard.

The Boy then smacked his whip, and fast
The horses scampered through the rain;
And soon I heard upon the blast
The voice, and bade him halt again.

Said I, alighting on the ground,
'What can it be, this piteous moan?'
And there a little Girl I found,
Sitting behind the Chaise, alone.

'My Cloak!' the word was last and first,
And loud and bitterly she wept,
As if her very heart would burst;
And down from off the Chaise she leapt.

'What ails you, Child?' She sobbed, 'Look here!'
I saw it in the wheel entangled,
A weather beaten Rag as e'er
From any garden scare-crow dangled.

'Twas twisted betwixt nave and spoke;
Her help she lent, and with good heed
Together we released the Cloak;
A wretched, wretched rag indeed!

'And wither are you going, Child,
Tonight along these lonesome ways?'
'To Durham' answered she half wild—
'Then come with me into the chaise.'

She sate like one past all relief;
Sob after sob she forth did send
In wretchedness, as if her grief
Could never, never, have an end.

'My child, in Durham do you dwell?'
She checked herself in her distress,
And said, 'My name is Alice Fell;
I'm fatherless and motherless.

And I to Durham, Sir, belong.'
And then, as if the thought would choke
Her very heart, her grief grew strong;
And all was for her tattered Cloak.

The chaise drove on; our journey's end
Was nigh; and, sitting by my side,
As if she'd lost her only friend
She wept, nor would be pacified.

Up to the Tavern-door we post;
Of Alice and her grief I told;
And I gave money to the Host,
To buy a new Cloak for the old.

'And let it be a duffil grey,
As warm a cloak as man can sell!'
Proud Creature was she the next day,
The little Orphan, Alice Fell!

From a new historicist perspective we might try to situate this poem
in relation to other contemporary discourses which deal with poverty,
charity and property. We could, for example, investigate the rhetorical
strategies and discursive conventions of debates surrounding the Poor
Law, economics, poverty and charity at the turn of the nineteenth century. One such text is Adam Smith's *The Wealth of Nations*, first published in 1776, one of the most influential works of political economy in
the early nineteenth century. In this work, Smith twice refers to beggars,
once when he argues that 'Before the invention of the art of printing, a
scholar and a beggar seem to have been terms very nearly synonymous'
(Smith 1986, 237), and once when he considers beggars as the only
people who do not take part in the circulation of exchange and barter.
In this latter passage, the second chapter of his multi-volume work,
Smith argues that there is 'a certain propensity in human nature' which
is 'to truck, barter, and exchange one thing for another' (117). It is this
'propensity' which distinguishes humans from animals: 'When an animal
wants to obtain something either of a man or of another animal, it has
no other means of persuasion but to gain the favour of those whose
service it requires' (118). But humans—unlike animals, consistently
dependent on others—cannot constantly expect others' benevolence.
Instead, a man must 'interest [another person's] self-love in his favour':
'Nobody but a beggar chooses to depend chiefly upon the benevolence
of his fellow-citizens' (118–19). Although Smith goes on to say that even

beggars take part in the circulation of monetary exchange by buying goods with the money that they are given, in this extraordinary passage he has managed to dehumanize beggars, to put them outside of humanity, on the level of the animal. By arguing that human relations are relations of exchange, based on the principle of 'self-love', however, Smith suggests an apparent paradox in the discourse of charity: he claims that 'the charity of well-disposed people' supplies the beggar with 'the whole fund of his subsistence' (119), but does not explain *why* such people should give to beggars. According to his own arguments, people would only give to beggars if they were to gain something in return. There is, in this sense, no pure gift, no possibility of a gift. A number of significant rhetorical manoeuvres, then, may be seen to be at work in Smith's discourse of charity and begging. In the first place, beggars are dehumanized. Secondly, charity becomes a paradoxical or perverse, even an impossible act. Thirdly, by saying 'a beggar *chooses* to depend', Smith implies freedom of choice where economic necessity may be at stake. Finally, and most generally, Smith makes it clear that questions of charity and begging are part of a larger discourse of property and the exchange of property, indeed, part of a specific ideology of free-market liberalism.

We might think about these points in relation to Wordsworth's poem for, although Alice Fell does not actually beg and is not referred to as a beggar, the poem puts her in the position of a beggar, and is specifically concerned with that particular kind of exchange of property named 'charity'. What we might then seek to do is not to produce a thematic reading of the poem: rather, we might consider how the rhetorical strategies at work in Smith's account of beggars, property and charity are reproduced and transformed in those of the poem.

We might start by thinking about ways in which the poem articulates questions of property. Property in 'Alice Fell' is not simply a question of the cloak, but of poetry itself as property. The very origins of the narrative are bound up with questions of ownership in that the story originated with Wordsworth's friend Robert Grahame. Moreover, Dorothy Wordsworth, the poet's sister, wrote an account of the same incident in her journal before Wordsworth wrote his poem. Dorothy's account goes as follows:

> Mr. Graham said he wished Wm had been with him the other day— he was riding in a post chaise and he heard a strange cry that he could not understand, the sound continued and he called to the

> chaise driver to stop. It was a little girl that was crying as if her
> heart would burst. She had got up behind the chaise and her cloak
> had been caught by the wheel and was jammed in and it hung there.
> She was crying after it. Poor thing. Mr. Graham took her into the
> chaise and the cloak was released from the wheel but the child's
> misery did not cease for her cloak was torn to rags; it had been a
> miserable cloak before, but she had no other and it was the greatest
> sorrow that could befal her. Her name was Alice Fell. She had no
> parents, and belonged to the next Town. At the next Town Mr. G.
> left money with some respectable people in the town to buy her a
> new cloak. (Wordsworth 1984, 702)

As with a number of William's most famous lyrics, 'Alice Fell' resembles
Dorothy's journalistic account in many ways: both poem and journal
entry are concerned with the strangeness of the girl's cry, with the girl's
continuing misery, with the ragged state of her cloak. More specifically,
there are numerous verbal echoes of the journal entry in William's poem,
most strikingly, the poem's 'she wept,/As if her heart would burst' and
the journal's 'crying as if her heart would burst'. In this respect, William
may be said to have appropriated the story from his friend and from his
sister. This leads us to the question of what property it is that constitutes
this text as a poem. Is it *properly* a poem? How is it different from
Grahame's oral account or from Dorothy's journal entry? And where
does the poem originate, who owns it and authorizes it? We might want
to follow these questions through to an investigation of the institution
of literature itself. How is the canon produced, for example, what factors
are at work in canon-formation in England such that women's diaries
have tended to be excluded, canonically marginalized? How is Dorothy's
account both reproduced and effaced in William's poem and in the critical tradition, and why? Rather differently, we could argue that Dorothy's diary entry is not simply supplementary to the poem but is an
essential part of it. Indeed, it becomes difficult to distinguish property
as regards the cloak and property as regards the Wordsworths. In these
respects, questions of property cannot be considered to be simply the
context or the thematic focus of the poem: the poem originates in certain
problematic exchanges, transfers or gifts of narrative property.

The poem is also 'about' an exchange of property. The girl loses her
cloak in the wheel of the carriage, and the speaker gives her enough
money to buy a new one. But along with this exchange go a series of
property disturbances. The girl's proper name, Alice Fell, for example,
is curious. It is not a name Wordsworth invented, it seems. But is it

'historical' or 'literary'? The poem, indeed, exacerbates the sense of uncertainty regarding the strange properties of this proper name. Not only is it transferred from the title to the main body of the poem, or from the girl to the poem, but it also has a curious grammatical status in itself: it is suspended between a name and a minimal sentence, a kind of mini-narrative in itself—Alice fell. The poem is not only called 'Alice Fell', but is also about the fall of Alice. And once we recognize that there is something strange about the girl's name, we might also notice that 'Alice Fell' is haunted by the figure of a 'fallen woman', a woman outside 'respectable' society. Dorothy's text seems to pick up on this in its use of the verb 'befal', just prior to naming the girl herself. Conversely, we might notice that 'fell' also means the skin or hide of an animal, so that Alice might be like her cloak, a kind of rag, caught up and torn apart by the moving carriage. Finally, 'fell' as 'wild', as 'fierce, savage, cruel, ruthless, dreadful, terrible' or 'intensely painful' and even (of poison) 'deadly', or 'shrewd, clever, cunning' (*OED*) gives us a sense of the outcast, inhuman, dangerous, improper nature of this figure, and perhaps partly explains her—and the poem's—haunting power. The dehumanization at work in Smith's account of beggars is also wildly at work in Wordsworth's poem.

If the poem is about the exchange of property, it is also about the question of charity. Every act of charity may be understood as an implicit assertion that the end of suffering is possible. Dorothy's account of the incident recognizes that, after the girl's cloak was released, her 'misery did not cease'. One of the key stanzas of Wordsworth's poem in this respect is stanza seven:

> She sate like one past all relief;
> Sob after sob she forth did send
> In wretchedness, as if her grief
> Could never, never, have an end.

The phrases 'like' and 'as if' point to the unspeakable possibility that the girl really is 'past all relief', and that her 'grief / Could never, never, have an end'. Much of the force of the poem may be said to reside precisely in this terrifying possibility—that nothing can be done, that charity cannot finally help. In this respect, it is significant that unlike Dorothy's account, the poem ends in a blustering statement of self-satisfaction: in the final stanza, the girl is said to be 'proud' on account of her new cloak. But the girl's poverty and orphanhood remain and the pride appears to be as much a projection of the speaker's emotions as the girl's. The *speaker* apparently does have reason to be proud—he can feel proud of his charitable action. Attributing pride to the girl simply increases the speaker's own reasons to be proud. It might be argued that the poem works against itself, implicitly exposing the self-deceptive nature of the charitable act. Given this logic of projection, the poem clearly suggests that self-deception is necessary to charity or that, in Adam Smith's terms, there is no pure gift, that in giving the cloak, the speaker receives the satisfaction of pride. Moreover, the poem's triumphant ending implies that charity can end suffering. But this sense of triumph and of an ending are simultaneously undone: we must give and to do so we must believe that our gift will help to end suffering, but suffering is never-ending. The hardly audible, ghostly historical counter-voice of the poem cries that, as an orphan, Alice Fell cannot but suffer (etymologically, 'orphan' means 'one who has lost'). Her suffering is never-ending because it cannot be ended. Unlike the speaker, who is on a journey that will end (see line 49, 'our journey's end'), the suffering of Alice Fell has no end. Just as the speaker is haunted by a strange voice at the beginning of the poem, so he is haunted by the uncanny disembodied voice of suffering, haunted by what he knows but cannot know—that suffering and the improper or 'fell' (wild, inhuman, fallen) disturbances of property are never ending.

Stephen Greenblatt argues that culture 'is a particular network of negotiations for the exchange of material goods, ideas, and—through institutions like enslavement, adoption, or marriage—people'. Greenblatt also contends that 'Great writers are precisely masters of these codes, specialists in cultural exchange' (Greenblatt 1990b, 229–30). Our account has sought to locate Wordsworth's poem in relation to the discourses of property and charity as articulated in one particular text. Wordsworth, we might say, is a master of—and is mastered by—the codes of property and charity. New historicism seeks to explore and revitalize such mastery but at the same time to remain alert to ways in which such codes continue to play themselves out in the discourses of the present—including, not least, the discourses of history and criticism. T.S. Eliot is not often read as a new historicist, but he did make at least one comment to which such critics might subscribe: writing of the task of the poet in 'Tradition and the Individual Talent', Eliot remarks that he (or she) needs a 'historical sense' which, he says, 'involves a perception, not only of the pastness of the past but of its presence' (Eliot 1975, 38). Perhaps what is most telling and most productive in those 'new' ways of thinking about literary texts in relation to history with which we have been concerned in this chapter is their sense of the transformative power of history, the way, finally, that the 'presence' of the past might also involve its transformation, as we write, of the future.

Further reading

For eloquent and readable accounts of a historicized theory of culture, see Stephen Greenblatt's essays 'Towards a Poetics of Culture' (1990a) and 'Culture' (1990b). And see his *Shakespearean Negotiations* (1988) and *Marvelous Possessions* (1991) for witty and penetrating readings of various Renaissance texts. For an important if somewhat intricate discussion of such issues in the context of the Romantic period, see James Chandler's *England in 1819* (1998). Useful collections of new historicist and cultural materialist essays include Dollimore and Sinfield, eds, *Political Shakespeare* (1994), Wilson and Dutton, eds, *New Historicism and Renaissance Drama* (1992), Veeser, ed., *The New Historicism* (1989) and *The New Historicism Reader* (1994), and Ryan, ed., *New Historicism and Culture Materialism* (1996). For a complex but important study of history and contemporary historiography, see Robert Young, *White Mythologies* (1990). For a good but demanding overview of historicisms old and new, see Paul Hamilton's *Historicism* (1996). For a sharp and engaging account of new historicism and cultural materialism, see Brannigan (1998). Todd (1988) provides a valuable feminist account of literary history.

Me

Who are we? What am I? What is an 'I'? What does it mean to say 'me'?
What is the relationship between an 'I' in a literary text and an 'I'
outside it? One of the central ideas of this book is literature's capacity
to question, defamiliarize and even transform the sense of who or what
we are. In the next few pages we would like to elaborate further on this,
by trying to look at the nature of personal identity or 'me' both in
broadly historical and theoretical terms and more specifically in terms
of what literary texts themselves may suggest on this topic.

In Flannery O'Connor's story 'Revelation' (1961) a woman called Mrs
Turpin has a traumatic and bizarre reaction when a strange girl sitting
in a doctor's waiting room tells her: 'Go back to hell where you came
from, you old wart hog' (217). Mrs Turpin is scandalized by this statement and that same evening, back at the farm, by herself, hosing down
the pigs, she demands an explanation. Being Christian and superstitious
(as well as grotesquely racist and class-prejudiced), Mrs Turpin regards
the girl's words as a message from God:

> 'What do you send me a message like that for?' she said in a low
> fierce voice, barely above a whisper but with the force of a shout in
> its concentrated fury. 'How am I a hog and me both?' (222)

What is striking here is not only the woman's confusion and indignation
at the apparently contradictory idea that she might be a human being
and an old wart hog at the same time, but also the fact that her 'fury' is
expressed in a direct, personal address to God. Mrs Turpin's sense of
outrage becomes outrageous in turn, as her questions addressed to God
culminate in a questioning *of* God: 'A final surge of fury shook her and
she roared, "Who do you think you are?"' (223) The strangeness of

putting this question to God comes from the fact that it is a question that should only be asked of another human. Only humans are supposed to be able to reflect on who they are and at the same time be obliged to take seriously a questioning of their own identity. If the question 'Who do you think you are?' is one that cannot or should not be asked of God, nor is it a question one would normally ask of a wart hog. In this respect it would seem that there is something characteristically human about the question. 'Who do you think you are?' is the question that humans ask of others and try to answer about themselves. As Socrates said, 'The unexamined life is not worth living' (Plato, *Apology*, 38a). And the definition of being human must remain in the form of a questioning: Mrs Turpin's 'final surge of fury' is, in this respect, pitifully, comically human.

At the same time, it could be said that this question ('Who do we think we are?') is most clearly raised and most fully explored in works of literature. This might in fact be another general definition: literature is the space in which questions about the nature of personal identity are most provocatively articulated. In the nineteenth century and earlier in the twentieth century, literary critics used to talk about 'the person' and 'the individual'. In more recent years, however, there has been a tendency to refer to 'the human subject'. This may sound jargonistic but there are good reasons, in fact, for talking about 'the human subject' rather than, say, 'the person' or 'the human individual'. The French poststructuralist Michel Foucault has written: 'There are two meanings of the word "subject": subject to someone else by control and dependence, and tied to one's own identity by a conscience or self-knowledge' (Foucault 1983, 212, cited by During 1992, 153). The word 'person', by contrast, perhaps too easily retains connotations of the 'I' or 'me' as detached from everything, a *free agent*. Likewise, the term 'individual' (etymologically from the Latin *individuus*, 'undivided' or 'not divisible') misleadingly suggests a sense of the 'I' as simply free, as being at one with itself and autonomous or self-ruling. It is this idea of the sovereignty of the 'I' that Freud gestures towards when he speaks of 'His Majesty the ego'.

The usefulness of the term 'subject', then, is that it encourages a more critical attentiveness to the fact that the 'I' is *not* autonomous, that it does not exist in a sort of vacuum. Rather an 'I' or 'me' is always *subject* to forces and effects both outside itself (environmental, social, cultural, economic, educational, etc.) and 'within' itself (in particular in terms of what is called the unconscious or, in more recent philosophical terms, otherness). We are subjects in the sense of being 'subject to' others 'by control or dependence' (in Foucault's phrase) right from birth and even before: not only are we radically dependent on the father who sires us and the mother who bears us, but also on the environment (ecological, economic, familial, social, etc.) into which we are born, as well as on the multiple forms of authority and government which condition our upbringing. A 'me' born to a single mother in Soweto is not the same kind of 'me' as a 'me' born to a duchess in Kensington, but they are both in their different ways *subjects*. Of course if the Kensington 'me' had been in line for the throne, things would have looked slightly different: in Britain, at least, one is subject not only to the authority of one's parent or parents, one's local authorities, the police and central government, but also—at least on paper—to the Queen (thus one is 'a British subject') and, beyond her (if only nominally), to the Christian God. That, then, is one way in which every 'I' is necessarily and fundamentally a *subject*. Rather differently, being a subject has specifically to do with language. You cannot be an 'I' without having a proper name, and in English-speaking countries you usually acquire a proper name around the time of birth or even before. We are born into language, we are born—more precisely—into patriarchal language, into being identified by a patronym, by a paternal proper name. (Even the mother's maiden name is, of course, a patronym.) We are also endowed with a forename and again this is not something *we* choose, it is something to which we are *subject*—even if, in Britain for example, people do legally have the right to change their names at the age of eighteen. Juliet's complaint is haunting and even tragic precisely because it highlights the way in which we are *subject to* names, even if we wish to ignore or disown them:

> Oh Romeo, Romeo, wherefore art thou Romeo?
> Deny thy father and refuse thy name;
> Or, if thou wilt not, be but sworn my love,
> And I'll no longer be a Capulet.
> (*Romeo and Juliet*, II, ii, 33–6)

More broadly what is being suggested here is that questions of personal or individual identity are indissociably bound up with language. We may like to suppose that there is some 'me' outside language or that there is some way of thinking about ourselves which involves a non-linguistic 'me'. But the *idea* of this non-linguistic 'me' must found itself in language. We cannot, in any *meaningful* way, escape the fact that we are *subject to* language.

We can also consider this topic from a historical perspective. The idea of the 'I' or 'me', in other words, is not unchanging and unchangeable. It is in many respects historically and ideologically determined. The way we think about 'I' today is inevitably different from the way in which 'I' was thought about and defined in, say, seventeenth-century France by René Descartes. The principle of the Cartesian cogito ('I think therefore I am')—that is to say, the model of the *rational subject* which Descartes theorizes in his *Discourse on Method* (1637; 1977)—in many respects continues to govern Western thinking. But there are other ways of thinking, and other ways of thinking about thinking. Earlier in the present century, for example, the German philosopher Martin Heidegger declared: 'Thinking begins only when we have come to know that reason, glorified for centuries, is the most stiffnecked adversary of thought' (Heidegger 1977, 112, cited by Judovitz 1988, 186). Likewise, and more recently, Jacques Derrida has been repeatedly concerned to demonstrate that, as he puts it: 'reason is only one species of thought—which does not mean that thought is "irrational"' (Derrida 1983, 16).

But perhaps the most obvious way of illustrating the changes over the past century in thinking about thinking, and in thinking about the model of the rational subject, is in terms of psychoanalysis. Psychoanalysis has changed the way in which we are obliged to think about 'the subject'. In the light of the psychoanalytic theory of the unconscious, the proposition 'cogito ergo sum' ('I think therefore I am') becomes manifestly problematic. I do not, and perhaps strictly speaking never can, know precisely *why* or *how* I think what I think, if only because of the extent to which what I think is necessarily determined by forces and effects of which I am (in many ways thankfully) unaware. In a short essay written as an encyclopaedia entry on 'Psychoanalysis' first published in 1923, Freud suggests that the unconscious is evident not only in dreams but in

> such events as the temporary forgetting of familiar words and names, forgetting to carry out prescribed tasks, everyday slips of the tongue and of the pen, misreadings, losses and mislayings of objects, certain errors, instances of apparently accidental self-injury, and finally habitual movements carried out seemingly without intention or in play, tunes hummed 'thoughtlessly', and so on. (Freud 1986, 136–7)

The significance of Freud's theory of the unconscious thus consists in the demonstration that the subject who thinks (the subject of 'I think') is composed of forces and effects which are at least in part unconscious. 'I', let us remind ourselves, is not 'God'—even if it may be *subject to* fantasies of being so.

Psychoanalysis, then, has been a particularly disturbing but valuable discourse in the twentieth century because it has promoted an awareness of the extent to which any 'I' or human subject is *decentred*: I, in other words, can never be simply or precisely who or what I think. What makes this idea disturbing and at the same time valuable is that it involves a dislocation of the notions of human mastery and autonomy of self and introduces instead the humility of recognizing that the human subject is not centred in itself, let alone centred in relation to the surrounding world or solar system. In an essay on 'The Resistances to Psychoanalysis' (1925), Freud talks about the 'emotional' difficulties people have in accepting the ideas of psychoanalysis and draws analogies between this and the theories of Darwin and Copernicus. In the case of psychoanalysis, he says, 'powerful human feelings are hurt by the subject-matter of the theory. Darwin's theory of descent met with the same fate, since it tore down the barrier that had been arrogantly set up between men and beasts.' Freud goes on to suggest that 'the psychoanalytic view of the relation of the conscious ego to an overpowering unconscious was a severe blow to human self-love', and that, 'as the *psychological* blow to men's narcissism', it compares 'with the *biological* blow delivered by the theory of descent and the earlier *cosmological* blow aimed at it by the discovery of Copernicus' (Freud 1986, 272–3). In this sense, psychoanalysis complements the Copernican revolution and nineteenth-century evolutionary theory in providing a powerful critique of anthropocentric values and ideas. Psychoanalysis demonstrates in uncomfortably clear terms how the 'arrogance' of anthropocentrism—that is to say, every kind of thinking, including every kind of philosophy and politics, which puts the human at the centre of the earth and solar system, if not of the universe—is both unwarranted and unsustainable.

The Cartesian 'I think therefore I am' can be further considered specifically in relation to language. Language determines the 'I' and the 'I think'. This can be illustrated simply by reflecting on the idea that Descartes's formulation was first published in Latin ('cogito ergo sum'). We anglophone subjects are already adrift in effects of language and translation, but so too was Descartes himself: after all, his works appeared not in some form of seventeenth-century French but in a foreign, 'dead' language. He was subject to the scholarly protocols of his own time and the requirement to write (and in some sense presumably think) in Latin. What is at stake in this logic of being *subject to language* is a conception of language as not simply *instrumental*: language is not simply something that we *use*. Language governs what we (can) say as much as we govern or *use* language. Language is not simply an instrument: we are, unavoidably, *agents* of language. Moreover we are, more precisely perhaps, secret or double agents of language: we do not necessarily know, from one moment to the next, *how* we are being used by language or where it might be leading us. As in the most compelling kind of espionage story, however, this is not a situation we can get out of. As the narrator neatly puts it, in Margaret Atwood's short story 'Giving Birth' (1977): 'These are the only words I have, I'm stuck with them, stuck in them' (225–6). The 'in' is, no doubt, more difficult to reflect on than the 'with', but it is no less important.

How do these various questions and ideas relate to literary works more generally? First of all let us emphasize that, if literature is concerned with exploring and reflecting on the nature of personal identity, it is also a space of exhilarating, even anarchic openness and imaginative or transformational possibility. Literature might be thought of as being, in Derrida's words, 'the institution which allows one to *say everything*, in *every way*' (Derrida 1992a, 36). In particular there is this astonishing, anarchic freedom in literature: at least in principle, the author of a literary work can be any 'I' he or she wishes to. To put it like this is to imply that the author is an 'I' before or outside the literary work. But who is to say that there is an 'I' anywhere that is not in part *literary*? This rather strange question is a focus of one of the greatest comical literary or philosophical works in the twentieth century, Samuel Beckett's *The Unnamable* (first published in English in 1959). This text is preoccupied with the idea that it is the 'I' itself that is in a sense the unnamable: the 'I' that speaks, or that seems to speak, is never true, never precisely itself, never the same, for example, as the 'I' who has spoken or the 'I' that writes 'I'. *The Unnamable*, then, starts off from the apparently simple but perhaps unfathomable remark, 'I, say I', and from the paradox that 'I seem to speak, it is not I, about me, it is not about me' (293). Nearly fifty pages later the narrator is still impelled to observe that 'on the subject of me properly so called . . . so far as I know I have received no information up to date' (338). In Beckett's wonderfully funny, but also dark and unnerving text, the Cartesian-rationalistic 'I think' becomes: 'I only think, if that is the name for this vertiginous panic as of hornets smoked out of their nest, once a certain degree of terror has been exceeded' (353). As with so much of Beckett's writing, this sentence is at once quite straightforward and semantically dense, unsettling, surprisingly resistant to a single interpretation. We might note, for example, the explicit attention to the uncertainties of language ('if that is the name') and of the relationship between terror and thinking. To think about this sentence can induce vertiginous panic and become terrifying. It succinctly illustrates literature's complex and unsettling effects when it comes to thinking about identity and about the I that claims to think.

We could conclude by trying to say a little more about the ways in which, as we suggested earlier, the 'I' or 'me' is in fact historically determined. One very broad but decisive example of this would be the question of the 'I' or 'me' in relation to romantic and post-romantic literature. In *Of Grammatology* (1967), Derrida argues that the importance of Jean-Jacques Rousseau's work consists in the fact that he 'starts from a new model of presence: the subject's self-presence within *consciousness* or *feeling*' (Derrida 1976, 98). European romanticism in general might be characterized in terms of this kind of 'new model of presence', and in particular in terms of a new emphasis on the centrality and importance of the 'I' as a subject who both thinks and feels. This could be exemplified by the fragment often published as the prologue or opening stanza to George Gordon Byron's *Don Juan* (1819–24):

> I would to heaven that I were so much clay,
>   As I am blood, bone, marrow, passion, feeling—
> Because at least the past were pass'd away—
>   And for the future—(but I write this reeling,
> Having got drunk exceedingly to-day,
>   So that I seem to stand upon the ceiling)
> I say—the future is a serious matter—
> And so—for God's sake—hock and soda-water!

The new emphasis on the 'I' in romantic culture is consistently articulated in terms of the polarity or gulf between a subject ('I feel') and an object (the clouds, a skylark, a nightingale). The (impossible) desire for a fusion between subject and object (the idea for example of being, in Matthew Arnold's words, 'in harmony with nature') is one of the most striking characteristics of the work of the English romantic poets. It is clear, for instance, in Keats's 'Ode to a Nightingale', in which the speaker is eventually compelled to admit to defeat in his attempt to fuse

or dissolve into the nightingale's song: the word 'forlorn' is 'like a bell /
To toll me back from thee to my sole self'. This emphasis on the 'sole
self' broaches the notion of solipsism, that is to say the refusal or
inability to believe in the reality of anything outside or beyond the self.
The idea of such an isolation of the self has its representatives in classical
philosophy and literature, but it is particularly pervasive in nineteenth-
and twentieth-century European culture. It is evoked by the pathos,
or bathos, of the opening lines of Matthew Arnold's poem, 'To
Marguerite—Continued' (1849):

> Yes! in the sea of life enisled,
> With echoing straits between us thrown,
> Dotting the shoreless watery wild,
> We mortal millions live *alone.*

It is also implicit in the work of Freud, to the extent that psychoanalysis
suggests that everything comes down to the power and significance of
projection, of the qualities, moods or emotions which we *project onto*
people and things. Wallace Stevens sums this up when he says:

> few people realize on that occasion, which comes to all of us, when
> we look at the blue sky for the first time, that is to say: not merely
> see it, but look at it and experience it . . .—few people realize that
> they are looking at the world of their own thoughts and the world
> of their own feelings. (Stevens 1951, 65–6)

But as we hope will by now be clear, solipsism is a myth, a delusion or
mirage. Solipsism presupposes the idea of something like what Wittgenstein calls a private language (Wittgenstein 1984). There is no such
thing as a private language: the phrase 'private language' is an oxymoron.
Language is social or, at least, language comes from elsewhere, from
others and from otherness in general. Even to say, as a self-avowed
solipsist might, 'I do not believe in the reality of anything apart from
myself', is to demonstrate a dependence on what is not 'me', not oneself.
It is to demonstrate that one is *subject to* language. As the voice, or one
of the voices, in *The Unnamable* puts it: 'I'm in words, made of words,
others' words . . .' (390).

Literature, like art more generally, has always been concerned with
aspects of what can be called the unconscious or 'not me' or other: it
is and has always been centrally concerned with dreams and fantasy,
hallucinations and visions, madness, trance, and other kinds of

impersonality or absences of self. But we could say that romantic and post-romantic literature has been increasingly sensitive to the role of otherness and increasingly aware of what might be described as our obligations in relation to otherness. Beckett's writing is perhaps only the most philosophically refined recent example of post-romantic literature which is concerned to explore, deflate and transform our understanding of the question, 'Who do we think we are?' In this respect his work might be seen to anticipate and encapsulate much of what is called post-structuralism. Poststructuralism demonstrates that the I or human subject is necessarily *decentred*. It argues against the reductiveness (and even the possibility) of rationalism, in particular through its attention to what is other (though not simply 'irrational') as regards Western 'rational' thinking. And it persistently shows up the presumptuousness of the model of an autonomous, supposedly masterful human being, and thus points beyond 'merely' literary questions, exposing the barbarities of anthropocentrism in general. Some of this may be felt in a faltering, haunting few words from *The Unnamable*:

> if only I knew if I've lived, if I live, if I'll live, that would simplify everything, impossible to find out, that's where you're buggered, I haven't stirred, that's all I know, no, I know something else, it's not I, I always forget that, I resume, you must resume . . . (417)

Further reading

For some very clear and stimulating introductory accounts of psycho-analysis and its implications for 'me', see Freud 1986; for a complex and challenging analysis of Freudian thinking on the idea of the subject, see Borch-Jacobsen, *The Freudian Subject* (1988). For a careful and thought-provoking discussion of the human subject from the perspective of the social sciences, see Paul Hirst and Penny Woolley, *Social Relations and Human Attributes* (1982). A highly influential account of romanticism stressing the importance of conflicts and disjunctions between subject and object, me and the world, etc., is M.H. Abram's classic study, *The Mirror and the Lamp* (1953). Another influential discussion of these issues, this time from the perspective of the history of philosophy (particularly from Descartes to the Romantic period) is Charles Taylor's wide-ranging and informative *Sources of the Self* (1989). For two very good general accounts of poststructuralism, see Robert Young's Intro-duction to *Untying the Text* (1981) and Josué Harari's Introduction to

Textual Strategies (1979); and see Joel Fineman's *The Subjectivity Effect in Western Literary Tradition* (1991) for a theoretically and critically astute exploration of such issues in a number of literary (especially Shakespearean) texts.

Ghosts

What has literature to do with ghosts? Before we consider this question we need to think about a prior question: what is a ghost? The word 'ghost' is related to and originates in the German *Geist*, a word that *Chambers Dictionary* defines as 'spirit, any inspiring or dominating principle'. The *OED* gives, as its first and fourth definitions of 'ghost', the 'soul or spirit, as the principle of life' and 'A person'. In these respects, the ghost is fundamental to our thinking about the human: to be human is to have a spirit, a soul, a *Geist* or ghost. But the more common modern sense of 'ghost' (albeit only listed seventh in the *OED*) involves the idea of a spectre, an apparition of the dead, a revenant, the dead returned to a kind of spectral existence—an entity not alive but also not quite, not finally, dead. Ghosts disturb our sense of the separation of the living from the dead—which is why they can be so frightening, so uncanny. These conflicting senses of the word 'ghost' suggest that ghosts are both exterior and central to our sense of the human. Ghosts are paradoxical since they are both fundamental to the human, fundamentally human, and a denial or disturbance of the human, the very being of the inhuman. We propose to devote this chapter, to dedicate it, to the living-dead, to the ghost(s) of literature. And we propose that this scandal of the ghost, its paradoxy, is embedded in the very thing that we call literature, endlessly inscribed in multiple and haunting ways, in novels, poems and plays.

Ghosts have a history. They are not what they used to be. Ghosts, in a sense, *are* history. They do not, after all, come from nowhere, even if they may appear to do just that. They are always inscribed *in a context*: they at once belong to and haunt the idea of a place (hence 'spirit of place' or *genius loci*), and belong to and haunt the idea of a time (what we could call a 'spirit of time' or rather differently what is called the

'spirit of the age' or *Zeitgeist*). In other words, it is possible to trace a
history of ghosts, as well as to think about history itself as ghostly, as
what can in some form or other always come back. We might, for
example, pursue a history of ghosts in terms of what J. Hillis Miller
calls 'the disappearance of God' (Miller 1963). If the Christian God is,
as Karl Marx claimed, 'Spectre No. 1' (Marx 1976, 157), it is fair to
suppose that his 'disappearance', especially from the nineteenth century
onwards, has altered the conception of ghosts, holy or otherwise. On
the other hand, we might pursue a history of ghosts in terms of the
nineteenth-century emergence of psychology and, in particular, psychoanalysis. Ghosts, that is to say, move into one's head. The ghost is
internalized: it becomes a psychological symptom, and no longer a thing
that goes bump in the night or an entity issuing commandments on a
mountain-top.

In particular, psychoanalytic accounts of ghosts have revolutionized
literary studies. We might illustrate this in terms of what is arguably the
greatest 'ghost work' in English literature, Shakespeare's *Hamlet* (1600–
1601). The play itself is cryptic and elusive about the apparition and
truthfulness of the figure of the ghost of Hamlet's father: why is it, for
instance, that when the ghost appears in Act III, scene iv, it is only seen
by Hamlet and not by his mother? But it is also clear that the play's
representation of the ghost is grounded in the Christian mythology of
Shakespeare's time—hence Hamlet's fear that 'The spirit that I have
seen / May be a devil' who 'Abuses me to damn me' (II, ii, 598–9, 603).
In twentieth-century psychoanalytic readings such as those advanced
by Jacques Lacan or Nicolas Abraham, however, the ghost has become
something very different. Lacan develops the ghostly or phantasmatic
dimensions of the basic Freudian reading of the play as Oedipal drama:
Hamlet cannot take revenge on his murderous uncle Claudius because
he is haunted by the sense that what Claudius has done is what he would
have wanted to do—kill his father and go to bed with his mother. In
Lacan's scandalous and brilliant development of this reading of *Hamlet*
(in a seminar in 1959), the ghost has to do with the phallus. As 'an
imaginary object which the child comes to accept as being in the father's
possession' (Wright 1992, 318), the phallus is in a sense the very symbol
of paternity. For Lacan, the reason for Hamlet's inability to kill Claudius
(until, at least, the moment of 'complete sacrifice', i.e. of his own death)
is that 'one cannot strike the phallus, because the phallus, even the real
phallus, is a *ghost*' (Lacan 1977b, 50–1). In this way, Lacan makes
Hamlet an allegory of phallocentric culture: phallocentrism (everything

in a culture that serves to equate the symbolic power of the father, the phallus, with authority, the proper, presence, truth itself) becomes a sort of farcical but terrible ghost story. In Lacan's reading, Hamlet's being haunted by his father is an allegory of the nature of the ego. In an appalling pun, he calls Hamlet an 'hommelette', a little man, a son, who is both dependent on his namesake King Hamlet and has his 'ego' scrambled—like an egg—by this haunting. As Maud Ellmann neatly summarizes it: 'the ego is a ghost' (Ellmann 1994, 17). There are problems with what Lacan does with a literary work like *Hamlet*, in particular in seeming to appropriate it simply as an allegorical means of presenting the 'truth' of psychoanalysis. But his thinking has proved extremely productive and stimulating for critics and theorists concerned to analyze the ghostliness of identity in literary texts and to question the nature and terms of the phallocentric ghost story in which we continue to have our being.

In the work of Nicolas Abraham, on the other hand, *Hamlet* is a central text for his theory that ghosts have to do with unspeakable secrets. The only reason why people think they see ghosts is because the dead take secrets with them when they die. In his essay 'Notes on the Phantom: A Complement to Freud's Metapsychology' (1975), Abraham observes that 'the theme of the dead—who, having suffered repression by their family or society, cannot enjoy, even in death, a state of authenticity—appears to be omnipresent (whether overtly expressed or disguised) on the fringes of religions and, failing that, in rational systems' (Abraham 1994, 171). Ghosts are everywhere, a painful fact of life. Abraham contends that 'the "phantom" [or "ghost"], whatever its form, is nothing but an invention of the living'. People see ghosts because 'the dead were shamed during their lifetime or . . . took unspeakable secrets to the grave'. These secrets remain, like a crypt, a gap, in the unconscious of the living. The ghost or phantom thus embodies 'the gap produced in us by the concealment of some part of a loved object's life . . . what haunts are not the dead, but the gaps left within us by the secrets of others' (171).

Abraham's account is helpful in illuminating the strangeness of Shakespeare's *Hamlet*, its obscure but persisting sense of secrets taken to the grave, of what the ghost calls the untellable 'secrets of my prison-house' (I, v, 14). But his 'Notes on the Phantom' also opens up new ways of thinking about ghosts in literature more generally: in effect, it inaugurates a theory of literature as a theory of ghosts. We can think of this ghostliness, first, in the relatively straightforward sense described by a character called Stella Rodney in Elizabeth Bowen's *The Heat of the Day* (1948): ' "What's unfinished haunts one; what's unhealed haunts one" ' (322). From the great fourteenth-century Middle English dream-elegy *Pearl* to Toni Morrison's very different dream-elegy *Beloved* (1987), literature is a place of ghosts, of what's unfinished, unhealed and even untellable. But more precisely, and perhaps more eerily, Abraham's work alerts us to a ghostliness about which characters, and even authors themselves, are unaware. Here we encounter the strangeness of the ghostly secret as, in Esther Rashkin's words, 'a situation or drama that is transmitted without being stated and without the sender's or receiver's awareness of its transmission' (Rashkin 1992, 4).

If psychoanalysis has been important in providing new ways of thinking about ghosts, however, this has not happened in a vacuum. As we suggested earlier, it is in fact part of a more general shift in how ghosts have been figured, theorized and experienced since the end of the nineteenth century. The emergence of psychology and psychoanalysis has its ghostly counterpart in literature, especially in the emergence of psychological realism and the psychological novel. Nowhere is this clearer than in the fiction of Henry James (1843–1916). In an essay on his ghost stories, published in 1921, Virginia Woolf writes:

> Henry James's ghosts have nothing in common with the violent old ghosts—the blood-stained sea captains, the white horses, the headless ladies of dark lanes and windy commons. They have their origin within us. They are present whenever the significant overflows our powers of expressing it; whenever the ordinary appears ringed by the strange. (Woolf 1988, 324)

Stories such as *The Turn of the Screw* (1898), 'The Beast in the Jungle' (1903) and 'The Jolly Corner' (1908) conjure and explore the ghostliness of experience in profoundly unsettling ways. All of these stories bear witness to the ungovernable, overflowing strangeness which Woolf evokes. More particularly, they also illustrate the sense of ghostly secrets, of what Abraham called the 'gaps left within us by the secrets of others', together with a sense of the ghostliness of the ego (or 'I') itself.

The last of these stories, 'The Jolly Corner', is especially forceful in its evocation of the idea of the 'I' as ghost. As in a number of other ghost stories—for example, Emily Brontë's *Wuthering Heights* (1848), Nathaniel Hawthorne's *The House of the Seven Gables* (1851) and George

Douglas Brown's *The House with the Green Shutters* (1901)—'The Jolly Corner' is both the name of a house and the name of the text itself. The literary work is a haunted house. 'The Jolly Corner' recounts how a 56-year-old, wealthy New Yorker called Spencer Brydon, long settled in Europe, makes a 'strangely belated return to America' (190), having been absent 33 years. He goes back to his childhood home, 'his house on the jolly corner, as he usually, and quite fondly, described it' (191). Rented out and a source of income for decades, the house is now, ostensibly, empty. Brydon becomes obsessed with the place, with visiting and wandering around it, increasingly caught up by the sense that it contains some ghostly secret of the past. Following a dense but queerly captivating third-person omniscient narration, we are drawn into a hunt, in which the protagonist turns out to be both hunter and hunted, haunter and haunted. As the narrator asks, with the bizarre tone of detachment characteristic of the text as a whole: 'People enough, first and last, had been in terror of apparitions, but who had ever before become himself, in the apparitional world, an incalculable terror?' (202). Of course—and this is where fiction is most manifestly a *haunt*—this 'apparitional world' to which James refers only appears through writing. The very strangeness of fiction may be said to consist in this idea of a 'medium', a text, in which the apparitional and non-apparitional are made of the same stuff, indistinguishable. As E.M. Forster put it, in *Aspects of the Novel* (1927): 'Once in the realm of the fictitious, what difference is there between an apparition and a mortgage?' (Forster, 1976, 103).

The greater the literary work, we might venture, the more ghostly it is. This might be one way of understanding what Derrida is getting at when he proclaims, in his book *Spectres of Marx*, that 'A masterpiece always moves, by definition, in the manner of a ghost' (Derrida 1994, 18). Playing on the earlier Latin sense of 'genius' as 'spirit', he says that a masterpiece is 'a work of *genius*, a *thing* of the *spirit* which precisely seems to *engineer itself* [*s'ingénier*]' (18). Masterpieces, such as *Hamlet* (which is the example Derrida is discussing) or James's 'The Jolly Corner' or Toni Morrison's *Beloved*, are *works* that give a sense of having been spirited up, of working by themselves. Great works call to be read and reread while never ceasing to be strange, to resist reading, interpretation and translation. This is one basis for thinking about canonicity in Harold Bloom's terms: the canon is always a spectral affair. As he declares, in *The Western Canon*: 'One ancient test for the canonical remains fiercely valid: unless it demands rereading, the work does not qualify' (Bloom 1994, 30). A great work will always seem uncanny, at once strange and familiar; a surprising, unique addition to the canon and yet somehow foreseen, programmed by the canon; at once readable and defiant, elusive, baffling. For Bloom, writing itself is essentially about a relationship (always one of anxiety, according to him) with the dead, with earlier great writers. The point is most succinctly made by Bloom's precursor, T.S. Eliot, when he says in his essay 'Tradition and the Individual Talent' (1919) that the 'best', 'most individual' parts of a literary work are 'those in which the dead poets . . . assert their immortality most vigorously' (Eliot 1975b, 38). It is a relationship eerily evoked in Eliot's 'Little Gidding' (1943), where the speaker describes an encounter in which he 'caught the sudden look of some dead master / . . . The eyes of a familiar compound ghost / Both intimate and unidentifiable' (Eliot 1975a, 193). For Bloom, as for Eliot, poetry is also a ghostly discourse in a more general sense. This is hauntingly exemplified by Wallace Stevens's 'Large Red Man Reading' (1948), in which the subject of the poem, the reader himself, evokes ghosts: 'There were ghosts that returned to earth to hear his phrases, / As he sat there reading, aloud, the great blue tabulae. / They were those from the wilderness of stars that had expected more' (423). We are all haunted: experience itself is never enough; and it is the ghostly discourse of literature which most sharply testifies to this.

One problem with talking about the canon in the way Bloom does is that it appears to be ahistorical: in other words, literature seems to belong to a timeless realm, the canon seems to be impervious to the material effects of social, political, economic and cultural history. Our argument in the present chapter, however, is that while literature is indeed 'ghost work', its haunt is historical. The ghosts of the twentieth are not the same as those of the nineteenth or any other century. We might, for example, reflect on the links between ghosts and technology. In the context of Western culture at the start of the third millennium, and from the point of view of so-called common sense, we may like to believe that we do not believe in ghosts any more; but in important respects the world has become and is continuing to become increasingly ghostly. As Jacques Derrida has observed:

> Contrary to what we might believe, the experience of ghosts is not tied to a bygone historical period, like the landscape of Scottish manors, etc., but . . . is accentuated, accelerated by modern technologies like film, television, the telephone. These technologies inhabit, as it were, a phantom structure . . . When the very *first* perception

of an image is linked to a structure of reproduction, then we are dealing with the realm of phantoms. (Derrida 1989, 61).

This recalls, or calls up, the image of Derrida in Ken McMullen's film *Ghost Dance* (1989) being asked if he believes in ghosts and replying: 'That's a hard question because, you see, I am a ghost.' In a film, everyone is a ghost. If the ghost is the revenant, that which uncannily returns without ever being properly present in the first place, it becomes clear that, more than ever, we live in the midst of ghosts: the voice on the telephone is only ever the reproduction of a voice, the image on television or movie-screen only ever a reproduction. Freud conveys his amazement at the surreal nature of telephones when he remarks in *Civilization and Its Discontents* (1930) that 'With the help of the telephone [one] can hear at distances which would be [regarded] as unattainable even in a fairytale' (1985e, 279). But since Freud's day (itself a somewhat spooky turn of phrase: what haunts this metaphor? why do we not say 'so-and-so's *night*'?), we have witnessed the new ghostly arrivals of the answer-phone, video-recorder, camcorder, personal computer, email, the Internet and World Wide Web, virtual reality, genetic engineering, hyperspace and so forth.

Whether in literature, psychoanalysis or philosophy, twentieth-century thought is irrevocably hooked up to developments in technology and telecommunications. Contemporary literature faces new kinds of challenge in terms of how to represent, assimilate or think the increasing ghostliness of culture. This does not mean that literary works are obliged to deal explicitly with 'new technologies' (though many do); but the question of literature today (or tonight) is inseparable from an increasing ghostliness. We would like to conclude by trying to explore this idea in relation to Toni Morrison's novel *Beloved*. This novel, first published in 1987, is set in America, in the years leading up to and following the abolition of slavery. It is about the unspeakable reality of slavery, about ghosts and the way in which US culture continues to be haunted by the atrocities of its past. The narrative of the novel rests on the dynamic of ghostly secrets and the untellable. 'Beloved' is a baby murdered by her mother, Sethe, because the mother sees death for her daughter as preferable to slavery; 'Beloved' is also a beautiful 'shining' ghost of a woman who, years later, haunts the lives of Sethe and her other daughter, Denver, and Sethe's drifting partner Paul D. The novel, in its very title, is a ghost, or gathering of ghosts. *Beloved* is about

> what it took to drag the teeth of that saw under the little chin; to
> feel the baby blood pump like oil in [Sethe's] hands; to hold her face
> so her head would stay on; to squeeze her so she could absorb, still,
> the death spasms that shot through that adored body, plump and
> sweet with life. (251)

This, 250 pages into the text, is the most 'graphic' description we are
given of what nevertheless haunts the book from the title onwards. The
haunting is inscribed in the passage just quoted, for example, in the
eerie double sense of 'still' (as adverb 'yet' and verb 'stop'): this is a
still, stilled moment, caught in time, which still haunts, is still to be
absorbed. On the final page of the novel we encounter the statement
that 'This is not a story to pass on' (275). This statement suggests that
the story should not or cannot be told, but also that it is not one we can
pass by. The history of the United States is an untellable ghost story
that must not, however, be forgotten. Every house in America is a
haunted house. As Baby Suggs says in grimly comic response to her
daughter-in-law Sethe's suggestion that they vacate the baby-haunted
house known by the grimly euphemistic name of 'Sweet Home': ' "Not
a house in the country ain't packed to its rafters with some dead Negro's
grief. We lucky this ghost is a baby. My husband's spirit was to come
back in here? or yours? Don't talk to me" ' (5).

 Beloved is set in the nineteenth century and is faithful to the modes
of ghostliness, spirits, tele-culture and telecommunications available at
that time: the text opens with an attempted exorcism and an instance of
apparent telekinesis ('The sideboard took a step forward but nothing
else did': 4); there are allusions to telegraphy and the recently invented
Morse code (110), to 'long-distance love' (95) and even to photography
(275). But in other ways *Beloved* is a profoundly contemporary novel, a
work of the late twentieth century not only in style and form but also in
terms of its conception and implacable analysis of ghosts. In particular, it
is written out of or through a psychoanalytically inflected understanding
of deferred meaning, a sense of trauma as ghostly, as that which comes
back again and again, which continues, hauntingly. Morrison's novel is
about the unspeakable not only now but in the future, slavery as a legacy
still, not as something belonging to what we call the history books. Marx
in 1848 saw communism as 'a spectre . . . haunting Europe' (the famous
opening words of *The Communist Manifesto*). One hundred and fifty
years later, Derrida too sees communism as spectral. Hence its rapport

with deconstruction which—in its concern with trying to think about the sense that 'everyone reads, acts, writes with *his or her* ghosts' (Derrida 1994, 139), with trying to think about presence (and absence) as necessarily haunted, about meaning as spectralized—offers perhaps the most important contemporary theory of ghosts. Communism is like democracy itself: 'it has always been and will remain spectral: it is always still to come' (Derrida 1994, 99).

Further reading

For two good and wide-ranging accounts of the ghostly in literature from a 'gothic' perspective, see David Punter, *The Literature of Terror*, 2nd edition (1996), and Fred Botting, *Gothic* (1997). Terry Castle (1995) has a good chapter on eighteenth- and nineteenth-century conceptions of ghosts, entitled 'Spectral Politics: Apparition Belief and the Romantic Imagination'. For a lucid and helpful exposition of Lacan's notoriously difficult essay on *Hamlet*, see Bruce Fink (1996). More generally, for some very good, clear and accessible readings of literature-with-Lacan, see Linda Ruth Williams (1995). More complex Lacanian accounts of the literary may be found in the brilliant work of Shoshana Felman (1987) and Jacqueline Rose (1996). Nicolas Abraham's 'Notes on the Phantom: A Complement to Freud's Metapsychology' and 'The Phantom of Hamlet *or* The Sixth Act, *preceded by* The Intermission of "Truth"' are collected in *The Shell and the Kernel* (1994). For a difficult but thought-provoking elaboration of Abraham's work on ghosts, see Esther Rashkin, *Family Secrets and the Psychoanalysis of Narrative* (1992). For a very rich but demanding account of spectrality and politics, focusing on *Hamlet* and the writings of Karl Marx, see Jacques Derrida, *Spectres of Marx* (1994). For the links between psychoanalysis, technology and telecommunications, see Derrida's challenging but fascinating *Archive Fever* (1995); for an account of the cultural and philosophical importance of the telephone, see Avital Ronell's *The Telephone Book* (1989). Peter Nicholls's essay, 'The Belated Postmodern: History, Phantoms and Toni Morrison' (1996), offers a subtle and stimulating reading of *Beloved* by way of many of the notions of the ghostly discussed in this chapter.

Sexual difference

John laughs at me, of course, but one expects that in marriage.

John is practical in the extreme. He has no patience with faith, an intense horror of superstition, and he scoffs openly at any talk of things not to be felt and seen and put down in figures.

John is a physician, and *perhaps*—(I would not say it to a living soul, of course, but this is dead paper and a great relief to my mind)—*perhaps* that is one reason I do not get well faster.

You see he does not believe I am sick! (9–10)

This passage from Charlotte Perkins Gilman's short story *The Yellow Wallpaper* (1892) presents a number of important issues concerning sexual difference. In particular it dramatizes conventional presuppositions about the differences between men and women. The phrase 'of course' may signal that the first sentence is satirical and ironic, but the implication remains: a woman is subordinate to her husband and cannot expect to be taken seriously. The differences between men and women, in this passage, are primarily a matter of recognizing certain kinds of gender stereotypes. Such stereotypes depend to a considerable extent on a conceptual opposition: man versus woman. And, like other binary oppositions, this involves a hierarchy. John, the man, is active, 'practical', dominant, unemotional. The narrator, the woman, appears to be passive, non-practical, subordinate, emotional. The opposition between the man and the woman is underscored by the insistent stress on the man's actions, qualities and characteristics (John does this, John is such-and-such) and the corresponding *absence* of information regarding the woman. Gilman is exposing a hierarchy, in other words, involving the dominance of the man and the subordination of the woman. *The Yellow Wallpaper* has become something of a modern classic as regards the literary representation of women and the idea of what Elaine Showalter has called, in a book of that name, 'A Literature of Their Own'.

The Yellow Wallpaper is a first-person narrative which tells the story of a woman whose husband insists that, because she is ill, she must remain confined in a room with revolting yellow wallpaper in a large old house where the couple and their baby are staying for the summer. The woman narrates the frightening process whereby she comes to believe that there is some *other* woman in the room, a woman behind or inside the wallpaper. The text culminates with the demonic turn by which she has *become* the woman behind the wallpaper but has got out. The husband comes into the room to discover his wife creeping around the walls: 'Now why should that man have fainted? But he did, and right across my path by the wall, so that I had to creep over him every time!' (36)

The Yellow Wallpaper offers a particularly striking example of what Sandra Gilbert and Susan Gubar talk about as 'the madwoman in the attic' (Gilbert and Gubar 1979). The story is a dramatic and powerfully ironic account of how a woman is repressed, confined and ultimately driven crazy, specifically by her husband, but more generally by the violence of patriarchy. It is no coincidence, therefore, that *The Yellow Wallpaper* should have been written by a woman known in her own lifetime for her contribution to the women's movement in the United States and, in particular, for her work of non-fiction, *Women and Economics* (1898). *The Yellow Wallpaper* can be read as a powerful satire on patriarchal society and values. In particular it emphasizes the ways in which violence against women need not be physical in a literal sense, but can nevertheless be all-pervading. It is what we could call the soft face of oppression that is satirically presented, for example, when the narrator notes: '[John] is very careful and loving, and hardly lets me stir without special direction' (12). Or when she says: 'It is so hard to talk with John about my case, because he is so wise, and because he loves me so' (23).

All literary texts can be thought about in terms of how they represent gender difference and how far they may be said to reinforce or question gender-role stereotypes. Take, for example, an early sixteenth-century sonnet, such as Thomas Wyatt's 'Whoso List to Hunt':

> Whoso list to hunt, I know where is an hind,
> But as for me, alas, I may no more.
> The vain travail hath wearied me so sore

I am of them that farthest cometh behind.
Yet may I, by no means, my wearied mind
Draw from the deer, but as she fleeth afore,
Fainting I follow. I leave off therefore,
Since in a net I seek to hold the wind.
Who list her hunt, I put him out of doubt,
As well as I, may spend his time in vain.
And graven with diamonds in letters plain
There is written, her fair neck round about,
'*Noli me tangere*, for Caesar's I am,
And wild for to hold, though I seem tame.'

Wyatt's sonnet figures men and women in a number of gender-stereotypical ways. Man is the hunter, woman is the hunted. Man is the subject, active, full of 'travail', whereas woman is the object, indeed she is not even figured as human but instead as simply 'an hind', a female deer. Moreover Wyatt's poem integrates this gender-stereotyping within its very structure of address. The poem, that is to say, is addressed to men (to those who wish, or 'list', to hunt), not to women: in this way it appears to offer a classic example of the construction or assumption of the reader as male. Gilman's short story and Wyatt's sonnet are radically different kinds of text, written at completely different periods and from within almost unimaginably heterogeneous cultures (England in the early sixteenth century, the United States in the late nineteenth century). Yet they do offer significant parallels. Both in their quite different ways invite us to reflect critically on the question of gender and more particularly on the power of gender-stereotypes. In both texts, we encounter such stereotypes (I am a woman and therefore subordinate, passive, hysterical, an object, etc.), but we are also provoked to a questioning of the very idea of gender opposition as such.

On one level, then, there is a valuable and perhaps unavoidable reading of literary texts in terms of essentialism: there is essentially one form of sexual difference and that is the difference between male and female, boys and girls, men and women. The notion of essentialism here consists primarily in anatomical or biological difference: the man has a penis, whereas the woman does not, or the woman has a pudendum, breasts and a child-bearing capacity whereas the man has none of these. Various kinds of gender-stereotypes are then articulated, as it were, onto this essentialism: the male is strong, active, rational, the female is weak, passive, irrational and so forth. Within the logic of this description—which has dominated the history of Western culture—having a penis seems to have been so important that it becomes appropriate to speak of its *symbolic* significance, in other words to speak of the *phallus*. Texts or particular aspects of texts can then be described not only in terms of the patriarchal but also in terms of the phallocentric or phallogocentric. Patriarchy involves upholding the supposed priority of the male. In Gilman's text, for example, John is the head (or patriarch) of the family, he makes the decisions and rules the household. The notion of phallocentrism, on the other hand, involves some of the more subtle, more symbolic and perhaps more fundamental ways in which the phallus can be equated with power, authority, presence, and the right to possession. The 'logo' of 'phallogocentrism' points us towards the argument (promoted by theorists such as Jacques Derrida, Hélène Cixous and Luce Irigaray) that the very notions of truth, reason, rationality, the proper, meaning, etc. are phallocentric. Jonathan Culler has summarized this as follows:

> Numerous aspects of criticism, including the preference for metaphor over metonymy, the conception of the author, and the concern to distinguish legitimate from illegitimate meanings, can be seen as part of the promotion of the paternal. Phallogocentrism unites an interest in patriarchal authority, unity of meaning, and certainty of origin. (Culler 1983, 61)

It is in this context, then, that the French theorist Irigaray speculates on the possibilities of kinds of language that would somehow break with the masculine. She remarks:

> For, a feminine language would undo the unique meaning, the proper meaning of words, of nouns: which still regulates all discourse. In order for there to be a proper meaning, there must indeed be a unity somewhere. But if feminine language cannot be brought back to any unity, it cannot be simply described or defined. (Irigaray 1977, 65)

As may already be clear from these very brief accounts of phallocentrism and phallogocentrism, reading literary texts in terms of sexual difference can be more complex and demanding than simply recognizing the gender oppositions and hierarchies by which a text is structured. As feminist criticism has established, such kinds of recognition are crucial. Inevitably perhaps, we start from an essentialist position and our reading of literary texts is guided by this. But what is most important about literary representations of gender is not merely that a particular text can be shown to be sexist or phallocentric, or even feminist. Rather it is that literary texts call into question many of our essentialist ideas about gender.

In other words it could be argued that there is no such thing as a feminist, or a masculinist or a sexist, literary work *in itself*: it all depends on how it is read. An obvious example of this would be the work of D.H. Lawrence. Kate Millett's *Sexual Politics* (1969) was a groundbreaking book because of the acuity and passion with which it attacked Lawrence's (and other male writers') work for its 'phallic consciousness' (238) and degradation of women. Millett's account still makes powerful reading, but it is also in important respects reductive—especially in its author-centred representations of the novels it discusses. For Millett, that is to say, the aim of literary criticism is to criticize the male author—a figure whose male voice, male presence and male ideas are unequivocally clear, for Millett, in everything Lawrence wrote. More recently, however, critics have tended to focus more on the tensions and paradoxes within Lawrence's writings in themselves, rather than on the author-figure thought to be looming behind them. Theorists such as Leo Bersani (1978) and Jonathan Dollimore (1991) have thus emphasized the idea of Lawrence's texts as in many ways working *against themselves* and as unsettling various assumptions that we may have (or Lawrence may have had) about gender as such. Thus Dollimore, for example, focuses on the fact that 'so much [in Lawrence's work] is fantasized from the position of the woman . . . and in a voice that is at once *blindingly heterosexist and desperately homoerotic'* (Dollimore 1991, 275).

We can consider these points by looking again at the Gilman and Wyatt texts. As we have suggested, *The Yellow Wallpaper* reads, on one level at least, as a literary case-study in the oppression and repression of a middle-class white woman in the United States in the late nineteenth century. It may be read as a dynamic feminist demand for liberation from the maddening claustrophobia of patriarchy. But the text is at the same time powerfully equivocal. For instance, simply in terms of the narrative and its conclusion, we must ask ourselves: how much of an affirmation is it, if the only possible liberation for a woman is madness? Is it possible to speak on behalf of women from the position of madness? If, as the narrative of Gilman's text implies, the only way out of patriarchy is to fall, or creep, into madness, is there in fact any way out at all? Isn't *The Yellow Wallpaper* as much caught up in the net of the patriarchal as, say, Henry Miller's *Sexus*? Such questions are not meant as a way of *closing down* the Gilman text by reducing it to the transmission of a merely negative message about the position of women in relation to patriarchy. Rather they are questions which the text itself can be said to pose: to read *The Yellow Wallpaper* critically is to engage with its equivocality, with its ironic and complex refigurations of essentialist notions of gender.

In this context it is not surprising that some of the most provocative feminist criticism since the mid-1970s has been closely bound up with what is referred to as deconstruction. Deconstruction could be defined as a strategy of disruption and transformation with regard to every and any kind of essentialism. 'Essentialism' here would include, for example, the assumption that everyone is essentially either male or female, that the literal is essentially different from the figurative, that speech is essentially different from writing and so on. In particular, deconstruction involves the desedimentation of those conceptual oppositions through which such essentialism operates. In the first place this has meant reversing the hierarchy of male and female, masculine and feminine, father and mother, phallic and (for example) clitoral, along with related couplings such as strong and weak, active and passive, rational and irrational, practical and impractical, presence and absence. Deconstruction, however, entails not only the reversal or overturning of hierarchies but also the transformation of the basis on which they have operated. This might be thought about in relation to the passage from *The Yellow Wallpaper* with which we began this chapter. The narrator tells us: 'John is practical in the extreme. He has no patience with faith, an intense horror of superstition, and he scoffs openly at any talk of things not to be felt and seen and put down in figures' (9). What we have here is an apparently straightforward assertion of the physician husband's practicality and rationalism, implicitly contrasted with the narrator's own lack of these. But on another level the passage might be said to disturb and even transform the very basis on which we presume to talk about the practical and impractical, the rational and irrational. After all, as George Eliot's great novel *Daniel Deronda* (1876) rhetorically asks: 'Who supposes that it is an impossible contradiction to be superstitious and rationalising at the same time?' (48). Indeed, as Gilman's text here intimates, rationalism can be construed as in turn a kind of superstition. To 'scoff openly', as John does, suggests exaggeration and defensiveness. To have 'an intense horror of superstition' is itself perhaps a mark of superstitiousness. There is, in short, a disturbance of the grounds of reason (here and elsewhere) in Gilman's text, and this has to do with deconstruction in the sense that deconstruction is specifically concerned with a suspension of the logic of non-contradiction. It is interested in subversions of what is perhaps the founding claim of Western philosophy, namely Aristotle's proposal that it is not possible for A to be A and not A at the same time. Deconstructive feminism puts this founding claim into question. It is rather like the Freudian argument that the unconscious knows no contradictions: one can dream of a compound figure, for example, someone who is (say) both your mother and not your mother but someone else at the same time. Feminism in its deconstructive mode, then, undermines the very basis on which identity and non-identity are constructed. A deconstructive reading of *The Yellow Wallpaper*, for example, might elaborate on the logic whereby the narrator is both mad and not mad at the same time. The narrator both is and is not the woman behind the wallpaper. The narrator both is and is not herself.

Over the past thirty years, feminism has revolutionized literary and cultural studies. But, as recent critical work such as Judith Butler's suggests, the political force of feminism remains limited so long as it promotes itself as an 'identity politics' (politics based on identifying oneself with a particular, usually marginalized and oppressed, group). The problem with the essentialism or (in Butler's terms) the *foundationalism* of 'identity politics' is that 'it presumes, fixes, and constrains the very "subjects" that it hopes to represent and liberate' (Butler 1990, 148). The subjects who empower themselves through 'identity politics' are in some sense disempowered by their very subjection to it. This, in part, is why we have titled this chapter 'Sexual difference' rather than, say, 'Gender and identity'. What the term 'sexual difference' may usefully gesture towards, then, is the idea that identity itself is perhaps most productively and critically seen as fissured, haunted, at odds with itself. 'Sexual difference' involves not only difference *between* but difference *within*. We are, in Julia Kristeva's phrase, 'strangers to ourselves' (Kristeva 1991). *The Yellow Wallpaper* could be seen to enact or allegorize this notion of difference *within*. That is to say, it subverts the idea of identity itself, in its presentation of a woman who is, in a sense, uncannily double, always already inhabited by another, in this case the woman behind the wallpaper. The text thus prompts us to ask: what is a woman (and conversely, what is a man) if she is double within herself?

This sort of disruption or subversion of identity is further suggested at the level of *writing* itself. The narrator of *The Yellow Wallpaper* presents herself as a writer. This is indicated in the passage we cited at the beginning of this chapter: 'I would not say it to a living soul, of course, but this is dead paper and a great relief to my mind.' The narrator attests to her own 'imaginative power and habit of story-making' (15). With this in mind we could suggest the following hypothesis: wherever there is writing, sexual or gender identity becomes equivocal, questionable, open to transformation. The hypothesis might be considered in relation to Thomas Wyatt's 'Whoso list to hunt'. We have suggested earlier how clearly this poem seems to categorize and distinguish between men and women, even to the extent of postulating its very addressee as a male. A conventional response to this poem is, in the first instance at least, firmly guided by essentialist and oppositional thinking: man vs. woman, hunter vs. hunted, etc. Originally, of course, Wyatt's poem would have circulated privately among a small group of aristocratic men. And indeed, as Marguerite Waller has remarked in her reading of this poem, even in the twentieth century the critical tendency has been to deny 'the position of any reader who is not male, heterosexual, and politically privileged' (Waller 1987, 6). But there are other ways in which to think about this poem and to appreciate that, like other literary works, it can be seen to call into question many of our essentialist ideas and assumptions. For example, through its implicit elision of a female reader it provokes the questions: How should a woman read this poem? Is it possible that the apparent *absence* of women as addressees might be construed as a testament to the idea that a woman reader is precisely what the poem calls for but cannot have, and that this absence is strangely figured in the rhetoric of the poem itself, for instance in the image of trying to hold the wind in a net? Is the wind that is woman more or less powerful than the net? Is the net of patriarchy that we mentioned earlier only so much wind in turn?

Or to put these questions in a somewhat different form: To whom does writing belong? The idea that writing (and therefore literature in general) is a site of questioning and possible transformation of sexual or gender identity applies to both the Wyatt sonnet as a whole and to its final couplet in particular:

> '*Noli me tangere*, for Caesar's I am,
> And wild for to hold, though I seem tame.'

Whose words are these? To whom are they addressed? Such writing, 'graven with diamonds in letters plain', renders paradoxical the distinctions between man and woman, man and man (the speaker and Caesar), the touchable and untouchable, wild and tame, addressor and addressee.

Literary texts at once encourage *and* exceed the parameters of essentialist or identity-oriented readings. By rendering the nature of sexual identity fundamentally questionable they provide a particularly disturbing as well as exhilarating space in which to reflect on the question that Foucault asks in the context of the memoirs of Herculine Barbin, a nineteenth-century French hermaphrodite: 'Do we truly need a true sex?' (Foucault 1980b, 3)

Further reading

Joseph Bristow's *Sexuality* (1997) provides a very clear and helpful account of contemporary theories of sexual desire and how these frame issues of identity and difference. Specifically on literature, sexuality and modernism, see Joseph Allen Boone's *Libidinal Currents: Sexuality and the Shaping of Modernism* (1998). For an accessible and clear account of contemporary feminist criticism and theory, see Toril Moi, *Sexual/Textual Politics* (1985). For a more challenging and radical view, see Judith Butler's *Gender Trouble* (1990) and *Bodies that Matter* (1993). *Speaking of Gender* (Showalter, ed., 1989) is a good collection of essays on gender, and Warhol and Herndl, eds, *Feminisms* (1997) is a comprehensive collection of over seventy classic and more recent essays on different aspects of feminist literary criticism and theory. Another good collection, oriented towards rethinking gender from within, is *Sexual Sameness* (Bristow 1992b). See, too, in this context, Jonathan Dollimore's extensive and provocative study, *Sexual Dissidence* (1991). Finally, for an important historical account of 'woman', see Denise Riley, *Am I That Name?* (1988).

God

John Lennon, playing his celestially white piano, begins the song entitled 'God' (1970) by singing: 'God is a concept / by which we measure / our pain'. What kind of concept is God? In this chapter we propose to explore this question and its relation to literature. In doing this we shall try to emphasize not only that literature is pervasively concerned with religious themes but also that the ways in which we think, read and write about literature are likewise pervaded by religious—and particularly Judaeo-Christian—ideas. The concept of God, in other words, has as much to do with the practice of literary criticism as with the nature of literature. To give three very brief instances. The most famous atheist in the history of English poetry, Percy Bysshe Shelley, asserts that 'A poem is the very image of life expressed in its eternal truth' (Shelley 1977, 485): in the phrase 'eternal truth', Shelley is being religious. In his Preface to *Poems* (1853), Matthew Arnold writes of the name 'Shakespeare' that it is 'a name the greatest perhaps of all poetical names; a name never to be mentioned without reverence' (Arnold 1965, 599): with the word 'reverence', Arnold is being religious. Finally, in his essay 'Tradition and the Individual Talent' (1919), T.S. Eliot declares that 'The progress of an artist is a continual self-sacrifice, a continual extinction of personality' (Eliot 1975, 40): by appealing to 'self-sacrifice', Eliot is being religious.

We would like to try to approach the question of 'God' and literary studies by presenting, with all due respect, a series of six edicts. As we hope will become clear, these edicts are not cut in stone. Nor do they add up to a list of systematic principles or rules. Our aim, as elsewhere in this book, is to provoke questions and further discussion, not to close them off or close them down.

First edict: God is an anthropomorphism. As we have noted elsewhere (for instance in Chapter 5), anthropomorphism is the rhetorical term by which something that is *not* human is attributed with the form or shape (Greek, *morphe*) of the human (*anthropos*). More specifically, as Nietzsche, Freud and others have argued, God is simply a projection of the human ego onto the surrounding universe. And it comes as no surprise to find that this ego or 'me' writ extremely large is, almost invariably, male. It is in this context that Freud suggests that God (here primarily the Judaeo-Christian God) is a kind of hyperbolic father-figure. He proposes that God is 'a father-substitute; or, more correctly . . . he is an exalted father . . . he is a copy of the father as he is seen and experienced in childhood' (Freud 1985c, 399). God is the figure of authority, the great progenitor, the Big Daddy who is sometimes angry (Old Testament), sometimes loving (New Testament). If one thinks for a moment about the idea of God as 'she', one might quickly sense the whole edifice of traditional Christianity tremble. This is no doubt the reason for the frisson of amusement that may accompany the reading of this car-sticker: 'When God made men-drivers she was only joking!' God, then, is not it: God is 'he' or, if you want to get people's backs up, 'she'. Either way, God would seem to be inconceivable without anthropomorphism.

Second edict: God is dead. This proposition is linked most often with the philosophy of Nietzsche, but it can be understood more generally in relation to the impact on European culture of biblical (especially German) scholarship and of (mainly British and German) fossil discoveries and subsequent developments in the theory of evolution in the nineteenth century. By the mid-nineteenth century it had become clear, at least to a significant number of educated European people, that the Bible was a tendentious collection of writings, many of which simply could no longer be trusted in terms of their historical fact and accuracy. The study of fossils made it impossible to suppose that the earth could be, as the Bible propounds, only a few thousand years old. Most famously, Charles Darwin's *The Origin of Species* (1859) offered a far more empirically and historically convincing account of how human beings came about and, at the same time, served to cut God out of the equation. Poets and novelists of all sorts were obliged to reckon with what J. Hillis Miller (in a book of that title) refers to as 'the disappearance of God'. It is this sense of disappearance that Matthew Arnold evokes in 'Dover Beach' (written around 1851), when he describes the retreating 'sea of faith':

> The Sea of Faith
> Was once, too, at the full, and round earth's shore
> Lay like the folds of a bright girdle furled.
> But now I only hear
> Its melancholy, long, withdrawing roar,
> Retreating, to the breath
> Of the night wind, down the vast edges drear
> And naked shingles of the world.

European culture, at least according to this story, has become increasingly secularized.

Of course things are inevitably more complex than this. Even to acknowledge, for example, that 'God is dead' is to think in anthropomorphic terms, and to imply that 'He' was once alive rather than (more plausibly) always already dead. The notion of the death of God runs into difficulties in many ways similar to those regarding the notion of the death of the author (see Chapter 3, above). As Virginia Woolf notes, in a somewhat different context: 'It is far harder to kill a phantom than a reality' (Woolf 1942, 151).

Third edict, then: to acknowledge the idea that God is an anthropomorphism or that he is dead is not the same as getting rid of him. As Barthes makes clear, the idea of God is inescapably linked to ideas of truth, presence, revelation and meaning in general. In this respect, the issue of God is liable to creep into the discussion of literary texts, wherever questions of meaning, truth and so on are at stake. Barthes sees the notion of the author as interdependent with that of God. And he presses for a theory and practice of literature that would no longer be theological, declaring:

> The space of writing is to be ranged over, not pierced; writing ceaselessly posits meaning ceaselessly to evaporate it, carrying out a systematic exemption of meaning. In precisely this way literature (it would be better from now on to say *writing*), by refusing to assign a 'secret', an ultimate meaning, to the text (and to the world as text), liberates what may be called an anti-theological activity, an activity that is truly revolutionary since to refuse to fix meaning is, in the end, to refuse God and his hypostases—reason, science, law. (Barthes 1977a, 147)

The intimate linkage between 'God' and 'meaning' is implicit in the Bible, in the opening sentence of the Gospel according to St John: 'In the beginning was the Word, and the Word was with God, and the Word was God' (St John 1:1). The original Greek for 'Word' here is 'logos', which means not only 'word' but also 'sense' or 'meaning'. It is in this context that we might consider the notion of what Jacques Derrida has called logocentrism, in other words the entire system (of Western thought, culture and philosophy) that is implicitly or explicitly governed by notions of essential and stable meaning and ultimately by what Derrida refers to as a transcendental signified (God, for example). To put this more specifically in terms of literary texts, we could say that perhaps our greatest desire in reading a poem or a novel is to know what it 'means'. Knowing what the text 'means' has often been seen as synonymous, for example, with knowing what the author (who here becomes a sort of substitute for God) meant by writing it. No doubt a crucial part of reading and doing criticism concerns precisely such a 'theological' activity. What Barthes helps us to see, however, is that this activity is *theological* in the sense that it presupposes and hearkens towards a single, stable and authoritative centre.

Barthes's account is extremely appealing—for instance in its associating literature, or *writing*, with the 'truly revolutionary'—but it is also in certain respects problematic. While he is doubtless right to link literature with notions of revolution, anarchy, transgression and liberation, things are trickier than his account may suggest. Barthes's own phraseology remains, at least to some extent, complicit with what it claims to be rejecting or refusing. Just as an atheist could be said to be complying with a kind of theistic thinking through the very gesture of denial (you cannot say, for example, that God does not exist without presupposing a kind of ultimate knowledge of the universe), so the idea of 'an *anti-theological* activity' inevitably remains bound up with an understanding of the 'theological' to which it is being opposed. Similarly Barthes's use of the word 'truly' ('truly revolutionary') could be said to reinstate the notions of 'reason, science, law' precisely at the moment that he is claiming to denounce or refuse them. This is not to say that the general value and significance of Barthes's observations can be discounted. Rather it is to suggest that non-theological thinking is considerably more difficult than one might imagine. It is in this respect that we could recall Nietzsche's assertion that we shall not get rid of God until we get rid of grammar. Like many of Nietzsche's more disturbing aphoristic remarks, this assertion borders on the unthinkable: What could one say about anything if there were no rules governing how to speak or what to say?

Fourth edict: Religion is everywhere. It perhaps becomes clearer how deeply Western culture is theologically embedded if we reflect on the way we structure time: in the most fundamental way, the year (2000, for example) is based on the Christian religion. Things look very different in a non-Christian framework: imagine, to begin with, a concept of the year that does not involve Christmas or Easter, or a concept of the week that does not have a Sunday. Christianity, in short, is far more pervasive and insidious than many people, including non-practising Christians, might suppose.

How should we think about this in relation to reading and writing about literary texts? In many ways, searching for religious and particularly Christian ideas and motifs in the field of literary studies is like being the Edgar Allan Poe character in 'The Purloined Letter' who is faced with a map and cannot see the name of the country he is looking at because the letters of the name are so big. Being critical of religion is also more unusual than one might think. As Jonathan Culler points out, in an essay entitled 'Political Criticism: Confronting Religion': 'literature departments these days contain people with all manner of views—Marxists, Lacanians, deconstructionists, feminists—but seldom anyone who seriously attacks religion' (Culler 1988b, 78). Culler goes on to provide a forceful summary of the responsibilities of the teacher and critic in this context:

> The essential step is to take up the relation of our teaching and writing to religious discourse and to maintain a critical attitude when discussing religious themes—that is, not to assume that theistic beliefs deserve respect, any more than we would assume that sexist or racist beliefs deserve respect. This might involve us in comparing Christianity with other mythologies when we teach works imbued with religion, or making the sadism and sexism of religious discourse an explicit object of discussion, as we now tend to do when teaching works containing overtly racist language. (Culler 1988b, 80)

Fifth edict: literature has an evil streak. Rather than innocently pretend that literature in its creativity and *joie de vivre* is somehow innately *good*, or ludicrously claim, as do critics such as Matthew Arnold (in the nineteenth century) and F.R. Leavis (in the twentieth), that reading and studying literature in some 'natural' way make you a 'better' person, we should recognize instead that literary creativity has at least as much to do with evil as with good. In his influential and characteristically religious essay 'The Function of Criticism at the Present Time' (1864),

Matthew Arnold described literature as 'the promised land' that contains 'the best that is known and thought in the world' (Arnold 1964, 34, 33). Very much within this Christian-spiritualistic critical tradition, F.R. Leavis propounded a theory of literature as the embodiment of 'our spiritual tradition . . . the "picked experience of ages"' (Leavis and Thompson 1964, 82). Such conceptions epitomize the sorts of spurious claims traditionally made of what Leo Bersani has described (and devastatingly criticized) as 'the authoritative, even redemptive virtues of literature' (Bersani 1990, 1). There is something diabolical about the literary. As Georges Bataille makes clear in his pathbreaking study, *Literature and Evil* (1953), a collusion between creation, imagination and evil, is characteristic of literary works in general. 'Literature is not innocent', writes Bataille: 'Literature, like the infringement of moral laws, is dangerous' (Bataille 1985, x, 25).

We can illustrate this by considering the example of John Milton's *Paradise Lost* (1667) and the following lines from Book I. In this passage Milton describes the unsettling ability that devils have of being able to change instantaneously from the size of giants to the size of pygmies or to the size of 'fairy elves':

> . . . they but now who seemed
> In bigness to surpass Earth's giant sons
> Now less than smallest dwarfs, in narrow room
> Throng numberless, like that Pygmean race
> Beyond the Indian mount, or fairy elves,
> Whose midnight revels, by a forest side
> Or fountain some belated peasant sees,
> Or dreams he sees, while overhead the moon
> Sits arbitress, and nearer to the earth
> Wheels her pale course: they on their mirth and dance
> Intent, with jocund music charm his ear;
> At once with joy and fear his heart rebounds. (777–88)

Unfolding the comparison of devils with 'fairy elves', these lines have to do with seduction and uncertainty, the charming power of music (or, by extension, poetry)—to which even the moon seems drawn—and the rebounding undecidability of 'joy and fear', the moment in which one does not know what one sees (or dreams one sees). Is one charmed by this vision or not? Milton leaves the comparison there, on the point of the rebound. And in a sense the whole of *Paradise Lost* is inscribed in the moment of this rebounding heart.

The passage from *Paradise Lost* demonstrates the workings of a powerful ambivalence and what we might call an aesthetic tribute (or subordination) to the devilish. This may help to explain William Blake's famous remark about *Paradise Lost*, in 'The Marriage of Heaven and Hell' (1790–3), that 'The reason Milton wrote in fetters when he wrote of Angels & God, and at liberty when of Devils & Hell, is because he was a true Poet and of the Devil's party without knowing it.' One of the most controversial literary critics of the late twentieth century, Harold Bloom, has elaborated an entire theory of poetry (Bloom 1973) in accordance with this Blakean insight: for Bloom, Milton's Satan is the very epitome of the strong modern (i.e. Miltonic and post-Miltonic) poet. In any case it seems clear that Milton's great epic poem, and Blake's poetry in turn, is profoundly indebted to a kind of aesthetic of evil. As Bataille shows, evil and the literary imagination are in cahoots. We could illustrate this quite succinctly in terms of Shakespeare's *Othello*, by supposing that this play were retitled *Iago*: Iago may indeed be abominable, but he is just as clearly the imaginative focus of Shakespeare's play, the embodiment of its creativity and dramatic energy.

A corresponding sense of the literary aesthetic of evil is suggested by Henry James when he offers an explanation of the power of *The Turn of the Screw* (1898), in his comments on that short but enthralling horror novel in a preface to *The Aspern Papers*: 'Only make the reader's general vision of evil intense enough', James says, '. . . Make him [*sic*] *think* the evil, make him think it for himself . . .' (James 1986, 343). Putting our fifth edict in slightly different terms, then, we could say that literature tends towards the demonic: it is about entrancement, possession, being invaded or taken over. The word 'demonic' in this context is significantly ambiguous and is best left that way: a demon is 'an evil spirit' or 'devil', but can also be 'a friendly spirit or good genius' (*Chambers*). To argue that literature has an evil streak is not to imply a moral denunciation of literary works any more than it is to provide support for the liberalist notion that reading literature makes you a better person. Literary texts are dangerous. No one, we might suggest, is more palpably aware of this fact than the author of *The Satanic Verses* (1988). Reading literary texts engages us, in a disturbing but creative and singular way, in the obligation to 'think the evil for oneself'. The paradoxically creative force of evil in literary texts is what makes them in turn the exemplary space for experiencing the undecidable and for thinking about ethics. Far from being immoral or even amoral, literature involves us in what Bataille calls a 'hypermorality' (Bataille 1985, ix). It confronts us with questions which call for different kinds of decision-making and critical responsibilities. Is *The Satanic Verses* an evil work? Is it any more evil than *Paradise Lost*, say, or Mary Shelley's *Frankenstein* (1818) or Elizabeth Bowen's *The House in Paris* (1935)? To rush to decisions in response to such questions is to turn a blind eye to the enigmatic powers of the literary and to ignore what could be called its peculiar ethical imperative.

Sixth edict: literature is sacred. This would be another side to what is paradoxical about the literary. Salman Rushdie's Herbert Read Memorial Lecture, 'Is Nothing Sacred?' was given in his absence by Harold Pinter, at the Institute for Contemporary Arts in London, on 6 February 1990: Rushdie himself, of course, was in enforced hiding and unable to appear in public for the occasion. Rushdie's lecture starts off by stating that nothing is sacred:

> nothing is sacred in and of itself . . . . Ideas, texts, even people can be made sacred—the word is from the Latin *sacrare*, 'to set apart as holy'—but . . . the act of making sacred is in truth an event in history. It is the product of the many and complex pressures of the time in which the act occurs. And events in history must always be subject to questioning, deconstruction, even to declaration of their obsolescence. (Rushdie 1990, 3)

But the lecture then moves on to cast doubt on this idea that nothing is sacred. Rushdie suggests that he may be obliged 'to set aside as holy the idea of the absolute freedom of the imagination and alongside it [his] own notions of the World, the Text and the Good' (5). He goes on to speculate on the idea that art can and must offer us something like 'a secular definition of transcendence' where transcendence is defined as 'that flight of the human spirit outside the confines of its material, physical existence which all of us, secular or religious, experience on at least a few occasions' (7). Finally Rushdie withdraws and appears to want to retract these earlier claims about art and, in particular, literature. He declares: 'now I find myself backing away from the idea of sacralizing literature with which I flirted at the beginning of this text; I cannot bear the idea of the writer as secular prophet' (14).

The shifts in Rushdie's position, the different kinds of flirtation going on in this brief text, 'Is Nothing Sacred?', are neatly illustrative of the seemingly paradoxical, contradictory nature of the concept of literature. We may, as readers or students or teachers, be powerfully motivated by a sense of the secular (and even, to phrase it more provocatively, by a sense that religion has been the greatest evil in human history, that it is nothing more than what Don Cuppit calls a 'hatred machine' (Cuppit 1997, 98)). But so long as we are concerned with the question of literature we are concerned with what is sacred. The murder of the Japanese translator of Rushdie's novel *The Satanic Verses* may allow us to reflect sombrely on the terrible blindness by which certain people have arrived at the belief that *The Satanic Verses* is an evil work, a blasphemous book which cannot or should not be read as fictional (or in that sense '*literary*') at all. But it also tragically gestures towards what may after all be the *something* that is sacred about literature, namely its untranslatability. Jacques Derrida has spoken of this, in the context of the German writer and philosopher Walter Benjamin, as follows:

> if there is something untranslatable in literature (and, in a certain way, literature is the untranslatable), then it is sacred. If there is any literature, it is sacred; it entails sacralization. This is surely the relation we have to literature, in spite of all our denegations in this regard. The process of sacralization is underway whenever one says to oneself in dealing with a text: Basically, I can't transpose this text such as it is into another language; there is an idiom here; it is a work; all the efforts at translation that I might make, that it itself calls forth and demands, will remain, in a certain way and at a given moment, vain or limited. This text, then, is a sacred text. (Derrida 1985b, 148)

Quite apart from the fact that, as critics such as Terry Eagleton (1996) have stressed, literary studies in Britain, for example, in many ways arose out of the desire or need to find a substitute for religion, literature is sacred in its singularity. As soon as we set it apart (*sacrare*) and recognize the singularity or uniqueness of a work, its demand that it be translated and its insistence on being untranslatable, we are engaging with the sacred.

> To be, or not to be, that is the question . . .

> Season of mists and mellow fruitfulness,
>   Close bosom-friend of the maturing sun . . .

> Sexual intercourse began
> In nineteen sixty-three . . .

Further reading

Salman Rushdie's 'Is Nothing Sacred?' (1990) is an accessible and very stimulating essay on literature and the sacred. Jonathan Culler's 'Political Criticism: Confronting Religion' (1988b) is clear and provocative, as is the book on which his discussion is centrally focused, William Empson's *Milton's God* (1965). On religion and the historical emergence of English Studies in Britain, see Eagleton 1996. For a very challenging reading of Nietzsche's 'God is dead', see Heidegger 1977. For a complex but fascinating account of God and language, see Jacques Derrida's 'Des Tours de Babel' (1985a). For two excellent studies which consider the Bible itself from a literary critical perspective, see Robert Alter, *The Art of Biblical Narrative* (1981) and *The Art of Biblical Poetry* (1985). A useful general survey of theology in relation to the work of various contemporary theorists and philosophers can be found in Graham Ward (1996). For two recent and powerful books on some of the paradoxes of religion today, see Don Cupitt, *After God* (1997), and Derrida and Vattimo, eds, *Religion* (1998).

Ideology

Between 1979 and 1997, despite economic crises, political mismanage-
ment, levels of unemployment that stubbornly refused to go much below
three million, a doubling in the figures for reported crime, repeated
disclosures of personal and institutional scandal and corruption, numerous ministerial resignations and 'betrayals', increased poverty and home-
lessness, and a return to Victorian standards of bigotry, hypocrisy and
political dishonesty (or economy with the truth), the Conservative Government in Britain held office and, indeed, were re-elected three times.
The reasons for this caused critics on the left to be increasingly puzzled
and frustrated. Writing in 1987, Stuart Hall explained the phenomenon
as follows:

> People don't vote for Thatcherism, in my view, because they believe
> the small print. People in their minds do not think that Britain is
> now a wonderfully blooming, successful, economy. Nobody believes
> that, with $3\frac{3}{4}$ million people unemployed, the economy is picking up.
> Everyone knows Lord Young's figures are 'economical with the
> truth'. What Thatcherism as an ideology does, is to address the fears,
> the anxieties, the lost identities, of a people. It invites us to think
> about politics in images. It is addressed to our collective fantasies,
> to Britain as an imagined community, to the social imaginary. Mrs
> Thatcher has totally dominated that idiom . . . (Hall 1988, 167)

It was ideology, then—as distinct from the economic and social reality—
that kept the Tories in power all this time. It was ideology as a false
representation of reality, as the *idea* of reality, ideology as the appeal to
fears, anxieties and nostalgia. Ideology is constituted by images and fantasies. This might be illustrated by the change in the fate of the Tory

party and the crisis of electability that they suffered in the final years of their rule. The difference between Margaret Thatcher and the unre-electable John Major may just have been their respective ability and inability to affirm a particular ideology. This would be the difference between Thatcher's sombre call to return to 'Victorian Values' and Major's immediately risible call of 'Back to Basics': the former seemed to fool at least some of the people some of the time, while the latter dug a hole into which Tory ministers proceeded to jump quicker than you could say 'marital infidelity'. While the Conservative Government's economic performance and political goals may have changed little, the fact that Major was deemed the most unpopular prime minister since records began might be understood simply in terms of his inability to reaffirm the ideological self-deception of the electorate.

But what is this thing called 'Ideology'? The word has something of a bad name: the 'crude' Marxist notion of ideology is as 'false consciousness', 'the system of ideas and representations which dominate the mind of a man [*sic*] or a social group' (Althusser 1977, 149), as contrasted with the underlying reality of economic and class relations. The influential theorist Louis Althusser summarizes Marx's notion of ideology as 'an imaginary assemblage (*bricolage*), a pure dream, empty and vain, constituted by the "day's residues" from the only full and positive reality, that of the concrete history of concrete material individuals materially producing their existence'. 'Ideology', Althusser continues, 'represents the imaginary relationship of individuals to their real conditions of existence' (Althusser 1977, 151, 153). In classical Marxism—which, as we shall see, Althusser radically develops—ideology is an imagined representation of reality: it is false, distorted by definition. Ideology is not, Terry Eagleton remarks, 'a set of doctrines': rather, it 'signifies the way men [*sic*] live out their roles in class-society, the values, ideas and images which tie them by their social functions and so prevent them from a true knowledge of society as a whole' (Eagleton 1976, 16–17).

For many traditional non-Marxist critics—humanists, pluralists, liberals and so on—ideology is often seen as a set of political theories which override any sensible or objective analysis of social relations. According to this view, thinking about ideology is something that gets in the way of reading literature: focusing on the political or ideological dimensions of a literary text results in a reductive simplification of its true value, a value that transcends local or contingent questions of class, race or gender. For such critics, the opening to the present chapter would be 'ideological' in a bad sense—it is, they might say, politically biased, not the way to write objective, academic literary criticism. Once again, but differently, ideology is a distortion.

Finally, for poststructuralist critics, the notion of ideology is fundamentally suspect, since it appears to rely on a classical opposition of true and false, of reality and false consciousness, which such critics would question. By this view, ideology appears too easily as a master term for totalizing readings of literary texts. It assumes a privileged position— outside ideology—through which the ideological may be examined and criticized. In this chapter, however, we shall attempt to suggest ways in which the work of the neo-Marxist critic Louis Althusser has effectively produced a poststructuralist Marxism by substantially modifying the 'crude' opposition of disguised or distorted representations on the one hand and an underlying political and material reality on the other.

In a famous essay entitled 'Ideology and Ideological State Apparatuses' (1969), Louis Althusser seeks to describe ways in which the state exerts its power outside such institutions as the army, the courts, the police, etc.—that is to say, in culture and society generally. The central insight of this essay is that ideology is bound up with the constitution of the subject, that 'man is an ideological animal by nature'—meaning that people constitute or define themselves *as humans* through ideology. Althusser argues that

> the category of the subject is constitutive of all ideology, but at the same time . . . the category of the subject is only constitutive of all ideology insofar as all ideology has the function (which defines it) of 'constituting' concrete individuals as subjects. (Althusser 1977, 160)

To put it simply: subjects—people—make their own ideology at the same time as ideology makes them subjects. The implications of this idea are enormous because it means that 'ideology' goes to the heart of personal identity, of how we conceive ourselves as subjects in the world and all that this involves. Althusser avoids a reductive opposition of ideology and reality by suggesting that ideology *makes* our reality in constituting us as subjects. Ideology, Althusser argues, 'hails or interpellates concrete individuals as concrete subjects' (162): it calls us or calls to us as subjects and we recognize ourselves as subjects in our response to this call. To become human, to identify oneself as a subject, then, is an effect of ideology. For Althusser, the function of Art is, as he remarks in 'A Letter on Art', 'to make us see', and what it allows us to see, what it forces us to see, is 'the ideology from which it is born' (Althusser

1977, 204). What is most terrifying and compelling about this is the fact that being a subject feels so real, so natural—and yet, as Althusser remarks, this very 'reality' or 'naturalness' of being a subject is itself an 'ideological effect'.

This is heady stuff, and rather abstract—if also, as Althusser suggests, terribly real. How can we begin to think about the workings of ideology in literary texts? Etienne Balibar and Pierre Macherey take us some way towards an understanding of the question in their important essay 'On Literature as an Ideological Form' (1981). They argue that literary texts produce the illusion of 'unity' and that a 'material analysis' needs to look for 'signs of contradictions' which appear 'as unevenly resolved conflicts in the text' (87). For these critics, indeed, literature *begins* with 'the imaginary solution of implacable ideological contradictions': literature is there because 'such a solution is impossible' (88). In capitalist society, literature itself is an 'ideological form', both produced by and producing ideology. The task of the critic would be to look beyond the unity that the literary text strives to present, and forcefully to explore the contradictions embedded within it. The strange case of detective fiction illustrates this point very well. The genre produces its own consoling fictions, its own ideology. While we may think of crime as eternally recurring, for example, as an unavoidable function of any sociopolitical context, detective fiction allows us to perceive it as both solvable and the result of the actions of specific, isolated and morally culpable individuals.

Tony Bennett has argued that a thoroughgoing Althusserian criticism would not simply restore or reveal the contradictions that are already in texts: rather, it would 'read contradictions into the text' in such a way that it would 'effect a work of transformation on those forms of signification which are said to be ideological' (Bennett 1979, 146–7). In this respect, an 'ideological criticism' is not one that understands the reality of a text better. Rather it is criticism that changes the text. Such a reading of, say, an Agatha Christie detective novel would not simply seek to expose ways in which such writing conforms to and reinforces the status quo of bourgeois capitalism. Instead, it would recognize reading as an intervention in and transformation of that text itself. Bennett argues that there can be no notion of '*the* text' underlying any reading: texts have 'historically specific functions and effects' (Bennett 1979, 148), they change in time, and what changes them is reading.

In order to think about some of these points and questions, we shall briefly consider Edgar Allan Poe's story 'The Purloined Letter' (1845). This story, together with two other stories by Poe, 'The Murders in the

Rue Morgue' (1841) and 'The Mystery of Marie Roget' (1842–3), is usually considered to constitute the origins of modern detective fiction. Set in Paris, the narrative concerns a detective named August C. Dupin, who is asked to solve a mystery concerning the theft of a letter from the 'royal apartments' belonging to 'a personage of the most exalted station' (495), that is to say, presumably, the Queen of France. The contents of the letter have the potential to compromise the Queen and leave her open to blackmail. As she is reading the letter she is interrupted by her husband, from whom the letter must be concealed. She does not have time to hide the letter so she lays it on the table as she talks to her husband, relying on the fact that it is *not* concealed to hide the fact that it *must* be concealed. While they are talking, another person, 'Minister D.', enters the room, notices the letter and manages to exchange it for a worthless letter that he happens to be holding. The Queen sees this exchange but can do nothing to stop it without drawing attention to the secret letter. She is now open to blackmail and her letter must be discreetly retrieved by the head of the police service. The police have surreptitiously searched Minister D.'s house but have been unable to find the letter. Dupin is asked to help. He goes to the minister's house and manages to spot the letter, turned inside out, but revealed for all to see, hanging from the Minister's mantelpiece. Later, by returning to the house with a copy of the letter and arranging for the minister to be distracted while he is there, Dupin manages to substitute his copy for the genuine article and retrieve the now doubly purloined letter.

Detective fiction may be understood to have a conservative ideological form because of its generic investment in the restoration of the status quo. A detective story typically involves a disturbance of order in the wake of an originary event of physical violence or theft of property, followed by the re-establishment of order by the discovery of the criminal—after which the jewels are returned or the murderer is punished (or both). Moreover, the genre conventionally relies on the idea of the criminal as an autonomous individual: he or she must be morally responsible for his or her actions and must not be insane. This is because the genre depends, on the one hand, on an outcome in which society's and the reader's desire for moral restitution is fulfilled and, on the other hand, on the detective's ability rationally to deduce the criminal's motives. If the criminal is mad, he or she cannot be punished (he or she must be cured), and his or her motives and actions cannot be rationally deduced because they will be, by definition, irrational. Similarly, any critique of society or social institutions is likely to be counterproductive in a work of detective fiction because of the danger that 'society', rather than a particular individual, will itself come to be seen as the culprit. This is a dilemma which is particularly acute in, for example, contemporary feminist detective fiction: the novels of such writers as Sara Paretsky and Amanda Cross are as much concerned with exposing the gross injustices of patriarchal society as with finding a specific criminal. In such cases there is a sense in which the criminal cannot finally be punished and the status quo restored because it is that very status quo which is responsible for the crime. Encoded within classic detective fiction, then, is a reactionary political agenda. This ideological form of the genre might be said to be an unspoken but necessary part of any conventional detective story. From this point of view, one could say that 'The Purloined Letter' involves the re-establishment of power relations, the assertion of the culprit as autonomous and independent, and the implementation of reason to restore the status quo.

But what is particularly interesting about Poe's story from this perspective is not so much the way in which it institutes and reinforces the ideological formation of a certain literary genre, as it is the fact that this formation also entails a number of paradoxes, sites of disturbance and displacement. One of the key elements of the story is the identification of the detective with the criminal. Dupin explains that he was able to discover the letter by identifying himself with Minister D. and, in particular, by identifying the minister's mode of thinking as both rational and poetic (like Dupin, he is both mathematician and poet). The story establishes what we might call 'inspired reasoning'—as contrasted with the rational approach of the regular police—as the characteristic technique for both detective and criminal in detective fiction. But the story also initiates a central paradox of the genre whereby the detective not only identifies with but is in some ways identical to the criminal. In this sense, it is no accident that the letter is, in fact, 'purloined' twice—once by the minister and once by Dupin. The detective in this story, and in detective fiction more generally, must obey the double bind of identity with, but difference from, the criminal. This intrinsic generic paradox suggests ways in which the ideological conservativism of the genre, its investment in a restoration of the status quo and reinforcement of an absolute distinction between criminal and non-criminal, may be undermined. Similarly, in establishing 'inspired reasoning' as the *modus operandi* for both detective and criminal, Poe's story opens the way for its own deconstruction. While detective and criminal, author and reader all need to employ reason to attain their ends, such reason is continually disturbed by its 'other', inspiration or unreason. It comes as no surprise, therefore, that Poe was also obsessed with occultism, spiritualism and the uncanny. Nor is it any surprise to discover that the inventor of Sherlock Holmes, Arthur Conan Doyle, was on the one hand a trained physician and, on the other, a keen amateur in the study of telepathy and the after-life. The detective in this context combines a doctor's empirical and scientific acumen with a telepath's ability to read the criminal's mind. More generally, detective fiction is continually threatened with its generic other—the gothic, tales of psychic phenomena, spiritualism—as is suggested by such gothic tales as Doyle's *The Hound of the Baskervilles* (1902), for example, or such apparently supernatural tales as his 'The Parasite' (1893). Finally, the genre of detective fiction is organized through a precarious relation with social critique. As we have pointed out, classic detective fiction must distance itself from an ideological critique of society which, however, can never be finally erased. In the Soviet Union, the authorities used to claim that there was a crime rate of zero. This laughable claim had to be made according to the contention that a Marxist society is necessarily free of crime. Detective fiction can only exist if there are crimes to detect, and if there are crimes to detect society cannot be perfect. Some of the most interesting exponents of detective fiction—Dashiel Hammett, Raymond Chandler, or more recently Paul Auster, William McIlvanney, Sara Paretsky, Philip Kerr—gain much of their narrative energy from precisely such a tension—the possibility that the constitution of their narratives as detective fiction will be dissolved by their unavoidable engagement in social and political critique.

Our final point concerning Poe's story and its relation to ideology concerns the way in which it is based on the idea that what is most open or revealed, most 'obvious', may itself be the most deceptive or most concealing. The fact that Minister D. conceals the purloined letter precisely by *not* hiding it, by leaving it where all can see it (the place where no one—except Dupin—will look, because it is too exposed), makes 'The Purloined Letter' an allegory of ideological formation. Ideology may be defined in terms of the obvious, in terms of common sense. It is, in the West, 'common sense' that a 'normal' subject or person is autonomous, for example, that crime is the result of individual actions, or that such an individual operates through rational motivation. But at the same time each of these obvious, self-evident or commonsensical points disguises a very specific concept of the self, an ideology.

Literary texts, then, rather than offering an escape from ideology, may be considered as places where the structures and fractures of ideology are both produced and reproduced. Literary texts do not simply or passively 'express' or reflect the ideology of their particular time and place. Rather, they are sites of conflict and difference, places where values and preconceptions, beliefs and prejudices, knowledge and social structures—all the complex formations of ideology by which history articulates itself—may be produced and, finally, transformed.

Further reading

Althusser's 'Ideology and the Ideological State Apparatuses' (1977) is a basic text for a consideration of the fundamental importance of ideology in the constitution of the human subject. The classic Althusserian account of literature is Macherey's astute and highly readable *A Theory of Literary Production* (1978); see also Balibar and Macherey (1981). A good brief account of ideology is the entry in Williams, *Keywords* (1976). More recent, more detailed and exhaustive is Terry Eagleton's *The Ideology of the Aesthetic* (1990). For two recent collections of essays see Eagleton, ed., *Ideology* (1994) and Mulhern, ed., *Contemporary Marxist Literary Criticism* (1992). The classic work on the ideology of detective fiction in particular is Stephen Knight's *Form and Ideology in Detective Fiction* (1980).

Desire

In 1954 Alan Turing, the inventor of one of the first modern electronic computers (the 'Turing Machine'), killed himself. Two years earlier, he had been prosecuted for 'gross indecency'—that is, for having an affair with another man. His crime had been to desire the wrong person, to have the wrong desire. The man who, with others, has transformed our world by the manipulation of a binary system (on/off), was prosecuted and persecuted thanks to another binary system—right/wrong, good/ evil, moral/immoral, legal/illegal, heterosexual/homosexual, normal/ perverse. There is a terrible irony here. Turing's machine and its descendants exploit a simple polarity to develop the most complex patterns imaginable (and those beyond imagination). Society's technology of ethics and legality, by contrast, has not progressed beyond a model based on rigid and unforgiving binary oppositions. Desire: right or wrong.

Is it possible that desire is more complex? The most influential philosopher of desire in the twentieth century has been Sigmund Freud. For Freud, all desire goes back to the child's original desire for the mother, for the mother's breast. This desire is so strong that it produces an absolute identification: ' "I am the breast" ', wrote Freud, ventriloquizing the unspoken words of the infant (Freud 1975b, 299). Beyond this originary desire, however, Freud tends to see the precise structure of desire as determined by socialization, by the way in which the child is brought up. In such texts as *On Sexuality: Three Essays on the Theory of Sexuality* (1905/1977), Freud argues that desire is 'essentially' mobile—it has no essence, no proper object, beyond the child's hallucinatory desire for the breast. Most justifications for the proscription of desire—against homosexual acts, for example—rely on assertions about what is 'natural'. But if we accept Freud's arguments, we find that the appeal to the natural is highly questionable.

The mobility of desire is demonstrated by a text such as Shakespeare's comedy *Twelfth Night* (c.1601). While his *Romeo and Juliet* (*c*.1595) may seem to reproduce the myth of an absolute and eternal love between one man and one woman, *Twelfth Night* is concerned rather with the contingency and mobility of desire. Duke Orsino sees himself as a true lover, a man overwhelmed by love and constant only in his desire:

> For such as I am, all true lovers are,
> Unstaid and skittish in all motions else,
> Save in the constant image of the creature
> That is belov'd. (II, iv, 17–20)

In love with an image of the woman he claims to love, Orsino is at the same time in love with the image of himself in love. A philosopher of love—most of his speeches meditate, often absurdly, on the nature of love and the lover—Orsino is unaware that 'true love', including his own, is love of love, that desire is desire for its own image. In spite of himself, Orsino illustrates the accuracy of Nietzsche's aphorism: 'In the end one loves one's desire and not what is desired' (Nietzsche 1989, 93). In fact, by the end of the play it has become clear that Orsino's desire is radically mobile and contingent. Orsino uses his servant Cesario as a messenger between himself and Lady Olivia, the woman he desires. Cesario is really a woman called Viola, dressed as a man, and is herself in love with the Duke. At the end of the play, Olivia marries Viola's twin brother and Viola reveals that she is really a woman. At this point, unabashed by the ease with which his desire can move from one object to another, Orsino proposes marriage to Viola. The 'true lover' in Shakespeare's play turns out to have mobile desires, and even gender seems to be more a comedy of convention than a matter of nature. Does Orsino finally desire Viola or Cesario?

In the context of literature more generally, we can begin to think about the importance of desire in two fundamental ways. In the first place, we would suggest that every literary text is in some way *about* desire. To say this, however, is not to suggest that it is everywhere and always the same desire. As Michel Foucault's influential three-volume *A History of Sexuality* (1981–8) makes particularly clear, desire is bound up with all sorts of social and institutional practices and discourses—

with questions of law, gender and sexuality, with the discourses of medicine, theology, economics and so on. Thinking about desire in literary texts—about representations of desire—inevitably opens onto questions of historical context. For example, nowadays we may take for granted the term 'homosexual' and the notion of homosexual desire. But as we show in more detail in Chapter 20, below, the term and indeed the concept is relatively recent. The *OED* suggests that the word 'homosexual' entered the English language in 1892. Critics such as Joseph Bristow have demonstrated that a critical appreciation of a play such as Oscar Wilde's *The Importance of Being Earnest* (1895) is crucially dependent on an understanding of the historical emergence of a homosexual lifestyle at the end of the nineteenth century (Bristow 1992a). While the term 'homosexual' can refer to both men and women, its entry into the English language in the late nineteenth century did not result in a sudden visibility for lesbians, however. Indeed, the most striking aspect of lesbianism in 'straight' culture generally has been the denial of its existence. In 1885, for example, Queen Victoria is said to have reacted to the suggestion that there should be a law for women corresponding to the new law against 'gross indecency' between men by remarking, simply, 'no woman could ever do that' (quoted in Castle 1992, 128). Similarly, Leonard Woolf's mother responded to Radclyffe Hall's lesbian novel *The Well of Loneliness* (1928) by saying 'I am seventy-six—but until I read this book I did not know that such things went on at all. I do not think they do' (quoted in Knopp 1992, 118). And, in literary criticism, it is only during the past decade or so, despite pioneering studies such as Jeannette Foster's *Sex Variant Women in Literature* from 1958, that a critical vocabulary for talking about lesbian writing has begun to emerge. As far as 'straight' culture goes, critics such as Joseph Allan Boone, for example, have shown how the very *form* of conventional nineteenth-century narrative is bound up with the Victorian social dynamics of courtship and marriage (Boone 1987).

But literary texts are not only *about* desire: they also produce or solicit desire. Literary texts produce desire in reading, textual desire. Literary texts, we might say, are machines of desire. Not only do they generate desire (such as the desire to read on), but they are generated by it (by the desire, for example, to tell). In this respect it might be useful to turn Freud's famous question of female desire, 'what does a woman want?'— and Gayatri Spivak's reformulation of it as 'what does a man want?'— into a question about literary texts: What does a text want? Does it want to tell us something or conceal something? Does it want to make us want it? How? And so on. But if texts can be thought to desire, readers desire, too: we desire solutions, we desire to get to the end of the story, we desire insight or wisdom, pleasure or sadness, laughter or anger. The fundamental paradox of reading, however, is that we always desire an end (a resolution, an explanation, the triumph of good), but that this end is not the end of desire. As Boone has shown, classic nineteenth-century narrative ends with the satisfaction of desire. But as Freud has taught us, this end of desire is not the end of the story: as he speculates in 'Civilization and Its Discontents', there is something in the very nature of sexual life which 'denies us full satisfaction' (Freud 1985e, 295).

The most important post-Freudian theorist of desire, especially in the context of literary studies, is the French psychoanalyst Jacques Lacan. His particular concern is with what he terms the 'paradoxical, deviant, erratic, eccentric, even scandalous character' of desire (Lacan 1977a, 286, quoted in Bowie 1991, 134). Lacan's texts are notoriously difficult to read, in part because they claim to (or are condemned to) speak on behalf of this strange figure of desire. Any attempt to summarize or explain what he has to say about desire is bound to be misguided— precisely to the extent that it will appear to be putting this scandalous figure in a conceptual strait-jacket. With that proviso in mind, however, we could be a bit scandalous in our own fashion and summarize Lacan's characterization of desire as follows: Lacan elaborates on Freud's contention that there is something about the nature of desire that is incompatible with satisfaction. His account of desire is more radical than Freud's, however. Freud emphasizes the ways in which we can never get what we want: we may think we have got it (pouring ourselves a gin and tonic, paying for a new car), but actually desire will always have moved on again (to the next gin and tonic, the chance to get on the road and drive and so on). Waiting for a final fulfilment of desire is, indeed, like waiting for Godot in Samuel Beckett's play. For Freud, this endlessly deferred complete satisfaction is seen simply as an unavoidable, if rather pathetic aspect of what it is to be human. For Lacan, on the other hand, the nature of desire is at once more alien and more subversive. This can be illustrated in two ways. First, for Lacan, the alien or alienating character of desire is not something that happens to come along and make life difficult for people. Instead, people have become alienated before they even become people (or 'subjects' in psychoanalytic terms). The human subject is always already 'split'—divided within itself by the scandalous nature of desire. Second, Lacan gives much greater emphasis than Freud to the role of langauge in relation to desire. One of Lacan's most famous dicta is that 'the unconscious is structured like a language' (see, for example, Lacan 1977a). For Lacan, language is not something that we can use in order to try to make ourselves more comfortable with the alien nature of desire: desire speaks through language and it speaks us. We are, in a way, the senseless puppets of desire as much when we speak or write as when we fall in love.

The interdependence of desire and language in turn is an overt concern of many literary texts. In such texts, there is a recognition that language or meaning can never finally be closed or completed and that desire can never be fulfilled. Robert Browning's poem 'Two in the Campagna', from 1855, is one such text:

1
I wonder do you feel today
   As I have felt since, hand in hand,
We sat down on the grass, to stray
   In spirit better through the land,
This morn of Rome and May?

2
For me, I touched a thought, I know,
   Has tantalized me many times,
(Like turns of thread the spiders throw
   Mocking across our path) for rhymes
To catch at and let go.

3
Help me to hold it! First it left
   The yellowing fennel, run to seed
There, branching from the brickwork's cleft,
   Some old tomb's ruin: yonder weed
Took up the floating weft,

4
Where one small orange cup amassed
   Five beetles,—blind and green they grope
Among the honey-meal: and last,
   Everywhere on the grassy slope
I traced it. Hold it fast!

5
The champaign with its endless fleece
   Of feathery grasses everywhere!

Silence and passion, joy and peace,
　　An everlasting wash of air—
Rome's ghost since her decease.

　　　6
Such life here, through such lengths of hours,
　　Such miracles performed in play,
Such primal naked forms of flowers,
　　Such letting nature have her way
While heaven looks from its towers!

　　　7
How say you? Let us, O my dove,
　　Let us be unashamed of soul,
As earth lies bare to heaven above!
　　How is it under our control
To love or not to love?

　　　8
I would that you were all to me,
　　You that are just so much, no more.
Nor yours nor mine, nor slave nor free!
　　Where does the fault lie? What the core
O' the wound, since wound must be?

　　　9
I would I could adopt your will,
　　See with your eyes, and set my heart
Beating by yours, and drink my fill
　　At your soul's springs,—your part my part
In life, for good and ill.

　　　10
No. I yearn upward, touch you close,
　　Then stand away. I kiss your cheek,
Catch your soul's warmth,—I pluck the rose
　　And love it more than tongue can speak—
Then the good minute goes.

　　　11
Already how am I so far
　　Out of that minute? Must I go
Still like the thistle-ball, no bar,
　　Onward, whenever light winds blow,
Fixed by no friendly star?

12
Just when I seemed about to learn!
  Where is the thread now? Off again!
The old trick! Only I discern—
  Infinite passion, and the pain
Of finite hearts that yearn.

The poem is about the impossibility of capturing the moment of desire, of capturing or 'holding' desire, of ending it. The speaker desires the 'good minute'—analogous to what James Joyce later calls 'epiphany' and Virginia Woolf 'moments of being'—but recognizes its inevitable escape. The second stanza makes it clear that this is also a poem about language, about the tantalizing nature of a moment which poetry attempts to but cannot capture. In stanza ten, the speaker 'pluck[s] the rose / And love[s] it more than tongue can speak' but the moment passes immediately and he asks 'Already how am I so far / Out of that minute?' Exploring the central trope of romantic love—the loss of identity in a merging with the other, the desire evoked in stanza nine in particular— Browning's poem suggests the impossibility and inevitable failure of this desire. The poem traces the paradoxes of romantic love while discerning the impossibility of expressing in language the flux of life, the fluidity and fragility of experience.

If literature and theory alike demonstrate that desire is mobile, endlessly displaced, they also suggest that it is 'mediated', produced through imitation and simulation. Particularly influential in this context has been the recent work of Eve Kosofsky Sedgwick. Developing the ideas of the French poststructuralist critic René Girard, Sedgwick argues that desire is everywhere mediated, that desire is structured by a triangular relation of rivalry. Take three people: A, B and C. A, let us say, desires B. Why? Normally, we would assume that A desires B because B is desirable (at least to A). For Girard and Sedgwick, however, things are rather different. For them, A desires B because B is desired by C. We learn to desire, Girard and Sedgwick argue, by copying others' desires, and our desire is produced, fundamentally, in response to the desire of another. 'The great novelists', Girard claims, 'reveal the imitative nature of desire' and expose what he terms 'the lie of spontaneous desire' (Girard 1965, 14, 16). Now, Sedgwick further points out that most of the examples in Girard's book, *Deceit, Desire, and the Novel* (1965), involve a specific relation of gender, wherein B is a woman and A and C men: the woman is the object of desire, while the two men are rivals. Love stories often concern the rivalry of two men for a woman, in which the rivalry itself indeed becomes more important than the desire for the woman. For Sedgwick, in fact, Western culture in general is structured by a 'crisis of homo/heterosexual definition': 'an understanding of virtually any aspect of modern Western culture must be, not merely incomplete, but damaged in its central substance to the degree that it does not incorporate a critical analysis of modern homo/heterosexual definition' (Sedgwick 1991, 1). Sedgwick develops these insights to suggest that, in Western discourse, in stories, novels, films and so on, relationships are most commonly structured in terms of what she calls 'homosocial desire'. Homosocial desire is not the same as homosexual desire. It does not need to be explicitly expressed as desire, and it is not necessarily physical. In fact, homosocial desire is often concerned rigorously to exclude the possibility of homosexual relations. The traditional male preserves of locker-room, boardroom and clubroom are sites of homosocial bonding which, at the same time, may be virulently homophobic. But in male-dominated society, such relations are fundamental: in all such societies, Sedgwick claims, 'there is a special relationship between male homosocial (*including* homosexual) desire and the structures for maintaining and transmitting patriarchal power' (Sedgwick 1985, 25). Sedgwick argues that a large proportion of the stories, films, songs and other narratives by which Western society imaginatively structures desire can be read as narratives of homosocial desire: while such narratives take as their overt subject the desire of a man for a woman, again and again the really important relationship is that between two men, either as rivals or as colleagues, friends, or associates. Developing the idea first proposed by the French structuralist anthropologist Claude Lévi-Strauss, that in many societies women tend to be tokens of exchange, Sedgwick argues that women are effaced in this triangular structure, as mere objects for barter. At some level, then, patriarchal society excludes women even from relations of desire. Homosocial desire in our society, Sedgwick suggests, is both the most required and the most carefully regimented desire.

Sedgwick offers a highly provocative model for thinking about desire in narrative. According to this model, the workings of desire are inextricably linked to the homophobic, homosocial and patriarchal structures of society. Many canonical works of literature might be reread in these terms. This is not to suggest that the Great Tradition is full of closet homosexuality, for example, just waiting to be 'outed'. Rather, it is to suggest that homosocial desire in all its forms is central to the workings of what we might like to think of simply as 'heterosexual' writing. The notions of heterosexual and homosexual need to be rethought. (For a fuller discussion of these issues, see 'Queer', Chapter 20, below.) Shakespeare's *Hamlet* (*c*.1601), for example, concerns not only the murder of Hamlet's father and its revenge, but also a relation of rivalry between Prince Hamlet (as a surrogate for his father, King Hamlet) and Hamlet's uncle, Claudius (the dead King's brother), over the Queen. Emily Brontë's *Wuthering Heights* (1847) may gain much of its power from the barely hidden conflicts of homosocial desire between Heathcliff and other men, resulting in rivalry and extraordinary violence. In its focus on the triangle of two men (Eugene Wrayburn and Bradley Headstone) and one woman (Lizzie Hexam), Charles Dicken's *Our Mutual Friend* (1865) is a superb, if disturbing, example of the potentially murderous erotic dynamic that exists between men. Thomas Hardy's *Tess of the D'Urbevilles* (1891), a novel that appears to focus on the eponymous and tragic heroine, is also structured by rivalry between two men who desire her, Angel Clare and Alec D'Urbeville. D.H. Lawrence's *Women in Love* (1921), while overtly about two men and their love for two women, is also, and perhaps more importantly, about the relationship between the two men, Gerald and Birkin.

Desire, then, is both a fundamental topic of literary texts and fundamental to the very experience of reading. But one of the things that literary texts consistently suggest is that desire is paradoxical, mobile, mediated. And perhaps the homophobia that may have ultimately resulted in the death of Alan Turing can itself be understood in terms of a distortion or displacement of desire—a fear of homosexuality, a fear of the other, which is bound up in society's anxieties about such mobilities and mediations. One of the principal responsibilities of contemporary literary criticism and theory lies in the exposure, questioning and transformation of the rigid oppositions that result in such fear and oppression.

Further reading

Foucault's *The History of Sexuality: An Introduction* (1981) is a crucial starting point for thinking about desire. Similarly influential is Deleuze and Guattari's difficult but compelling *Anti-Oedipus* (1983). Peter Brooks offers a fascinating account of the reader's desire in *Reading for the Plot* (1984), while Catherine Belsey presents a readable poststructuralist account of a number of literary texts of desire in her *Desire: Love*

Stories in Western Culture (1994). For two excellent brief accounts of the work of Lacan, see the introductory books by Bowie (1991) and the Weber (1992). On the discourse of homosexual desire and homophobia, see Jonathan Dollimore's influential book *Sexual Dissidence* (1991), and for a collection of essays on lesbian criticism and theory, see Munt, ed., *New Lesbian Criticism* (1992). On the importance of heterosexual desire for the development of the novel in the nineteenth century, see Joseph Allen Boone, *Tradition and Counter Tradition* (1987). For a historically wide-ranging discussion of issues of desire in relation to death, see Dollimore's *Death, Desire and Loss in Western Culture* (1998).

Queer

Queer's a queer word.

The entry of the word 'queer' into the English language is itself a study in the queer ways of words. *Chambers Dictionary* defines the adjective as follows: 'odd, singular, quaint: open to suspicion: counterfeit: slightly mad: having a sensation of coming sickness: sick, ill (*dial[ect]*): homosexual (*slang*)'. What's queer about this synonymatic definition is the way in which it includes three apparently unrelated senses for the 'same' word—clustering around ideas of strangeness, sickness and homosexuality. One question immediately arises: how do you get from 'queer' as 'singular' or 'quaint' or 'slightly mad' or 'ill' to 'queer' as 'homosexual'? While the answer may seem to some to be self-evident, the process is worth examining in greater detail. The *Oxford English Dictionary* shows the slippage from one sense to the other in action: its extensive historical account of the word reveals that in fact there was a delay of more than four hundred years between the introduction of the 'odd' or 'singular' sense of the word into English and the introduction of its 'homosexual' sense. The first entry for 'queer' in the *OED* comes from the early sixteenth century (Dunbar's 'Heir cumis awin quir Clerk', from 1508), while the first entry for the word in its homosexual sense is from 1922 in a publication by the Children's Bureau of the US Department of Labor. The latter comes from the straight (but also rather queer) language of a report entitled *The Practical Value of the Scientific Study of Juvenile Delinquents*, which refers to the idea that 'A young man, easily ascertainable to be unusually fine in other characteristics, is probably "queer" in sex tendency'. The sentence, immortalized as an entry in the *OED* simply by virtue of its priority as the first recorded usage of the word, is intriguing for a number of reasons. It makes stereotypical assumptions about certain 'characteristics', it expresses the idea that queerness is written on the body and implicitly identifies it with delinquency or illness. But it also holds the word at arm's length—with so-called 'scare-quotes'—as if the term is not fully accepted or acceptable, or as if the word is still in process, moving from a sense of oddness to a (related) sense of homosexuality. Homosexuality is 'queer', then, because of the perceived queerness of queers, their difference from 'us' (scientists, US Department of Labor officials, sociologists, and so on): queers are a category apart, a self-defining and identifiable group determined precisely by the queer difference of its members from the regime of the normal—from what Adrienne Rich, the contemporary lesbian poet and critic, calls 'compulsory heterosexuality' (Rich 1986).

But the story of 'queer' is not over yet. For the next seventy years or so, 'queer' gained currency in the English language in the United States and elsewhere as (usually) a derogatory term for (usually male) homosexual; it was combined with 'coot' to form the dismissive phrase 'queer as a coot'; and, in the 1960s and 1970s, was combined with 'bashing' to denote (and doubtless to help legitimize) verbal and physical violence against those who were, or who were perceived to be, homosexual. In the late 1980s and early 1990s, however, partly in response to the spread of AIDS among gay men, the word took a queer turn: homosexuals themselves began to 'reclaim' the word, to use it in place of the gender-specific and arguably effete term 'gay' or the clinical and cheerless 'homosexual' or the polite and even mythological-sounding 'lesbian'. 'Queer' becomes a term of pride and celebratory self-assertion, of difference affirmed and affirmative difference. The very reason for the use of 'queer' to denote homosexuality in the first place—the sense that homosexuality is associated with singularity and difference—is also inherited in this act of linguistic reappropriation, but the values afforded such strangeness are reversed. The fact that queers are different from 'straight' people is seen as a source of power and pride—and 'straight' now becomes a term with potentially negative connotations (conventional, dull, unadventurous). 'Queer' also has the advantage of being an inclusive term which gains in prestige and power just in so much as it shakes up our codes and codings of male and female, or masculinity and femininity, or bi-, hetero- and homo-. As Eve Kosofsky Sedgwick comments, 'queer' can refer to 'the open mesh of possibilities, gaps, overlaps, dissonances and resonances, lapses and excesses of meaning when the constituent elements of anyone's gender, of anyone's sexuality aren't made (or *can't be* made) to signify monolithically' (Sedgwick

1994, 8). Essentially, then, 'queer' challenges all gender and sexual essentialisms.

In homage to this brilliant queering of 'queer', its (re-)appropriation as a device for the social and political empowerment of certain more or less defined, more or less discrete, more or less oppressed sexual identities, and linking up with our comments elsewhere on the association of literary texts with the uncanny or the strange, we would like to suggest that literature is itself a little (and sometimes more than a little) queer. By this we mean two things. Firstly, we want to suggest that there is an eminent tradition of queer writing in English, writing by men and women who are more or less permanently, more or less openly, more or less explicitly, queer and writing about queerness. For reasons that will become clear, this tradition is all but invisible before the late nineteenth century, although it arguably includes Marlowe, Shakespeare, the debauchee Lord Rochester, the eighteenth-century poet Katherine Philips, Henry Mackenzie (author of the novel of exquisite sensitivity *The Man of Feeling* [1771]), Matthew Lewis (author of the Gothic high-camp novel *The Monk* [1796]), Lord Byron, Walt Whitman and Herman Melville. But the late nineteenth- and twentieth-century canon is full of authors who are queer, who write homoerotic poetry or write about the experience of homosexual desire—including Gerard Manley Hopkins, Algernon Swinburne, Oscar Wilde, A.E. Housman, Virginia Woolf, Vita Sackville-West, Djuna Barnes, D.H. Lawrence, Dorothy Richardson, Charlotte Mew, H.D., Rosamund Lehmann, Radclyffe Hall, T.E. Lawrence, E.M. Forster, Elizabeth Bowen, W.H. Auden, Christopher Isherwood, Compton Mackenzie, Tennessee Williams, Alan Ginsberg, Gore Vidal, Truman Capote, James Baldwin, Patrick White, William Burroughs, Edmund White, Thom Gunn, Adrienne Rich, Joe Orton, Alice Walker, Jeanette Winterson, John Ashbery, Hanif Kureishi and innumerable others. We might say that there is a canon of queer writers in modern literature, except that the 'straight' canon is itself everywhere inhabited by queers (many of the writers listed above, that is to say, are central to the canon of literature in English, whether they are read as queer or straight).

Our second reason for talking about literature as 'a little (and sometimes more than a little) queer' is to suggest that literary texts in general might be open to what has been called 'queer reading'. Some of the strangeness or uncanniness, some of the power and fascination of literary texts, that is to say, has to do with the singular space which they offer for thinking (differently) about gender and sexuality. This point is illustrated by the work of Eve Sedgwick, one of the most influential queer theorists of recent years, whose notion of 'homosocial desire' we discuss, above, in our chapter on 'Desire'. In an essay entitled 'The Beast in the Closet' (first published in 1986), Sedgwick discusses Henry James's short story 'The Beast in the Jungle' (1903). James's story is an apparently 'straight' story about John Marcher, a confirmed bachelor, who has a terrible and overwhelming secret (the 'beast' of the title), a secret which never is, never could be, articulated, but which is nevertheless understood by his friend May Bartram, a woman who supports him and who, it is clear, could—or should—have been his lover or wife. In a stunning reading of the story, Sedgwick examines a number of aspects of the story and its discursive contexts. She discusses the figure of the bachelor in the late nineteenth century, for example, as a role that allowed certain men to avoid the rigorous demands of the compulsorily heterosexual society in which they lived. (James himself, Sedgwick argues, was a bachelor whose complex sexuality seems to have been notable as much for the obstinacy of its heterosexuality as for anything else.) Sedgwick considers the dynamics of 'male homosexual panic' as the unmanageable fear of homosexuality among heterosexuals, a fear that would also appear to be based on the heterosexual male's fear of his own desire for other men. Sedgwick then examines certain linguistic and rhetorical aspects of the apparently heterosexual story and shows how, viewed in this light, the story turns queer. Thus Sedgwick notes that the story uses the word 'queer' on a number of occasions to denote John Marcher's condition: while it is clear that the primary sense of the word denotes a certain 'strangeness' (after all, the homosexual sense of 'queer' was not an explicit part of its official meaning in 1903), nevertheless, as we have seen, the move within 'queer' from 'strange' to 'homosexual' is never far away—and is not as queer as it might seem. In this respect, James's use of the word may be seen to be haunted by its semantic developments a few years later and to raise the spectre of an unacknowledged difficulty concerning Marcher's sexual identity. Sedgwick also notes a number of less specific 'lexical pointers', all of which are 'highly equivocal' but which add up to a queering of the whole story. Phrases such as Marcher's 'singularity', 'the thing [May Bartram] knew, which grew to be at last . . . never mentioned between them save as "the real truth" about him', 'his queer consciousness', 'dreadful things . . . I couldn't name', 'his unhappy perversion', and so on (quoted in Sedgwick 1994, 203), convey a strong sense of specifically *sexual* disturbance in Marcher's character. In a complex and enthralling piece of literary critical detective-work, Sedgwick develops a reading of the text which compellingly suggests the 'cataclysm' of Marcher's condition to be that of (in Oscar Wilde's poignant formulation) the 'love that dare not speak its name', the unacknowledged and unacknowledgeable homosexuality of his queerness. As far as the normative values of straight society are concerned, queerness is devastatingly and catastrophically *queer*: the 'straight' Marcher's problem is his inability to deal with the problem of (his) queerness.

In her reading of the story, however, Sedgwick is not attempting to argue, definitively, that Marcher (or James, for that matter) is in any simple sense homosexual. Instead, she is queering the narrative by thinking through its linguistic and conceptual slippages and their engagements with the discourse that emerges out of and indeed energizes the otherwise bland, monolithic certainties of heterosexuality. Sedgwick attempts to bring out (from the closet, so to speak) the extent to which the discourse of homosexuality—the heterosexual discourse of homosexuality, that is to say, the way that homosexuality is conceived and expressed by so-called 'heterosexuals'—may be read in a text that is apparently concerned with very different matters. And Sedgwick's reading powerfully demonstrates that the discourse of heterosexuality is itself dependent upon that of homosexuality, governed, even defined, by that which it excludes. There is something rather queer, in other words, about being straight.

As well as opening up new ways of reading 'straight' literary texts, then, queer theory—such as recent work by Michel Foucault, Eve Sedgwick, Judith Butler, Leo Bersani, Alan Sinfield, Jonathan Dollimore, Joseph Bristow and others—has begun to challenge our ideas about gender and sexuality by querying (or queerying) the very basis of the categories we use to talk about ourselves, us queers and us straights. Queer theory, that is to say, queers the pitch as far as sexuality is concerned. As a number of theorists have commented, there is something rather curious, rather queer, about the way in which we divide our human and social worlds into two supposedly discrete (if not always discreet) categories. Of all the possible categories that are available to us to define ourselves and others—our wealth (or lack of it), class, height, hair colour, dietary preferences, shoe size, baldness or otherwise, political or religious beliefs, aesthetic preferences, choice of holiday destination or hi-fi manufacturer—the one that our culture has fixed upon to define us most profoundly, in some respects perhaps even beyond that of ethnic origin, race or skin colour, is that of sexual preference, the sex of the person whom we desire. Indeed, as Leo Bersani remarks, 'Unlike racism, homophobia is entirely a response to an internal possibility' (Bersani 1995, 27). As David Halperin has commented, however, 'it is not immediately evident that differences in sexual preference are by their very nature more revealing about the temperament of individual human beings, more significant determinants of personal identity, than, for example, differences in dietary preference' (Halperin 1990, 26). The comment invites us to imagine a world, or a society, in which one's identity would be defined by one's choice of food, a world in which, say, vegetarians would regularly be discriminated against in terms of their careers (they would not be allowed to join the army, for example, for fear that they might seduce others into vegetarianism); would be subject to physical and verbal abuse while walking quietly in the streets of our cities (veggie-bashing, it would be called, and would be caused by veggiephobia, the fear of being forced to eat a plate of vegetables or even of finding out that one is, deep down, oneself a vegetarian); would be disqualified from adopting children because of the fear that such children would lack a balanced diet in the crucial early years of their physical and mental development; would often socialize in special veggie bars and clubs avoided by carnivores; and would be, or would be thought to be, immediately recognizable by the way they walked, their clothes, their hairstyles, and their general demeanour. This imagined world might remind us of the pervasiveness and power of sexual preference as a determiner of our everyday lives. Indeed, the absurdity of this fictional scenario brings home how deeply embedded in our thinking is our definition of gender and sexual preference: Michel Foucault makes the point forcefully in an interview when he remarks that 'ever since Christianity, the West has not stopped saying: "To know who you are, find out about your sex." Sex has always been the focal point where, besides the future of our species, our "truth" as human subjects is tied up' (Foucault 1980a, 3). In this context we might think about how odd it is, how queer, that our social worlds and our social prejudices are organized around a choice—the sex of our sexual partners—which in some ways is similar to choices about eating, or not eating, meat.

One of the major projects of queer theory has been to examine the ways in which, in fact, the categories of desire by which we regulate our social and sexual worlds are not as fixed and immutable, not as 'natural' and self-evident, as we might like to think. Indeed, according to the influential argument of Michel Foucault, our ideas about hetero- and homo-sexuality are a function of the 'invention' of homosexuality in the late nineteenth century. While the precise historical configurations of any such 'invention' have been challenged by historians of sexuality, many of whom see the late eighteenth century as the crucial period of redefinition, Foucault's argument has been highly important in the development of queer theory. But it is crucial to understand that when Foucault claims that homosexuality was invented at a particular time in the recent past he is not arguing that men did not love, desire and have sex with other men, or women with women, before that time. Rather, he is suggesting that what many people tend to think of as the clear, unequivocal distinction between *being* homosexual or *being* straight—the sense that you *are* one or the other, and the sense that *who you are* is defined by that distinction—is an aspect of sexual relationships and personal identity which has developed only very recently. According to Foucault, during the nineteenth century a series of shifts in the discourses of medicine, law, religion, politics and social analysis combined to produce the homosexual as a discrete identity. In particular, while medicine began to define a certain type of behaviour and certain desires as characteristic of a certain 'type' of person (the so-called 'invert'), the law redefined sexual acts between men as 'gross indecency' (an offence instituted in the so-called 'Labouchére Amendment' added to a law passed in the United Kingdom in 1885 which was primarily concerned with the regulation of prostitution). The new law criminalized sex between men (it simply ignored sex between women), by contrast with an older law, against 'sodomy', which covered certain forms of sex between men and women as well as various other kinds of 'unspeakable' acts, sexual and otherwise. Thus, for example, Jeffrey Weeks points out that nineteenth-century society imprisoned together atheists, the mute and sodomites, suggesting a strange homology of criminality (Weeks 1998, 693). As a result, the homosexual comes to be seen as a particular type of person, as having a particular identity. In an eloquent and forceful passage from *The History of Sexuality: An Introduction*, Foucault argues as follows:

> As defined by the ancient civil or canonical codes, sodomy was a category of forbidden acts; their perpetrator was nothing more than the juridical subject of them. The nineteenth-century homosexual became a personage, a past, a case history, and a childhood, in addition to being a type of life, a life form, and a morphology, with an indiscreet anatomy and possibly a mysterious physiology. Nothing that went into his total composition was unaffected by his sexuality.

It was everywhere present in him: at the root of all his actions because it was their insidious and indefinitely active principle; written immodestly on his face and body because it was a secret that always gave itself away. It was consubstantial with him, less as a habitual sin than as a singular nature . . . Homosexuality appeared as one of the forms of sexuality when it was transposed from the practice of sodomy onto a kind of interior androgyny, a hermaphrodism of the soul. The sodomite had been a temporary aberration; the homosexual was now a species. (Foucault 1981, 43)

Foucault is arguing that homosexuality as an *identity* is more or less invisible before the mid to late nineteenth century. In other words, in the context of thinking about, say, Shakespeare, asking the question of whether or not he was homosexual is, in effect, an anachronism, inappropriate to the specific ways in which sexuality and sexual identity were constructed, experienced and defined in the late sixteenth and early seventeenth centuries.

The notion of the historically and culturally constructed nature of sexuality, the idea that sexualities are differently defined and differently experienced at different times, is taken one step further by the influential theorist of gender and sexuality Judith Butler. For Butler, gender and sexuality are performative, rather than fixed or determined by biology or 'nature': gender identity 'is performatively constituted by the very "expressions" that are said to be its results' (Butler 1990, 25). 'I'm queer' is not simply a descriptive statement but makes something happen: it not only states but affirms and even creates the identity it refers to. According to this argument, in fact, the more of a man or the more of a woman you are, the more obviously your masculinity or femininity is a performative construct, the more overtly it is acted out. Both gender and sexuality, for Butler, are always kinds of drag acts so that theatrical drag acts play out the implicit logic of sex and gender identity according to which our lives are, more generally, determined. As an example of such a performance of gender and sexuality Butler reminds us of Aretha Franklin's line 'you make me feel like a natural woman'. As Butler remarks, on first sight the line seems to be affirming the notion of the naturalness of gender and sexuality: the singer's love for the man makes her a *natural* woman. Butler comments that the line seems to indicate that 'there is no breakage, no discontinuity between "sex" as biological facticity and essence, or between gender and sexuality' (Butler 1991, 27). But when we think a little more carefully we see that this naturalness is both something that is *learnt* or *produced* ('you *make* me feel . . .'), and something that is *imitated* ('you make me feel *like* . . .'). Playing out and articulating the performative logic of gender and sexuality, Aretha Franklin is singing about it, wittingly or not, as a kind of 'heterosexual drag' (28). This, for Butler, is indicative of the way that all sexualities—homo-, hetero-, bi- and other—are forms of drag, performances of sex and of gender.

'Shakespeare', declares Harold Bloom, 'largely invented us' (Bloom 1994, 40). One way of understanding this claim would be in relation to the cultural construction of gender and sexuality. Reading Shakespeare can help us to think about ways in which sexuality is an unstable site of conflict and transgression, historically contingent, mobile, a performance. Writing at a time before categories of homo- and heterosexual desire had been institutionalized, medicalized, rigidified and policed, Shakespeare's writing questions what it means to be a man or a woman, and what it means, as a man and as a woman, to desire men and to desire women. We might end by thinking about Shakespeare's sonnet 20, a key text in debates surrounding his representations of sexuality and sexual identity: in this sonnet, as Bruce Smith comments, 'for the poet, for his readers, and presumably for the young man', issues of love and sexuality 'reach a crisis' (Smith 1994, 249). Here is a poem that has fascinated (and indeed horrified) readers and critics through the centuries, a poem by a man addressed to a man, his 'master mistress', which thinks about masculinity and femininity and thinks about the different ways in which they inhabit male and female bodies, thinks about how homo- and hetero-eroticism are performed, played out in language. It is a poem that both plays on stereotypes of gender and sexuality (including misogyny) and, at the same time, disorientates them, queers them, plays with the idea of a 'natural' gender and sexuality but also with the idea of the constructedness of such identities. This is a natural wo/man: a man who is all man, by nature 'pricked out', but who is at the same time, curiously, queerly, female, his 'woman's face' by 'nature' 'painted':

> A woman's face, with nature's own hand painted,
> Hast thou, the master mistress of my passion—
> A woman's gentle heart, but not acquainted
> With shifting change, as is false women's fashion;
> An eye more bright than theirs, less false in rolling,
> Gilding the object whereupon it gazeth;
> A man in hue all hues in his controlling,
> Which steals men's eyes and women's souls amazeth.

And for a woman wert thou first created,
Till nature as she wrought thee fell a-doting,
And by addition me of thee defeated,
By adding one thing to my purpose nothing.
But since she pricked thee out for women's pleasure,
Mine be thy love, and thy love's use their treasure.

Further reading

Eve Kosofsky Sedgwick's books *Between Men* (1985), *The Epistemology of the Closet* (1991) and *Tendencies* (1994) present highly influential accounts of homosocial and homosexual desire focusing on a series of (mainly) nineteenth- and twentieth-century texts. The opening two chapters of the groundbreaking *Between Men* offer a good starting point. Alan Sinfield's brisk, polemical and entertaining books *Cultural Politics—Queer Reading* (1994) and *The Wilde Century: Effeminacy, Oscar Wilde and the Queer Moment* (1994) provide accessible accounts of many of the ideas encountered in this chapter. A more detailed and scholarly discussion of queer sexuality in Renaissance England is Bruce Smith's *Homosexual Desire in Shakespeare's England* (1994). Correspondingly, for a study of 'effeminate England' since 1885, see Joseph Bristow (1995). For a brilliant and often excoriating examination of some of the presuppositions and prejudices surrounding cultural representations of homosexuality (including those of 'queer theorists' themselves), see Leo Bersani's *Homos* (1995).

Suspense

In a moment, we shall say something that may be rather shocking. In the meantime, we propose to describe two kinds of suspense, resolved and unresolved. 'Resolved' suspense is usually associated with thrillers, detective stories, gothic novels, tales of mystery and the supernatural, and romances. The Italian novelist and literary theorist Umberto Eco uses the term 'closed texts' for such narratives, as contrasted with 'open texts' which leave the reader in doubt or uncertainty (Eco 1979). In closed texts, the murderer is found, the mystery resolved, the ghost exposed as a mechanical illusion, or the lovers are able to consummate their love. In these cases, suspense relies for its resolution on the revelation of a secret or secrets. Characteristically, it involves the construal or repeated withholding of a particular answer to the question of what will happen next. Resolved suspense can also be created by delaying an event that we know will happen. This is especially clear in examples from cinema. We feel certain that the woman behind the shower curtain cannot escape the raised dagger of the psycho-killer, but for a few seemingly endless moments the fulfilment of this expectation is delayed. Similarly, in *Fatal Attraction* the pet rabbit is never going to avoid the boiling pot, and in *Silence of the Lambs* it is only a matter of time before Hannibal the cannibal lives up to his name and gets his unjust dessert. Here suspense is not so much created by a hermeneutic gap, by the reader's ignorance, as by our expectation of an event which is delayed: we know *what* is going to happen, we just don't know *when*. These are kinds of narrative suspense, then, that can be defined in terms of expectation, delay and resolution.

One of the most notorious instances of literary suspense is Henry James's novella *The Turn of the Screw* (1898). In this story, the reader's expectation of an ending is screwed to an excruciating pitch of tension (the story is, not least, about suspense itself, as its title might indicate). The suspense of this haunting story rests largely on whether the governess actually sees ghosts and detects real evil, or whether the story is, rather, a psychological case-study of a disturbed mind. The critical response to the story has tended to argue for one reading or the other. Recently, however, critics have recognized that the choice of interpretation—the choice, finally, of which story we think we are reading—is irresolvable. Indeed, critics have realized that this uncanny and unsettling suspense of interpretation is itself part of what makes the story so terrifying: *The Turn of the Screw* is *suspended* between two mutually exclusive readings. While the tale builds up to an extraordinary pitch of narrative suspense, our sense of what happens at the end of the story may never finally be resolved. James manages to exploit a fundamentally ambivalent narrative structure (the story is told by the governess herself, so there is no one to tell us whether or not she is mad), and to 'end' his story in a kind of *open* suspense, a suspense without end. In particular, James continually provides us with pointers or markers to a final resolution, with suggestions of ghosts, telepathy and evil on the one hand, and of madness on the other, making us wait for a final resolution of ambiguities which never arrives. In Chapter 9, for example, the governess says of the two children Miles and Flora that 'There were moments when, by an irresistible impulse, I found myself catching them up and pressing them to my heart' (131). The sentence foreshadows in a suspenseful and undecidable way the extraordinary ending of the story, where the governess does, literally, 'catch' Miles: 'I caught him, yes, I held him— it may be imagined with what a passion' (198). In both cases, however, the *force* of this catching—how forceful it is, and how conscious or rational, what its intention is—is suspended. Is the governess protecting Miles or smothering him? We are left, then, in a state of hermeneutic suspense, of interpretative uncertainty—unable to know, finally, how to read James's story. Suspense, in this case, is open.

Another way to think about this is in terms of a suspense which, according to Jacques Derrida, is peculiarly literary: 'There is no literature', claims Derrida, 'without a *suspended* relation to meaning and reference' (Derrida 1992a, 48). We might want to think of the irresolution of James's suspense simply as carelessness or as a mistake—the author has not made his meaning clear. As Derrida suggests, however, literary texts can be characterized precisely in terms of unresolved suspense. And this suspense concerns, in the first place, the status of the very worlds to which literary texts refer. Critics use various terms to describe

such suspenseful effects: ambiguity, ambivalence, equivocality, indeterminacy, undecidability, uncertainty, aporia, gap, hiatus. All of these
words may be applied to the effects of suspense achieved by James's
story.

In addition to such narrative suspense, effects of suspense can be
produced on a more local and less melodramatic scale by aspects of
syntax and versification, by the very language of the text. James, in
fact, is famous for a peculiarly suspenseful sentence structure which
complements the intensity of narrative suspense in stories such as *The
Turn of the Screw*. The story opens in the form of a 'frame narrative': a
group of people get together to tell stories, one of which is that of the
governess. Here is the opening sentence of the story:

> The story had held us, round the fire, sufficiently breathless, but
> except the obvious remark that it was gruesome, as, on Christmas
> eve in an old house, a strange tale should essentially be, I remember
> no comment uttered till somebody happened to say that it was the
> only case he had met in which such a visitation had fallen on a child.
> (81)

Not only is this sentence *about* suspense—the suspense of being 'held'
by a story, the holding of breath and the withholding of comments—but
it is also syntactically structured by suspense. The final word, 'child', is
the kernel of the sentence, its centre, but the word is withheld until the
end of the sentence. Before that, the sentence develops through multiple
subclauses and syntactical digressions. Henry James's prose, then, the
syntax of his sentences, is highly suspenseful.

The Turn of the Screw turns on suspense—indeed turns, self-
reflexively, on the very idea of 'turns'. Chapter 9, again, is exemplary.
The governess is reading Henry Fielding's *Amelia* alone at night: 'I
found myself, at the turn of a page and with his spell all scattered,
looking straight up . . .' (133). She leaves her room and walks into the
hall, where at 'the great turn of the staircase' (134) she sees, for the
third time, the ghost of Peter Quint. The chapter ends with a description
of this ghost disappearing into 'the silence itself': 'I definitely saw it
turn, as I might have seen the low wretch to which it had once belonged
turn on receipt of an order' as it disappears 'into the darkness in which
the next bend was lost' (135). The 'next bend' may be in the darkness
of the staircase, but it is also the next chapter of the story, the dark
bend or turn of narrative. It is not only the governess, then, who sees

or hallucinates a ghostly presence in the turns: our own reading is suspended on the turns of the narrative.

Verse also relies on turns. In particular, the fact that the word 'verse'
comes from the Latin *vertere*, 'to turn', might alert us to the way in
which verse is wedded to the turns of line endings, suspenseful places
of ghostly pausation. In addition to the suspense as we turn from one
line to the next, verse produces its own forms of suspense through the
exploitation of the possibilities of rhythm. Comparatively rudimentary
verse-forms, such as those of nursery rhymes and ballads, for example,
are notable for the way in which they generate suspense through rhythmical repetition, by building into the poetry the expectation of a repetition. The opening to the traditional Scottish ballad 'Sir Patrick Spens'
is one such example:

> The King sits in Dumferling toune,
>   Drinking the blude-reid wine:
> O whar will I get a guid sailor,
>   To sail this schip of mine?

Much of the force of this powerfully haunting and uncanny poem (one
that, in many ways, anticipates such pseudo-medieval ballads as Coleridge's 'The Ancient Mariner' and Keats's 'La Belle Dame sans Merci') is
achieved through the regularity of its metrical arrangement (the regular
four-beat first line and three-beat second line, which continues throughout the poem). Together with the regular rhyming of lines two and four
of each stanza, the prosody of the poem adds up—in the expectation
and fulfilment of rhythmical suspense—to one of the most compelling
of its pleasures.

Effects of rhythmical suspense are also explored in more complex
ways by poets such as Thomas Hardy. Hardy's poetry is notable not
least for the wide range of its verse-forms. 'Neutral Tones' (written in
1867, first published in 1898) enacts various effects of suspense through
rhythm:

> We stood by a pond that winter day,
> And the sun was white, as though chidden of God,
> And a few leaves lay on the starving sod;
>   —They had fallen from an ash, and were gray.
>
> Your eyes on me were as eyes that rove
> Over tedious riddles of years ago;

> And some words played between us to and fro
> On which lost the more by our love.
>
> The smile on your mouth was the deadest thing
> Alive enough to have strength to die;
> And a grin of bitterness swept thereby
> Like an ominous bird a-wing . . .
>
> Since then, keen lessons that love deceives,
> And wrings with wrong, have shaped to me
> Your face, and the God-curst sun, and a tree,
> And a pond edged with grayish leaves.

While not strictly regular, the rhythm of the first three lines of each stanza is more or less regular, consisting of four sets of one or two weak (or 'short') [·] stresses followed by one strong (or long) one [—]: Wė stōōd | bẏ ȧ pōnd | thȧt wīn | tėr dāy. The final line of each stanza, however, lacks one 'foot', having only three combinations of weak and strong stress: Thėy hȧd fāllen | frȯm ȧn ash, | ȧnd wėre grāy. The regularity of the first three lines of each stanza is disappointed. This gives an effect of blankness, of something missing, of incomplete suspense. This effect is related to the theme of the poem, its sense of blank hopelessness: the poem is concerned with something missing, a lack, which is inexpressible. This, then, is just one example of the many ways in which poetry is able to create effects of suspense in rhythm such that the *form* of the poem is inseparable from its *content*.

As we have already suggested, poetry can also exploit line endings for effects of suspense. The neo-classical poetry of Alexander Pope, for example, plays on the suspenseful formalities of rhyming couplets. The following lines from Pope's poem 'An Essay on Criticism' (1711) generate suspense through rhyme, rhythm and antithesis:

> *True wit* is *Nature* to Advantage drest,
> What oft was *Thought*, but ne'er so well Exprest . . .
> (lines 297–8)

The fact that the whole of this long poem is in the form of rhyming couplets means that the first line creates the expectation of a second line which will end in the rhyme 'est' and either develop, answer, or repeat its sense. And we are not disappointed. The second line both develops and explains the first, creating an analogy between thought and nature on the one hand, and clothing and expression on the other, to define 'true wit'. Owing to the regularity of the verse-form, the first line creates an expectation of such an answering line and, although the lines are end-stopped (they do not continue syntactically from one line to the next), they produce the expectation of such an answer: the sense of the first line is suspended until its completion in the next.

Writing almost a century later, William Wordsworth also exploits the suspenseful effects of verse, in particular of line endings, but does so very differently. Consider, for example, his famous lyric 'A Slumber did my Spirit Seal' (1800):

> A slumber did my spirit seal;
> I had no human fears:
> She seemed a thing that could not feel
> The touch of earthly years.
>
> No motion has she now, no force;
> She neither hears nor sees,
> Rolled round in earth's diurnal course
> With rocks and stones and trees.

This poem is usually understood to be about a young girl who has died, and critics usually relate it to other poems which were written by Wordsworth at about the same time and which concern a girl named Lucy. The speaker appears to be lamenting not only the girl's death, but also his own ignorance, the fact that he remained unaware that she might die when she was alive. Unlike Pope's poem in almost every other respect, Wordsworth's poem is similar in that most of its lines are end-stopped. Only line three is run on or enjambed: there is no punctuation after the word 'feel', and the next line is required for syntactical completion. In fact, the end of this line exploits not only syntactical but also hermeneutic suspense. After all, it would be possible to read line three as syntactically complete: 'She seemed a thing that could not feel'. But this produces a very different meaning from what we find if we continue to the next line—'She seemed a thing that could not feel / The touch of earthly years'. There is a significant difference between not being able to feel, and not being able to feel 'the touch of earthly years'. The first possibility gives us the sense that she—like, apparently, the speaker, in line one—is anaesthetized, closed off, to all sensation and all emotion. The second possibility gives us the sense that this was a young girl who seemed as if she would never grow old or die. What the poem achieves with this line-break, this turn, is to keep both meanings in suspense.

While the latter is no doubt the 'correct' reading—we cannot simply ignore line four, once we have read it—the apparent completion offered by line three in isolation remains to haunt this latter sense.

As with our discussion of Henry James, we find that examples of resolved or closed suspense can in fact be read as open—as examples of the unresolved. Wordsworth's poem prompts a number of undecidable questions, sites of irresolvable suspension. In the very opening line of the poem, for example, it is not clear whether 'my spirit' sealed a slumber or a slumber sealed 'my spirit': in any case it is very difficult to know what the three words ('slumber', 'spirit', 'seal'), either separately or together, are referring to. Likewise, while we have assumed that the referent of 'she' in line three is a girl, Lucy, the word can also be understood to refer back to 'my spirit' in line one. There is, in fact, no final way of determining which reading is 'correct'. While we may want to choose one reading over the other, we have no way to justify such a choice: the point is undecidable or equivocal. And the difference has significant implications for any reading of the poem. In the first place, while the poem appears to be about the relationship between the speaker and a girl, the equivocal reference of 'she' means that we can no longer be sure that the object of the speaker's interest is a person outside of himself, rather than his own 'spirit'. As Paul de Man comments in his reading of this poem in his essay 'The Rhetoric of Temporality', 'Wordsworth is one of the few poets who can write proleptically about their own death and speak, as it were, from beyond their own graves. The "she" in the poem', de Man continues, 'is in fact large enough to encompass Wordsworth as well' (de Man 1983, 225). Rather differently, it may be that this equivocal reference suggests something very important about mourning itself—that in mourning, the object of our grief is neither simply inside nor simply outside the one who mourns. The suspense of reference in this context might be connected to another of the themes of the poem—closure. The speaker talks of his spirit being 'sealed', of 'she' being untouchable in the first stanza, and in the second of 'she' being without motion, force or sensory perception, 'rolled round' with the earth as if sealed in a grave. This sense of closure may even be reinforced by the end-stopped rhymes of each stanza. In all of these ways, the poem is 'about' a sense of closure—being sealed, enclosed, finished, dead. And yet the closure that the poem so intensively suggests is in dynamic tension with the undecidable suspense of reference—with, indeed, the poem's *meaning*. Far from being closed, in fact, the poem is undecidably suspended. Once we recognize the central importance of the tension between what we have called closed and open suspense in the poem, it becomes available as a means with which to map many of the poem's features. In particular, we might recognize that the poem is suspended by the uncanny gap of time between stanza one and stanza two, that moment outside the poem when 'she' dies, the unspoken, perhaps unspeakable event of a death which at once haunts and generates the poem. Wordsworth's poem thus enacts a drama of suspense, an allegory of closure *and* undecidability.

Ambiguity and undecidability have been central to literary criticism and theory in the twentieth century. One of the most influential works of modern Anglo-American criticism, for example, is William Empson's *Seven Types of Ambiguity* (1930; 3rd edn 1953). In the middle decades of the century, partly as a response to Empson's book, the so-called new critics focused on ambiguity as a major concern of literary texts. More recently, poststructuralist critics have emphasized the notion of undecidability. The difference between new critical ambiguity and poststructuralist undecidability, though apparently minimal, is, in fact, fundamental. For the new critics, ambiguity produces a complex but organic whole, a unity wherein ambiguity brings together disparate elements. For poststructuralist critics, by contrast, undecidability opens up a gap, a rift in the text which can never be fully sealed. Undecidability opens the text to multiple readings, it destabilizes the reader's sense of the certainty of any particular reading, and ultimately threatens to undermine the very stability of any reading position, the very identity of any reader (as Søren Kierkegaard remarks, 'the moment of decision is madness'). Suspensions of meaning bypass the reductive and constricting determination of what is now recognized to be the illusion of a single, final, determined 'meaning'. To think in terms of undecidability, however, is not to advocate the equal legitimacy of any and every interpretation: to acknowledge aporias or suspensions of meaning involves the responsibilities of the most thoughtful and scrupulous kinds of reading.

Readers tend to want to resolve suspense: like foreplay, suspense carried on beyond a certain point seems to be undesirable, indeed intolerable. We want answers, and we want them soon. And there are all sorts of ways of terminating suspense, of closing it or resolving it. We can appeal to the notion of authorial intention and try to argue that Wordsworth 'meant' this or that, or we can appeal to 'historical evidence' and try to establish whether Lucy 'really is' the referent of this poem, or in line with the dentistry school of literary criticism to which we referred in Chapter 2, we can simply argue for a single extractable molar of meaning for the text. Rather than immediately attempting to resolve suspense, however, we might think about literary texts as themselves sites of suspense, places where suspense can occur without being closed off, without being finished. We might consider that it is the function of literary texts to go beyond the trite, the comforting, the easy resolution of suspense, to take us to imagined places where suspense cannot be resolved, where questions are more complex and more challenging than can be reduced to a single determined meaning. In this respect, there are reasons to welcome the threatening uncertainty of undecidability, this challenge to our desire to master the text.

Further reading

For a brilliant exploration of Wordsworth's line endings, see Christopher Ricks's 'William Wordsworth 1' (1984). For a comprehensive introduction to rhythm and metre, see Derek Attridge's *Poetic Rhythm* (1992). An excellent and imaginative exploration of prosody in terms of the sounds of English poetry is John Hollander's *Vision and Resonance* (1985). On suspense in the sense of ambiguity or undecidability, there is, perhaps, no better place to start than William Empson's classic *Seven Types of Ambiguity* (1953), first published in 1930. On the idea of literature as suspended in relation to meaning and reference, see the interview with Jacques Derrida in his *Acts of Literature* (1992a). A classic argument concerning the 'undecidability' of contending meanings in literary texts is J. Hillis Miller's 'The Figure in the Carpet' (1980). For a rather different approach, see D.A. Miller, ' "Cage aux folles": Sensation and Gender in Wilkie Collins's *The Woman in White*' (1989), which offers a fascinating consideration of the physiological effects of suspense fiction on readers.

Racial difference

Charlotte Brontë's *Jane Eyre* (1847) is one of the classic nineteenth-century novels in English. It describes a love affair between the epony-mous heroine, a governess, and her aristocratic master, Rochester. The novel ends with the marriage of Jane and Rochester after Jane has become both professionally and economically independent. Jane's struggle for independence marks the novel as centrally engaged with the oppression of women in nineteenth-century England and with the possibility of their liberation from constricting roles of subservience to their male 'masters'. Alongside the question of gender, however, *Jane Eyre* raises other questions. These are questions of racial difference and they will form the focal point of this chapter. Jane and Rochester are unable to marry because Rochester is already married to Bertha Mason, a creole woman from the West Indies. This woman, who is mad, is kept locked up in Rochester's attic. Occasionally she escapes, and at one point attempts to set light to Rochester's bed while he is in it. Finally, in a pyromaniacal frenzy, she sets light to the house and dies in the blaze. Her death leaves the way clear for Jane and Rochester to marry, although not before Rochester is blinded and crippled in trying to save Bertha from the fire.

While the novel has long been recognized as an exploration and cri-tique of the position of women in nineteenth-century society, more recently critics have begun to see questions of racial and ethnic differ-ence as central to the novel. The delayed recognition of the importance of these questions is telling. As in the English literary tradition more generally, such questions have been marginalized or effaced. They have simply not been seen or have been ignored. Such an effacement is, in fact, inscribed in the novel itself. Indeed, representations of race in *Jane Eyre* may be said to constitute a sort of textual unconscious: like the repressed contents of the Freudian unconscious, they repeatedly return in disguised form. In the following passage, for example, racial and ethnic difference becomes part of the flirtatious courtship ritual of Jane and Rochester. At one point, Jane, the narrator, sees Rochester smile: 'I thought his smile was such as a sultan might, in a blissful and fond moment, bestow on a slave his gold and gems had enriched.' This image of sultan and slave then develops into a whole discourse on slavery and racial otherness:

> 'I would not exchange this one little English girl for the Grand Turk's whole seraglio—gazelle-eyes, houri forms, and all!'
>
> The Eastern allusion bit me again. 'I'll not stand you an inch in the stead of a seraglio', I said; 'so don't consider me an equivalent for one. If you have a fancy for anything in that line, away with you, sir, to the bazaars of Stamboul, without delay, and lay out in extensive slave-purchases some of that spare cash you seem at a loss to spend satisfactorily here.'
>
> 'And what will you do, Janet, while I am bargaining for so many tons of flesh and such an assortment of black eyes?'
>
> 'I'll be preparing myself to go out as a missionary to preach liberty to them that are enslaved—your harem inmates amongst the rest. I'll get admitted there, and I'll stir up mutiny; and you, three-tailed bashaw as you are, sir, shall in a trice find yourself fettered amongst our hands: nor will I, for one, consent to cut your bonds till you have signed a charter, the most liberal that despot ever yet conferred.' (197–8)

Ironically, Jane is to gain her financial independence and her freedom from what Rochester calls her 'governessing slavery' (298) when she inherits a fortune derived, we can only assume, from the slave-trade of the West Indies. Moreover, although she seriously contemplates it, she does not finally leave England with another man, St John Rivers, who wishes to marry her and take her with him as a missionary to India. Most importantly, however, this passage presents us with the intersection of the discourses of sexual desire and racial otherness. These discourses organize the novel but do so in a way that the novel itself seems to repress. Both Jane and Rochester figure the racially other as sexually active and even passionate, while at the same time being available for purchase, like goods to be bought in a market. By contrast, Jane herself is repeatedly figured in terms of resisting both her own sexual desires and the financial temptations of Rochester's wealth: her sexuality is governed by self-control and she cannot be bought. The passage also brings together questions of sexuality and gender, race and economics, through its references to slavery. Slavery, the buying and selling of the dehumanized and racially other, is central to the novel's plot in that Jane gains her financial and therefore social independence after inheriting a fortune made in the Caribbean, where slavery had been the main source of wealth. Rather differently, the novel repeatedly figures slavery through metaphors of chains and imprisonment. A few paragraphs after the above quotation, for example, Rochester expresses a desire to imprison Jane when he says that ' "when once I have fairly seized you, to have and to hold, I'll just—figuratively speaking—attach you to a chain like this" (touching his watch-guard)' (299). The expression 'figuratively speaking' denies but at the same time exposes the structure of gender and race relations organizing the novel: it exposes the fact that Rochester is *not* only speaking 'figuratively'. Indeed, the phrase marks a textual anxiety concerning the precise status of slavery in the novel—literal or figurative. And this anxiety is compounded by the fact that while Rochester is flirtatiously threatening Jane with enchainment, incarcerated in his attic, imprisoned in chains, is his wife, the racially other Bertha.

A brief reading of a second passage might clarify some of these issues concerning the novel's representations of race. The first time that Jane and the reader see Bertha is a crucial moment. Jane and Rochester are prevented from marrying by the revelation that he is already married. Rochester tells Jane the truth and, in order to excuse his attempted bigamy, takes her into the attic to look at Bertha:

> In the deep shade, at the farther end of the room, a figure ran back-
> wards and forwards. What it was, whether beast or human being,
> one could not, at first sight tell: it grovelled, seemingly, on all fours;
> it snatched and growled like some strange wild animal: but it was
> covered with clothing, and a quantity of dark, grizzled hair, wild as
> a mane, hid its head and face. (321)

No longer a woman, Bertha is the other of humanity, unrecognizable as human, a beast with a purely animal physiognomy. Almost invisible, Bertha cannot be seen. Invisibility, as this suggests, and as we observe in our reading of the opening to Ralph Ellison's *Invisible Man* in Chapter 10, above, is the condition of racial otherness. As Henry Louis Gates has commented, 'The trope of blackness in Western discourse has signified absence at least since Plato' (Gates 1984, 315). In this novel, Bertha cannot and must not be seen. Despite (or because of) her invisibility as an individual, Bertha embodies the very idea of difference for Rochester and for the novel itself. Rochester explicitly contrasts Bertha with Jane: 'look at the difference! Compare these clear eyes with the red balls yonder—this face with that mask—this form with that bulk' (322). By contrasting the two women, Rochester makes it clear that Bertha should be understood as the other of Jane. But, as we have seen elsewhere, otherness is a tricky business. If you say that one thing is the opposite of another, you are at the same time asserting their mutual dependence, in that it is pointless to contrast two things from different categories. You would not say that a cricket match is the *opposite* of a submarine, for example, if only because there are no obvious points of comparison. In the context of Brontë's novel it would seem strange to say that Rochester, rather than Jane, is the opposite of Bertha, because their structural roles or social positions contain few if any similarities. What is being asserted in Rochester's comparison, then, is not only difference but also likeness: in particular, they are both women who are, in different ways, imprisoned, and both are partners for Rochester. Bertha is what Jane is not but *could be*. This is what we might term the 'subtext' of the novel: while only opposition is announced, *Jane Eyre* is haunted by the possibility that Bertha is not simply other to but also, in some ways, identical with Jane.

In these respects, then, *Jane Eyre* articulates how racial otherness is constituted—both absolutely other, non-human, bestial, and at the same time an integral element in what defines racial sameness, in this case 'Englishness', in other words part of the self-same, part of Western identity. And it is this ambiguous status of the other (racial or otherwise) that makes it so threatening, so disturbing, so dangerous. This dangerous (racial) other, far from being unusual is, in fact, quite common in canonical works of English literature. Figures of the racially other— more or less threatening, more or less destructive—appear as, for example, the Moor in Shakespeare's *Othello* (c.1602), the Jew in *The Merchant of Venice* (c.1596), Man Friday in Daniel Defoe's *Robinson Crusoe* (1719), Heathcliff in Emily Brontë's *Wuthering Heights* (1847), and in the colonial stories and novels of Rudyard Kipling (1865–1936), Joseph Conrad (1857–1924) and E.M. Forster (1879–1970), to name only some of the most famous examples. Far from being a marginal concern of English Literature, in fact, racial otherness is central.

We have tried to suggest elsewhere in the present book that many of the major developments in literary criticism and theory of the past few years have been associated with what is known as a critique of the subject—with a deconstruction of the stable, coherent and autonomous 'self'. This critique explores the ways in which personal identity is dependent on language: it investigates the idea that there is nothing *essential* about the nature of any individual or about the human more generally. It is not for nothing that this critique of the subject and of essentialism has been mounted. Our brief reading of the dehumanization of Bertha in *Jane Eyre* has begun to suggest that Western humanism necessarily defines itself through racial otherness, by constructing a racial other which then stands in opposition to the humanity of the racially homogeneous. Such essentializing of race is at once philosophically untenable and very dangerous. Racism is, before anything else, the delusion of essentialism. As Robert Young points out, the invention of modern concepts of 'human nature', together with ideas about the universal nature of humanity and the human mind, occurred during the centuries characterized in the West by colonization, 'those particularly violent centuries in the history of the world now known as the era of Western colonization' (Young 1990, 121). Critics such as Frantz Fanon, Edward Said, Gayatri Spivak and Homi Bhabha have argued that the Western discourse of colonialism is constituted by the other subject— by alterities of race, colour or ethnic origin. The Western constitution of human identity itself as universal or unchanging may be recognized as a historical construct constituted by the exclusion, marginalization and oppression of racial others.

Literary studies is far from free of the discursive marginalization of racial and ethnic others. For example, it was long thought possible for writers and critics to appeal to 'universal' values. A notorious instance of this is a series of comments made by the nineteenth-century politician, literary critic and historian Thomas Babington Macaulay in his *Minute on Law and Education* (1835). This Minute, presented to the Committee of Public Instruction for Bengal, was destined to have a decisive influence on the education of the indigenous population in colonial India. Macaulay argues for the teaching of English and against the teaching of Arabic and Sanscrit to the Indian population. His argument relies on assertions concerning the aesthetic value of Western culture:

> I have no knowledge of either Sanscrit or Arabic. But I have done what I could to form a correct estimate of their value. I have read translations of the most celebrated Arabic and Sanscrit works. I have conversed, both here and at home, with men distinguished by their

proficiency in the Eastern tongues. I am quite ready to take the oriental learning at the valuation of the orientalists themselves. I have never found one among them who could deny that a single shelf of a good European library was worth the whole native literature of India or Arabia. The intrinsic superiority of the Western literature is indeed fully admitted by those members of the committee who support the oriental plan of education . . . . It is, I believe, no exaggeration to say that all the historical information which has been collected in the Sanscrit language is less valuable than what may be found in the paltry abridgements used at preparatory schools in England. In every branch of physical or moral philosophy, the relative position of the two nations is nearly the same. (Quoted in Said 1983, 12)

While expressing appalling prejudice, this passage appeals to standards of objectivity, academic authority and apparently rational statements about 'intrinsic superiority'. The passage is evidence that, as Frantz Fanon remarks, for the native, 'objectivity is always directed against him' (quoted in Said 1993, 196)—that 'objectivity' is ideological. In Macaulay's statement, such objectivity is, in fact, blatantly ideological in its dependence on judgements of aesthetic value. By their very nature, such statements can *only* be culturally, ethnically and historically specific. To judge the aesthetic standards of one culture by those of another is self-evidently problematic. Judged by the standards of Japanese Noh drama, for example, Shakespeare's plays are absurdly verbose and thoroughly incompetent. And yet the history of Western aesthetics is dominated by precisely such notions of the universality of art.

To end this chapter, we shall suggest two ways of going beyond such judgemental and naive ways of reading and writing. Implicit in our discussion has been the idea that there is a connection between the differences of race and of gender. In this respect, Patrick Williams and Laura Chrisman have recently argued that any 'discussion of ethnicity is always also by implication a discussion of gender and sexuality'. The reason for this is, not least, that 'Women, as the biological "carriers" of the "race", occupy a primary and complex role in representations of ethnicity . . . and it is women's exercise of their sexuality which is an often unacknowledged major concern underlying such representations' (Williams and Chrisman 1993, 17). In Western literature black women have been doubly effaced. As novels such as Alice Walker's *The Color Purple* (1982) and Toni Morrison's *The Bluest Eye* (1970) make clear, black women are silenced both as black and as female. But it is precisely this doubled otherness which might help us begin to move beyond racial essentialism, beyond the repressive politics of identity. In an attempt to get beyond a constricting notion of identity and of a simple and reductive notion of otherness, Mae Gwendolyn Henderson has argued that black women's writing is 'interlocutionary, or dialogic' owing to their position as 'not only the "Other" of the Same, but also as the "other" of the other(s), [which] implies . . . a relationship of difference and identification with the "other(s)"' (Henderson 1993, 258–9). The value of this analysis is that it allows us to recognize the plurality of identity, to recognize that any identity is constituted by a multiplicity of positions and differences. Black women's writing, in particular, being marginalized twice over, figuring the other of the other, reinforces a sense of the polymorphic nature of identity in all discourse. In addition, Henry Louis Gates has argued that all black texts are necessarily 'two toned', or 'double-voiced', that they both engage with white canonical discourse and, at the same time, express a black consciousness. This, for Gates, leads to a discourse which is duplicitous, potentially subversive, one that undermines the universalizing and essentializing tendencies of hegemonic white discourse: 'Black people have always been masters of the figurative: saying one thing to mean something quite other has been basic to black survival in oppressive Western cultures' (Gates 1984, 6).

Our second suggestion for displacing the monolithic and oppressive drive to identify simply in terms of racial difference is the possibility of *reading* otherwise—the possibility of what Edward Said calls 'contrapuntal reading' (Said 1993, 78). A number of critics and theorists have suggested different ways of reading, guided by an acceptance of multiplicity, a questioning of binary oppositions and an affirmation of radical otherness. Said suggests that we might read such texts as Brontë's *Jane Eyre* or Jane Austen's *Mansfield Park* 'with an understanding of what is involved when an author shows . . . that a colonial sugar plantation is . . . important to the process of maintaining a particular style of life in England' (78). Such a reading, a contrapuntal reading, two-toned or double-voiced, cannot ignore the discourse of slavery by which Jane's liberation as a woman is mediated.

Further reading

Frantz Fanon's impassioned and politically charged *The Wretched of the Earth* (1967) is the classic work on race, nationalism and decolonization. Much of the most interesting work on race and ethnicity in literature has been that associated with studies of postcolonialism: two important collections of essays are Homi Bhabha, ed., *Nation and Narration* (1990) and Williams and Chrisman, eds, *Colonial Discourse and Post-Colonial Theory* (1993). The work of Spivak, who comes at the subject of race and ethnicity from a specifically feminist position, has been particularly influential: see her *In Other Worlds* (1987). For another collection of poststructuralist essays, see Henry Louis Gates, ed., *'Race', Writing and Difference* (1986). Gates's *The Signifying Monkey* (1988) is the most sustained elaboration of his theory of writing and racial difference from the perspective of black writing in the United States. From a more specifically feminist perspective, see Toni Morrison's brief and highly readable *Playing in the Dark: Whiteness and the Literary Imagination* (1993).

The colony

Colonialism, postcolonialism, neocolonialism: three *isms* that depend upon the figure of the colony. In the Preface to this book we remark that theory—particularly when it takes the form of *isms*—can seem intimidating or simply boring. Deeply desiring to be neither, we also have good theoretical reasons for feeling wary of *isms*. As Martin Heidegger put it: 'Every mere *ism* is a misunderstanding and the death of history' (Heidegger 1967, 60–1). This assertion draws attention to the ways in which *isms* inevitably encourage generalization, abstractness, and lack of critical clarity and of historical awareness. But saying this of course does not make *isms* go away. *Isms* are convenient, as well as deadly. Here are three convenient, if deadly, definitions: 'colonialism' is 'the policy or practice of obtaining, or maintaining hold over, colonies, *esp* with the purpose of exploiting them' (*Chambers Dictionary*); 'postcolonialism' is concerned with what 'occur[s] or exist[s] after the end of colonial rule' (*Shorter OED*); 'neocolonialism' is concerned with the *continuing effects* of colonialism after the end of colonial rule, and thus with a questioning of the apparently straightforward break implied by the *post-* of 'postcolonial'. Much *ism*-izing energy has been spent on the distinctions or lack of distinctions between these various terms. For example, the authors of the influential book *The Empire Writes Back* (1989) argue that the term 'postcolonial' should be seen as covering 'all the culture affected by the imperial process from the moment of colonization to the present day' (Ashcroft, Griffiths and Tiffin 1989, 2). This definition mingles colonialism and 'postcoloniality', and also mixes itself up with the arguably more rigorous and precise conception of 'neocolonialism' as involving 'the half-hidden narratives of colonialism's success in its continuing operations' (Young 1991b, 3). Rather than engage directly with these various *isms*, we propose in this chapter to try to reflect on them indirectly, by focusing on what is common to them all (the colony) and by considering a series of related topics: language, time, point of view, writing, law, justice and drama.

The word 'colony' itself is suggestive: in etymological terms a patriarchal and agricultural metaphor (Latin *colonia* a colony, from *colonus* a husbandsman, from *colere* to till), 'colony' is, according to *Chambers*, 'a name vaguely applied to a state's dependencies overseas or abroad . . .; a body of persons settled in a foreign country, or forming a separate ethnic, cultural or occupational group; the settlement so formed; the place they inhabit'. One thing is already clear from this dictionary definition: the colony, and all the *isms* it colonizes, has to do with the colonizing power and effects of language itself, with language *as* colonization. There is no concept of the colony in the English language that does not depend on the colonization of English by Latin—which is also to say, the colonization of Latin by English. Correspondingly, we might ask, is US English colonized by British English or is it the other way round? Colonization here, as always, works in two directions: to colonize is, how ever imperceptibly or insidiously, to be colonized. If, as William Burroughs claimed, language is a virus, this is because it is a colonizer. In particular as 'dependency overseas or abroad' or 'settlement in a foreign country', a colony always involves the imposition of a foreign language; and all the colonialist wars in history (there are perhaps no other) are also wars in and over language. Indeed, as some linguists like to say, a language is a dialect with an army and a navy. Finally, however, we may suppose that there is no way of thinking about any of these matters *in one's own language* without being already *colonized by* language. Colonization is at the origin: we are always already dependants of language, colonized by one or more languages.

To be 'always already' is to be unsure, among other things, about one's sense of time. In this and other respects, the notion of colony has a strange relation to time. As its etymology indicates, 'colony' is fundamentally a spatial term: originally it has to do with tilling the land. When we think about colonies we think, first perhaps, of space, of the appropriation and exploitation of land. But questions of time are just as important when trying to think in a (post- or neo-) colonialist context. Indeed, as we indicated a few moments ago, the very terms 'post-' and 'neo-' are temporal, concerned with what comes after or continues to haunt the colony. Literary texts offer especially good illustrations of how the colony deranges and disorders the sense not only of place but also of time. We could consider this, for example, in relation to Conrad's

Heart of Darkness (1902). On the one hand, there is a clear and irrefutable historical context for the narrative: it is a novel about the European (especially Belgian and British) colonial exploitation of Africa (especially the Congo) in the late nineteenth century. On the other hand, however, and *at the same time*, the novel conveys a particularly strong sense of this journey to the colonial heart of darkness as a journey into another time. As Marlow recounts:

> Going up that river was like travelling back to the earliest beginnings of the world . . . The broadening waters flowed through a mob of wooded islands; you lost your way on that river as you would in a desert, and butted all day long against shoals, trying to find the channel, till you thought yourself bewitched and cut off for ever from everything you had once known—somewhere—far away—in another existence perhaps. (48)

Conrad's novel is both historically specific (it illuminates the barbarity of European colonialism in Africa) and pervasively dreamlike (at once timeless and primordial). Jean Rhys's *Wide Sargasso Sea* (1966) also characterizes the colony as unsettling any 'homely' sense of time, in particular by evoking the strange timelessness of dreaming and trance. For the unnamed Mr Rochester (the colonizer who is also colonized by his time in the West Indies) the unnamed Windward island, where he and Antoinette spend their honeymoon, is 'quite unreal and like a dream' (49). Indeed his colonial experience as a whole may be described as 'all . . . a nightmare' (76). But the strangeness works in two directions. Thus England in turn is repeatedly evoked in terms of the timelessness of a dream for Antoinette (49, 70). Just as *Heart of Darkness* traces a disturbing circular structure which returns the narrative, finally, to London as the 'heart of darkness', so Rhys's novel complicates our sense of time in more general narrative terms. Its disordering of temporality has to do, above all, with its status as a prequel to Charlotte Brontë's *Jane Eyre*: post- but also pre-*Jane Eyre*, it exposes the colonialist dimensions of the earlier novel *before the event*.

Finally, we could consider the example of Chinua Achebe's *Things Fall Apart* (1958). Achebe's novel recounts the rise and fall of a man called Okonkwo, and tells how Christian white men come to colonize and largely destroy the culture and identity of the Igbo tribe to which he belongs. Like *Heart of Darkness* and *Wide Sargasso Sea*, *Things Fall Apart* is temporally deranged and deranging: it is impelled by Achebe's own 'decolonizing' mission of seeking to write an alternative version of Conrad's novel, specifically from the perspective of the *colonized*. Yet Achebe's narrator is obliged to occupy a sort of double-time—at once from the late nineteenth-century time of the novel's action (narrating as if from *within* the Igbo tribe) and from the mid-twentieth-century time of its telling (narrating from a position *outside* the tribe and from a considerable distance in time). Achebe's novel is an extraordinary meditation on the difficulty of saying *when* 'things fall apart', of determining when, for example, colonization happens, or when the colonial becomes postcolonial. This difficulty is marked, above all, in the title of the novel, with its haunting suspension in the present tense, and in the fact that it is a quotation. The phrase 'things fall apart' is taken from W.B. Yeats's 'The Second Coming' (1919), a poem that is inseparable from Christian mythology and inseparable in turn from the colonialist context of the First World War and the Irish Troubles. Achebe's novel, from its title onwards, is written (however critically or ironically) in the language of the Christian colonizer.

If from a literary perspective the twentieth century is 'the age of Kafka', as Harold Bloom asserts (Bloom 1994, 448), Kafka's work is perhaps not the most obvious to turn to for thinking about issues of the colony. Let us, however, consider a short story that may help to dislodge this assumption. 'In the Penal Colony' (*In der Strafkolonie*) was written in October 1914 and first published shortly after the First World War, in 1919. It is one of Kafka's most grim and least funny stories. Set in an unnamed penal colony, on an unnamed island, it focuses on a number of unnamed characters and is told—primarily from the perspective of an unnamed 'explorer'—by an omniscient third-person narrator. The explorer has been invited by the Commandant of the colony to witness the execution of a soldier who has been 'condemned to death for disobedience and insulting behaviour to a superior' (140). The story focuses on the terrifying, uncanny machine that is to bring this execution about, and on the 'officer' whose proud, even sacred, responsibility it is to explain the machine to the explorer and ensure it does its work. By a characteristically eerie Kafkaesque twist, the officer ends up freeing the prisoner and putting himself to death in his place; the story concludes with the explorer leaving the island on a boat with an unnamed ferryman.

The interest of Kafka's narrative in terms of issues of (post- or neo-) colonialism has to do with four related ideas: point of view, writing, law and justice. First, it dramatizes the problem and importance of 'point of view', both in a narratological and also in a more broadly cultural and political sense. It offers a basis for thinking about questions such as: From what perspective or point of view can or should one think about, say, Shakespeare's *Othello* (1604), Austen's *Mansfield Park* (1814), Forster's *A Passage to India* (1924), Rushdie's *Midnight's Children* (1981) or indeed any other literary work that engages with colonial differences? And more broadly, from what point of view does one make ethical and other judgements about other people, other societies and cultures? Kafka's story does this by *exploring* (a word in our critical vocabulary that suddenly takes on a new 'colonialist' dimension) the explorer's dilemma from his own point of view: 'The explorer thought to himself: It's always a ticklish matter to intervene decisively in other people's affairs. He was neither a member of the penal colony nor a citizen of the state to which it belonged' (151). The explorer is a foreigner, a stranger, but he is also described as being 'conditioned by European ways of thought' (155). How should the man respond to the seemingly undeniable 'injustice of the procedure and the inhumanity of the execution' (151)? Kafka's text does not offer any simple answer to this question, focusing instead on the increasingly intolerable suspense of withholding judgement. At the same time it generates an overwhelming sense of the explorer's unique position and responsibility: he is seen as 'an illustrious foreigner' (155) in a privileged position to pass comment and influence events. Indeed Kafka's story gives a further, more deranging inflection to the dilemma. For while there *is* judgement and decision within the story (the explorer makes clear his strong disapproval of the machine and the punishment; the officer in turn makes a firm decision to free the condemned man and take his place), the reader is left finally with what is in some respects the most 'ticklish matter' of all, namely: who is the narrator of this story, what point of view does he or she have on everything that goes on in the text, and what, in the light of this, is our own point of view? As Gilles Deleuze and Félix Guattari have observed, 'It is by the power of his noncritique that Kafka is so dangerous' (Deleuze and Guattari 1986, 60). 'In the Penal Colony' dramatizes an extraordinary experience of solitude, by posing the question of point of view as a necessary but radically uncertain experience of *responsibility* for each and any reader. To read the story is to be colonized by this dangerous power.

Second, Kafka's text foregrounds the importance of writing itself, of textuality. One of the continuing controversies within the general area of postcolonialist thinking concerns the theoretical complexity of some of its best-known practitioners. Thus postcolonialist theory is perceived as being 'depressingly difficult' (Williams and Chrisman 1993, ix), above all on account of its seemingly abstract, unworldly focus on 'discourse' and 'textuality'. Edward Said, Gayatri Spivak and Homi Bhabha in particular have come to be seen as what Dennis Walder calls 'the three police officers of the postcolonial' (Walder 1998, 4). In his engaging book *Post-colonial Literatures in English*, Walder seeks to evade the long arm of the law while trying to keep his sights trained on postcolonial literary works themselves. This is a bold but perhaps questionable strategy. As Ania Loomba puts it: 'Many writings on colonial or postcolonial discourse may not expressly privilege the textual, but they implicitly do so by interpreting colonial relations through literary texts alone' (Loomba 1998, 95). As Kafka's story suggests, when it comes to thinking about the colony, there is no getting away from the founding complexity of questions of textuality, from the uncanny character of writing, from the limits of the readable. For law itself is inseparable from textuality, writing, inscription. Moreover, Kafka's story is also a disturbing account of law in terms of different, even mutually unintelligible, incommensurable languages or discourses: different characters speak, read and fail to understand different languages. The punishment for the condemned man in Kafka's story involves a Harrow which inserts innumerable needles into the prisoner's body and gradually inscribes in his flesh 'whatever commandment [he] has disobeyed' (144). The officer patiently explains:

> 'there are two kinds of needles arranged in multiple patterns. Each long needle has a short one beside it. The long needle does the writing, and the short needle sprays a jet of water to wash away the blood and keep the inscription clear.' (147)

The words being inscribed in this case are 'HONOUR THY SUPER-IORS!' (144). For the condemned man the sentence is unreadable, unknown, until it is literally written on his body, by which time he will be at the point of death, beyond all sense of honour, beyond any sense at all.

Finally, Kafka's story provokes the thought that every colony is a penal colony. Every colony entails the imposition of codes of law, justice and punishment from elsewhere, from back 'home' or from a foreign country. This is indeed a central issue in many colonial or postcolonial novels. Forster's *A Passage to India*, for example, turns on the question of justice and the law, culminating in the drama of the trial scene and the attempt to have Dr Aziz found guilty of attempted rape. Likewise in Rhys's *Wide Sargasso Sea*, everything depends on the colonizing power of 'English law' (see 5, 11, 69) and what Christophine calls the 'damn cold lie' of that English word, ' "justice" ' (94). Similarly we may recall that *Heart of Darkness* concludes with Marlow's meditation on the idea that Kurtz had 'wanted only justice' (111), while *Things Fall Apart* ends with the self-justificatory cogitations of the District Commissioner who is to write a mere paragraph about what we as readers have spent a book experiencing and who has decided, 'after much thought', to entitle his work *The Pacification of the Primitive Tribes of the Lower Niger* (148). 'Be just': these are the key words of Kafka's brief and terrifying text, 'In the Penal Colony'. The dictum appears, according to the officer, among the papers of the former Commandant of the colony. But the explorer cannot read it:

> Now the officer began to spell it, letter by letter, and then read out the words. ' "BE JUST!" is what is written there,' he said, 'surely you can read it now.' . . . [T]he explorer made no remark, yet it was clear that he still could not decipher it. (161)

Issues of law and justice are at the heart of all (post- or neo-) colonial literature. On the one hand, as 'In the Penal Colony' suggests, these issues are always context-specific; they can, and perhaps must, call for a dangerous experience of solitude in any and every reader. The reader is judge: Be just! The reader is put in the impossible position of trying to see from the perspective of both the explorer and the narrator at the same time and, alone, to judge accordingly. On the other hand, the study of such literature is not confined to the realm of fiction. Such texts also remind us of the extent to which ethical and juridical decisions are determined within a context of specific national and state identities. Thus Kafka clarifies the need for a revolution in the very concept of international law, beyond the boundaries of any state or colony. As Jacques Derrida has proposed in *Spectres of Marx*: 'international law should extend and diversify its field to include, if at least it is to be consistent with the idea of democracy and of human rights it proclaims, the *worldwide* economic and social field, beyond the sovereignty of States' (Derrida 1994, 84).

In Plato's philosophical colony, his imagined Republic, mimetic art, including poetry and drama, is to be excluded. It is dangerous because it 'waters and fosters' (Plato 1961, 832) false feelings: art embodies the uncomfortable truth that imitation is formative. This recalls the idea, proposed at the outset of this chapter, that language and colonization are inextricable. To imitate is to be uncertainly colonized *and* colonizing. We could consider this further in relation to the important essay called 'Of Mimicry and Man: The Ambivalence of Colonial Discourse', by Homi Bhabha, one of the 'police officers' mentioned earlier. Bhabha demonstrates how post-Enlightenment English colonialism is dependent on a logic of imitation or mimicry: the colonized other is obliged to mimic the language, and to varying degrees to imitate the customs, gestures and even dress of the colonizers. This mimicry, however, is never pure: mimicry, Bhabha argues, 'is at once resemblance and menace' (Bhabha 1996, 362). There is a fundamental *ambivalence* in the act of colonial appropriation: the colonizer at once desires and fears that the colonized be like him (or, less frequently, her). Colonial mimicry, in other words, is governed by a logic of what Bhabha describes as 'almost the same, *but not quite*' (361). In order to succeed, colonial appropriation must fail. As Angela Smith describes it, in the context of V.S. Naipaul's *The Mimic Men* and Rhys's *Wide Sargasso Sea*: 'The presence of the colonial other imitating the white male colonizer disrupts the authority of the colonizer's language, and [reveals] an inherent absurdity in the colonial enterprise' (Smith 1997, xviii). The appeal and effectiveness of Homi Bhabha's argument is that it undermines the 'authoritative discourse' (362) of colonialism from within: by imitating this discourse, the colonized subject shows it to be different from itself, never at home with its own innermost desires.

One of the understated effects of Bhabha's essay is to suggest how important the notions of theatre, acting and drama are for thinking about (post- or neo-) colonialism. Indeed it encourages us to reflect more broadly on the extent to which personal identity is based on imitation, is inherently theatrical. These are hardly new concerns in the context of literature. Work by critics such as Barker and Hulme (1985) and Paul Brown (1994), for example, has emphasized how deeply Shakespeare's *The Tempest* (1611) is a play about these issues. A play about strange derangements in the experience of time as well as place, and pervasively concerned with questions of legitimacy, authority and justice, *The Tempest* is also profoundly engaged with the 'colonial' paradoxes of language, acting and identity. It is a play not least about teaching and mimicry. Just as Prospero is Miranda's 'schoolmaster' (I, ii, 172), so she in turn becomes the teacher of Caliban, the 'slave' whom they find when first coming to the island. In a celebrated exchange near the beginning of the play she reminds Caliban: 'I pitied thee, / Took pains to make thee speak, taught thee each hour / One thing or other' (I, ii, 355–7). Caliban retorts: 'You taught me language; and my profit on 't / Is, I know how to curse. The red plague rid you / For learning me your language!' (I, ii, 365–7). There are a number of paradoxes in play here. This exchange suggests how thoroughly language determines who or what we are or might become: there is no escape from the colonizing and mimicking power of language as it annexes one subject (Caliban) after another (Miranda). As the quibble on 'red' and 'rid' intimates, one cannot be rid of what is read, what is read cannot be unread: language in *The Tempest* is itself a sort of plague. Caliban's capacity to curse, indeed his very capacity to embody any meaning at all, is an effect of linguistic colonization. Yet his cursing at the same time can only ever be based on a reflection or mimicking of the colonizers and, no doubt, of their own 'innermost desires'. Caliban presents Miranda and Prospero with a disturbing and uncertain mirroring of themselves which nothing in the play can finally efface. This is evident in the very syntax and versification of Prospero's final declaration of recognition regarding Caliban: 'this thing of darkness I / Acknowledge mine' (V, i, 275–6). The inverted syntax and the hesitancy of the enjambment underscore this ambivalent sense of Prospero as not merely owning but also, and paradoxically, *being* 'this thing of darkness'.

As critics such as Barker and Hulme have emphasized, *The Tempest* is, in various paradoxical and intractable respects, 'a play imbricated within the discourse of colonialism' (204). It is also, as we have tried to make clear, a play about acting, imitation and mimicry. Finally, we would like to suggest that *The Tempest* is also a kind of colony in itself. Indeed in a sense this is just what every dramatic work is. It establishes itself in a strange time and place of its own, linked to but distinct from the rest of the world: the dramatic work is a site of derangement, mimicry, power and transformation. As Captain Phillip, the Governor of New South Wales, observes, in Timberlake Wertenbaker's *Our Country's Good* (1988): 'A play is a world in itself, a tiny colony we could almost say' (Act 2, Scene 2). Engaged in casting a different and complex theatrical light on that penal colony the British called Australia, *Our Country's Good* is also, like any other dramatic work, strangely resistant to being seen merely as a representation or part of the world in which it is set. In its very title, like Shakespeare's *The Tempest* or *A Midsummer Night's Dream*, it establishes a peculiar colony, it 'gives to airy nothing / A local habitation and a name' (*A Midsummer Night's Dream*, V, i, 16–17).

Further reading

Much valuable material is available in anthologies such as Ashcroft, Griffiths and Tiffin, eds, *The Post-Colonial Studies Reader* (1995) and Williams and Chrisman, eds, *Colonial Discourse and Post-Colonial Theory* (1993). For a good general introductory work, see Ania Loomba's *Colonialism/Postcolonialism* (1998); see also Robert Young's *Postcolonialism: A History* (1999). Loomba is particularly stimulating for the emphasis she gives to how far issues of gender and sexuality are implicated in (post- or neo-) colonialism. Young provides more detailed coverage of some of these issues in his earlier book *Colonial Desire: Hybridity in Theory, Culture and Race* (1995). Related to this (and indeed apposite in the context of the tacitly homoerotic dimensions of Kafka's 'In the Penal Colony'), increasing critical attention has recently been given to the links between the colony and queerness. On this, see, for example, Christopher Lane's challenging but fascinating *The Ruling Passion: British Colonial Allegory and the Paradox of Homosexual Desire* (1995) or Yonatan Touval's playful and thought-provoking essay on *A Passage to India*, 'Colonial Queer Something' (1997). Finally, Edward Said's work on (post- and neo-) colonial issues is both very accessible and highly influential: his most important books are *Orientalism* (1978) and *Culture and Imperialism* (1993).

The performative

'I confess my ignorance': *Chambers Dictionary* gives this as an example of a performative. The word 'performative', declared J.L. Austin in 1956, 'is a new word and an ugly word, and perhaps it does not mean anything very much. But at any rate there is one thing in its favour, it is not a profound word' (Austin 1970, 233). The present chapter is concerned to sort out what this rather odd, perhaps unprofound word does mean. A performative is a statement that not only describes an action but actually performs that action. A performative is, in principle at least, the opposite of a constative statement. A constative statement involves a description of how things seem to be, a statement or assertion of something that can be true or false. 'The teachers are ignorant', for example.

All language can be thought about in terms of the constative and the performative. On the one hand, there is language as *descriptive*, as saying something about something. On the other, there is language as performative, as not only saying something but *doing* or *performing* something at the same time. 'I do' (as words spoken by the prospective wife or husband in answer to a particular question in the marriage service), 'I declare this meeting inquorate', 'I promise to pay the bearer the sum of twenty pounds': these are all examples in which language is clearly supposed to be doing something. If it were not, marriage would be impossible, committee meetings would never end (or, more happily, might never take place at all) and a twenty-pound note would be quite worthless, a mere curiosity. The distinction between constative and performative statements is derived from a particular strand of Anglo-American philosophy known as speech-act theory. Speech-act theory is most famously associated with the work of the Oxford philosopher J.L. Austin and in particular with his book entitled *How to do Things with Words*

215

(1962). It has become an important area of contemporary philosophy and linguistics but has also proved extraordinarily provocative in the field of literary criticism.

At first this idea may seem baffling. Surely, we may tell ourselves, literary texts are simply 'words on a page' and moreover words that relate to fictional or poetic worlds, not to the so-called real world in which marriage ceremonies are genuinely performed, committee meetings truly take place and money is real. But the truth of the matter is a little more complicated than this. Literary texts can indeed be considered from the perspective of the performative. Thus we may recall that the very word 'poetry' comes from the Greek verb *poieein*, 'to make', 'to create': this suggests that poetry might in fact be a making or *doing*, as much as a saying or *stating*.

In order to start exploring this idea in more detail, we will look at one or two poems which are particularly interesting in the context of the performative. First of all, John Keats's 'This Living Hand' (written in c.1819):

> This living hand, now warm and capable
> Of earnest grasping, would, if it were cold
> And in the icy silence of the tomb,
> So haunt thy days and chill thy dreaming nights
> That thou would wish thine own heart dry of blood
> So in my veins red life might stream again,
> And thou be conscience-calm'd—see here it is—
> I hold it towards you—

These chilling lines, which as it happens were not published until 1892, more than seventy years after Keats's death, are apparently *about* this death. The text functions as a bizarre and complex kind of curse or threat: it suggests that if the writer were dead (if this hand were no longer living but cold and in the grave), 'you'—the reader—would be so haunted that you would be willing to die in order that the writer could live again. The last words then weirdly suggest that this hand really is still living, despite the fact that we know the poet is dead: 'see here it is—I hold it towards you—'.

Keats's poem may or may not be 'unfinished': we only have the text as recorded in the margin of a manuscript of another poem. Our doubt as to whether it is a fragment or a finished poem is part of a more general sense of uncertainty. 'This Living Hand' promotes a strong sense of the strangeness of writing as such. It testifies on the one hand (as it were) to the fact that a hand, the writer's or anyone else's, is always capable of being outlived by the writing which it produces. Paradoxically, what lives on is the writing and not the hand. On the other hand (so to speak), the poem insists—in a quite threatening and disturbing way—on the power that language has to be *deictic*, to point (like, precisely, a hand) and to say 'this' ('This living hand') and 'here' ('here it is'), now, in a strangely 'icy' or frozen present. We may not know how we feel about this poem, we may not know how to understand or earnestly 'grasp' it. But however we may want to think about it, one thing seems clear: the poem is *doing* something to us as readers. It is performative in at least two ways: first, in that it is a threat and, second, in that it *enacts* the curious logic of holding out a hand ('This living hand') to us as readers, here and now. Austin notes, in *How to do Things with Words*, that the classic examples of performatives are 'all with verbs in the first person singular present indicative active . . . Examples are "I name", "I do", "I bet", "I give"' (Austin 1962, 56). And he adds that another 'useful criterion' for a performative statement is the presence, whether explicit or implicit, of the word 'hereby' (57). Keats's poem, whether considered as finished or unfinished, is clearly saying in some sense: I hereby threaten and haunt you.

Here is another example ('we hereby offer it to you'), a three-line poem by the contemporary English poet Michael Ayres, entitled 'Bittersweet' (1993):

> Survivors again. I never thought we'd make it.
> I never thought I could be forgotten,
> Or that it would be so bittersweet.

There are intriguing similarities between the Keats and Ayres poems. Both are concerned with the idea of survival and both can be read as poems about themselves, in other words as poems that are self-reflexive or self-referential. And like 'This Living Hand', 'Bittersweet' is self-reflexive in a decidedly paradoxical sense. The deployment of the title-word 'bittersweet' at the very end of the poem establishes the self-reflexive or self-referential dimension: it invites us to suppose that what 'would be so bittersweet' would be the poem of that title, the poem we are or have just been reading. The word 'bittersweet' at the end of the poem leads us back to the beginning of the poem, or rather to the very title of the poem, in a way that calls to mind Coleridge's favourite image for a story—that of a snake with its tail in its mouth. If the sense of time in this poem is paradoxical, so too of course is the very word 'bittersweet'. This word is an oxymoron—an apparent contradiction in terms, comparable to Milton's phrase 'darkness visible' (*Paradise Lost*, I, 63). Finally, Ayres's poem is paradoxical as regards the idea of being forgotten. The 'I' of this poem declares, 'I never thought I could be forgotten'. This can be read as saying 'I never thought I could be forgotten and look, sure enough, I haven't been', but it can also be read as saying the opposite: 'I never thought I could be forgotten but the truth is that I have been.' The more plausible of these interpretations would perhaps be the latter, but if we read the poem in this way we encounter what appears to be its central paradox: being a survivor involves being forgotten. How should we make sense of this? One way would be to say that this is a love poem about the bittersweet experience of surviving some crisis or great difficulty in a relationship: the 'I' of the poem survives but only at the cost of no longer being the 'I' he (or she) used to be. We are left, in this case, with the enigma of an 'I' who has been forgotten, but who nevertheless survives in writing, that is to say, in the very words of the poem. If 'I' simply depends on writing, then perhaps so does the 'we' referred to in the first line. This 'we', in turn, could be read not only as referring to the speaker and the speaker's lover, for example, but also as referring to *ourselves*, the poem's readers. In this sense the poem would be doing something to us, turning us into survivors: reading becomes bittersweet.

As if haunted by an aftertaste, we could carry on trying to describe here what 'This Living Hand' and 'Bittersweet' seem to be doing as poems. The basic point, however, is precisely that: they are not poems that are simply descriptive, they are also performative. Keats's text pulls us into its strange and icy grasp, Ayres's poem makes reading bittersweet. Both poems are indeed kinds of riddle. Each is saying, in effect: without your being able fully to understand it, this is a poem about the fact that you have read it. Each of these poems draws particular attention to the fact that it is writing and that it can survive its author, like a monument. In this respect both poems exploit the monumentalizing character of writing in a way similar to that of Shakespeare's sonnet 55:

> Not marble, nor the gilded monuments
> Of princes, shall outlive this pow'rful rime,
> But you shall shine more bright in these contents

Than unswept stone, besmear'd with sluttish time.
When wasteful war shall statues overturn,
And broils root out the work of masonry,
Nor Mars his sword nor war's quick fire shall burn
The living record of your memory.
'Gainst death and all-oblivious enmity
Shall you pace forth; your praise shall still find room,
Even in the eyes of all posterity
That wear this world out to the ending doom.
   So till the judgment that yourself arise,
   You live in this, and dwell in lovers' eyes.

This is a love poem which asserts that it will 'outlive' marble, gilded monuments, masonry and so on. It is thus concerned with the idea that writing—and this text in particular—has a capacity for monumentalization greater than that of anything else that humans might create. Because the poem itself will last until the end of the world ('the ending doom'), so will the memory of the lover who is being addressed. The haunting irony of Shakespeare's poem is that it constitutes not only the 'living record' of the lover's 'memory' but also the very existence of this lover: 'You live in this, and dwell in lovers' eyes.' The poem is not simply a 'record'. Rather, the lover ('you') only exists thanks to these fourteen lines. Poetry, then, in keeping with its etymology, can be performative in the most radical way: it can create 'you'.

The notion of the performative is extremely helpful for thinking about literature, then, because it allows us to appreciate that literary texts not only describe but perform. Literary texts not only say but do things: they do things with words and do things to us. More precisely they do things *by* saying. After declaring, in his poem 'In Memory of W.B. Yeats (d. Jan. 1939)', that 'poetry makes nothing happen', the poet W.H. Auden qualifies and even contradicts this by observing that 'it survives', as 'A way of happening, a mouth'. Alongside this we could juxtapose a remark made by Jacques Derrida, who says: 'promising is inevitable as soon as we open our mouths—or rather as soon as there is a text' (Derrida 1986a, 98). A promise is, of course, a classic example of a performative. This is not to say that we should scan poems or other literary texts for examples of the poet, author, narrator or characters literally making promises to the reader or to other characters. Rather it is a matter of recognizing that literary texts are, in their very structure, promises. To recall an example that Derrida gives: 'A title is always a promise' (Derrida 1986a, 115). Even (or especially) with its title, a literary text has begun to promise. As soon as there is a text, perhaps before anyone (the poet, author, narrator or character) even opens their mouth, the performativity of a promise is underway. In order to get a sharper sense of the way a title works as a promise, we could consider how a text might be read if it had a different title from the one it has been given. Imagine Shakespeare's *King Lear* if it were retitled *Cordelia*, or Emily Brontë's *Wuthering Heights* if it were retitled *The Two Catherines*, or Sylvia Plath's 'Daddy' if it were retitled 'Why I Love a Fascist'. With a different title, there would be a quite different kind of promise being made: the work would be doing something quite different to us.

Let us conclude with a few words about this last example, Sylvia Plath's poem 'Daddy'. This poem is about the speaker's love and hatred of her father and describes the process by which she comes to exorcise him—by 'killing' him twice and finally driving a stake through his heart. 'Daddy' neatly encapsulates many of the points we have been discussing in this chapter. If 'Daddy' is a particularly crucial word for this poem, starting from its very title, so too is the word 'do'. Plath's text is fundamentally about *doing* and most of all, we can suggest, about doing by saying, about doing things with words. 'You do not do', the poem emphatically opens. 'I do, I do', the speaker exclaims. A powerfully disturbing rhetorical mixture of a marriage and an execution, Plath's poem at once describes *and performs* the process by which the speaker can finally disconnect herself from the addressee ('The black telephone's off at the root') and conclude finally: 'Daddy, daddy, you bastard, I'm through'. The force of the poem involves the sense that the speaker is exorcising her father as she speaks, that these words are what finally get rid of him. The text is like a poetic equivalent of psychoanalysis as 'the talking cure'.

We have been dealing mainly with poems in this chapter, since they provide an especially clear sense of how the 'I' of the text, or how the text itself, can be seen to create and transform—to perform. But as the example of titles indicates, the idea of the performative is of fundamental importance for all literary texts. A simple way of illustrating this would be to say that every literary text is a kind of letter. It is a text addressed privately to each of us, me or you in isolation, at the same time as being a letter that has been made public, published. To read a literary text is to agree to the idea of a possible relationship. The literary text—whether poem, play, short story or novel—is a letter, and by reading it you become its recipient. Pursuing this analogy between a literary text and a letter, J. Hillis Miller argues that what is particularly striking about the performative dimension of literature is that it is in some ways fundamentally unpredictable. Literary texts give a 'twist' to the conventional, Austinian notion of the performative. Miller writes: 'The "twist" lies in the fact that the performative power of the letter is not foreseen or intended. This is contrary to the strict concept of a performative utterance as defined by Austin' (Miller 1991, 172). We have tried to suggest the workings of such a 'twist' in the paradoxical and 'riddling' effects of the poems we have looked at: poems are performative but not in ways that we can necessarily expect or completely, earnestly grasp. The 'twist' of performatives in literature might be illustrated in relation to the final words of Sylvia Plath's poem 'Daddy': 'Daddy, daddy, you bastard, I'm through'. Something is happening here, something is being performed, but what? Is calling daddy 'bastard' a way of renouncing his legitimacy and thus, as it were, excommunicating him? What does 'I'm through' mean? Can the 'I' say this, while still addressing 'daddy'? Does 'I'm through' mean 'I *am* finished' or 'I *have* finished'? Or does it mean, paradoxically, that the 'I' is finally *through to* 'daddy', only now, beyond the last word of the poem, finally able to address him?

Further reading

J. Hillis Miller's work on performatives is particularly accessible. See his book, *Tropes, Parables, Performatives* (1991). More difficult but extremely good are the essays of Paul de Man, for instance in his *Allegories of Reading* (1979). De Man gives some startling accounts of literary texts as works of persuasion. From a more psychoanalytically oriented perspective, see also Shoshana Felman's challenging but thought-provoking study, *The Literary Speech Act* (1983). Judith Butler's work, especially *Gender Trouble* (1990), *Bodies That Matter* (1993) and *Excitable Speech* (1997), offers a complex but compelling account of identity, gender and politics in general as 'performative' in ways explicitly indebted to J.L. Austin, even if he would not readily have recognized them. Jonathan Culler has a helpful and stimulating account of Butler and performative language in his *Literary Theory: A Very Short Introduction* (1997).

Secrets

Why do we read works of literature? What do we hope to get out of reading a novel, for example? In an essay entitled 'Secrets and Narrative Sequence', Frank Kermode writes: 'To read a novel expecting the satisfactions of closure and the receipt of a message is what most people find enough to do; they are easier with this method because it resembles the one that works for ordinary acts of communication' (Kermode 1983, 138). Most people, according to Kermode, read novels in the hope of reading something that adds up to a complete whole—a story with a clear structure and 'message'. They are looking for a good story line—something to get their teeth into on a long train-journey, for example, something which has a strong sense of what Kermode calls 'narrative sequence'. This is what is implied by the term 'consumer-fiction': to read a novel is to consume it. If a good novel is like a good meal, some novels are no doubt easier to chew and swallow than others. Stephen King's *The Shining* would be fast food in comparison with the feast of Henry James's *The Golden Bowl*. Kermode is working with a very basic model: novels can be compared with 'ordinary acts of communication' (by which he presumably means things like successfully negotiating your order with the person behind the service counter at Burger King) and most novel-reading is as simple and as sequential as abc. There are, however, things which get in the way of narrative sequence, and these are what Kermode calls *secrets*: 'secrets', he argues, 'are at odds with sequence' (138). What he is referring to here is the idea of textual details, specific aspects of the language of a text, particular patterns of images or rhetorical figures that a reader may not even notice on a 'consumerist' reading, but that are nevertheless present and which can provoke a sense of mystery. Thus in his essay, Kermode focuses on the enigmatic, repeated but apparently superfluous references to black and white in Joseph Conrad's *Under Western Eyes* (1911).

It may be that what draws many people towards the study of literature (the desire not only to consume the novels of, say, Stephen King, but also to reflect on their cultural, historical and ideological context, on how these novels work and what effects they produce) is a fascination with the possibilities of secrets. As we shall try to show in this chapter, the relationship between literature, secrecy and secrets is fundamental. Indeed, we would like to suggest that in many respects the question, 'What is literature?' can be considered as synonymous with the question, 'What is a secret?'

A secret is what is concealed, deliberately or inadvertently hidden, kept separate and apart. (The word 'secret' comes from the Latin *secernere*, where *se-* signifies 'apart' and *cernere* is 'to separate'.) Even the most rapidly consumed of novels involve secrets, if only because narratives are linear and the contents of a work cannot be presented all at once. Every narrative can be defined as a process of unfolding and revelation. It is precisely because there are things that remain hidden from us, and because we want to know what these things are, that we continue to read. This is the general context in which Roland Barthes elaborates his notion of the 'hermeneutic code'. The hermeneutic code concerns everything in a narrative text that has to do with the creation of an enigma and its possible clarification and explanation. In this respect it is perhaps helpful to recall that etymologically the word 'enigma' is linked to fable and storytelling. It derives from the Greek verb *ainissesthai*, 'to speak darkly', from *ainos*, 'a fable'. The most obvious example of enigma in the context of literary narratives is the whodunnit detective story: the question 'whodunnit?' forms the central enigma of the text and the hermeneutic code involves 'the various (formal) terms by which an enigma can be distinguished, suggested, formulated, held in suspense, and finally disclosed' (Barthes 1990b, 19). Why is this character doing this, for instance phoning the police or watching a letter burn on the fire? What is the significance of such and such an object, for instance the concrete-mixer in the cellar? How does this moment in the narrative throw light on the enigma of the crime? What is about to be revealed? All these questions are hermeneutic—they have to do with a work of interpretation and the hope or expectation or desire that the text will provide the answers. The mystery story or whodunnit is a particularly striking example, since (as its name indicates) it is explicitly concerned with drawing the reader into a mystery, and with manipulating her or him into asking questions, being watchful for 'clues' and looking for an explanation. In this sense, the pleasure of detective stories involves reading as itself a form of detecting.

But the mystery story or whodunnit is only one example of something that is much more general about the relationship between narratives and secrets. For, in an important sense, Chandler's *The Little Sister* (1949) or William McIlvanney's *Laidlaw* (1977) are no different from, say, D.H. Lawrence's *The Virgin and the Gipsy* (1930) or Toni Morrison's *The Bluest Eye* (1970). These novels likewise involve various kinds of mystery and concealment: they inevitably hold back a full revelation of what happens, releasing this information only gradually. More importantly perhaps, they generate a sense of mystery and secrecy through the very institution of the omniscient narrator. The idea of such a narrator is basically magical or occult (the word 'occult', it may be noted, literally means 'hidden', 'secret'): such narratives are structured by powers of foresight. For it is invariably part of the nature of omniscient narration (including all of what is known as 'realist fiction') that the narrator 'knows' the future and that this power of foresight is implicitly or explicitly articulated at numerous moments in a given narrative.

The Virgin and the Gipsy, for example, opens as follows:

> When the vicar's wife went off with a young and penniless man the scandal knew no bounds. Her two little girls were only seven and nine years old respectively. And the vicar was such a good husband. True, his hair was grey. But his moustache was dark, he was handsome, and still full of furtive passion for his unrestrained and beautiful wife.
>
> Why did she go? Why did she burst away with such an *éclat* of revulsion, like a touch of madness?
>
> Nobody gave any answer. Only the pious said she was a bad woman. While some of the good women kept silent. They knew.
>
> The two little girls never knew. (167)

This passage not only plays on the idea of secrecy as something related to a particular character (the vicar's 'furtive passion') but, through its omniscient narration, sets up various kinds of secret knowledge. The 'good women kept silent' because they 'knew': 'knew what?' we ask ourselves. 'The two little girls never knew': this, too, the narrator knows though does not, at least for the moment, reveal to us. What is it that the narrator knows? What is it that the two little girls 'never knew'?

The 'never' in particular is a subtle and eerie word, suggesting that the perspective from which the narrator speaks is in fact posthumous as regards the girls themselves. On rereading—that is to say, with the benefits of readerly hindsight—we may find this word 'never' even more peculiar, since the two girls who 'never knew' do not die, in fact, in the course of the narrative. In this context one might want to ask: What planet, or fictional world, does this narrator come from?

Of course, narrators are just linguistic fabrications, merely textual creatures. Nevertheless, we are drawn into their worlds and a crucial part of the magic, sorcery or 'occultism' of literary narratives has to do with the mysterious but seductive 'reality' of the narrator. An omniscient narrator is a strange figure, by its very nature. The strangeness consists not only in the basic idea of omniscience itself, but also in what is concealed within that omniscience. Narrators may appear to be all-knowing but they are certainly not all-telling. A narrator is always secretive, in other words, and this secretiveness concerns both the notion of storytelling-as-gradual-revelation and the question of what we do not and perhaps can never know about this narrator. Thus we may recognize that one of the most secretive or enigmatic aspects of a literary narrative may concern the character of its narrator (whether omniscient or not): what, for example, are we to make of the narrator of Henry James's *Washington Square*, or Joseph Conrad's *Heart of Darkness*, or Virginia Woolf's *Mrs Dalloway*?

Toni Morrison's *The Bluest Eye*, on the other hand, involves the final revelation that the two primary narrators (an omniscient narrator and one of the characters, Claudia) are apparently the same: such a revelation does not serve to clarify or rationalize the nature of the storytelling but, on the contrary, exacerbates the reader's sense of the narrator-as-enigma. *The Bluest Eye* indeed begins with mystery—with the enigmatic presentation (and equally enigmatic repetition or re-presentation) of the text of what appears to be a US school primer: 'Here is the house. It is green and white. It has a red door. It is very pretty. Here is the family' (7). In a forcefully disjunctive way this opening switches, without any explanation, to a passage of italicized text which starts: 'Quiet as it's kept, there were no marigolds in the fall of 1941. We thought, at the time, that it was because Pecola was having her father's baby that the marigolds did not grow' (9). There is a sense here of a narrator speaking knowledgeably from a position of hindsight ('We thought, at the time'), of someone who knows things which may or may not be revealed as the narrative unfolds. More provocatively, however, we are left with the mysteriousness of the first four words, 'Quiet as it's kept'. What is 'it'? Who or what is keeping quiet? Why are we being alerted to what appears to be secret and why should it be kept quiet? Is the narrator imparting information to the reader or keeping quiet about it?

If a logic of secrecy, concealment and revelation is crucial to the workings of any novel, it is also evident in less obviously narrative texts such as lyric poetry. Consider the following poem (No. 180), written around 1859, by Emily Dickinson:

> Our lives are Swiss—
> So still—so Cool—
> Till some odd afternoon
> The Alps neglect their Curtains
> And we look farther on!
>
> *Italy* stands the other side!
> While like a guard between—
> The solemn Alps—
> The siren Alps—
> Forever intervene!

This poem is about what is concealed or hidden from us: it gestures towards something secret. It suggests that there are moments of revelation or epiphany ('some odd afternoon') when we are able to 'look farther on'—beyond the Alps. These moments, or this moment (since technically only one 'odd afternoon' is mentioned), might be compared to what Wordsworth calls 'spots of time' or Hardy 'moments of vision'. Dickinson's poem appears, at least on one level, to describe or relate such a moment and to attribute great significance to it. But if there is a revelation, if the secret and perhaps the meaning of our lives is being referred to here, what is it? The poem says only that 'we look farther on' and that '*Italy* stands the other side': it remains unclear what it is that is being revealed at this moment when 'The Alps neglect their Curtains'. Is it '*Italy*' simply? But what does '*Italy*' mean? The word 'Forever' in the final line of the poem underlines the strangeness of what is going on here and the continuing or unresolved *enigma* of what the poem has to tell us. The definiteness and absoluteness of 'forever' confirms, in effect, the sense that this poem at once reveals and can never reveal its secret.

Dickinson's poem could in fact be described as exemplary of literary texts in general. In particular it dramatizes the fact that the notion of a secret is paradoxical. Jacques Derrida has formulated the paradox as follows: '*There is something secret.* But it does not conceal itself' (Derrida 1992b, 21). In an essay called 'Derrida's Topographies', J. Hillis Miller offers a helpful account of this paradox. On the one hand, Miller points out, 'We normally think of a secret as in principle discoverable' (Miller 1994, 16): Kermode's 'satisfactions of closure' and 'the receipt of a message' and Barthes's 'hermeneutic code' make sense only if we accept this principle. There is closure and there is a message to the extent that 'All is revealed'. There is a valid hermeneutic effort or labour of interpretation because there is something to be interpreted, seized, comprehended. On the other hand, however, there is the question of what Miller calls a 'true secret'. He notes: 'a true secret, if there is such a thing, cannot ever, by any means, be revealed' (17). And Miller then elaborates on the Derridean paradox: 'A true secret . . . is not hidden somewhere . . . A true secret is all on the surface. This superficiality cannot by any hermeneutic procedures, material or linguistic, be gone behind. A literary text (and any text may be taken as literary) says what it says' (17). Thus, in Dickinson's poem, there would be the enigmatic, perhaps ultimately cryptic status of '*Italy*': there is nothing 'within' or 'behind' this appositely italicized '*Italy*'. The text says (only) what it says: '*Italy* stands the other side!' It does not say that 'Italy' symbolizes 'romance' or that it represents 'revolution' or even that it can be taken as a synonym for 'the secret'. However superficial or profound or elliptical, it simply says what it says. In these terms, then, it is not only a question of literature as involving secrets that are concealed and that are gradually or finally brought to light. It is also—and perhaps more enigmatically—a matter of a secrecy that does not involve any kind of concealment at all.

A literary text 'says what it says': it says, for example, that 'we look farther on!' Or it says, at the very outset, what its title is. Perhaps the secrecy of literary works begins with titles themselves. Perhaps what makes a work 'literary' is in part that its title remains enigmatic. A literary text says that it is called 'The Virgin and the Gipsy' or 'The Bluest Eye' or, say, 'The Shining'. What do these titles refer to? Does Lawrence's text, for example, finally and clearly establish what is to be understood by 'the dark, tremulous potent secret of . . . virginity' (207), or what is meant by the idea of a gipsy, of a figure that is apparently outside 'the vast and gruesome clutch of our law' (236)? And what is the status and significance of the conjuctive ('and') in the title of this Lawrence text? What does 'and' mean? Conversely, what is signified by 'the bluest eye' and in the eyes of which reader or beholder? Or again, what do those two words, 'the shining', have to tell us? Each of these examples, in fact, resists what Kermode refers to as 'the satisfactions of closure' and 'the receipt of a message'. It is their readability *and* their resistance to being read that makes them 'literary', in Hillis Miller's terms. This is in part at least why the question 'What is literature?' is inseparable from the question 'What is a secret?'

It has been traditional to think of meaning as something behind or within the words of a text. Reading has conventionally been thought of on the basis of a surface-depth model, with the words of the text as the surface and the meaning lurking somewhere inside or underneath. The text has secrets and often explicitly conveys and exploits the idea that it has the power to disclose or preserve these secrets. With poststructuralist accounts of literature, however, there has been an important shift away from this surface-depth model. This is not to say that the surface-depth model is no longer relevant. Indeed it is very difficult to think about meaning or about reading without relying to a considerable extent on the values and assumptions of this model. Moreover, as we have been trying to suggest, virtually every literary text can be seen to work with this model. It is, in short, the theory and practice of secrets as (in principle) discoverable. Poststructuralism, however, is generally suspicious about any reading of a literary text that would equate a secret with the 'true' or 'ultimate ' meaning. Poststructuralism pays particular attention to the paradoxical nature of secrets—to the fact that secrets can be undiscoverable and yet at the same time unconcealed. In this sense the secrets of a literary text may be right in front of our eyes and yet they remain secret, like 'the purloined letter' on the mantelpiece in Edgar Allan Poe's story of that title, or like the solemn, siren Alps, some odd afternoon.

To conclude, we could briefly consider secrets in two further ways. At the beginning of this chapter we put forward the hypothesis that what attracts many people to the study of literature is a fascination with the idea of secrets. We have sought to elaborate on this by considering some of the many respects in which literary texts are bound up with the enigmatic, mysterious, secret and (in a double sense) occult. And we have attempted to emphasize the important paradox whereby secrets can be discoverable but that a 'true secret', if there is such a thing, can never be discovered. Our focus has been on texts and on how they compel, manipulate and fascinate their readers. But there is also another perspective from which to think about literature and secrets. This would be from that of the reader rather than the text, and in particular as regards the notion of a reader who is interested not so much in the idea of secrets *in the text* (whodunnit? what is going to happen next? and so on) but rather in the possibilities of secrets *within herself* or *within himself*, secrets that may have to do with dreams, memories, fantasies, speculations and desires set off by the text, thoughts and feelings that may never have been experienced before—that is to say, in a surprising way, secret thoughts and feelings. It is in this context that literary texts can be acknowledged as having uncanny powers, including an ability to alter people's very sense of themselves, of their identity and 'place'.

Secondly, we might try to think about the possibility of a 'true secret' within ourselves, about the paradox of what a 'true secret' might be. This touches on what we refer to in the following chapter as 'the unpresentable'. The name which is sometimes given to this notion of a true secret is 'death'. The Ghost of Hamlet's father comes to Hamlet and says:

> But that I am forbid
> To tell the secrets of my prison-house,
> I could a tale unfold whose lightest word
> Would harrow up thy soul, freeze thy young blood,
> Make thy two eyes like stars start from their spheres,
> Thy knotted and combined locks to part,
> And each particular hair to stand an end
> Like quills upon the fretful porpentine.
> But this eternal blazon must not be
> To ears of flesh and blood. (I, v, 14–21)

The Ghost at once tells and does not tell. The Ghost keeps the secrets of its prison-house even as it evokes the effects of their disclosure. This is another way of talking about the enigma of literature: whether in the form of Shakespearean tragedy or a twentieth-century whodunnit, literature is about what cannot be told, and in particular about that impossible package holiday which Hamlet refers to as that 'undiscover'd country, from whose bourn / No traveller returns' (III, i, 78–9). This undiscovered country is neither inside us nor outside us. It is a secret that does not conceal itself: the fact that we are going to die but that, as Freud puts it, 'It is indeed impossible to imagine our own death; and whenever we attempt to do so we can perceive that we are in fact still present as spectators' (Freud 1985a, 77).

Further reading

Besides the readable and stimulating essay on 'Secrets and Narrative Sequence' (1983), Frank Kermode has written an important study entitled *The Genesis of Secrecy* (1979) which deals with various questions about, for example, 'why narratives are obscure', why we prefer an enigma to 'a muddle', and so on. Barthes's *S/Z* (1990b) contains brilliant insights into senses of secrecy and enigma in reading. Especially in its focus on silence and the unspoken, Pierre Macherey's *A Theory of Literary Production* (1978) is a powerful account of literary secrets in relation to politics and ideology. From a quite different, intensively psychoanalytic perspective, Esther Rashkin's *Family Secrets* (1992) is a thought-provoking though somewhat cryptic study of mainly nineteenth-century literary works. Jacques Derrida has written numerous essays about secrets: see, in particular, the fascinating but difficult 'Fors' (Derrida 1986b) and 'Passions' (Derrida 1992b). In his essay on 'Derrida's Topographies' (1994), on the other hand, J. Hillis Miller provides an excellent account of Derrida's work on secrets (especially 'Fors') and more generally a valuable and accessible introduction to 'Derrida and literature'.

The postmodern

Since this book does not attempt to introduce different critical schools or historical periods of literature, it may seem inappropriate to include a chapter on the postmodern. In the following pages, however, we wish to suggest that this topic provides us with an invaluable set of terms for thinking about literary and other cultural texts, that to a significant degree it involves ways of thinking which are unavoidable at the start of the twenty-first century.

The word 'postmodern' itself is evocative of ways of thinking characteristic of the postmodern, in that it paradoxically refers to what is after ('post') the contemporary ('modern'). How can something be *after* the contemporary? In this respect, in as much as they are confronting the importance of paradox in relation to the contemporary study of literature, other chapters in this book are also dealing with the postmodern. But this paradox of the time of the postmodern also points to the fact that, strictly speaking, the postmodern should not be thought of as a term of periodization: the postmodern challenges our thinking about time, challenges us to see the present in the past, the future in the present, the present in a kind of no-time.

Because it is paradoxical, the postmodern resists definition. It resists the totalizing gesture of a metalanguage, the attempt to describe it as a set of coherent explanatory theories. Rather than trying to explain it in terms of a fixed philosophical position or as a kind of knowledge, we shall instead present a 'postmodern vocabulary' in order to suggest its mobile, fragmented and paradoxical nature.

A postmodern vocabulary

Undecidability

Undecidability involves the impossibility of deciding between two or more competing interpretations. As we point out in Chapter 16, classical logic is founded on the law of non-contradiction: something cannot be both A and not A at the same time. The postmodern gives particular emphasis to ways in which this law may be productively questioned or suspended. A classical example of this is the Cretan liar paradox. If someone says 'I am a liar', how can we tell if that person is lying or not? Our ability to make a decision about the validity of such a statement is, at least temporarily, suspended. According to classical logic, the Cretan liar paradox is an isolated and particular instance of a paradoxical statement. For the postmodern, by contrast, the suspension of the law of non-contradiction is endemic. In the postmodern, all absolute values—such as the traditional values of God, Truth, Reason, the Law and so on—are understood to be in suspense. They become sites of questioning, of rethinking, of new kinds of affirmation. The postmodern, that is to say, does not simply reject the possibility of making decisions. Rather, it gives new attention to the value of the undecidable. What the new critics of the middle of the twentieth century called ambiguity or paradox is now considered in terms of undecidability. The difference is that for the new critics literary texts tended to exploit the polysemic potential of language to create a unified whole in which ambiguity produced an enriching of the text's final unity. For the postmodern critics, by contrast, undecidability radically undermines the very principle of unity—of literary wholeness. Undecidability splits the text, disorders it. Undecidability dislodges the principle of a single final meaning in a literary text. It haunts. As Derrida puts it, there is no decision, nor any kind of moral or political responsibility that is not haunted, that is not 'structured by [the] *experience and experiment of the undecidable*' (Derrida 1988, 116).

A new enlightenment

Theorists of the postmodern are drawn into that exhilarating as well as terrifying 'play' of a text thrown up by its forms of undecidability. For those nervous of the postmodern, this results directly in nihilism and chaos. But for postmodernists it is precisely those monolithic, unthinking assumptions about a fixed grounding for political, ethical and textual decisions that lead to abhorrent results. It is the belief in a transcendent explanatory system—such as God, national identity or historical materialism, to name just three—which leads to terror, persecution and oppression. In each case, there is a transcendental value (God, the Nation-State, a certain reading of the writings of Marx) which can justify any excess. Postmodernists suggest that reason itself has been used to justify all sorts of oppression. Reason may be said to lie behind the Stalinist terror, for example, in the form of a rational or 'scientific' development of Marx's thinking. Alternatively, in the science of eugenics, 'rational' argument or so-called empirical science helped to justify the Jewish holocaust on grounds of racial difference. This is why, writing in 1944, Theodor Adorno and Max Horkheimer argue that 'Enlightenment is totalitarian' (quoted in Docherty 1993, 5). 'Enlightenment' here can be understood very generally as a way of characterizing Western thought since the seventeenth century. Very simply, the notion of the Enlightenment entails the assertion of the power of reason over both superstition and nature, the belief that a combination of abstract reason and empirical science will lead to knowledge and eventually to political and social progress. By contrast, the postmodern is sceptical about claims of progress in history, not least because of the necessary marginalization (of the apparently non-progressive) which it entails.

A common misunderstanding of the postmodern is that it involves simply an assertion and celebration of the irrational. The postmodern can more helpfully be understood, however, as a *suspension and deconstruction* of the opposition between the rational and the irrational. Irrationalism in itself is only another form of rationalism because it is dependent for its definition on its opposite (only someone who is *rational* could conceive of someone or something as *irrational* and the irrational can only be defined in opposition to the rational). The postmodern could be seen as concerned rather with what Jacques Derrida calls 'a new enlightenment' (Derrida 1988, 141) concerned to explore the value and importance of ways of thinking that cannot be reduced to an opposition between the rational and the irrational.

Dissemination

Postmodern resistance to totalizing forces such as rationalism or irrationalism means that its characteristic form is fragmentary. Fragmentation, in fact, is commonly associated with the romantic and modern periods: poems such as Percy Bysshe Shelley's 'Ozymandias' (1818) from the romantic period and T.S. Eliot's *The Waste Land* (1922) from the modern period are crucially concerned with the notion of the fragment. In this sense, fragmentation is not unique to the postmodern. But the postmodern entails a new kind of critique of the very ideas of fragment and totality. This has taken the form of, among other things, a fundamental questioning of the notion of originality and correspondingly a new kind of emphasis on citation and intertextuality, parody and pastiche. In this respect, originality, which has been of such importance as an aesthetic value since at least the nineteenth century, is seen as a kind of ideological fetish, rather than the overriding criterion in aesthetic judgements. Moreover, we might remark a significant difference between notions of fragmentation in the postmodern and those in romanticism and modernism: fragmentation in the postmodern does not depend on the possibility of an original 'unity' which has been lost. The romantics and modernists, by contrast, tend to figure fragmentation in terms of the loss of an original wholeness. Another way of thinking about postmodern fragmentation is in terms of dissemination. Dissemination involves a sense of scattering (as in a scattering of seeds or 'semes'), a scattering of origins and ends, of identity, centre and presence. Postmodern fragmentation is without origins, it is dissemination without any assurance of a centre or destination.

Little and grand narratives

One of the best-known distinctions in the postmodern is that made by Jean-François Lyotard concerning what he calls 'grand' narratives and 'little' narratives. 'Grand narratives' such as Christianity, Marxism, the Enlightenment attempt to provide a framework for everything. Such narratives follow a 'teleological' movement towards a time of equality and justice: after the last judgement, the revolution, or the scientific conquest of nature, injustice, unreason and evil will end. Lyotard argues that the contemporary 'world-view', by contrast, is characterized by 'little narratives'. Contemporary Western discourse is characteristically unstable, fragmented, dispersed—not a *world-view* at all. 'Little narratives' present local explanations of individual events or phenomena but do not claim to explain everything. Little narratives are fragmentary, non-totalizing and non-teleological. Lyotard claims that, in the West, grand narratives have all but lost their efficacy, that their legitimacy and their powers of legitimation have been dispersed. Legitimation is now plural, local and contingent. No supreme authority—Marx, Hegel or God—can sit in judgement. In his provocatively titled book *The Gulf War Did Not Take Place* (1995), for example, Jean Baudrillard offers an analysis of the way that such an event is as much a function of televisual and other media representations as of anything else. Despite the controversial nature of his title, Baudrillard is not so much suggesting that there was no war as that in an unprecedented way its very actuality was and remains indissoluble from media representations.

The phenomenon described here has also been described by the phrase 'legitimation crisis', borrowed from the German thinker Jürgen Habermas. Habermas uses this phrase to denote a situation in which all 'master codes' or grand narratives, all conventions, institutions, final authorities have been put into a state of crisis. And in the last century or so, the announcements of the death of God, 'man' and the author have successively dramatized this dissolution of authority.

Simulation

The Western philosophical tradition of aesthetics has relied heavily on a distinction between the real and its copy. This goes back at least as far as Plato, who argued that painters, actors, dramatists and so on, all produce representations or 'imitations' of the real world. (In fact, Plato argues that even a bed is an imitation of the concept or idea of a bed, so that a picture of a bed is a second-degree copy of an essential but unobtainable bed, the essence of bedness.) This way of thinking has given rise to a hierarchical opposition between the real and the copy. And the hierarchy corresponds to that of nature and fabrication, or nature and artifice. The postmodern, however, challenges such hierarchies and shows how the set of values associated with these oppositions can be questioned. As the film *Falling Down* (1993) starring Michael Douglas makes clear, the photograph of the hamburger in the fast-food restaurant is infinitely superior to the rather sad and surprisingly expensive artifact that you have just bought. Even nature, in this postmodern reversal, is subject to improvement. To adopt Umberto Eco's words, 'technology can give us more reality than nature can' (Eco 1993, 203). Films such as *Wag the Dog* (1997) and *The Truman Show* (1998) demonstrate a postmodern fascination with the technologies of virtual reality. In the first, uncannily prescient film, war is created by a Hollywood producer to distract public attention from a sex scandal involving the U.S. President, while in the second a man unwittingly lives his life in the fabricated studio world of a 24-hour-a-day soap opera.

Another way of thinking about this phenomenon is to use Jean Baudrillard's term 'simulation' (or 'the simulacrum'). Simulation is contrasted with representation. The latter works on the basis that there is a distinction between what the linguist Ferdinand de Saussure calls the signifier and the signified, between a word or 'sound-image', and the idea or the 'mental concept' that it represents. In classical terms, there is an absolute distinction between the word 'hamburger' and what that word represents. Similarly, common sense tells us that there is a clear and necessary distinction between a photograph of a hamburger and a hamburger. Simulation, by contrast, short-circuits such distinctions. Saturated by images—on computers, TV, advertising hoardings, magazines, newspapers and so on—the 'real' becomes unthinkable without the copy. In other words, simulation involves the disturbing idea that the copy is not a copy of something real; the real is inextricable from the significance and effects of the copy. That hamburger that looks so tempting is far more delicious than any you could ever taste. But, paradoxically, when you taste *your* hamburger, you are at the same time tasting what is created by advertising images of hamburgers. If Coke really is it, then, it is because our experience of drinking Coca Cola cannot be disengaged from the seductive lifestyle images of its advertising, from those insidious effects of the brand name, whereby the desirability of a given product is in a sense *branded* into our consciousness and unconscious. This leads to the world of what Jean Baudrillard calls the hyperreal, in which reality is fabricated by technology. As Baudrillard puts it 'simulation is no longer that of a territory, a referential being or substance. It is the generation by models of a real without origin or reality; a hyperreal . . . Henceforth it is the map that precedes the territory' (Baudrillard 1988, 166).

Depthlessness

Another way of talking about simulation or the simulacrum is in terms of depthlessness. If one governing opposition for Western thought has been between the real and the copy, between nature and artifice, another has been between surface and depth. An obvious example of this would be the notion of 'expression', which involves the idea that the words which we write or speak *express* something 'inside' our heads (thoughts). The words are the surface, whereas our thoughts or consciousness represent depth. Similarly, the idea of the self, the very possibility of being human, has conventionally relied on such an opposition: the subject or self is constituted as a relation between surface and depth, inside and outside.

Fredric Jameson provides a useful account of four depth models that, he argues, have dominated the West in the twentieth century (Jameson 1993, 70):

1. Marxism: Marxism crucially depends on the notion of ideology. Put simply, this involves the idea that we do not see the reality of the world around us but only what we have been indoctrinated into seeing.
2. Psychoanalysis: Freud's theories are based on the distinction between the conscious and the unconscious, whereby the unconscious is held to be the truth behind or beneath the distorted representation which we call consciousness.
3. Existentialism: in its various forms, existentialism relies on a distinction between, on the one hand, authentic existence and, on the other hand, inauthenticity: authenticity is the truth of selfhood underlying the distortions effected by a state of inauthenticity.
4. Semiotics: as we have seen, Saussurean notions of language presuppose a distinction between the signifier on the one hand and the signified on the other. The word or sound-image indicates an underlying idea or mental concept.

In each case, the authentic or real is understood to be hidden or disguised, while the surface phenomenon, the facade, is an inauthentic distortion or arbitrary offshoot of the underlying truth. With the postmodern, all of these surface-depth models are shaken up. The postmodern suspends, dislocates and transforms the oppositional structures presupposed by major Western modes of thought—by classical Marxism, psychoanalysis, existentialism, semiotics.

Pastiche

Jameson also distinguishes between parody and pastiche. Both rely on imitation of earlier texts or objects. In parody, there is an impulse to ridicule by exaggerating the distance of the original text from 'normal' discourse. The postmodern, however, no longer accepts the notion of 'normal' language: pastiche is 'blank' parody in which there is no single model followed, no single impulse such as ridicule and no sense of a distance from any norm (see Jameson 1992, 166–7). Postmodern architecture, for example, borrows elements from various earlier periods of architecture and puts them in eclectic juxtaposition. In what the architectural critic Charles Jencks has termed 'radical eclecticism' (Jencks 1993, 283), there is no single stable reference. Similarly, a Madonna video parodies, for example, *film noir*, Marilyn Monroe, contemporary pornography, avant-garde erotic art and Catholic icons, in an apparently random dissonance of combination. Indeed this sense of eclecticism is what distinguishes contemporary culture for Lyotard:

> Eclecticism is the degree zero of contemporary general culture: one listens to reggae, watches a western, eats McDonald's food for lunch and local cuisine for dinner, wears Paris perfume in Tokyo and retro clothes in Hong Kong; knowledge is a matter for TV games. (Lyotard 1992, 145)

This hybridization, a radical intertexuality which mixes forms, genres, conventions, media, dissolves boundaries between high and low art, between the serious and the ludic. Genre becomes unstable, especially in such texts as D.M. Thomas's *The White Hotel* (1981) which exploits the genres of poetry and psychoanalytic case-study, or John Fowles's *The French Lieutenant's Woman* (1969), which uses history textbooks to tell a love story. Two of the most creative and powerful television drama series yet produced are exemplary in this respect: David Lynch's *Twin Peaks* mixes up the detective story with forms such as horror, avant-garde or art-house movies, soap opera and so on, while Dennis Potter's *The Singing Detective* dissolves the borders between the detective story and Hollywood musicals, psychological dramas, the *Bildungsroman* and so on.

One of the most dramatic recent examples of this mixing of genres concerns the Gulf War. In a 'docudrama' about the war entitled *The Heroes of Desert Storm*, broadcast in the United States by ABC, the audience is told that the film 'interweaves news footage and dramatizations with actors and actual participants. To achieve realism, no distinction is made among these elements' (quoted in Rogin 1994, 26). How can you tell if people are really dying or if they are only pretending?

The unpresentable

Since the postmodern challenges the distinction between mimesis or copy on the one hand, and the real on the other, it contests the modes of its own representation, of representation itself. Thus it paradoxically *defines* itself in terms of liminal phenomena which defy both categorization and, finally, expression—the unpresentable, or in some of its other formulations, the sublime (Lyotard), the abject (Kristeva), the unnamable (Beckett). Thus Samuel Beckett's writing, for example, may be said to be constituted by the paradoxical impossibility and necessity of discourse—'I can't go on, I'll go on' (*The Unnamable*, 418).

If in 'going on' there are no clear rules of representation, mimesis, temporality, then the artist is working within the terms of the radically undecidable, or the yet to be decided, as Lyotard remarks:

> The postmodern would be that which, in the modern, puts forward the unpresentable in presentation itself: that which denies itself the solace of good forms, the consensus of a taste which would make it possible to share collectively the nostalgia for the unattainable; that which searches for new presentations, not in order to enjoy them but in order to impart a stronger sense of the unpresentable . . . the artist and the writer, then, are working without rules in order to formulate the rules of what *will have been done*. Hence the fact that work and text have the characters of an *event* . . . *Post modern* would have to be understood according to the paradox of the future (*post*) anterior (*modo*). (Lyotard 1992, 149–50)

The unpresentable is an effect, not least, of a disturbance of temporality, of the linear progression of time. The postmodern is grammatically specified as inhabiting the future perfect, what will have been. There is no present, no presence of the present, on the basis of which representation may take place.

Decentring

Everything that we have said in this chapter may be summarized in terms of the notion of decentring. The postmodern challenges the 'logocentric' (the authority of the word, the possibility of final meanings or of being in the presence of pure 'sense'). It challenges the ethnocentric (the authority of one ethnic 'identity' or culture—such as Europe or 'the West'). It challenges the phallocentric (everything that privileges the symbolic power and significance of the phallus). As Ihab Hassan remarks, the postmodern may be summarized by a list of words prefixed by 'de-' and 'di-': 'deconstruction, decentring, dissemination, dispersal, displacement, difference, discontinuity, demystification, delegitimation, disappearance' (Hassan 1989, 309).

In place of the centre, but not in its place, there is alterity, otherness, a multiplicity and dispersal of centres, origins, presences.

Further reading

Two good collections of essays are Brooker's *Modernism/Postmodernism* (1992) and Docherty's *Postmodernism* (1993), both of which have reasonably accessible introductions to the subject. Lyotard's *The Postmodern Condition* (1984) is, by now (paradoxically) a classic text to start with—'Answering the Question: What is Postmodernism?' (1992) is particularly useful. His more recent *Postmodern Fables* (1997) offers a series of brief, elliptical and often enigmatic essays on postmodern topics. Jameson's 'The Politics of Theory' (1988) and Linda Hutcheon's books *A Poetics of Postmodernism* (1988) and *The Politics of Postmodernism* (1989) provide strong, politicized accounts of the postmodern. Steven Connor offers an excellent overview of the postmodern in his *Postmodernist Culture* (1997). For an engaging study of the postmodern in relation to romance, romanticism and politics, see Elam (1992). Readings and Schaber, eds, *Postmodernism Across the Ages* (1993) is a useful collection of essays which seek to challenge the common assumption that postmodernism is a period term referring to the late twentieth century.

Pleasure

Whether in a seminar or at the pub, often the first thing that gets asked about a book is: Did you enjoy it? This is not just a way of making conversation, but also suggests the fundamental importance of pleasure when it comes to reading. In fact, the question 'Did you enjoy it?', far from breaking the ice and starting a passionate discussion, is generally followed by a terse 'Yes' or 'No' and then forgotten. We may talk about things we enjoy in a work of literature—the gripping narrative, the appealing characters, the power of the language, the comedy and pathos—but we do not very often talk about the enjoyment itself, about what enjoyment or pleasure *is*. There are at least two reasons for this. In the first place, pleasure, enjoyment, emotional and indeed erotic excitement are extremely difficult, or even impossible, to talk about. Secondly, such pleasures tend to border on the transgressive or taboo. But as we hope to show in the course of this chapter, pleasure is crucial to, and even synonymous with, literature itself. This is not to construe the literary as 'mere' play, as simply hedonistic or self-indulgent. Instead we will seek to describe a sense of pleasure and of literature that may be both disconcerting and subversive.

Take a text that might seem relatively innocuous, a story called 'Bliss' (1920) by the New Zealand writer Katherine Mansfield. 'Bliss' concerns a 30-year-old woman called Bertha Young and her feelings of extreme pleasure before and during a dinner-party at her home. She and her husband Harry entertain an erotically powerful blond woman called Pearl Fulton, a ludicrous poet called Eddie Warren and a more or less equally risible couple, Mr and Mrs Norman Knight. Bertha is consistently described as feeling a 'fire of bliss' (311) inside her: 'Everything was good—was right. All that happened seemed to fill again her brimming cup of bliss' (311). She is 'as much in love as ever' (308) with her

241

husband, but she has also fallen in love with the beautiful Pearl Fulton: 'she always did fall in love with beautiful women who had something strange about them' (307). Whether it is the lovely appearance of the dinner table or the blossoming pear tree which Bertha takes Pearl to look at from the drawing-room balcony, everything helps to give Bertha the feeling of being (like Keats in 'Ode to a Nightingale') 'too happy' (308). The story ends with an excruciating moment of revelation, however, as Bertha inadvertently discovers that her husband and Pearl Fulton are lovers: unaware that Bertha can see them, the couple exchange intimacies in the hall. Bertha's feelings of bliss are finally, brutally effaced.

This is how 'Bliss' begins:

> Although Bertha Young was thirty she still had moments like this when she wanted to run instead of walk, to take dancing steps on and off the pavement, to bowl a hoop, to throw something up in the air and catch it again, or to stand still and laugh at—nothing—at nothing, simply.
>
> What can you do if you are thirty and, turning the corner of your own street, you are overcome, suddenly, by a feeling of bliss—absolute bliss!—as though you'd suddenly swallowed a bright piece of that late afternoon sun and it burned in your bosom, sending out a little shower of sparks into every particle, into every finger and toe? (305)

Bertha can scarcely contain herself, she is overcome by such a feeling of bliss that she does not know what to do with herself. The passage suggests a number of significant things about the nature of pleasure. First, there is an evocation of laughter which may complement some of the remarks we make about laughter in Chapter 11: Bertha wants 'to stand still and laugh at—nothing—at nothing, simply'. Laughter, the desire to laugh, is one manifestation of Bertha's feelings of extreme pleasure or 'bliss'. But more precisely laughter is identified with a sense of 'nothing, simply'. We may recall here Georges Bataille's remark: '[when I laugh,] I am in fact nothing other than the laughter which takes hold of me' (Bataille 1973, 364). There is, for Bertha, the desire to laugh but a desire for laughter that would be 'at nothing', a sense of laughter as pointless, as itself nothing.

Second, and related to this, there is the sense of bliss (like the force of uncontrollable laughter) as something by which a subject—Bertha Young—is 'overcome'. The subject is no longer in control, but rather is in danger of no longer being a subject. She is in danger of shattering, as if into a 'shower of sparks'. Third, the passage suggests a striking correlation between 'bliss' and the inexpressible. The language of the extract resorts to the metaphorical, figurative and paradoxical (it was '*as though* you'd suddenly swallowed a bright piece of that late afternoon sun') precisely because it would appear that there is no other way of describing this 'feeling of bliss'. This feeling of bliss is like having a foreign body inside you (as if you'd suddenly swallowed a piece of the sun): it's alien to yourself but burning inside you. Fourth, and leading on from this, there is the suggestion that pleasure can be painful at the same time: the burning bosom here might be compared with the 'aching Pleasure' evoked in Keats's 'Ode to Melancholy'.

Finally, and perhaps most crucially, the passage draws the reader into the experience that is being described. It intimates a subtle kind of performative (see Chapter 24), that is to say we can think about the passage as not only describing something but also *doing something*. Pleasure, up to and perhaps even beyond the extreme form of pleasure to which Bertha gives the name 'bliss', is not just a topic or theme *in* the text: it also *is* the text, it is the title of the text and it is a potential effect of reading and interacting with the text. The text draws us into a sense of what Wordsworth refers to when he declares, of his experience of the first days of the French Revolution, in *The Prelude*: 'Bliss was it in that dawn to be alive' (Book XI, 108). Through its evocations of the loveliness of the world (a blue dish, a pear tree in blossom), Mansfield's story affirms and calls on us to affirm the inexpressible pleasures of being alive: it evokes the experience of a revolution in sensibility. It also gives us the pleasure of reading about eroticism, about the subtleties of erotic feelings between people. It gives us the pleasures of identification, irony, suspense and social satire. Last but not least, 'Bliss' gives us all of these things in language: the experience of pleasure is an experience of words, a pleasure in words, even as it points towards a sense of pleasure that is inexpressible, beyond words.

The pleasure of reading 'Bliss' starts with the deceptive simplicity of its narrative perspective. We are confronted here with an apparently omniscient or telepathic narrator who is capable of inhabiting the mind, body and feelings of the protagonist. The narrator gives us Bertha Young's thoughts and feelings: she does this not only through a third-person narration ('she still had moments', 'she wanted to run') but also, in the second paragraph of the extract, in the second-person ('you are overcome'). This is unusual—though an important characteristic of

Mansfield's work generally—and strangely insidious: the 'you', after all, may not finally stop short of *you*, the reader. The subtle, almost imperceptible way in which the text draws us into the experience of what is being described can be illustrated in the very opening words of the story: 'Although Bertha Young was thirty she still had moments like this'. The word 'this' seems to call on the reader to acknowledge or accept something already evident, already presented to her or him. Discreetly, deftly, it draws the reader into the immediate here and now of the experience of bliss.

Another aspect of the pleasure of Mansfield's story has to do with its creation of irony and suspense. The text works through suspense, through the pleasure of suspension and an ominous suspension of pleasure. For while the narrative perspective invites us to identify with Bertha and her feelings of bliss, the text also generates other, more specifically *readerly* kinds of pleasure. Bertha's feelings of 'bliss', for example, are at various moments represented in ironic terms. The reader is given a strong sense that—despite the repeated evocations of the 'fire of bliss', the incredible beauty of the table, the pear tree and so on—Bertha Young may have a rather limited experience of bliss, especially in sexual terms. Near the end of the story we are told that, as people are about to start leaving the party, 'For the first time in her life Bertha Young desired her husband' (314). Bliss in this case seems to have been postponed. The reader takes pleasure, then, in being able to identify with the protagonist but to experience at the same time a sense of ironic detachment. Above all, readerly pleasure is generated by the pervasive sense that something is going to happen, that the narrator knows something (and soon perhaps the reader will know something too) which fundamentally complicates Bertha's feelings of 'bliss'. Bliss, then, seems to involve a state of suspension—for Bertha, for the reader and, differently, for the very structure of narration.

On this basis we can perhaps formulate one or two more general propositions about pleasure and literature. Literature is about the possibilities of pleasure. It is about the idea that readerly pleasure is erotic. Literature is erotic (even if it is not literally concerned with erotic or sexual topics or themes) because it is always concerned with seducing the reader. Literary texts can seduce us, or, put more strongly, they need to seduce us. In a sense there is no reason to read a literary text, it serves no purpose, has no function. And this is why, as Ross Chambers has argued, in his book *Story and Situation: Narrative Seduction and the Power of Fiction* (1984), the essential 'power' of a literary text is its power of seduction. In particular, a literary text can seduce us through a logic of what Freud calls 'disavowal'. Disavowal involves the situation in which someone knows that such and such is not true but nevertheless thinks, speaks or acts as if it is true. Disavowal involves thinking: 'I know, but still . . .'. The process of disavowal whereby we can be seduced into the world of literature, into fictional worlds, has been neatly phrased by Roland Barthes in his book, *The Pleasure of the Text* (1973): the reader *disavows*, in other words he or she keeps thinking, '*I know these are only words, but all the same* . . .' (Barthes 1990a, 47). The logic of disavowal perhaps offers a more precise way of thinking about how we read works of literature than Coleridge's famous idea of a willing suspension of disbelief: the notion of disavowal more dramatically highlights the contradictoriness of what is going on in the act of reading. The work of the text, its task of seduction, is to ensure this disavowal, to put the reader into this state of what is at once 'truth' and 'fiction'.

This principle is disavowal—of reading a work of fiction as though it were not only words—permits us to suggest a way of distinguishing between literature and pornography. Both have a capacity for erotic and sexual stimulation but the difference between them could be said to consist in the fact that a literary work does not allow the reader to forget the process by which he or she is being seduced, whereas pornography calls for the abolition of the 'as though' altogether. In other words, pornography entails what John Forrester (following Jean Baudrillard) describes as 'a fantasy of a real in which representation does not exist, i.e. a real without seduction' (Forrester 1990, 332). Katherine Mansfield's 'Bliss' is not likely to be classified as pornography, but it is certainly about erotic and sexual feelings—both in what it tells and in its telling, both in its characters and narrative and in ourselves as readers. More particularly, the story explores some of the limits of pleasure: it dramatizes the ways in which pleasure is concerned with strangeness (the nothingness of laughter), paradox (the inarticulable) and contradiction (disavowal). Fundamental to this is what Mansfield's text suggests about the curious temporality of pleasure. To recall the opening words once more: 'Although Bertha Young was thirty she still had moments like this when she wanted to run instead of walk, to take dancing steps on and off the pavement, to bowl a hoop, to throw something up in the air and catch it again, or to stand still and laugh at—nothing—at nothing, simply.' This sentence is set in the past tense, but at the same time the word 'this' ('moments like this') suggests something immediate, here and now. In fact, the time of 'this' is uncertain and strange: it is as if the present of 'moments like this' is already gone. 'Moments like this' are presented in the past tense in such a way as to suggest that they are already 'moments like that' or 'moments like those'. The ambiguity of the this-ness of 'this' is compounded by multiplicity: Bertha wanted to run, to dance, to bowl a hoop, to throw and catch something, to stand still and laugh. Are these all different moments or are they different ways of figuring one single moment ('moments like this [one]')? The sense of time, in the context of extreme pleasure or 'bliss', seems to involve an undecidable, uncontainable multiplicity. Time cannot contain itself when it comes to bliss.

Katherine Mansfield's special focus on moments of intense feeling belongs to a specific historical context and in particular to the literary and cultural aftermath of late nineteenth-century aestheticism. This is to say that pleasure and bliss can be thought about in historical terms: they are experienced and represented differently at different times. A full-scale account of the aestheticism of such figures as Walter Pater, Oscar Wilde, Algernon Swinburne, Aubrey Beardsley and others need not detain us here. Its principal concerns were with the idea of art for art's sake, beauty as truth, and the appeal of the moment for the moment's sake (there is no past, no future, only ever the present moment). In recent times it is the aesthetes above all who made of pleasure a philosophy, a moral creed, a way of being. At the heart of aestheticism is a focus on the beauty and power of the present moment. It is concerned with the experience and expression of the intense pleasure of the present. The most succinct and eloquent text for an understanding of aestheticism is Walter Pater's Conclusion to his book *The Renaissance* (1873). This Conclusion, only a few pages in length, offers us remarkable insight into the work of many modernist writers, including Joseph Conrad, James Joyce, D.H. Lawrence, Virginia Woolf, Elizabeth Bowen, Ezra Pound, Wallace Stevens, T.S. Eliot and Mansfield herself. All of these writers are singularly concerned with the power of particular moments. On the one hand they are concerned with exploring a sense that the only time of *any* feeling or experience (painful or pleasurable) is right now, this very moment now. On the other hand, however, these writers are concerned with showing that even the present moment is already a ghost of itself. In the Conclusion to *The Renaissance*, Pater puts this concisely when he describes the present moment as 'gone while we try to apprehend it'. The present moment is that 'of which it may ever be more truly said that it has ceased to be than that it is' (196). Pater's Conclusion urges us to make the most of the ecstatic and passionate possibilities of experience, given the 'awful brevity' of our lives: life is defined as 'this short day of frost and sun' (197) and (one of the things that made this text quite scandalous at the time of its first publication) there is no sense of any afterlife or consolations beyond the grave. Here is the conclusion to Pater's Conclusion:

> our one chance lies in expanding that interval [i.e. life], in getting as many pulsations as possible into the given time. Great passions may give us this quickened sense of life, ecstasy and sorrow of love, the various forms of enthusiastic activity, disinterested or otherwise, which come naturally to many of us. Only be sure it is passion— that it does yield you this fruit of a quickened, multiplied consciousness. Of such wisdom, the poetic passion, the desire of beauty, the love of art for its own sake, has most. For art comes to you proposing frankly to give nothing but the highest quality to your moments as they pass, and simply for those moments' sake. (198–9)

Pater's unprecedented emphasis on the present moment played a crucial role in the development of aestheticism in Britain, the United States and elsewhere. It haunts modernist writing in turn—whether in the form of epiphanies (in James Joyce's *A Portrait of the Artist as a Young Man* for example), or of what Virginia Woolf famously refers to as 'moments of being', or of what Mansfield, at the start of 'Bliss', refers to as 'moments like this'. All of these writers in their different ways are concerned with the uncontainable, delirious, ecstatic, inexpressible quality of individual moments, of time as (only) now. It is not simply a question of a '*carpe diem*' ('seize the day') motif in modern literature. Rather, it is a matter of how the present moment resists any attempt to appropriate or 'seize' it. It is a matter of how moments of extreme pleasure (including orgasm) are at the same time moments of loss: such moments involve, indeed, a kind of dissolution and more generally suggest a sense of experience in terms of what Pater calls 'that continual vanishing away, that strange, perpetual weaving and unweaving of ourselves' (196).

In other words, as Mansfield's story suggests, pleasure can be thought about in terms of a subversion of identity. It is for this reason, among others, that it is not possible to say that the kinds of pleasures with which this chapter is concerned are simply hedonistic. Nor can one say that the kind of thinking and experience that Pater calls for constitutes mere self-indulgence or a contemptible neglect of political and social realities. As a way of illustrating this we will focus on what is perhaps the most important and most pleasurable work on the topic of pleasure and literature in recent years, Roland Barthes's *The Pleasure of the Text*. Barthes stresses that 'hedonism has been repressed by nearly every philosophy' (Barthes 1990a, 57) and he is at pleasurable pains to argue against such repression. The value and originality of his study consists not in the politically suspect project of advocating hedonism in a traditional sense but rather in the critical delineation of the paradoxes of pleasure, specifically in the experience of reading. Barthes offers a sort of critical anatomy of pleasure in reading. In particular, he distinguishes between two sorts of pleasure: pleasure of the 'comfortable' sort and pleasure of a more disturbing and subversive kind. Barthes writes:

> Text of pleasure: the text that contents, fills, grants euphoria; the text that comes from culture and does not break with it, is linked to a *comfortable* practice of reading. Text of bliss: the text that imposes a state of loss, the text that discomforts (perhaps to the point of a certain boredom), unsettles the reader's historical, cultural, psychological assumptions, the consistency of his tastes, values, memories, brings to a crisis his relation with language. (14)

Barthes's book suggests, then, that there are two ways in which we could think about pleasure. One is basically recuperative: it does not break with culture but rather reinforces traditional or comfortable notions of meaning, society, ideology, etc. The other sense of pleasure ('bliss') is more unsettling and strange. No doubt all literary and other cultural texts are susceptible to being read in both of these ways. Barthes's own emphasis, however, falls on 'bliss' ('jouissance' in French). 'Bliss' has to do with the inexpressible: 'pleasure can be expressed in words, bliss cannot' (21). Bliss has to do with a deconstruction of the political: it is thus engaged in 'de-politicizing what is apparently political, and in politicizing what apparently is not' (44). Or as Barthes puts it: 'The text is (should be) that uninhibited person who shows his behind to the *Political Father*' (53). Above all, bliss has to do with the subversion of identity itself. As with the uncontrollable force of laughter or the moment of orgasm, the extreme pleasure of bliss involves a shattering of self, a (momentary) dissolution of identity. The subject is thus 'never anything but a "living contradiction": a split subject, who simultaneously enjoys, through the text, the consistency of his selfhood and its collapse, its fall' (21).

By way of conclusion, we would like to suggest that—while Barthes

refers to the reader as 'he'—the 'living contradiction' he describes may
be thought about as, in the final analysis, undecidably gendered. Partly
what makes Barthes's work unusual and challenging is that it explicitly
centres on the importance of 'emotion', defining this as 'a disturbance,
a bordering on collapse' (25). For Barthes, we could say, the pleasure of
reading inevitably involves 'getting hysterical'. But the collapse of selfhood, the shattering force of bliss which he talks about, is a collapse in
which it is no longer clear whether there is a subject, let alone what
gender it might belong to. Mansfield's story can also be considered in
these terms. Insofar as it is a text about 'women and hysteria', it suggests
that 'getting hysterical' (306) is just as much a male as a female tendency.
'Bliss', that is to say, is as much about male hysteria as it is about female
hysteria. This is evident, in particular, in Mansfield's characterization
of Eddie Warren, the poet who is '(as usual) in a state of acute distress',
and whose first words for example provide a hysterical account of his
journey to the Youngs':

> 'I have had such a *dreadful* experience with a taxi-man; he was *most*
> sinister. I couldn't get him to *stop*. The *more* I knocked and called
> the *faster* he went. And *in* the moonlight this *bizarre* figure with the
> *flattened* head *crouching* over the *lit-tle* wheel . . .' (309)

But it is also evident in Mansfield's characterization of Bertha's husband
Harry, who is one moment 'rush[ing] into battle where no battle was'
(310) and at others 'extravagantly [i.e. hysterically] cool and collected'
(310, 315). More radically, however, 'Bliss' is a story about the condition
of 'living contradiction' which Barthes evokes. It suggests that that
extreme of pleasure called 'bliss' is the very undoing of identity, including the undoing of gender-identity..

The story concludes with Harry locking up and Bartha recalling Pearl
Fulton's final words to her ('Your lovely pear tree!'):

> And then she was gone, with Eddie following, like the black cat
> following the grey cat.
> 'I'll shut up shop,' said Harry, extravagantly cool and collected.
> 'Your lovely pear tree—pear tree—pear tree!'
> Bertha simply ran over to the long windows.
> 'Oh, what is going to happen now?' she cried.
> But the pear tree was as lovely as ever and as full of flower and
> as still. (315)

'Bliss' ends with this 'still'. It leaves the question of bliss itself in suspense, inexpressible, unbearable. As Barthes remarks: 'Pleasure's force of *suspension* can never be overstated' (Barthes 1990a, 65). Pleasure remains resistant and enigmatic, like 'literature'. At its most extreme, the pleasure of literature is less to do with the fact that it 'holds a mirror up to nature' and offers a reflection of 'life' and much more to do with an experience of 'living contradiction'—with what suspends or momentarily shatters our very identity.

Further reading

For a contemporary classic account, see Michel Foucault's *The Use of Pleasure (The History of Sexuality*, vol. 2, 1985). On pleasure and reading in general, see Roland Barthes's *The Pleasure of the Text* (1990a). For reading and seduction, Ross Chambers's *Story and Situation: Narrative Seduction and the Power of Fiction* (1984) is a fascinating and quite accessible work. Jean Baudrillard's *Seduction* (1990) is an important study but difficult. On the power of the moment in modern literature a good place to start is Morris Beja's clear and very readable *Epiphany in the Modern Novel* (1971). For an advanced study of pleasure and self, see Carolyn J. Dean's *The Self and Its Pleasures* (1992). On literature and the gendering of hysteria, see Elaine Showalter's fine essay 'On Hysterical Narrative' (1993). For a useful collection of essays on pleasure in relation to cultural studies, see Stephen Regan, ed., *The Politics of Pleasure* (1992).

The end

Fin. The British comedians French and Saunders do a parody of Ingmar Bergman films, in which they occupy an isolated clifftop house and moan at one another about alienation, death and damnation. The skit—shot, naturally, in black and white—concludes as the two women look out at the dismal grey seascape and see the letters 'FIN' appear amid the waves. One turns to the other and asks, 'What does it mean?' As with all jokes perhaps, amusement here depends on a force of recognition: 'fin' is not a dorsal fin or an abbreviation for 'Finland' but is immediately recognizable as a word (rather pretentiously taken from the French language) meaning 'The End'. And we all know what 'The End' means. It's obvious. Or is it? What is an end?

In 'Little Gidding' (1942), T.S. Eliot observes: 'to make an end is to make a beginning. / The end is where we start from.' Certainly when it comes to reflecting critically on our reading of a literary text, thinking about the end is a good way of starting. We can ask ourselves various questions: How does the text end? What effects does this ending have? Where does the text leave *us* as readers? More specifically, what *kind* of ending does the text have? Is it abrupt, surprising, inevitable, apocalyptic, bathetic? And why? All of these are questions which assume that the end or ending is indeed final, conclusive, closed. But what happens when we think about texts as having open endings? In what ways might the text be seen as having an ending that is haunting, ambiguous, suspenseful, unfinished, equivocal, undecidable? Again, it may be that the end of a literary text is both obvious and not so obvious—in some senses closed, but in others open. In any case, a particularly helpful way of reflecting on the overall force of a literary text is to analyze the nature and impact of its ending.

To provide a typology or systematic account of different kinds of endings, in poems, plays, short stories and novels, would be an endless task, not least because every ending is by definition different from every other and each calls on the reader to respond to this singularity. It may be a characteristic of many short stories that they end with a twist, and it may be a characteristic of many sonnets that they end with a rhyming couplet, but every short story and every sonnet still has to be thought about on its own terms. In this way we might take the final line of Adrienne Rich's poem, 'A Valediction Forbidding Mourning' (1970), to be emblematic: 'To do something very common, in my own way.' Every poem, every literary work, must have an ending—however open, suspended or apparently non-conclusive—but each one has its own way of doing this 'very common' thing.

More than this, every literary work is open to rereading, and the way in which its ending is appreciated or understood will vary, however imperceptibly, not only from one reader to another but from one reading to another. The idea of rereading can help us to clarify two important points about endings. First, to consider the end, to reflect critically on how a text ends and what effects it produces, is already to reread and, consequently, to recognize that there is no single end to a literary work: the end is always multiple. It is always possible to consider the end as happening in a number of different ways and in the light of more than one reading. Second, to reflect critically on how a text ends, and what impact it produces, is inevitably to think back, to think again and in effect to reread everything that has led up to this end. Thus it may be argued that, rather than being unusual or perverse, rereading is in fact unavoidable. In this sense we never get to the end of a text.

Literary texts call for rereading in various ways. Elizabeth Taylor's short story 'Mr Wharton' (1965) is about a girl called Pat Provis who has left her home near Nottingham to work in London, and about her mother Hilda who insists on coming down to help her move into a new flat in the suburbs. Pat rather reluctantly puts up with her mother's presence and begrudgingly accepts her maternal attentions and assistance. A significant topic of conversation, when Pat gets back from her day working as a secretary in an office, is how disgusting her boss, Mr Wharton, is. He is one of those sorts of men who (in Pat's words) go out for lunch, 'Eat and drink themselves stupid, and then go home and tell their wives what a hard day they've had' (229). The story ends with Hilda Provis on the train back to Nottingham and her daughter returning home to the flat. Here is the twist:

In a positive deluge, Pat and Mr Wharton drove up to Number
Twenty. He, too, had an umbrella, and held it carefully over her as
they went down the garden path and round the side of the house.
    'Excusez-moi', she said, stooping to get the key from under the
dustbin.
    'Could be a nice view on a nice day,' he said.
    'Could be,' she agreed, putting the key in the door. (234)

The revelation that Pat and her boss are apparently having (or are about
to begin having) an affair overturns the sense that we had been given
that Pat finds Mr Wharton repulsive. The twist, then, calls for a
rethinking or rereading of the text, even as it provides a final justification
or clarification as to why the text should be entitled 'Mr Wharton'. It is
also worth stressing, however, that while this is an apparently straightforward, even banal example of what Jeffrey Archer would call a story
with 'a twist in the tale', and while it ends in a clear and specific way,
still the ending is open and multiple. It is not, for example, entirely
clear how these two characters feel about one another or what kind of
relationship is involved. More generally, this ending forces us to rethink
everything in the story up to that point: we cannot help but revise our
reading of the text. Finally, it is important to recognize that the end of
Taylor's text, like that of many literary works, is explicitly future-
oriented. The words 'Could be' mark an openness to the future in relation to the recounted time of the narrative but they also mark an openness of ending and of interpretation.

Other texts call for other kinds of thinking about ends and rereading.
Coleridge's 'The Rime of the Ancient Mariner' (1798) ends with a
description of the effect of the tale of the Ancient Mariner on the Wedding-Guest who has been forced to listen to it:

> He went like one that hath been stunned,
> And is of sense forlorn:
> A sadder and a wiser man,
> He rose the following morn.

The final stanzas of Coleridge's poem constitute a sort of epilogue. We
might reasonably ask ourselves what status such an epilogue has in relation to the idea of the end of a work: does the end come before the
epilogue or is the epilogue itself the end? As in many of Shakespeare's
plays (*As You Like It, All's Well That Ends Well* and *The Tempest*, for
instance), the epilogue functions as a kind of supplement, and thus

conforms to the paradoxical logic of both coming *after* the end and at the same time *being the end*. Such a supplement is paradoxical in that it both completes and adds to the story. More generally, such endings are self-referential: just as the epilogues to Shakespeare's plays are explicitly about the fact that (as the King puts it, at the end of *All's Well That Ends Well*) 'the play is done', so the end of 'The Rime of the Ancient Mariner' specifically talks about the telling of the tale and the effect of this telling on its listener ('He went like one that hath been stunned / And is of sense forlorn'). The Mariner's tale, in other words, has already ended. Or has it? These are the final words of the Ancient Mariner:

> Since then, at an uncertain hour,
> That agony returns:
> And till my ghastly tale is told,
> This heart within me burns.
>
> I pass, like night, from land to land;
> I have strange power of speech;
> That moment that his face I see,
> I know the man that must hear me:
> To him my tale I teach.

In a transfixing and haunting way, the tale of the Ancient Mariner both ends and does not end. The 'ghastly tale is told' but what the tale tells is that it can never finally be told: it is at once the product and the articulation of an interminably recurring 'agony'. It is a tale about demonization, about being possessed by an 'agony' and by 'strange power of speech': it is a tale about its own telling and, in situating the reader in the position of the Wedding-Guest, it suggests that the end is only a beginning. Reading, or rereading, is interminable. From start to finish, reading is *it*: to recall the bizarre first word of Coleridge's poem, 'It is an Ancient Mariner . . .'.

In a very different fashion, Jean Rhys's novel *Wide Sargasso Sea* (1966) ends with the Creole female narrator (Bertha or, more correctly perhaps, Antoinette) preparing to set fire to the house in England belonging to the male narrator (the never specifically named Mr Rochester). Antoinette/Bertha waits for her guard, Grace Poole, to fall asleep:

> I waited a long time after I heard her snore, then I got up, took the keys and unlocked the door. I was outside holding my candle. Now

at last I know why I was brought here and what I have to do. There must have been a draught for the flame flickered and I thought it was out. But I shielded it with my hand and it burned up again to light me along the dark passage. (124)

Rhys's novel depends on the reader's acknowledgement of an intertextual relationship with Charlotte Brontë's *Jane Eyre*, but it is only at the end that the two dramatically collide. One of the things that makes this final passage so extraordinary is the fact that it is *not* final. Rather, it leads us directly into another text, into the fire that engulfs Thornfield Hall and kills Bertha Mason, in *Jane Eyre*. More fundamentally still, it puts a light to all our assumptions about Brontë's novel, it calls on us to reread and rethink the whole of *Jane Eyre* and its place and significance in the (white, middle-class or aristocratic) English literary canon. With the end of *Wide Sargasso Sea, Jane Eyre* can never be the same again.

The end of *Wide Sargasso Sea* is both an end and not an end. It is both closed and open. It is closed or conclusive in the sense that it leads us to the dramatic and terrible moment of setting fire to the house, and of the narrator in effect setting fire to herself. And it is closed or conclusive in the sense that it leads us into a decisive, radically different encounter with another text. *Wide Sargasso Sea* then dislocates everything in *Jane Eyre* that marginalizes or silences the otherness of a non-white (in this case West Indian Creole) subject and everything that marginalizes or silences the otherness of madness. But the ending of Rhys's novel is at the same time open in the sense that it calls for a rereading or for rereadings that are, in principle, limitless. What is involved here is a notion of intertextuality not only in its weak sense (*Wide Sargasso Sea* 'quotes' or alludes to *Jane Eyre*) but also in the strong sense of a text's strictly unbounded capacity for referring to or linking up with other texts. Thus the text of *Wide Sargasso Sea* is linked up not only with the text of *Jane Eyre*, for example, but with any and every other text that might be classified as representative of 'the traditional English novel', with any and every other text that portrays what Gilbert and Gubar call 'the madwoman in the attic' and so on. The end of Rhys's text is also open in the sense that it is future-oriented. The novel ends with a suspension of time: 'Now at last I know why I was brought here and what I have to do.' It leads us towards a terrible event, it leads us (in short) towards death, but it leaves us on the threshold—or rather, to recall the very last words of the text, it leaves us with suspended movement, in a 'dark passage'. It leaves us waiting to make connections, of potentially limitless kinds—for example with the Talking Heads, burning down the house.

Jane Eyre itself 'ends' with intertextuality. Specifically it cites the end of what is probably the most intertextually pervasive book in Western history, the Bible: ' "Amen; even so come, Lord Jesus!" ' (Revelation 22:20). The end of *Jane Eyre*, like the end of *Wide Sargasso Sea*, would then seem to confirm a sense that texts are inevitably linked up with other texts and that there is no simple end (or beginning) to any text. It may be, in fact, that to emphasize texts as unfinished and unfinishable is characteristically modern or, perhaps, postmodern. The writings of Franz Kafka and Samuel Beckett are often thought of as being representative of twentieth-century European literature. In this respect it should not seem surprising that Kafka's novels are unfinished and that they are about experiencing the interminable, or that Beckett's great trilogy (*Molloy, Malone Dies, The Unnamable*) ends with the paradoxical words, 'I can't go on, I'll go on' (418). Poststructuralism in particular challenges us to think critically about the ways in which the idea of the end is in various ways paradoxical. It calls on us to acknowledge—rather than to deny or ignore (as more traditional literary criticism has done)— the importance and value of aporia, suspense and the undecidable.

We can briefly illustrate this in terms of the endings of two very different twentieth-century novels, Elizabeth Bowen's *The Death of the Heart* (1938) and J.D. Salinger's *The Catcher in the Rye* (1951). Bowen's magnificent novel ends with a housemaid called Matchett taking a taxi to an obscure hotel somewhere in Kensington, intending to collect and take home the heartbroken heroine of the novel, the 16-year-old orphan called Portia:

> Matchett straightened her hat with both hands, gripped her bag more firmly, mounted the steps. Below the steps the grey road was all stucco and echoes—an occasional taxi, an occasional bus. Reflections of evening made unlit windows ghostly; lit lights showed drawing-rooms pallid and bare . . .
>
> Through the glass door, Matchett saw lights, chairs, pillars—but there was no buttons, no one. She thought: 'Well, what a place!' Ignoring the bell, because this place was public, she pushed on the brass knob with an air of authority. (318)

Bowen's novel ends with this endless moment of suspense—before Matchett enters the hotel. In this way Bowen's novel dramatizes the idea that the end of a text always figures a threshold or passing place, a place that is liminal and uncertain. Moreover it is a threshold which we can never go beyond: Matchett never goes into the hotel. Her intention (of collecting Portia) is never fulfilled.

Uncertainty or undecidability also marks the end of *The Catcher in the Rye*. Its final chapter is a kind of epilogue, which begins with Holden Caulfield declaring 'That's all I'm going to tell about' and goes on to conclude:

> . . . D.B. [Holden's brother] asked me what I thought about all this stuff I just finished telling you about. I didn't know what the hell to say. If you want to know the truth, I don't *know* what I think about it. I'm sorry I told so many people about it. About all I know is, I sort of *miss* everybody I told about. Even old Stradlater and Ackley, for instance. I think I even miss that goddam Maurice. It's funny. Don't ever tell anybody anything. If you do, you start missing everybody. (220)

The ending of Salinger's novel emphasizes that the narrator is in some kind of psychiatric institution but leaves in suspense the question of whether or not he will stay there or what will happen if he leaves. The final passage is equivocal and paradoxical: it suggests that the story or 'stuff' is 'finished' but that there is more 'to tell about'. We are presented not only with the narrator's own powerful ambivalence ('I don't *know* what I think') but also with a sense of uncertainty as to whether or not we as readers have really been told anything or where we are being left. What kind of end is this? Is it an end?

Poststructuralism entails a kind of thinking that tries to proceed by putting the very idea of the end into question. 'End' here involves not only the sense of 'conclusion' (the end of a text, for instance) but also the sense of 'goal' and 'purpose' (the goal or purpose of reading a text, for instance). As regards the sense of 'the end' as 'the conclusion of the text', poststructuralism shows how this is problematic and even impossible: as we have been trying to make clear, intertextuality and rereading (or rereadability) mean that, in important respects, there is no end to any text. As regards the sense of 'the end' as 'the goal' or 'purpose', poststructuralism again highlights what is paradoxical. At issue here is the very nature of human desire and the paradox of the idea that, as we argue in greater detail in Chapter 19, desire is endless. The poststructuralist

Jacques Derrida, for example, emphasizes that we cannot do without the notion of end as goal or purpose (or, in its Greek form, *telos*). Nor can we do without the idea of a fulfilment or plenitude of desire. But there is a paradox which means that we can never get to the end of desire. As Derrida puts it: 'Plenitude is the end (the goal), but were it attained, it would be the end (death)' (Derrida 1988, 129).

The poetry of John Ashbery is suggestive in this context. In a poem entitled 'Soonest Mended' (1970), he writes:

> To step free at last, minuscule on the gigantic plateau—
> This was our ambition: to be small and clear and free.

Part of what makes Ashbery's poetry 'postmodern' is that it repeatedly articulates the desire to 'step free at last' but at the same time repeatedly ironizes, dislocates, writes off this gesture or 'ambition'. Ashbery has described his poems as being like dreams, and as texts for a reader to pick up, to start reading and put down again at whatever point she or he chooses: like dreams, Ashbery's poems give no coherent or comfortable sense of how or why they end, and yet they also convey a strong sense of the desire and need to think in terms of ends.

Ultimately, of course, the end is death and, more generally perhaps, the end of the world. It is not surprising, in this respect, that *Jane Eyre* should end with a quotation from the end of the book which tells of the end of the world ('The Book of Revelation' or, in Greek, 'The Apocalypse'). As Frank Kermode demonstrates, in his book *The Sense of an Ending* (1967), 'the paradigms of apocalypse continue to lie under our ways of making sense of the world' (Kermode 1967, 28). Thus, for example, the great systems of Western philosophy—such as Christianity and Marxism—make sense of the world by imagining a future in which the world is fundamentally different, in which *our* world has ended forever. Christianity and Marxism, then, engage with desires that can be called apocalyptic. Such desires are crucial, also, for an appreciation of literature. Literature offers at once an imaginative experiencing and a critical questioning of the end, and it does so in ways that can be both at once exhilarating and terrifying. Literary texts, and particularly the ends of literary texts, open onto the future. And as Derrida has observed: 'The future can only be anticipated in the form of an absolute danger' (Derrida 1976, 5). The end is coming, this is it, it's now, right now, any moment now.

Further reading

Frank Kermode's *The Sense of an Ending* (1967) is a readable and very thought-provoking account of literature and what he sees as the human need for ends. Norman Cohn's *The Pursuit of the Millennium* (1970) remains a standard and accessible work of reference for the apocalyptic nature of religious and political systems (especially Christianity and Nazism). Jacques Derrida's entire œuvre can be described as a sustained meditation on 'the end': see, in particular, 'The Ends of Man', in *Margins of Philosophy* (Derrida 1982), 'No Apocalypse, Not Now (full speed ahead, seven missiles, seven missives)' (1984), and 'Of an Apocalyptic Tone' (Derrida 1992c). On the way that poems end, see Barbara Herrnstein Smith, *Poetic Closure* (1968). For a highly engaging account of gender and culture at the *fin de siècle*, see Elaine Showalter's *Sexual Anarchy* (1991). Finally, see D.A. Miller, *Narrative and its Discontents* (1981), a fascinating book on the endings of traditional nineteenth-century novels.

Glossary

Affective fallacy: term used by W.K. Wimsatt and Monroe Beardsley to designate what they see as the error of making subjective responses (cognitive or emotional) the criteria for interpretive, critical or aesthetic judgements.

Allegory: (Gk. 'other speaking') a narrative which—through allusion, metaphor, symbolism, etc.—can be read not simply on its own terms but as telling another, quite different story at the same time.

Alliteration: repeated consonant sounds, particularly at the beginning of words, e.g. 'kiddies' clobber', 'mountains of moonstone'. (See also *assonance.*)

Allusion: a reference, often only implicit or indirect, to another work of literature or art, person, event, etc.

Ambiguity: where a word, phrase or text may be interpreted in more than one way, but often taken to suggest an uncertainty between two (rather than three or more) meanings or readings. (See also *equivocality, polysemia, undecidability.*)

Animism: the rhetorical figure whereby something inanimate or lifeless is given attributes of life or spirit, e.g. Emily Brontë, *Wuthering Heights*: 'I believe at Wuthering Heights the kitchen is forced to retreat altogether into another quarter . . . the chairs, high-backed, primitive structures, painted green, one or two heavy black ones lurking in the shade . . .'; or the opening of Shelley's 'Ode to the West Wind': 'O wild West Wind, thou breath of Autumn's being . . .'.

Anthropocentrism: refers to everything in a culture that asserts or assumes that the human (Gk. *anthropos*, 'man') is at the centre—whether of the universe, the world, or the meaning of a text.

Anthropomorphism: the rhetorical figure whereby the non-human is described in human terms (e.g. the legs of a table, the face of truth).

Aporia: a rhetorical figure for doubt. Especially associated with deconstructive thinking, an aporia may arise when the reader encounters two or more contradictory codes, 'messages' or 'meanings' in a text. It involves an impasse or site of undecidability. (See also *undecidability*.)

Assonance: correspondence or 'rhyming' of vowel sounds, e.g. eat, sleep; ooze, droop.

Bathos: artistic falling-away; a sense of disappointment or anti-climax, expressed by the writer or felt by the reader, e.g. the bathos in Matthew Arnold's 'The Buried Life', in the use of the word 'melancholy' at the culmination of a sentence which might have been expected to conclude on a note of triumph or joy: 'Yet still . . . / As from an infinitely distant land, / Come airs, and floating echoes, and convey / A melancholy into all our day'.

Catachresis: (Gk. 'misuse') rhetorical term for misuse or misapplication of language.

Catharsis: (Gk. 'purgation', 'purification') according to Aristotle, something that can happen to a spectator or reader at the end of a tragedy, due to a release of emotional tension arising from the experience of a paradoxical mixture of pity and terror.

Chiasmus: (from the Gk. letter χ) a rhetorical figure involving repetition and reversal, e.g. 'If you fail to plan, you plan to fail'. More broadly the term is used to refer to forms of intercrossing or reversal whereby each of the two sides of a conceptual opposition (e.g. man/woman, text/world, etc.) is shown to be reversible and paradoxically to be present and functionally active in its opposite.

Close reading: 'method' of reading emphasized by new critics which pays careful attention to 'the words on the page' rather than the historical and ideological context, the biography or intentions of the author and so on. Close reading, despite its name, brackets questions of readers and reading as arbitrary and irrelevant to the text as an artifact (see *affective fallacy*). It assumes that the function of reading and criticism is simply to read carefully what is already 'there' in the text.

Closure: an ending, the process of ending.

Connotation: an association, idea or image evoked by a word or phrase. Roughly equivalent to 'suggestion', connotation is distinct from denotation (what words denote or signify).

Couplet: two successive rhyming lines in a poem, e.g. Alexander Pope's 'Epigram Engraved on the Collar of a Dog I Gave to His Royal Highness': 'I am his Highness' Dog at Kew: / Pray tell me, sir, whose dog are you?'

Cultural materialism: cultural materialism may be considered as the British version of new historicism. Both schools of criticism are characterized by newly theorized and politicized readings of history and of literary texts. While new historicism is particularly concerned with the textuality of history, however, cultural materialism, influenced by Raymond Williams's version of Marxist criticism, focuses on the material conditions of the production and reception of literary texts. Cultural materialists are thus concerned to expose the ideological and political dimensions of such texts.

Deconstruction: a term particularly associated with the work of Jacques Derrida. Roughly speaking, deconstruction is desedimentation: to deconstruct is to shake up and transform.

Defamiliarization: the Russian formalist critic Viktor Shklovsky uses the term *ostranenie*, usually translated as 'making strange' or 'defamiliarization', to denote what he sees as the primary function of literary texts—to make the familiar unfamiliar, to renew the old, or make the habitual appear fresh or strange.

Deixis: a term from linguistics, referring to the use of words concerning the place and time of utterance, e.g. 'this', 'here'.

Dénouement: (Fr: 'unknotting') either the events following the climax of a plot, or the resolution of this plot's complications at the end of a short story, novel or play.

Discourse: can mean simply 'speech or language generally', or 'language as we use it'. But the term is often used in more theoretical contexts to signify the use of language associated with a particular institution, cultural identity, profession, practice or discipline. In this way each discourse is one of a number of discourses (the discourse of the colonizer, for instance, as distinct from that of the colonized). Whether general or particular, discourse is always inscribed within relations of power, within the structures and strictures of institutions.

Double bind: a double bind involves the kind of double or contradictory statement or order which deconstructive criticism tends to focus on, e.g. the sentence 'This sentence is not true' is both true and not true at the same time (if it's true then it's not true and if it's not true then it's true). Rather differently, the sentence 'Do not read this sentence' involves an order which can only be obeyed if it is disobeyed (we have to read the sentence in order to know that we should not read it).

Elegy: (Gk. 'lament') a poem of mourning for an individual or a lament for a tragic event; an an adjective 'elegiac' may be used to describe a sense of mourning or loss encountered in any text—poem or prose.

End-stopping: where lines of poetry end with punctuation, usually with strong punctuation such as full-stops, semi-colons or colons, e.g. in the penultimate section of Wallace Stevens's 'An Ordinary Evening in New Haven': 'The wind has blown the silence of summer away. / It buzzes beyond the horizon or in the ground: / In mud under ponds, where the sky used to be reflected'. End-stopping is the opposite of *enjambment*.

Enjambment: the phenomenon whereby one line of poetry carries over into the next line without any punctuation whatever. Especially characteristic of poetry such as Milton's, Wordsworth's and Shelley's.

Epic: long narrative dealing with heroic deeds usually employing elevated language and traditionally involving a heroic or 'superhuman' protagonist, e.g. *The Odyssey, Paradise Lost*.

Epistemophilia: (Gk. 'a love of knowledge') epistemophilia is the desire for knowledge which literary texts produce in readers—the desire for the 'truth' or 'meaning' of the text, for example. Peter Brooks argues that epistemophilia is a dimension of the sex drive, and that it involves a 'dynamic of curiosity' which may be thought to be 'the foundation of all intellectual activity' (Brooks 1993, xiii).

Equivocality: like 'ambiguity', this suggests that a word, phrase, etc., has more than one meaning, but while 'ambiguous' suggests that it may be possible to decide on one primary meaning, 'equivocal' suggests that the meaning cannot be resolved. (See also *undecidability, polysemia*.)

Essentialism: refers to ways of conceiving people, cultures, etc. as having certain innate, natural or universal characteristics. Essentialism is strongly contested in most contemporary literary theory. The following three statements are all examples of essentialist thinking: (1) 'I have a personality and individuality which is completely unaffected by anything out there in the "real" world, such as language, economics, education, nationality, etc.'; (2) 'Women are more intelligent, caring and sensitive than men'; and (3) 'At bottom, you are either white or black, and that's all there is to it'.

Fabula: (also referred to as 'story' or '*histoire*') the events of a narrative.

Feminist criticism: feminist criticism seeks on the one hand to investigate and analyze the differing representations of women and men in literary texts and, on the other hand, to rethink literary history by exploring an often marginalized tradition of women's writing. Feminist criticism is concerned to question and challenge conventional notions of masculinity and femininity; to explore ways in which such conventions are inscribed in a largely patriarchal canon; and to consider the extent to which writing, language and even literary form itself are themselves bound up with issues of gender difference.

Figure (of speech), figurative language: this is usually defined in negative terms, that is to say as non-literal language. Figurative language involves the entire field of what is known as rhetoric and includes, for example, metaphor, simile, hyperbole, anthropomorphism, etc.

Formalism: refers generally to kinds of criticism that emphasize the importance of the formal dimensions of literary texts, such as prose style, rhyme, narrative structure, verse-form and so on. In this respect formalism is seen to stress the importance of form as (supposedly) distinct from content, meaning, social and historical context, etc. The term can be encountered in two quite different contexts, namely Russian formalism and the formalist concerns of American New Criticism (or 'close reading'). In fact the Russian formalists were not simply formalist: their close attention to the specificity of literary form was consistently subordinate to more general political, even revolutionary concerns.

Genre: a kind; a literary type or style. Poetry, drama, novel may be subdivided into lyric (including elegy, ode, song, sonnet, etc.), epic, tragedy, comedy, short story, biography, etc.

Hermeneutic: a term formerly used to designate attempts to establish a set of rules governing the interpretation of the Bible in the nineteenth century; in the context of contemporary criticism, the term refers to theories of interpretation more generally.

Heteroglossia: (Gk. 'other/different tongues') term used by Mikhail Bakhtin to describe the variety of voices or languages within a novel, but can be used of any text to give the sense that language-use does not come from one origin but is multiple and diverse, a mixing of heterogeneous discourses, sociolects, etc. (See also *polyphony*.)

Hyperbole: a figure of speech which involves exaggeration, excess or extravagance, e.g. 'I'm starving' instead of simply 'I am hungry,' 'incredible' instead of 'very good'.

Ideology: while the term 'ideology' has a long history, its most common usage in contemporary literary criticism and theory originates in Marx's distinction between base and superstructure and refers to the way in which literary texts may be said to engage with—to reinforce or resist—the governing social, cultural and especially political ideas, images and representations of a society. Ideology, in the work of writers such as Louis Althusser and Pierre Macherey, is seen as fundamental to the very production of subjectivity itself, and for these writers, all cultural signification (including that of literary texts) is 'ideological'. According to this thinking, ideology reflects the fact that no writer is merely 'free' to express him- or herself, but is necessarily constrained by the conditions of the production of his or her text, by his or her social, cultural, economic and political circumstances. Ideology is thus held to be ineradicably inscribed in the literary text and the task of the critic is to analyze the work's often disguised or hidden ideological subtext.

Implied reader: Wolfgang Iser uses this term to denote a hypothetical reader towards whom the text is directed. The implied reader is to be distinguished from the so-called 'real reader'.

Indeterminacy: see *undecidability*.

In medias res: (L. 'in the middle of things') starting a story in the middle of the action.

Intentional fallacy: W.K. Wimsatt and Monroe Beardsley's term for what they see as the mistake of attempting to interpret a literary text by appealing to the supposed intentions of its author.

Interpretation: usually understood to involve an attempt to define the meaning or meanings of a specific text, with the assumption that a text has a limited meaning or meanings.

Intertextuality: a term coined by Julia Kristeva to refer to the fact that texts are constituted by a 'tissue of citations', that every word of every text refers to other texts and so on, limitlessly. Often used in an imprecise or weak sense to talk about echoes or allusions.

Irony: a rhetorical figure referring to the sense that there is a discrepancy between words and their meanings, between actions and their results, or between appearance and reality: most simply, saying one thing and meaning another.

Logocentrism: term introduced by Jacques Derrida in order to refer to everything in Western culture that puts *logos* (the Gk. term for 'word', more broadly translatable as 'meaning' or 'sense') at the centre. As Derrida argues, there is no simple escape from logocentric thinking.

Lyric: usually a fairly short poem supposedly expressing the thoughts and emotions of a speaker. Lyrics tend to be non-narrative in form.

Metafiction: a short story or novel which exploits the idea that it is (only) fiction, a fiction about fiction. Arguably, however, there are metafictional dimensions in any work of fiction. (See also *self-reflexivity*.)

Metaphor: a basic trope or figure of speech in which one thing is described in terms of its resemblance to another thing, e.g. the verb 'to fly' in 'she flew into his arms'. (See also *simile*.)

Metonymy: a basic trope or figure of speech in which the name of an attribute of an object is given for the object itself (e.g. in 'the pen is mightier than the sword', pen is a metonym for writing; sword is a metonym for fighting or war).

Metre: the pattern of stressed and unstressed syllables in verse—one of the primary characteristics which may be said to distinguish verse from prose.

Mimesis: (Gk. 'imitation') the idea that literature attempts to represent 'life' or 'the world' more or less accurately, as it 'actually' is, etc. (See also *realism*.)

Monologue: a text (or part of a text) consisting of the speech of a single person (usually a fictional narrator, character or persona) speaking in actual or virtual solitude. In drama, referred to as a 'soliloquy'.

Narrative: may be defined in terms of the recounting of a series of events and the establishing of some (causal/temporal) relation between them.

Narratology: the field of critical and theoretical inquiry concerned with analysis of the underlying narrative structure or form of literary and other texts. Originating in the structuralist desire to produce a quasi-mathematical modelling of the deep structure of all narrative texts, recent developments in the field have encompassed poststructuralism, psychoanalytic criticism, feminism and other tendencies and have tended to move away from such scientism to examine the cultural and political significance of the workings of specific narrative texts in their historical context.

Narrator: the person or persona (as distinguished from the author) who is telling a story. Narrators can be variously categorized: an omniscient narrator appears to know everything, an intrusive narrator gives his or her own comments and opinions on the story, an unreliable narrator cannot be trusted for some reason (e.g. he or she is prejudiced, exaggerating, lying), a first-person narrator presents himself or herself in the story as 'I', a third-person narrator speaks of his or her characters as 'she', 'he', etc.

New historicism: like its British version, cultural materialism, new historicism in the USA is concerned with a newly politicized and theorized historical criticism. While cultural materialism traces its roots back to Raymond Williams, new historicism is particularly influenced by Foucault's investigations of the workings of the institutions and discursive practices of medicine, psychology, the law, the university and so on, by which subjects are constructed, by which ideas are formed, and within which contexts literary texts are produced. New historicists are concerned with what Louis Montrose, in a now famous chiasmus, calls the 'historicity of texts and the textuality of history' (in Veeser 1989): history is itself 'textual' and open to interpretation, while literary texts are subject to the circulation of political and other currents of power.

Oxymoron: (Gk. 'wise foolishness') a trope which combines contradictory words or ideas, e.g. 'bittersweet', 'darkness visible'.

Paradox: an apparently contradictory or strange statement of how things are: that which is apparently illogical or absurd but may be understood to be meaningful or 'true'.

Parody: an imitation of another work of literature (usually with exaggeration) in order to make it seem ridiculous and/or amusing.

Paronomasia: word play. (See also *pun*.)

Pastiche: a work made up of imitation of other work(s); unlike parody, pastiche is not necessarily designed to ridicule.

Performative: pertaining generally to performance and, in the context of drama, to the active, dynamic effects of theatre. More specifically in the context of speech-act theory and the analysis of literary texts, however, 'performative' is an adjective referring to the capacity that statements have for *doing* as well as *saying* things. A promise or a curse, for example, is a performative.

Phallocentrism: refers to everything in a culture that asserts or assumes that the phallus (the symbolic significance of a penis and more generally the patriarchy linked to this) is at the centre.

Phallogocentrism: a term conflating logocentrism and phallocentrism, used to refer to everything in language or meaning (*logos*) which is phallocentric. See also 'logocentrism' and 'phallocentrism'.

Point of view: refers to the way in which the narrator 'sees' or interprets her or his material: also referred to as 'narrative perspective'.

Polyphony: literally, 'having many voices': the idea that, rather than originating in a 'single voice' (cf. 'univocal'), a literary text has multiple origins or voices. Cf. 'heteroglossia', 'intertextuality'.

Polysemia or **polysemy:** (Gk. 'many meanings') the quality of having several or many meanings.

Protagonist: the leading character in a story (hero or heroine).

Pun: a play on words alike or nearly alike in sound but different in meaning (e.g. the word 'grave' in 'Ask for me tomorrow and you shall find me a grave man', *Romeo and Juliet*, III, i).

Queer theory: taking as its starting point an assumption about the constructedness of human sexualities, queer theory argues that sexuality is neither 'innate' nor 'natural' but subject to social, cultural, religious, educational, intellectual and other influences. Following Michel Foucault, theorists such as Eve Kosofsky Sedgwick, Judith Butler, Jonathan Dollimore and Joseph Bristow examine ways in which masculinity and femininity, and homo- and heterosexuality, are represented in literary and other texts and question traditional notions of the stability of such categories. In the work of such critics, 'queer theory' is in fact central to any thinking about literary representation, homosexual, heterosexual or other.

Realism: a descriptive term particularly associated with the nineteenth-century novel to refer to the idea that texts appear to represent 'the world' 'as it really is'.

Rhyme: like assonance and alliteration, rhymes are everywhere, in prose as well as in strictly 'poetic' texts. There are several varieties of rhyme, of which the most common are (i) full rhyme, e.g. 'cat'/'sat'; (ii) half-rhyme or off-rhyme, e.g. 'beat'/'keep', 'crime'/'scream'; (iii) internal rhyme, where a rhyme occurs within a line of verse, e.g. the '-ell' rhymes in Keats's ode 'To Autumn': 'To swell the gourd, and plump the hazel shells / With a sweet kernel; to set budding . . ./'; (iv) eye-rhyme, which should be seen but not heard, e.g. 'love'/'prove'; (v) masculine or strong rhymes, that is words of one syllable, e.g. 'cat'/'sat', etc.; (vi) feminine or weak rhymes, which extend over more than one syllable, e.g. 'follow'/ 'hollow', 'qualify'/'mollify', etc.

Satire: the humorous presentation of human folly or vice in such a way as to make it look ridiculous, e.g. Jonathan Swift's *A Modest Proposal*.

Self-reflexivity: the phenomenon whereby a piece of writing refers to or reflects on itself. Often used interchangeably with 'self-referentiality'. (See also *metafiction*.)

Sibilance: an emphatic presence of 's' or 'z' sounds.

Simile: a trope in which one thing is likened to another, specifically through the use of 'like' or 'as' (a species of metaphor): in 'The barge she sat in, like a burnish'd throne / Burn'd on the water' (*Antony and Cleopatra*, II, ii) there is a metaphor in 'The barge . . . burn'd' (it is not literally on fire), and a simile in 'the barge . . . like a burnish'd throne'.

Sjuzhet: (Russian 'plot') term used by the Russian formalist critics and borrowed by certain narratologists to denote the way in which a story is told, its 'discourse' or telling, as opposed to the events of the narrative, the *fabula* or story.

Sonnet: a lyric poem of (usually) fourteen lines, most commonly divided into units of eight lines (octave) plus six (sestet), or of three quatrains (four lines each) and a couplet.

Stanza: a grouping of lines of verse, usually forming a self-contained pattern of rhymed lines—thus stanzas of a poem are normally of equal length.

Symbol: a figure in which one object represents another object (often an abstract quality): conventional symbols include, for example, scales for justice, a dove for peace, a goat for lust, a lion for strength, a rose for beauty or love, etc. A symbol is a kind of metaphor in which the subject of the metaphor is not made explicit, and may be mysterious or undecidable.

Teleology: literally, 'to do with the study of the end, goal or purpose'. In contemporary literary studies, 'teleology' has to do with the idea that we think about texts (or about our activities as readers) as having a particular kind or particular kinds of *telos* (goal, purpose or end). One way of defining deconstruction or poststructuralism would be as a sustained questioning of the meaning, value and effects of teleological assumptions and ideas.

Trope: (Gk. 'turn'): any rhetorical figure or device.

Undecidability: the phenomenon or experience of being unable to come to a decision when faced with two or more possible readings or interpretations. In a weak and imprecise sense, used interchangeably with 'indeterminacy'. 'Indeterminacy' is a negative term, however, implying that a decision (about being unable to determine a reading or interpretation) has already been reached. 'Undecidability', on the other hand, stresses the active, continuing challenge of being unable to decide.

Univocal: the quality of supposedly having only one meaning. 'The cat sat on the mat' might (and at some level must) be considered as a statement with univocal meaning: everyone knows what it is referring to. But at another level univocality is always open to question, in particular insofar as the context of a statement is never stable but is always susceptible to alteration or recontextualization. For example: Does 'cat' mean 'lion' here? One person's sense of 'mat' may not be someone else's (it may be their prize Persian rug). And so on.

Select bibliography of other introductory texts and reference works

Introductions

Barry, Peter. 1995. *Beginning Theory: An Introduction to Literary and Cultural Studies*. Manchester: Manchester University Press.

Belsey, Catherine. 1980. *Critical Practice*. London: Methuen.

Culler, Jonathan. 1983. *On Deconstruction: Theory and Criticism after Structuralism*. London: Methuen.

Culler, Jonathan. 1997. *Literary Theory: A Very Short Introduction*. Oxford: Oxford University Press.

Eagleton, Terry. 1996. *Literary Theory: An Introduction*. 2nd edn. Oxford: Basil Blackwell.

Furniss, Tom and Michael Bath. 1996. *Reading Poetry: An Introduction*. London: Harvester Wheatsheaf.

Jefferson, Ann and David Robey. 1986. *Modern Literary Theory: A Comparative Introduction*. 2nd edn. London: Batsford.

Lentricchia, Frank and Thomas McLaughlin, eds. 1990. *Critical Terms for Literary Study*. London and Chicago: Chicago University Press.

Selden, Raman, Peter Widdowson and Peter Brooker, 1997. *A Reader's Guide to Contemporary Literary Theory*. 4th edn. Hemel Hempstead: Prentice Hall.

Reference works

Brogan, T.V.F. 1994. *The New Princeton Handbook of Poetic Terms*. Princeton: Princeton University Press.

Coyle, Martin, Peter Garside, Malcolm Kelsall and John Peck, eds. 1990. *Encyclopaedia of Literature and Criticism*. London and New York: Routledge.

Cuddon, J.A., ed. 1992. *The Penguin Dictionary of Literary Terms and Literary Theory*. Harmondsworth: Penguin.

Gray, Martin. 1992. *A Dictionary of Literary Terms*. 2nd edn. Harlow, Essex and Beirut: Longman York Press.

Groden, Michael and Martin Kreiswirth, eds. 1994. *The Johns Hopkins Guide to Literary Theory and Criticism*. Baltimore: Johns Hopkins University Press.

Laplanche, J. and J.-B. Pontalis. 1973. *The Language of Psycho-Analysis*, trans. Donald Nicholson-Smith. London: Hogarth Press and the Institute of Psycho-Analysis.

Makaryk, Irena R., ed. 1993. *Encyclopaedia of Contemporary Literary Theory: Approaches, Scholars, Terms*. Toronto: University of Toronto Press.

Sim, Stuart. 1995. *The A–Z Guide to Modern Literary and Cultural Theorists*. Hemel Hempstead: Prentice Hall/Harvester Wheatsheaf.

Wright, Elizabeth, ed. 1992. *Feminism and Psychoanalysis: A Critical Dictionary*. Oxford and Cambridge, Mass.: Basil Blackwell.

Literary works discussed

Achebe, Chinua. *Things Fall Apart*. London: Heinemann, 1986.

Achebe, Chinua. *Anthills of the Savannah*. London: Heinemann, 1987.

Anon. 'Sir Patrick Spens', in *The Penguin Book of Ballads*, ed. Geoffrey Grigson. Harmondsworth: Penguin, 1975.

Arnold, Matthew. Preface to *Poems* (1835), 'To Marguerite—Continued', 'Dover Beach', in *The Poems of Matthew Arnold*, ed. Kenneth Allott. London: Longman, 1965.

Ashbery, John. 'Soonest Mended', in *The Double Dream of Spring*. New York: Ecco Press, 1975.

Atwood, Margaret. 'Giving Birth', in *Dancing Girls and Other Stories*. London: Virago, 1985.

Auden, W.H. 'In Memory of W.B. Yeats (d. Jan. 1939)', in *Collected Poems*, ed. Edward Mendelson. London: Faber and Faber, 1991.

Austen, Jane. *Pride and Prejudice*, ed. Frank W. Bradbrook. London: Oxford University Press, 1970.

Ayres, Michael. 'Bittersweet', in *Poems 1987–1992*. Nether Stowey, Somerset: Odyssey Poets, 1994.

Beckett, Samuel. *Molloy, Malone Dies, The Unnamable*. London: Calder and Boyars, 1959.

Beckett, Samuel. *Murphy*. London: Picador, 1973.

Beckett, Samuel. *Waiting for Godot*. London: Faber and Faber, 1986.

Blake, William. 'The Marriage of Heaven and Hell', in *Blake: The Complete Poems*, 2nd edn, ed. W.H. Stevenson. London: Longman, 1989.

Bowen, Elizabeth. *The Heat of the Day*. Harmondsworth: Penguin, 1976.

Bowen, Elizabeth. *The Death of the Heart*. Harmondsworth: Penguin, 1987.

Bowen, Elizabeth. *A World of Love*. Harmondsworth: Penguin, 1988.

Brontë, Charlotte. *Jane Eyre*. Harmondsworth: Penguin, 1966.

Brontë, Emily. *Wuthering Heights*. Harmondsworth: Penguin, 1965.

Browning, Robert. 'Two in the Campagna', in *Robert Browning: Selected Poetry*, ed. Daniel Karlin. Harmondsworth: Penguin, 1989.

Byron. *Poetical Works*. Oxford: Oxford University Press, 1970.

Carver, Raymond. 'Fat' and 'Cathedral' in *Where I'm Calling From: The Selected Stories*. London: Harvill, 1993.

Chandler, Raymond. *The Little Sister*. New York: Vintage Books, 1988.

Chaucer, Geoffrey. *The Canterbury Tales: Nine Tales and the General Prologue*, ed. V.A. Kolve and Glending Olson. New York: Norton, 1989.

Coleridge, S.T. 'The Rime of the Ancient Mariner', 'Kubla Khan', in *The Oxford Authors Samuel Taylor Coleridge*, ed. H.J. Jackson. Oxford: Oxford University Press, 1985.

Conrad, Joseph. *Heart of Darkness*. Harmondsworth: Penguin Popular Classics, 1994.

Dante Alighieri. *The Divine Comedy. Inferno I: Italian Text and Translation*, trans. Charles S. Singleton. New Jersey: Princeton University Press, 1970.

Dickens, Charles. *Great Expectations*. Harmondsworth: Penguin, 1965.

Dickinson, Emily. 'Our Lives are Swiss', 'A Bird came Down the Walk', in *The Complete Poems of Emily Dickinson*, ed. Thomas H. Johnson. London: Faber and Faber, 1970.

Eliot, George. *Middlemarch*. Harmondsworth: Penguin, 1965.

Eliot, George. *The Lifted Veil*. London: Virago, 1985.

Eliot, George. *Daniel Deronda*. Harmondsworth: Penguin, 1987.

Eliot, T.S. *The Waste Land*, 'Little Gidding', in *Complete Poems and Plays*. London: Faber and Faber, 1975a.

Ellison, Ralph. *Invisible Man*. New York: Random House, 1952.

Ford, Ford Madox. *The Good Soldier* in *The Bodley Head Ford Madox Ford*, vol. 1. London: Bodley Head, 1962.

Gilman, Charlotte Perkins. *The Yellow Wallpaper*. London: Virago, 1981.

Hardy, Thomas. 'Neutral Tones', 'The Voice', 'The Darkling Thrush', in *The Oxford Authors Thomas Hardy*, ed. Samuel Hynes. Oxford: Oxford University Press, 1984.

Heaney, Seamus. *North*. London: Faber and Faber, 1975.

Ibsen, Henrik. *Four Major Plays*. Oxford: Oxford University Press, 1981.

James, Henry. *The Turn of the Screw*, in *The Bodley Head Henry James*, vol. XI, ed. Leon Edel. London: Bodley Head, 1974.

James, Henry. 'The Jolly Corner', in *Major American Short Stories*, ed. A. Walton Litz. Oxford: Oxford University Press, 1994.

Jonson, Ben. 1988. *A Critical Edition of the Major Works*, ed. Ian Donaldson. Oxford: Oxford University Press.

Joyce, James. 'The Dead', in *Dubliners*. London: Everyman, 1991.

Kafka, F. 'In the Penal Colony', in *The Complete Short Stories of Franz Kafka*, ed. Nahu N. Glatzer. London: Minerva, 1992.

Keats, John. 'Ode to a Nightingale', 'Ode on Melancholy', 'This Living Hand', in *The Poems of John Keats*, ed. Jack Stillinger. London: Heinemann, 1978.

Larkin, Philip. 'This Be The Verse', in *Collected Poems*, ed. Anthony Thwaite. London: Faber and Faber, 1988.

Lawrence, D.H. 'The Rocking-Horse Winner', in *The Collected Short Stories of D.H. Lawrence*. London: Heinemann, 1974.

Lawrence, D.H. *St. Mawr. The Virgin and the Gipsy*. Harmondsworth: Penguin, 1950.

Mansfield, Katherine. 'Bliss', in *The Stories of Katherine Mansfield*, ed. Antony Alpers. Oxford: Oxford University Press, 1984.

Marvell, Andrew. 'To His Coy Mistress', in *The Oxford Authors Andrew Marvell*, ed. Frank Kermode and Keith Walker. Oxford: Oxford University Press, 1990.

Melville, Herman. *Moby Dick; or, The Whale*, ed. Harold Beaver. Harmondsworth: Penguin, 1972.

Miller, Arthur. *The Crucible*. Harmondsworth: Penguin, 1988.

Milton, John. *Complete Shorter Poems*, ed. John Carey. London: Longman, 1971.

Milton, John. *Paradise Lost*, ed. Scott Elledge, 2nd edn. New York: Norton, 1993.

Monty Python's Flying Circus. *Just the Words*, 2 vols. London: Methuen, 1989.

Morrison, Toni. *The Bluest Eye*. London: Triad/Panther, 1981.

Morrison, Toni. *Beloved*. London: Picador, 1988.

O'Connor, Flannery. 'Revelation', in *The Secret Self: Short Stories by Women*, ed. Hermione Lee. London: Everyman, 1991.

Pater, Walter. *The Renaissance*. New York: Modern Library, 1919.

Plath, Sylvia. 'Daddy', in *Collected Poems*, ed. Ted Hughes. London: Faber and Faber, 1981.

Poe, Edgar Allan. 'The Premature Burial', 'The Purloined Letter', in *Tales of Mystery and Imagination*. London: Dent, 1984.

Pope, Alexander. 'An Essay on Criticism', in *The Poems of Alexander Pope*, ed. John Butt. London: Methuen, 1963.

Proust, Marcel. *A la recherche du temps perdu*. Paris: Gallimard, 1954.

Rhys, Jean. 'Let Them Call It Jazz', in *The Secret Self: Short Stories by Women*, ed. Hermione Lee. London: Everyman, 1991.

Rhys, Jean. *Wide Sargasso Sea*, ed. Angela Smith. Harmondsworth: Penguin, 1997.

Rich, Adrienne. 'A Valediction Forbidding Mourning', in *The Fact of a Doorframe: Poems Selected and New, 1950–84*. New York: Norton, 1984.

Rushdie, Salman. *Midnight's Children*. London: Picador, 1982.

Rushdie, Salman. *The Satanic Verses*. New York: Viking, 1988.

Salinger, J.D. *The Catcher in the Rye*. Harmondsworth: Penguin, 1987.

Shakespeare, William. *All's Well That Ends Well, Romeo and Juliet, Twelfth Night, Hamlet, Othello, King Lear, Macbeth, The Tempest*, Sonnet 20, Sonnet 50, in *The Riverside Shakespeare*. Boston: Houghton Mifflin, 1974.

Shelley, Percy Bysshe, 'Ozymandias', 'To a Sky-Lark', 'A Defence of Poetry', in *Shelley's Poetry and Prose*, ed. Donald H. Reiman and Sharon B. Powers. New York: Norton, 1977.

Sheridan, Richard Brinsley. *The Rivals*, ed. Elizabeth Duthie. London: Ernest Benn, 1979.

Sheridan, Richard Brinsley. *The School for Scandal*, ed. F.W. Bateson. New York: Norton, 1979.

Sidney, Sir Philip. *An Apology for Poetry*, ed. Geoffrey Shepherd. London: Nelson, 1965.

Sophocles. *The Three Theban Plays: Antigone, Oedipus the King, Oedipus at Colonus*, trans. Robert Fagles. Harmondsworth: Penguin, 1984.

Sterne, Laurence. *The Life and Opinions of Tristram Shandy, Gentleman*, ed. Ian Campbell Ross. Oxford: Clarendon Press, 1983.

Stevens, Wallace. 'Large Red Man Reading' in *The Collected Poems of Wallace Stevens*. New York: Alfred Knopf, 1954.

Stevens, Wallace. 'Adagia', in *Opus Posthumous*. New York: Alfred A. Knopf, 1957.

Swift, Jonathan. 'A Modest Proposal', in *The Writings of Jonathan Swift*, ed. Robert A. Greenberg and William Bowman Piper. New York: Norton, 1973.

Taylor, Elizabeth. 'Mr Wharton', in *The Secret Self: Short Stories by Women*, ed. Hermione Lee. London: Everyman, 1991.

Twain, Mark. *The Adventures of Huckleberry Finn*, ed. Walter Blair and Victor Fischer. Berkeley: University of California Press, 1988.

Wertenbaker, Timberlake. *Our Country's Good*. London: Methuen, 1988.

Winterson, Jeanette. *Sexing the Cherry*. London: Bloomsbury, 1989.

Winterson, Jeanette. *Written on the Body*. London: Jonathan Cape, 1992.

Woolf, Virginia. 'The Mark on the Wall', in *A Haunted House and Other Short Stories*. London: Grafton, 1982.

Woolf, Virginia. *Orlando: A Biography*. Oxford: Oxford University Press, 1992.

Wordsworth, William. 'Alice Fell', 'A Slumber did my Spirit Seal', in *The Oxford Authors William Wordsworth*, ed. Stephen Gill. Oxford: Oxford University Press, 1984.

Wyatt, Sir Thomas. 'Whoso List to Hunt', in *Collected Poems*, ed. Joost Daalder. London: Oxford University Press, 1975.

Bibliography of critical and theoretical works

Abraham, Nicolas. 1994. 'Notes on the Phantom: A Complement to Freud's Metapsychology' (1975) and 'The Phantom of Hamlet *or* The Sixth Act, *preceded by* The Intermission of "Truth"' (1975), in *The Shell and the Kernel: Renewals of Psychoanalysis*, Nicolas Abraham and Maria Torok, trans. Nicholas Rand. Chicago: Chicago University Press.

Abrams, M.H. 1953. *The Mirror and the Lamp: Romantic Theory and the Critical Tradition*. Oxford: Oxford University Press.

Alter, Robert. 1981. *The Art of Biblical Narrative*. London: George Allen and Unwin.

Alter, Robert. 1985. *The Art of Biblical Poetry*. New York: Basic Books.

Althusser, Louis. 1969. 'Ideology and Ideological State Apparatuses' and 'A Letter on Art', in *Lenin and Philosophy and Other Essays*, trans. Ben Brewster, 2nd edn. London: New Left Books, 1977.

Appelbaum, David. 1990. *Voice*. New York: State University of New York.

Apter, Terry E. 1982. 'The Uncanny', in *Fantasy Literature: An Approach to Reality*. London: Macmillan.

Aristotle. 1965. *On the Art of Poetry*, in *Classical Literary Criticism*, Trans. T.S. Dorsch. Harmondsworth: Penguin.

Arnold, Matthew. 1964. 'The Function of Criticism at the Present Time', in *Essays in Criticism*. New York: Everyman's Library.

Ashcroft, Bill, Gareth Griffiths and Helen Tiffin, eds. 1989. *The Empire Writes Back*. London: Routledge.

Ashcroft, Bill, Gareth Griffiths and Helen Tiffin, eds. 1995. *The Post-Colonial Studies Reader*. London: Routledge.

Attridge, Derek. 1992. *Poetic Rhythm*. Cambridge: Cambridge University Press.

Austin, J.L. 1962. *How to do Things with Words*. Oxford: Clarendon Press.

Austin, J.L. 1970. 'Performative Utterances', in *Philosophical Papers*, 2nd edn, eds J.O. Urmson and G.J. Warnock. Oxford: Oxford University Press.

Bakhtin, M.M. 1981. *The Dialogic Imagination: Four Essays*, trans. M. Holquist and C. Emerson. Austin: University of Texas Press.

Bakhtin, M.M. 1992. From 'Discourse in the Novel', in *Modern Literary Theory: A Reader*, eds Philip Rice and Patricia Waugh. London: Edward Arnold.

Balibar, Etienne and Pierre Macherey. 1981. 'On Literature as an Ideological Form', in *Untying the Text: A Post-Structuralist Reader*, ed. Robert Young. London: Routledge and Kegan Paul.

Barker, Francis and Peter Hulme. 1985. 'Nymphs and Reapers Heavily Vanish: The Discursive Con-Texts of *The Tempest*', in *Alternative Shakespeares*, ed. John Drakakis. London: Routledge.

Barker, Howard. 1989. *Arguments for a Theatre*. London: John Calder.

Barthes, Roland. 1972. *Mythologies*, trans. Annette Lavers. London: Jonathan Cape.

Barthes, Roland. 1977a. 'The Death of the Author', in *Image Music Text*, trans. Stephen Heath. London: Fontana.

Barthes, Roland. 1977b. 'From Work to Text', in *Image Music Text*, trans. Stephen Heath. London: Fontana.

Barthes, Roland. 1981. 'Theory of the Text', in *Untying the Text: A Post-Structuralist Reader*, ed. Robert Young. London: Routledge and Kegan Paul.

Barthes, Roland. 1990a. *The Pleasure of the Text*, trans. Richard Miller. Oxford: Basil Blackwell.

Barthes, Roland. 1990b. *S/Z*, trans. Richard Miller. Oxford: Basil Blackwell.

Barthes, Roland. 1990c. *A Lover's Discourse: Fragments*, trans. Richard Howard. Harmondsworth: Penguin.

Bataille, Georges. 1973. *Oeuvres Complètes*, vol. V. Paris: Gallimard.

Bataille, Georges. 1985. *Literature and Evil*, trans. Alistair Hamilton. London: Marion Boyars.

Baudrillard, Jean. 1988. 'Simulacra and Simulations', in *Selected Writings*, ed. Mark Poster. Cambridge: Polity.

Baudrillard, Jean. 1990. *Seduction*, trans. Brian Singer. London: Macmillan.

Baudrillard, Jean. 1995. *The Gulf War Did Not Take Place*, trans. Paul Patton. Sydney: Power Publications.

Beja, Morris. 1971. *Epiphany in the Modern Novel*. London: Peter Owen.

Belsey, Catherine. 1994. *Desire: Love Stories in Western Culture*. Oxford: Blackwell.

Bennett, Andrew, ed. 1995. *Readers and Reading*. London: Longman.

Bennett, Tony. 1979. *Formalism and Marxism*. London: Methuen.

Bergson, Henri. 1921. *Laughter: An Essay on the Meaning of the Comic*, trans. Cloudesley Brereton and Fred Rothwell. London: Macmillan.

Berry, Francis. 1962. *Poetry and the Physical Voice*. London: Routledge and Kegan Paul.

Bersani, Leo. 1978. *A Future for Astyanax: Character and Desire in Literature.* Boston: Little Brown.

Bersani, Leo. 1990. *The Culture of Redemption.* Cambridge, Mass.: Harvard University Press.

Bersani, Leo. 1995. *Homos.* Cambridge, Mass.: Harvard University Press.

Bhabha, Homi, ed. 1990. *Nation and Narration.* London: Routledge.

Bhabha, Homi K. 1996. 'Of Mimicry and Man: The Ambivalence of Colonial Discourse', in eds Philip Rice and Patricia Waugh, *Modern Literary Theory: A Reader.* 3rd edn. London: Edward Arnold.

Biriotti, Maurice and Nicola Miller, eds. 1993. *What is an Author?* Manchester: Manchester University Press.

Blanchot, Maurice. 1981. 'The Narrative Voice (the "he", the neuter)', in *The Gaze of Orpheus and Other Literary Essays*, trans. Lydia Davis. New York: Station Hill.

Bloom, Harold. 1973. *The Anxiety of Influence: A Theory of Poetry.* Oxford: Oxford University Press.

Bloom, Harold. 1990. 'The Analysis of Character', in *Holden Caulfield*, ed. Harold Bloom. New York: Chelsea House.

Bloom, Harold. 1994. *The Western Canon: The Book and School of the Ages.* London: Macmillan.

Boone, Joseph Allen. 1987. *Tradition and Counter Tradition: Love and the Form of Fiction.* Chicago: University of Chicago Press.

Boone, Joseph Allen. 1988. *Libidinal Currents: Sexuality and the Shaping of Modernism.* Chicago: Chicago University Press.

Borch-Jacobsen, Mikkel. 1987. 'The Laughter of Being', in *Modern Language Notes*, 102, no. 4: 737–60.

Borch-Jacobsen, Mikkel. 1988. *The Freudian Subject*, trans. Catherine Porter. Stanford: Stanford University Press.

Botting, Fred. 1997. *Gothic.* London: Routledge.

Bourdieu, Pierre. 1984. *Distinction: A Social Critique of the Judgment of Taste*, trans. Richard Nice. Cambridge, Mass.: Harvard University Press.

Bowie, Malcolm. 1991. *Lacan.* London: Fontana.

Bradley, A.C. 1904. *Shakespearean Tragedy: Lectures on Hamlet, Othello, King Lear, Macbeth.* London: Macmillan.

Brannigan, John. 1998. *New Historicism and Cultural Materialism.* London: Macmillan.

Brecht, Bertolt. 1978. 'A Short Organum for the Theatre', in *Brecht on Theatre: The Development of an Aesthetic*, ed. and trans. John Willett. London: Eyre Methuen.

Bristow, Joseph. 1992a. 'Introduction' to Oscar Wilde, *The Importance of Being Earnest and Related Writings.* London: Routledge.

Bristow, Joseph, ed. 1992b. *Sexual Sameness: Textual Differences in Lesbian and Gay Writing.* London: Routledge.

Bristow, Joseph. 1995. *Effeminate England: Homoerotic Writing after 1885*. Buckingham: Open University Press.

Bristow, Joseph. 1997. *Sexuality*. London: Routledge.

Bronfen, Elisabeth. 1992. *Over Her Dead Body: Death, Femininity and the Aesthetic*. Manchester: Manchester University Press.

Brooke-Rose, Christine. 1958. *A Grammar of Metaphor*. London: Secker and Warburg.

Brooker, Peter, ed. 1992. *Modernism/Postmodernism*. London: Longman.

Brooks, Peter. 1984. *Reading for the Plot: Design and Intention in Narrative*. Oxford: Oxford University Press.

Brooks, Peter. 1993. *Body Work: Objects of Desire in Modern Narrative*. Cambridge, Mass.: Harvard University Press.

Brown, Paul. 1994. ' "This thing of darkness I acknowledge mine": *The Tempest* and the Discourse of Colonialism', in *Political Shakespeare: Essays in Cultural Materialism*, eds Jonathan Dollimore and Alan Sinfield. 2nd edn. Manchester: Manchester University Press.

Burke, Sean. 1992. *The Death and Return of the Author: Criticism and Subjectivity in Barthes, Foucault and Derrida*. Edinburgh: Edinburgh University Press.

Burke, Sean, ed. 1995. *Authorship: From Plato to the Postmodern: A Reader*. Edinburgh: Edinburgh University Press.

Butler, Judith. 1990. *Gender Trouble: Feminism and the Subversion of Identity*. London: Routledge.

Butler, Judith. 1991. 'Imitation and Gender Insubordination', in *Inside/Out: Lesbian Theories, Gay Theories*, ed. Diana Fuss. New York: Routledge.

Butler, Judith. 1993. *Bodies that Matter: On the Discursive Limits of 'Sex'*. New York: Routledge.

Butler, Judith. 1997. *Excitable Speech: A Politics of the Performative*. New York: Routledge.

Castle, Terry. 1992. 'Sylvia Townsend Warner and the Counterplot of Lesbian Fiction', in *Sexual Sameness: Textual Differences in Lesbian and Gay Writing*, ed. Joseph Bristow. London: Routledge.

Castle, Terry. 1995. *The Female Thermometer: Eighteenth-Century Culture and the Invention of the Uncanny*. Oxford: Oxford University Press.

Chambers, Ross. 1984. *Story and Situation: Narrative Seduction and the Power of Fiction*. Manchester: Manchester University Press.

Chambers, Ross. 1991. *Room for Maneuver: Reading (the) Oppositional (in) Narrative*. Chicago: University of Chicago Press.

Chandler, James. 1998. *England in 1819: The Politics of Literary Culture and the Case of Romantic Historicism*. Chicago: University of Chicago Press.

Chase, Cynthia. 1986. *Decomposing Figures: Rhetorical Readings in the Romantic Tradition*. Baltimore: The Johns Hopkins University Press.

Chatman, Seymour. 1990. *Coming to Terms: The Rhetoric of Narrative in Fiction and Film*. Ithaca: Cornell University Press.

Cixous, Hélène. 1974. 'The Character of "Character" ', *New Literary History*, 5: 383–402.

Cixous, Hélène. 1976. 'Fiction and Its Phantoms: A Reading of Freud's *Das Unheimliche*', *New Literary History*, 7: 525–48.

Cixous, Hélène. 1990. 'The Laugh of the Medusa', trans. Keith Cohen and Paula Cohen, in *New French Feminisms: An Anthology*, eds Elaine Marks and Isabelle de Courtirvon. Amherst: University of Massachusetts Press.

Clark, Timothy. 1997. *The Theory of Inspiration: Composition as a Crisis of Subjectivity in Romantic and Post-Romantic Writing*. Manchester: Manchester University Press.

Cohn, Dorrit. 1978. *Transparent Minds: Narrative Modes for Presenting Consciousness in Fiction*. Princeton, NJ: Princeton University Press, 1978.

Cohn, Norman. 1970. *The Pursuit of the Millennium: Revolutionary Millenarians and Mystical Anarchists of the Middle Ages*. Oxford: Oxford University Press.

Connor, Steven. 1992. *Theory and Cultural Value*. Oxford: Blackwell.

Connor, Steven. 1997. *Postmodernist Culture: An Introduction to Theories of the Contemporary*. 2nd edn. Oxford: Blackwell.

Cordner, Michael, Peter Holland and John Kerrigan, eds. 1994. *English Comedy*. Cambridge: Cambridge University Press.

Crane, R.S. 1967. 'History Versus Criticism in the Study of Literature', in *The Idea of the Humanities and Other Essays Critical and Historical*, vol. 2. Chicago: University of Chicago Press.

Culler, Jonathan. 1981. 'Story and Discourse in the Analysis of Narrative', in *The Pursuit of Signs: Semiotics, Literature, Deconstruction*. London: Routledge and Kegan Paul.

Culler, Jonathan. 1983. *On Deconstruction: Theory and Criticism After Structuralism*. London: Routledge and Kegan Paul.

Culler, Jonathan, ed. 1988a. *On Puns: The Foundation of Letters*. Oxford: Basil Blackwell.

Culler, Jonathan. 1988b. 'Political Criticism: Confronting Religion', in *Framing the Sign: Criticism and Its Institutions*. Oxford: Basil Blackwell.

Culler, Jonathan. 1997. *Literary Theory: A Very Short Introduction*. Oxford: Oxford University Press.

Cupitt, Don. 1997. *After God: The Future of Religion*. London: Weidenfield and Nicolson.

Curti, Lidia. 1998. *Female Stories, Female Bodies: Narrative, Identity and Representation*. London: Macmillan.

Dean, Carolyn J. 1992. *The Self and Its Pleasures: Bataille, Lacan, and the History of the Decentered Subject*. Ithaca: Cornell University Press.

Deleuze, Gilles and Félix Guattari. 1983. *Anti-Oedipus: Capitalism and Schizophrenia*, trans. Robert Hurley *et al*. Minneapolis: University of Minnesota Press.

Deleuze, Gilles and Félix Guattari. 1986. *Kafka: Toward a Minor Literature*, trans. Dana Polan. Minneapolis: University of Minnesota Press.

de Man, Paul. 1979. *Allegories of Reading: Figural Language in Rousseau, Nietzsche, Rilke, and Proust.* New Haven: Yale University Press.

de Man, Paul. 1983. *Blindness and Insight: Essays in the Rhetoric of Contemporary Criticism.* 2nd edn. London: Methuen.

de Man, Paul. 1984. *The Rhetoric of Romanticism.* New York: Columbia University Press.

Derrida, Jacques. 1976. *Of Grammatology*, trans. Gayatri Chakravorty Spivak. Baltimore: The Johns Hopkins University Press.

Derrida, Jacques. 1979. 'Living On', trans. James Hulbert, in *Deconstruction and Criticism*, eds Harold Bloom *et al.* New York: Seabury Press.

Derrida, Jacques. 1982. 'White Mythology', in *Margins of Philosophy*, trans. Alan Bass. Chicago: University of Chicago Press.

Derrida, Jacques. 1983. 'The Principle of Reason: The University in the Eyes of Its Pupils', trans. Catherine Porter and Edward P. Morris, in *Diacritics*, vol. 13, no. 3: 3–20.

Derrida, Jacques. 1984. 'No Apocalypse, Not Now (full speed ahead, seven missiles, seven missives)', trans. Catherine Porter and Philip Lewis, *Diacritics*, vol. 14, no. 3: 20–31.

Derrida, Jacques. 1985a. 'Des Tours de Babel', trans. Joseph F. Graham, in *Difference in Translation*, ed. Graham. Ithaca: Cornell University Press.

Derrida, Jacques. 1985b. *The Ear of the Other: Otobiography, Transference, Translation. Texts and Discussions with Jacques Derrida*, trans. Peggy Kamuf. New York: Schocken Books.

Derrida, Jacques. 1986a. *Mémoires: for Paul de Man*, trans. Cecile Lindsay, Jonathan Culler and Eduardo Cadava. New York: Columbia University Press.

Derrida, Jacques. 1986b. 'Fors: The Anglish Words of Nicolas Abraham and Maria Torok', trans. Barbara Johnson, in Nicolas Abraham and Maria Torok, *The Wolf Man's Magic Word: A Cryptonymy*, trans. Nicholas Rand. Minneapolis: University of Minnesota Press.

Derrida, Jacques. 1988. 'Afterword: Toward an Ethic of Discussion', trans. Samuel Weber, in *Limited Inc.* Evanston: Northwestern University Press.

Derrida, Jacques. 1989. 'The Ghost Dance: An Interview with Jacques Derrida', trans. Jean-Luc Svobada, in *Public*, no. 2: 60–73.

Derrida, Jacques. 1992a. *Acts of Literature*, ed. Derek Attridge. London: Routledge.

Derrida, Jacques. 1992b. 'Passions: "An Oblique Offering" ', trans. David Wood, in *Derrida: A Critical Reader*, ed. David Wood. Oxford: Basil Blackwell.

Derrida, Jacques. 1992c. 'Of an Apocalyptic Tone Newly Adopted in Philosophy', trans. John P. Leavey, Jr, in *Derrida and Negative Theology*, eds Harold Coward and Toby Foshay. Albany, New York: State University of New York Press.

Derrida, Jacques. 1994. *Spectres of Marx: The State of the Debt, the Work of*

Mourning, and the New International, trans. Peggy Kamuf. New York: Routledge.

Derrida, Jacques. 1995. *Archive Fever: A Freudian Impression*, trans. Eric Prenowitz. Chicago: Chicago University Press.

Derrida, Jacques, and Gianni Vattimo, eds. 1998. *Religion*. Cambridge: Polity.

Descartes, René. 1977. *Discourse on Method and the Meditations*, trans. F.E. Sutcliffe. Harmondsworth: Penguin.

Docherty, Thomas. 1983. *Reading (Absent) Character: Towards a Theory of Characterization in Fiction*. Oxford: Oxford University Press.

Docherty, Thomas. ed. 1993. *Postmodernism: A Reader*. 2nd edn. Hemel Hempstead: Harvester Wheatsheaf.

Dollimore, Jonathan. 1989. *Radical Tragedy: Religion, Ideology and Power in the Drama of Shakespeare and his Contemporaries*. Hemel Hempstead: Harvester Wheatsheaf.

Dollimore, Jonathan. 1991. *Sexual Dissidence: Augustine to Wilde, Freud to Foucault*. Oxford: Clarendon Press.

Dollimore, Jonathan. 1998. *Death, Desire and Loss in Western Culture*. London: Penguin.

Dollimore, Jonathan and Alan Sinfield, eds. 1994. *Political Shakespeare: New Essays in Cultural Materialism*. 2nd edn. Manchester: Manchester University Press.

Donaldson, Ian, ed. 1988 *Ben Jonson: A Critical Edition of the Major Works*. Oxford: Oxford University Press.

Drakakis, John, ed. 1992. *Shakespearean Tragedy*. London: Longman.

Drakakis, John and Naomi Liebler, eds. 1998. *Tragedy*. London: Longman.

During, Simon. 1992. *Foucault and Literature: Towards a Genealogy of Writing*. London: Routledge.

Eagleton, Terry. 1976. *Marxism and Literary Criticism*. London: Routledge.

Eagleton, Terry. 1990. *The Ideology of the Aesthetic*. Oxford: Blackwell.

Eagleton, Terry, ed. 1994. *Ideology*. London: Longman.

Eagleton, Terry. 1996. *Literary Theory: An Introduction*. 2nd edn. Oxford: Basil Blackwell.

Eco, Umberto. 1979. 'The Poetics of the Open Work', in *The Role of the Reader: Explorations in the Semiotics of Texts*. Bloomington: Indiana University Press.

Eco, Umberto. 1992. 'Postmodernism, Irony, the Enjoyable', in *Modernism/Postmodernism*, ed. Peter Brooker. London: Longman.

Eco, Umberto. 1993. 'The City of Robots', in *Postmodernism: A Reader*, ed. Thomas Docherty. Hemel Hempstead: Harvester Wheatsheaf.

Elam, Diane. 1992. *Romancing the Postmodern*. London: Routledge.

Eliot, T.S. 1975b. *Selected Prose of T.S. Eliot*, ed. Frank Kermode. London: Faber and Faber.

Ellmann, Maud, ed. 1994. *Psychoanalytic Literary Criticism*. London: Longman.

Empson, William. 1953. *Seven Types of Ambiguity*, 3rd edn. London: Chatto and Windus.

Empson, William. 1965. *Milton's God*. London: Chatto and Windus.

Fanon, Frantz. 1967. *The Wretched of the Earth*, trans. Constance Farrington. Harmondsworth: Penguin.

Felman, Shoshana. 1983. *The Literary Speech Act: Don Juan with J.L. Austin, or Seduction in Two Languages*, trans. Catherine Porter. Ithaca: Cornell University Press.

Felman, Shoshana. 1987. *Jacques Lacan and the Adventure of Insight: Psychoanalysis in Contemporary Culture*. Cambridge, Mass.: Harvard University Press.

Felman, Shoshana. 1993. *What Does a Woman Want? Reading and Sexual Difference*. Baltimore: The Johns Hopkins University Press.

Fetterley, Judith. 1978. *The Resisting Reader: A Feminist Approach to American Fiction*. Bloomington: Indiana University Press.

Fineman, Joel. 1991. *The Subjectivity Effect in Western Literary Tradition: Essays Toward the Release of Shakespeare's Will*. Cambridge, Mass.: MIT Press.

Fink, Bruce. 1996. 'Reading Hamlet with Lacan', in Willy Apollon and Richard Feldstein, eds, *Lacan, Politics, Aesthetics*. Albany, NY: State University of New York Press.

Fish, Stanley. 1980. *Is There A Text in This Class? The Authority of Interpretive Communities*. Cambridge, Mass.: Harvard University Press.

Forrester, John. 1990. *The Seductions of Psychoanalysis: Freud, Lacan and Derrida*. Cambridge: Cambridge University Press.

Forster, E.M. 1976. *Aspects of the Novel*. Harmondsworth: Penguin.

Foster, Jeanette H. 1958. *Sex Variant Women in Literature: A Historical and Quantitative Survey*. London: Frederick Muller.

Foucault, Michel. 1970. *The Order of Things: An Archeology of the Human Sciences*. New York: Random House.

Foucault, Michel. 1979. 'What Is an Author?', in *Textual Strategies: Perspectives in Post-Structuralist Criticism*, ed. Josué V. Harari. London: Methuen.

Foucault, Michel. 1980a. 'The History of Sexuality: Interview', trans. Geoff Bennington, in *Oxford Literary Review*, vol. 4, no. 2: 3–14.

Foucault, Michel. 1980b. Introduction to *Herculine Barbin: Being the Recently Discovered Memoirs of a Nineteenth-Century French Hermaphrodite*, trans. Richard McDougall. New York: Pantheon Books.

Foucault, Michel. 1981. *The History of Sexuality: An Introduction*, trans. Robert Hurley. Harmondsworth: Penguin.

Foucault, Michel. 1983. 'The Subject and Power', in *Michel Foucault: Beyond Structuralism and Hermeneutics*, eds Hubert L. Dreyfus and Paul Rabinow. Chicago: University of Chicago Press.

Foucault, Michel. 1985. *The Use of Pleasure (The History of Sexuality*, vol. 2). Harmondsworth: Penguin.

Fowler, Roger. 1986. *Linguistic Criticism*. Oxford: Oxford University Press.

Freud, Sigmund. 1957a. 'The Antithetical Meaning of Primal Words' (1910), in *The Standard Edition of the Complete Psychological Works of Sigmund Freud*, vol. XI, trans. James Strachey. London: Hogarth.

Freud, Sigmund. 1957b. 'Findings, Ideas, Problems', in *The Standard Edition of the Complete Psychological Works of Sigmund Freud*, vol. XXIII, trans. James Strachey. London: Hogarth.

Freud, Sigmund. 1976. *Jokes and their Relation to the Unconscious* (1905), in *Pelican Freud Library*, vol. 6, trans. James Strachey. Harmondsworth: Penguin.

Freud, Sigmund. 1977. *On Sexuality: Three Essays on the Theory of Sexuality* (1905), in *Pelican Freud Library*, vol. 7, trans. James Strachey. Harmondsworth: Penguin.

Freud, Sigmund. 1985a. 'Thoughts for the Times on War and Death' (1915), in *Pelican Freud Library*, vol. 12, trans. James Strachey. Harmondsworth: Penguin.

Freud, Sigmund. 1985b. 'The "Uncanny"' (1919), in *Pelican Freud Library*, vol. 14, trans. James Strachey. Harmondsworth: Penguin.

Freud, Sigmund. 1985c. 'A Seventeenth-Century Demonological Neurosis' (1923), in *Pelican Freud Library*, vol. 14, trans. James Strachey. Harmondsworth: Penguin.

Freud, Sigmund. 1985d. 'Humour' (1927), in *Pelican Freud Library*, vol. 14, trans. James Strachey. Harmondsworth: Penguin.

Freud, Sigmund. 1985e. 'Civilization and Its Discontents' (1930), in *Pelican Freud Library*, vol. 12, trans. James Strachey. Harmondsworth: Penguin.

Freud, Sigmund. 1986. 'Psychoanalysis' (1923) and 'The Resistances to Psychoanalysis' (1925), in *Pelican Freud Library*, vol. 15, trans. James Strachey. Harmondsworth: Penguin.

Freund, Elizabeth. 1987. *The Return of the Reader: Reader-Response Criticism*. London: Methuen.

Fussell, Paul. 1975. *The Great War and Modern Memory*. Oxford: Oxford University Press.

Gates, Henry Louis, Jr, ed. 1984. *Black Literature and Literary Theory*. London: Methuen.

Gates, Henry Louis, Jr, ed. 1986. *'Race', Writing, and Difference*. Chicago: University of Chicago Press.

Gates, Henry Louis, Jr, 1988. *The Signifying Monkey: A Theory of Afro-American Literary Criticism*. Oxford: Oxford University Press.

Gates, Henry Louis, Jr, 1992. *Loose Canons: Notes on the Culture Wars*. New York: Oxford University Press.

Genette, Gérard. 1986. *Narrative Discourse: An Essay in Method*, trans. Jane E. Lewin. Oxford: Basil Blackwell.

Genette, Gérard. 1987. *Seuils*. Paris: Seuil.

Gibson, Andrew. 1996. *Towards a Postmodern Theory of Narrative*. Edinburgh: Edinburgh University Press.

Gilbert, Sandra M. and Susan Gubar. 1979. *The Madwoman in the Attic: The Woman Writer and the Nineteenth-Century Literary Imagination*. New Haven: Yale University Press.

Girard, René. 1965. *Deceit, Desire, and the Novel: Self and Other in Literary Structure*, trans. Yvonne Freccero. Baltimore: The Johns Hopkins University Press.

Gray, Frances. 1994. *Women and Laughter*. London: Macmillan.

Green, André. 1979. *The Tragic Effect: The Oedipus Complex in Tragedy*, trans. Alan Sheridan. Cambridge: Cambridge University Press.

Greenblatt, Stephen. 1988. *Shakespearean Negotiations: The Circulation of Social Energy in Renaissance England*. Oxford: Clarendon Press.

Greenblatt, Stephen. 1990a. 'Toward a Poetics of Culture', in *Learning to Curse: Essays in Early Modern Culture*. London: Routledge.

Greenblatt, Stephen. 1990b. 'Culture', in *Critical Terms for Literary Study*, eds Frank Lentricchia and Thomas McLaughlin. Chicago: University of Chicago Press.

Greenblatt, Stephen. 1991. *Marvelous Possessions: The Wonder of the New World*. Oxford: Clarendon Press.

Griffiths, Eric. 1989. *The Printed Voice of Victorian Poetry*. Oxford: Clarendon Press.

Guillory, John. 1993. *Cultural Capital: The Problem of Literary Canon Formation*. Chicago: Chicago University Press.

Hall, Stuart. 1988. 'Gramsci and Us', in *The Hard Road to Renewal: Thatcherism and the Crisis of the Left*. London: Verso.

Halperin, David. 1990. *One Hundred Years of Homosexuality and Other Essays on Greek Love*. New York: Routledge.

Hamilton, Paul. 1996. *Historicism*. London: Routledge.

Harari, Josué V. 1979. 'Critical Factions/Critical Fictions', in *Textual Strategies: Perspectives in Post-Structuralist Criticism*, ed. Josué V. Harari. London: Methuen.

Hartman, Geoffrey H. 1981. 'Words and Wounds', in *Saving the Text: Literature/Derrida/Philosophy*. Baltimore: The Johns Hopkins University Press.

Hassan, Ihab. 1989. 'Beyond Postmodernism? Theory, Sense, and Pragmatism', in *Making Sense: The Role of the Reader in Contemporary American Fiction*, ed. Gerard Hoffmann. München: Wilhelm Fink.

Hawkes, Terence. 1972. *Metaphor*. London: Methuen.

Hazlitt, William. 1910. 'On Shakespeare and Milton', in *Lectures on the English Poets and The Spirit of the Age*. London: Dent.

Heidegger, Martin. 1967. *What Is A Thing?*, trans. W.B. Barton, Jr and Vera Deutsch. Chicago: Henry Regnery.

Heidegger, Martin. 1977. 'The Word of Nietzsche: "God Is Dead"', in *The*

Question Concerning Technology and Other Essays, trans. William Lovitt. New York: Harper Torchbooks.

Henderson, Mae Gwendolyn. 1993. 'Speaking in Tongues. Dialogics, Dialectics and the Black Woman Writer's Literary Tradition', in *Colonial Discourse and Post-Colonial Theory: A Reader*, eds Patrick Williams and Laura Chrisman. Hemel Hempstead: Harvester Wheatsheaf.

Hertz, Neil. 1979. 'Freud and the Sandman', in *Textual Strategies: Perspectives in Post-Structuralist Criticism*, ed. Josué V. Harari. London: Methuen.

Hirst, Paul and Penny Woolley. 1982. *Social Relations and Human Attributes*. London: Tavistock.

Hobbes, Thomas. 1840. *The English Works of Thomas Hobbes*, ed. Sir William Molesworth, vol. IV. London: John Bohn.

Holland, Norman N. 1980. 'Unity Identity Text Self', in *Reader-Response Criticism: From Formalism to Post-Structuralism*, ed. Jane P. Tompkins, Baltimore: The Johns Hopkins University Press.

Hollander, John. 1985. *Vision and Resonance: Two Senses of Poetic Form*, 2nd edn. New Haven: Yale University Press.

Homans, Margaret. 1994. 'Feminist Fictions and Feminist Theories of Narrative', in *Narrative* 2: 3–16.

Hough, Graham. 1967. *The Romantic Poets*, 3rd edn. London: Hutchinson.

Hutcheon, Linda. 1988. *A Poetics of Postmodernism: History, Theory, Fiction*. London: Routledge.

Hutcheon, Linda. 1989. *The Politics of Postmodernism*. London: Routledge.

Irigaray, Luce. 1977. 'Women's Exile', in *Ideology and Consciousness*, no. 1:62–76.

Irigaray, Luce. 1985. 'This Sex Which Is Not One', in *This Sex Which Is Not One*, trans. Catherine Porter and Carolyn Burke. Ithaca: Cornell University Press.

Iser, Wolfgang. 1995. 'Interaction Between Text and Reader', in *Readers and Reading*, ed. Andrew Bennett. London: Longman.

Jacobus, Mary. 1986. *Reading Woman: Essays in Feminist Criticism*. London: Methuen.

Jakobson, Roman. 1960. 'Closing Statement: Linguistics and Poetics', in *Style in Language*, ed. Thomas A. Sebeok. Cambridge, Mass.: MIT.

James, Henry. 1986. *The Art of Criticism: Henry James on the Theory and Practice of Fiction*, eds William Veeder and Susan M. Griffin. Chicago: University of Chicago Press.

Jameson, Fredric. 1988. 'The Politics of Theory: Ideological Positions in the Postmodernism Debate', in David Lodge, ed., *Modern Literary Theory*. London: Longman.

Jameson, Fredric. 1992. 'Postmodernism and Consumer Society', in *Modernism/Postmodernism*, ed. Peter Brooker. London: Longman.

Jameson, Fredric. 1993. 'Postmodernism, or the Cultural Logic of Late

Capitalism', in *Postmodernism: A Reader*, ed. Thomas Docherty. Hemel Hempstead: Harvester Wheatsheaf.

Jencks, Charles. 1993. 'The Emergent Rules', in *Postmodernism: A Reader*, ed. Thomas Docherty. Hemel Hempstead: Harvester Wheatsheaf.

Johnson, Samuel. 1969. *Dr Johnson on Shakespeare*, ed. W.K. Wimsatt. Harmondsworth: Penguin.

Judovitz, Dalia. 1988. *Subjectivity and Representation in Descartes: The Origins of Modernity*. Cambridge: Cambridge University Press.

Kant, Immanuel. 1988. *The Critique of Judgement*, trans. James Creed Meredith. Oxford: Clarendon Press.

Kermode, Frank. 1967. *The Sense of an Ending: Studies in the Theory of Fiction*. Oxford: Oxford University Press.

Kermode, Frank. 1975. *The Classic*. London: Faber and Faber.

Kermode, Frank. 1979. *The Genesis of Secrecy: On the Interpretation of Narrative*. Cambridge, Mass.: Harvard University Press.

Kermode, Frank. 1983. 'Secrets and Narrative Sequence', in *Essays on Fiction 1971–82*. London: Routledge and Kegan Paul.

Knight, Stephen. 1980. *Form and Ideology in Detective Fiction*. London: Macmillan.

Knopp, Sherron E. 1992. ' "If I saw you would you kiss me?": Sapphism and the Subversiveness of Virginia Woolf's *Orlando*', in *Sexual Sameness: Textual Differences in Lesbian and Gay Writing*, ed. Joseph Bristow. London: Routledge.

Koestler, Arthur. 1964. *The Act of Creation*. London: Hutchinson.

Kristeva, Julia. 1986. 'Word, Dialogue and Novel', in *The Kristeva Reader*, ed. Toril Moi. Oxford: Basil Blackwell.

Kristeva, Julia. 1991. *Strangers to Ourselves*, trans. Leon C. Roudiez. Hemel Hempstead: Harvester Wheatsheaf.

Lacan, Jacques. 1977a. *Écrits: A Selection*, trans. Alan Sheridan. London: Tavistock.

Lacan, Jacques. 1977b. 'Desire and the Interpretation of Desire in *Hamlet*', trans. James Hulbert, *Yale French Studies*, no. 55/56. *Literature and Psychoanalysis. The Question of Reading: Otherwise*, ed. Shoshana Felman.

Lakoff, George and Mark Johnson. 1980. *Metaphors We Live By*. Chicago: University of Chicago Press.

Lane, Christopher. 1995. *The Ruling Passion: British Colonial Allegory and the Paradox of Homosexual Desire*. Durham: Duke University Press.

Leavis, F.R. 1948. *The Great Tradition*. London: Chatto and Windus.

Leavis, F.R. and Denys Thompson. 1964. *Culture and Environment: The Training of Critical Awareness*. London: Chatto and Windus.

Leavis, F.R. 1972. *Revaluation: Tradition and Development in English Poetry*. Harmondsworth: Penguin.

Lecercle, Jean-Jacques. 1990. *The Violence of Language*. London: Routledge.

Loomba, Ania. 1998. *Colonialism/Postcolonialism*. London: Routledge.

Lyotard, Jean-François. 1984. *The Postmodern Condition: A Report on Knowledge*, trans. Geoff Bennington and Brian Massumi. Manchester: Manchester University Press.

Lyotard, Jean-François. 1992. 'Answering the Question: What is Postmodernism?', in *Modernism/Postmodernism*, ed. Peter Brooker. London: Longman.

Lyotard, Jean-François. 1997. *Postmodern Fables*, trans. Georges van den Abbeele. Minneapolis: University of Minnesota Press.

Macherey, Pierre. 1978. *A Theory of Literary Production*, trans. Geoffrey Wall. London: Routledge and Kegan Paul.

Machor, James L., ed. 1993. *Readers in History: Nineteenth-Century American Literature and the Contexts of Response*. Baltimore: The Johns Hopkins University Press.

Manguel, Alberto. 1997. *A History of Reading*. London: Harper Collins.

Martin, Wallace. 1986. *Recent Theories of Narrative*. Ithaca: Cornell University Press.

Marx, Karl. 1976. *The German Ideology*, in Karl Marx and Frederick Engels, *Collected Works*, vol. 5. London: Lawrence and Wishart.

Meltzer, Françoise. 1994. *Hot Property: The Stakes and Claims of Literary Originality*. Chicago: University of Chicago Press.

Miller, D.A. 1981. *Narrative and its Discontents: Problems of Closure in the Traditional Novel*. New Jersey: Princeton University Press.

Miller, D.A. 1989. ' "Cage aux folles": Sensation and Gender in Wilkie Collins's *The Woman in White*', in *Speaking of Gender*, ed. E. Showalter. London: Routledge.

Miller, J. Hillis. 1963. *The Disappearance of God: Five Nineteenth-Century Writers*. Cambridge, Mass.: Belknap Press.

Miller, J. Hillis. 1980. 'The Figure in the Carpet', in *Poetics Today* 1, 3: 107–18.

Miller, J. Hillis. 1982. '*Wuthering Heights*: Repetition and the "Uncanny"', in *Fiction and Repetition: Seven English Novels*. Oxford: Basil Blackwell.

Miller, J. Hillis. 1987. *The Ethics of Reading: Kant, de Man, Eliot, Trollope, James, and Benjamin*. New York: Columbia University Press.

Miller, J. Hillis. 1990. 'Narrative', in *Critical Terms for Literary Study*, eds Frank Lentricchia and Thomas McLaughlin. Chicago: University of Chicago Press.

Miller, J. Hillis. 1991. 'Thomas Hardy, Jacques Derrida, and the "Dislocation of Souls"', in *Tropes, Parables, Performatives: Essays in Twentieth-Century Literature*. Hemel Hempstead: Harvester Wheatsheaf.

Miller, J. Hillis. 1992. *Ariadne's Thread: Story Lines*. New Haven: Yale University Press.

Miller, J. Hillis. 1994. 'Derrida's Topographies', in *South Atlantic Review*, 59, 1: 1–25.

Miller, Karl. 1989. *Authors*. Oxford: Clarendon Press.

Millett, Kate. 1969. *Sexual Politics*. London: Rupert Hart-Davis.

Mills, Sara, ed. 1994. *Gendering the Reader*. Hemel Hempstead: Harvester Wheatsheaf.

Moi, Toril. 1985. *Sexual/Textual Politics: Feminist Literary Theory*. London: Routledge.

Morrison, Toni. 1993. *Playing in the Dark: Whiteness and the Literary Imagination*. London: Picador.

Mulhern, Francis, ed. 1992. *Contemporary Marxist Literary Criticism*. London: Longman.

Munt, Sally, ed. 1992. *New Lesbian Criticism: Literary and Cultural Readings*. Hemel Hempstead: Harvester Wheatsheaf.

Nancy, Jean-Luc. 1987. 'Wild Laughter in the Throat of Death', in *Modern Language Notes*, vol. 102, no. 4: 719–736.

Nancy, Jean-Luc. 1993. 'Laughter, Presence', in *The Birth to Presence*, trans. Brian Holmes *et al*. Stanford: Stanford University Press.

Nicholls, Peter. 1996. 'The Belated Postmodern: History, Phantoms and Toni Morrison', in Sue Vice, ed., *Psychoanalytic Criticism: A Reader*. Oxford: Polity.

Nietzsche, Friedrich. 1968. *The Will to Power*, trans. Walter Kaufmann and R.J. Hollingdale. New York: Vintage.

Nietzsche, Friedrich. 1980. 'On Truth and Lie in an Extra-Moral Sense', in *The Portable Nietzsche*, ed. Walter Kaufmann. New York: Random.

Nietzsche, Friedrich. 1989. *Beyond Good and Evil: Prelude to a Philosophy of the Future*, trans. Walter Kaufmann. New York: Vintage.

Nuttall, A.D. 1992. *Openings: Narrative Beginnings from the Epic to the Novel*. Oxford: Clarendon Press.

Pask, Kevin. 1996. *The Emergence of the English Author: Scripting the Life in Early Modern England*. Cambridge: Cambridge University Press.

Patterson, Annabel. 1990. 'Intention', in *Critical Terms for Literary Study*, eds Frank Lentricchia and Thomas McLaughlin. Chicago: Chicago University Press.

Phelan, James, ed. 1989. *Reading Narrative: Form, Ethics, Ideology*. Columbus: Ohio State University Press.

Pinker, Steven. 1995. *The Language Instinct: The New Science of Language and Mind*. London: Penguin.

Plato. 1961. *The Collected Dialogues of Plato, Including the Letters*, eds Edith Hamilton and Huntington Cairns. New Jersey: Princeton University Press.

Price, Martin. 1983. *Forms of Life: Character and Moral Imagination in the Novel*. New Haven: Yale University Press.

Punter, David. 1996. *The Literature of Terror*. 2nd edn, 2 vols. London: Longman.

Rashkin, Esther. 1992. *Family Secrets and the Psychoanalysis of Narrative*. Princeton, NJ: Princeton University Press.

Raven, James, Helen Small and Naomi Tadmor, eds. 1995. *The Practice and Representation of Reading in England*. Cambridge: Cambridge University Press.

Readings, Bill and Bennet Schaber, eds. 1993. *Postmodernism Across the Ages*. Syracuse, New York: Syracuse University Press.

Regan, Stephen, ed. 1992. *The Politics of Pleasure: Aesthetics and Cultural Theory*. Buckingham: Open University Press.

Rich, Adrienne. 1986. 'Compulsory Heterosexuality and Lesbian Existence', in *Blood, Bread, and Poetry: Selected Prose, 1979–1985*. London: Virago.

Ricks, Christopher. 1984. 'William Wordsworth 1: "A pure organic pleasure from the lines"', in *The Force of Poetry*. Oxford: Clarendon Press.

Ricoeur, Paul. 1978. *The Rule of Metaphor: Multi-Disciplinary Studies of the Creation of Meaning in Language*, trans. Robert Czerny. London: Routledge and Kegan Paul.

Riley, Denise. 1988. *'Am I That Name?': Feminism and the Category of 'Women' in History*. Basingstoke: Macmillan.

Rogin, Michael. 1994. 'Sucking Up'. *London Review of Books* 16, 9 (12 May): 26.

Ronell, Avital. 1989. *The Telephone Book: Technology, Schizophrenia, Electric Speech*. Lincoln: Nebraska University Press.

Rose, Jacqueline. 1996. *States of Fantasy*. Oxford: Clarendon Press.

Royle, Nicholas. 1991. *Telepathy and Literature: Essays on the Reading Mind*. Oxford: Basil Blackwell.

Rushdie, Salman. 1990. *Is Nothing Sacred?* Cambridge: Granta.

Russell, Bertrand. 1967. *Autobiography 1872–1914*. London: George Allen and Unwin.

Ryan, Kiernan, ed. 1996. *New Historicism and Cultural Materialism: A Reader*. London: Arnold.

Said, Edward W. 1975. *Beginnings: Intention and Method*. New York: Basic Books.

Said, Edward W. 1978. *Orientalism*. London: Routledge and Kegan Paul.

Said, Edward W. 1983. *The World, the Text, and the Critic*. London: Faber and Faber.

Said, Edward W. 1993. *Culture and Imperialism*. London: Chatto and Windus.

Schwartz, Hillel. 1996. *The Culture of the Copy: Striking Likenesses, Unreasonable Facsimiles*. New York: Zone Books.

Sedgwick, Eve Kosofsky. 1985. *Between Men: English Literature and Male Homosocial Desire*. New York: Columbia University Press.

Sedgwick, Eve Kosofsky. 1991. *Epistemology of the Closet*. Hemel Hempstead: Harvester Wheatsheaf.

Sedgwick, Eve Kosofsky. 1994. *Tendencies*. London: Routledge.

Shklovsky, Viktor. 1965. 'Art as Technique', in *Russian Formalist Criticism: Four Essays*, eds Lee T. Lemon and Marion J. Reis. Lincoln: University of Nebraska Press.

Showalter, Elaine. 1977. *A Literature of Their Own: British Women Novelists from Brontë to Lessing*. New Jersey: Princeton University Press.

Showalter, Elaine, ed. 1989. *Speaking of Gender*. London: Routledge.

Showalter, Elaine. 1991. *Sexual Anarchy: Gender and Culture at the* Fin de Siècle. London: Virago.

Showalter, Elaine. 1993. 'On Hysterical Narrative', in *Narrative*, 1, 1: 24–35.

Sinfield, Alan. 1994. *Cultural Politics—Queer Reading*. London: Routledge.

Sinfield, Alan. 1994. *The Wilde Century: Effeminacy, Oscar Wilde and the Queer Moment*. London: Cassell.

Smith, Adam. 1986. *The Wealth of Nations*, Books I-III, ed. Andrew Skinner. Harmondsworth: Penguin.

Smith, Angela, ed. and introd. 1997. *Wide Sargasso Sea*. Harmondsworth: Penguin.

Smith, Barbara Herrnstein. 1968. *Poetic Closure: A Study of How Poems End*. Chicago: University of Chicago Press.

Smith, Barbara Herrnstein. 1981. 'Narrative Versions, Narrative Theories', in *On Narrative*, ed. W.J.T. Mitchell. Chicago: University of Chicago Press.

Smith, Barbara Herrnstein. 1988. *Contingencies of Value: Alternative Perspectives for Critical Theory*. Cambridge, Mass.: Harvard University Press.

Smith, Bruce R. 1994. *Homosexual Desire in Shakespeare's England: A Cultural Poetics*. Chicago: University of Chicago Press.

Spivak, Gayatri Chakravorty. 1987. *In Other Worlds: Essays in Cultural Politics*. London: Routledge.

Steiner, George. 1961. *The Death of Tragedy*. London: Faber.

Stevens, Wallace. 1951. *The Necessary Angel: Essays on Reality and the Imagination*. New York: Alfred A. Knopf.

Stewart, Garrett. 1990. *Reading Voices: Literature and the Phonotext*. Berkeley: University of California Press.

Still, Judith and Michael Worton, eds. 1990. *Intertextuality: Theories and Practices*. Manchester: Manchester University Press.

Suleiman, Susan R. and Inge Crosman, eds. 1980. *The Reader in the Text: Essays on Audience and Interpretation*. New Jersey: Princeton University Press.

Sypher, Wylie, ed. 1956. *Comedy*. New York: Doubleday.

Taylor, Charles. 1989. *Sources of the Self: The Making of Modern Identity*. Cambridge: Cambridge University Press.

Thomas, Keith. 1971. *Religion and the Decline of Magic: Studies in Popular Beliefs in Sixteenth and Seventeenth Century England*. London: Weidenfeld and Nicolson.

Todd, Jane Marie. 1986. 'The Veiled Woman in Freud's *Das Unheimliche*', in *Signs* 2/3: 519–28.

Todd, Janet. 1988. *Feminist Literary History: A Defence*. Cambridge: Polity Press.

Todorov, Tzvetan. 1981. *Introduction to Poetics*, trans. Richard Howard, Minneapolis: University of Minnesota Press.

Touval, Yonatan. 1997. 'Colonial Queer Something', in *Queer Forster*, eds Robert K. Martin and George Piggford. Chicago: University of Chicago Press.

Veeser, H. Aram, ed. 1989. *The New Historicism*. New York: Routledge.

Veeser, H. Aram, ed. 1994. *The New Historicism Reader*. New York: Routledge.

Vickers, Brian, ed. 1981. *Shakespeare: The Critical Heritage, Volume 6, 1774–1801*. London: Routledge and Kegan Paul.

Walder, Dennis. 1998. *Post-Colonial Literatures in English: History, Language, Theory*. Oxford: Blackwell.

Waller, Marguerite. 1987. 'Academic Tootsie: The Denial of Difference and the Difference It Makes', in *Diacritics*, vol. 17, no. 1: 2–20.

Ward, Graham. 1996. *Theology and Contemporary Critical Theory*. London: Macmillan.

Warhol, Robyn R. and Diane Price Herndl, eds. 1997. *Feminisms: An Anthology of Literary Theory and Criticism*, revised edn. London: Macmillan.

Weber, Samuel. 1973. 'The Sideshow, or: Remarks on a Canny Moment', in *Modern Language Notes*, 88: 1102–33.

Weber, Samuel. 1987. 'Laughing in the Meanwhile', in *Modern Language Notes*, vol. 102, no. 4: 691–706.

Weber, Samuel. 1992. *The Return to Freud: Jacques Lacan and the Dislocations of Psychoanalysis*. Cambridge: Cambridge University Press.

Weeks, Jeffrey. 1998. 'Introduction to Guy Hocquenghem's *Homosexual Desire*', in *Literary Theory: An Anthology*, eds Julie Rivkin and Michael Ryan. Oxford: Blackwell.

Wellek, René. 1963. 'Literary Theory, Criticism, and History', in *Concepts of Criticism*. New Haven: Yale University Press.

Wesling, Donald and Tadeusz Slawek. 1995. *Literary Voice: The Calling of Jonah*. Albany, NY: State University of New York Press.

White, Hayden. 1978. *Tropics of Discourse: Essays in Cultural Criticism*. Baltimore: The Johns Hopkins University Press.

Whiteside, Anna and Michael Issacharoff, eds. 1987. *On Referring in Literature*. Bloomington: Indiana University Press.

Williams, Linda Ruth. 1995. *Critical Desire: Psychoanalysis and the Literary Subject*. London: Edward Arnold.

Williams, Patrick and Laura Chrisman, eds. 1993. *Colonial Discourse and Post-Colonial Theory: A Reader*. Hemel Hempstead: Harvester Wheatsheaf.

Williams, Raymond. 1969. *Modern Tragedy*. London: Chatto and Windus.

Williams, Raymond. 1976. *Keywords: A Vocabulary of Culture and Society*. London: Fontana.

Williams, Raymond. 1992. *The Long Revolution*. London: Hogarth.

Wilson, Richard and Richard Dutton, eds. 1992. *New Historicism and Renaissance Drama*. London: Longman.

Wimsatt Jr, W.K. and Monroe C. Beardsley. 1972. 'The Intentional Fallacy', in *Twentieth Century Literary Criticism: A Reader*, ed. David Lodge. London: Longman.

Winters, Yvor. 1957. 'The Audible Reading of Poetry', in *The Function of Criticism: Problems and Exercises*, 2nd edn. Denver: Alan Swallow.

Wittgenstein, Ludwig. 1984. *Philosophical Investigations*. Oxford: Blackwell.

Wood, Sarah, ed. 1995. *Home and Family*. Special issue of *Angelaki*, 2:1.

Woolf, Virginia. 1942. *The Death of the Moth and Other Essays*. London: Hogarth Press.

Woolf, Virginia. 1988. 'Henry James's Ghost Stories', in *The Essays of Virginia Woolf*, vol. 3, 1919–1924, ed. Andrew McNeillie. New York: Harcourt Brace Jovanovich.

Wright, Elizabeth, ed.1992. *Feminism and Psychoanalysis: A Critical Dictionary*. Oxford and Cambridge, Mass.: Basil Blackwell.

Wright, Elizabeth. 1998. *Psychoanalytic Criticism: A Reappraisal*. 2nd edn. Cambridge: Polity.

Young, Robert. 1981. 'Introduction', in *Untying the Text: A Post-Structuralist Reader*, ed. Robert Young. London: Routledge and Kegan Paul.

Young, Robert. 1990. *White Mythologies: Writing History and the West*. London: Routledge.

Young, Robert. 1991a. 'Poems That Read Themselves', *Tropismes* 5: 233–61.

Young, Robert, ed. 1991b. *Neocolonialism*. Special issue of *Oxford Literary Review*, 13.

Young, Robert. 1995. *Colonial Desire: Hybridity in Theory, Culture and Race*. London: Routledge.

Young, Robert. 1999. *Postcolonialism: A History*. Oxford: Blackwell.

Index